Russian Entrepreneur

Ivan Sytin. Portrait by A.V. Moravov. From *Polveka dlia knigi*, edited by N.V. Tulupov (Moscow 1916).

Russian Entrepreneur

Publisher Ivan Sytin of Moscow 1851–1934

CHARLES A. RUUD

McGill-Queen's University Press
Montreal & Kingston • London • Buffalo

ISBN 0-7735-0773-6

Legal deposit third quarter 1990
Bibliothèque nationale du Québec

Printed in Canada on acid-free paper

This book has been published with the help of a grant from the Canadian Federation for the Humanities, using funds provided by the Social Sciences and Humanities Research Council of Canada. Publication has also been assisted by a grant from the J.B. Smallman Fund, The University of Western Ontario.

Canadian Cataloguing in Publication Data

Ruud, Charles A., 1933-
Russian entrepreneur
Includes bibliographical references.
ISBN 0-7735-0773-6
1. Sytin, Ivan Dmitrievich, 1851-1934. 2. Newspaper publishing - Soviet Union - History. 3. Publishers and publishing - Soviet Union - Biography. 4. Entrepreneurs - Soviet Union - Biography. I. Title.
Z368.S98R88 1990 077′.092 C90-090031-8

This book was set in $10\frac{1}{2}$ pt. on 12 pt. leading Baskerville regular.
By Nancy Poirier Typesetting Limited, Ottawa.

For Margie

Contents

Preface

I am indebted to several persons who helped in the preparation of this book. Two who participated actively are Marjorie L. Ruud, who made a substantial editorial contribution, and Professor Ken Papmehl, who freely gave of his knowledge of pre-revolutionary Russian culture and language. Professor Papmehl also deciphered and translated four letters.

Several colleagues in Moscow lent invaluable assistance. The first is V.A. Vdovin of the history faculty of Moscow State University, who was twice my generous-spirited adviser. S.I. Inikova, who knows the Sytin archives better than anyone else, gave me the benefit of her knowledge, as did E.A. Dinershtein of the All-Union Bibliographical Centre in Moscow, the author of the first book-length study of Sytin. V.I. Bovykin, also of the history faculty of Moscow University, was the willing impresario of a spirited seminar that included A.S. Bokhanov and N.A. Chlenova of the Institute of History, Academy of Sciences, USSR.

In the spring and summer of 1989 I benefited enormously from my informal association with the Sytin Museum recently established at 12 Gorky Street and with its staff: I.E. Matveeva, the director, and N.N. Aleshina, L.I. Maksimova, and V.V. Kirillov, her colleagues. I cannot thank them enough for their warm hospitality and for sharing with me their special knowledge of Sytin; and I owe much to Aleshina and Maksimova for the hours they spent deciphering Sytin's handwriting and making sense of his convoluted and ungrammatical Russian prose. I also had skilled assistance with translation from E.A. Khvostova, a senior editor with the Academy of Sciences.

Thanks go, as well, to Linda Brock, Joanne Burns, Lori Morris, Pat Rosen, and Melanie Wolfe of The University of Western Ontario, who so willingly and expertly typed my manuscript.

Most of the research for this book was conducted in Moscow and, to a lesser degree, in Leningrad in 1981, 1984, and 1989, while I was a participant in the Exchange of Senior Research Scholars with the USSR Ministry of Higher and Specialized Secondary Education (now the State Committee for Education) administered by the International Research and Exchanges Board. Further study took place at Harvard University, when I was a Senior Scholar at the Russian Research Center in the spring of 1982, and in the D.B. Weldon Library, University of Western Ontario, through funds provided by the Dean of Social Science, The University of Western Ontario.

C.A.R.
London, Ontario
September 1989

A Note on Style

The names of Soviet archives, all of which are abbreviated in the notes, appear in full in the bibliography. The names of most Russian journals and newspapers are cited in English translations in the text, with the Russian titles given in parentheses upon first mention.

All dates cited through January 1918 are "old style": that is, using the Julian calendar, which lagged behind the western Gregorian calendar by twelve days in the nineteenth century and by thirteen days in the twentieth century. All subsequent dates comply with the Gregorian calendar adopted by the Soviets on 1 February 1918 (old style), as 14 February 1918 (new style).

To render Russian words into English, I have followed the Library of Congress system of transliteration with some modifications. In both text and notes, the frequent ending of Russian surnames that is rendered "ii" in the LC system, I have transliterated as "y" ("Gorky," rather than "Gorkii"), and I have not used the LC symbol for the Russian soft "e." In the text alone, but not in the notes, I have eliminated the LC symbol for the soft sign (') and for the hard sign ('').

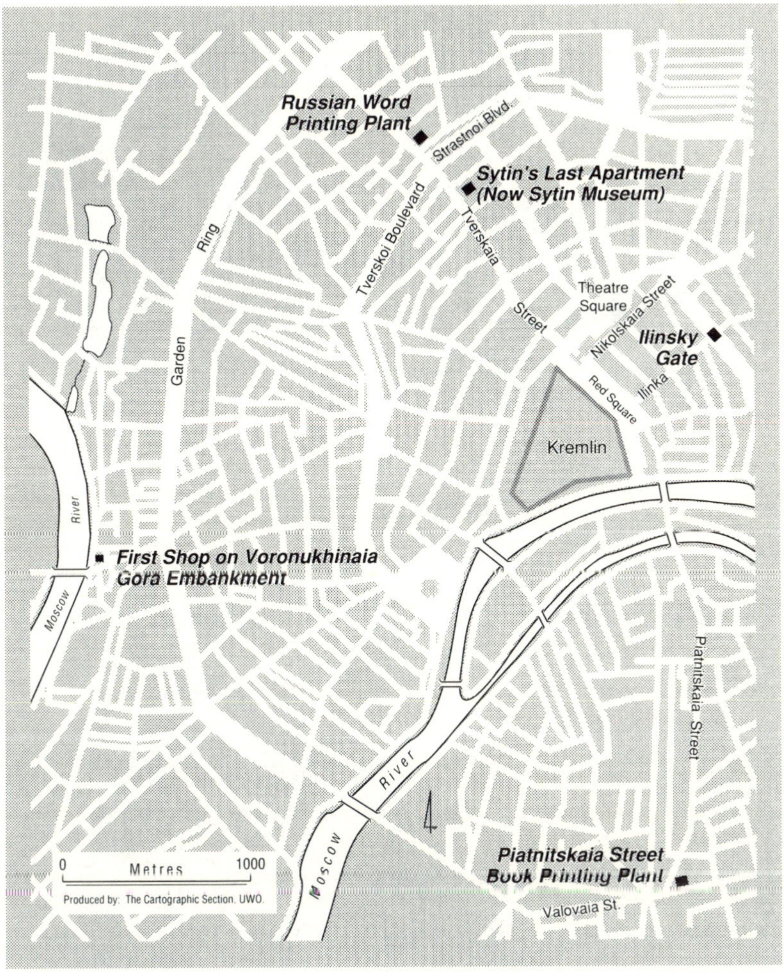

Turn-of-the-century Moscow showing the locations of the main printing and publishing plants of Sytin's career.

The print shop of Sytin's mentor, Sharapov, stood near this old Moscow landmark, Ilinsky Gate, not far from the Kremlin. From *Polveka dlia knigi*, edited by N.V. Tulupov (Moscow 1916).

Sytin's first print shop was located inside this building on Voronukhinaia Gora embankment overlooking the Moscow River.

These buildings made up the Piatnitskaia Street book printing plant, which also produced pictures, brochures, and calendars. It was the home of the Sytintsy, who were among the most radical print workers.

The *Russian Word* printing plant, left above, fronted on Tverskaia Street. The lower sketch shows carts arriving in the back courtyard with rolls of paper for the rotary presses. From *Polveka dlia knigi*, edited by N.V. Tulupov (Moscow 1916).

Russian Entrepreneur

Introduction

This book describes how an unlettered villager used the skills of an entrepreneur to become the premier publisher of the Russian Empire. Not only did I.D. Sytin (1851–1934) build the largest publishing company in Russia prior to the Revolution, but he also transformed what began as an obscure, conservative newspaper into Russia's largest daily.

As a newspaper and book baron of great wealth and influence, Sytin (rhymes with PREteen) replicated the publishing success of such western contemporaries as Joseph Pulitzer and William Randolph Hearst in America and Lord Northcliffe in England. But Sytin is not, like them, well known today. This Russian Orthodox believer and capitalist was anathema to most Bolsheviks, except Lenin; and for forty years after Lenin's death, what little the Soviets said about Sytin was dismissive. Only in the 1960s did the Soviet government begin to praise Sytin as a worthy exemplar in the publishing industry. As for accounts in the West, scholars have so far given little attention to Sytin or other large publishers in studies either of Russian industrialists or of the years before the Revolution.

In this study Sytin emerges as an important player in Russia's national history. Precisely because he made millions in publishing, Sytin helped significantly to spread literacy, shape opinion, and widen the limits of discussion under the autocracy – and he did so in ways that contributed to the general discontent preceding the fall of the Tsar. This book interweaves the history of Sytin as a force for change with the histories of the two institutions that gave him influence: his publishing house, Sytin & Co., and his Moscow daily, *Russian Word*.

Sytin was an uncommon Russian – so much so that some contemporaries, whether praisingly or pejoratively, called him an "American." A more useful term for assessing him is "entrepreneur."

Modern lexicographers define entrepreneur (from the French *entreprendre*, "to undertake") to mean a risk-taking organizer and director of a business or enterprise. From another source of current usage comes a definition even more relevant to Sytin: "the lover of risk with the gifts to turn opportunity into success, and the businessman who, even after amassing millions, is still driven to start another, and yet another venture."[1]

Most appropriate of all for this study is the definition set forth by the economist Joseph Schumpeter at a time when Sytin was becoming a world-ranking publisher. In 1911, in his book on the theory of economic development, Schumpeter singled out a significant but largely unnoticed developmental force in the West - the entrepreneur; and by that term he meant an enterpriser spurred by lowly birth who became a great success by employing "new combinations of productive means." The entrepreneur had gone unnoticed, said Schumpeter, because he rises to a higher social level through economic success only to be dismissed there as an uncultivated and merely laughable "upstart."[2]

Schumpeter drew on new findings in psychology to argue that entrepreneurs make sense only to those who understand personal drives. In his formulation, childhood deprivation causes the entrepreneur to be singularly bent on overcoming obstacles and formulating something new or better, and the end result is a business-venture kingdom that provides the "nearest approach to medieval lordship available to modern man."[3] By making that venture succeed, the upstart proves his worth - both to himself and to the world - and wins respect. Schumpeter held that material wealth was of minor importance to the men he defined as entrepreneurs.

Today we have entrepreneurial studies, "a new field of specialization not firmly attached to any discipline,"[4] to discover the traits and methods of successful risk-taking enterprisers, and Schumpeter's archetypal imagery still enjoys wide acceptance among these specialists.[5] In one study researchers found that two-thirds of the entrepreneurs they examined had learned self-reliance growing up in poor families and that many of them described leaving school at an early age, striving to outdo improvident fathers, and getting their start as the protégé of a mentor/sponsor.[6] The subjects of another such study showed a predominant inclination, like juvenile delinquents, to break established norms of behaviour. Those in still another were found to be consistently open to ideas and information and very flexible in setting goals.[7]

Detail after detail in the life of Ivan Sytin shows him to be an entrepreneur par excellence in the publishing business, especially in his meeting Schumpeter's criterion of employing "new combinations of productive means." This book shows how he accomplished what he did during a time when the autocratic government still ruled Russia.

My prime sources for this book came from archives in the Soviet Union. I mainly read reports on Sytin from the censorship administration, the police, and the courts before 1917 and from the new Soviet government after 1917; records of the business and publishing activities of Sytin & Co.; contemporary periodicals; letters and memoranda by and about Sytin; and documentary materials previously in the hands of the Sytin family and now on deposit at the Sytin Museum in Moscow. I found Sytin's published prose clear and logical because others had edited it. What the former peasant scrawled on his own, however, is barely legible and textually difficult even for native speakers of Russian. Perhaps the best description of Sytin's fragmentary, ungrammatical, unpunctuated, unedited "sentences" is to liken them to prerevolutionary popular speech. Because their literal translation into English renders them incomprehensible, I have worked with persons more adept in Russian than I to decipher and then extensively edit the colloquial writings of Sytin that I quote. We have made every effort to convey the sense, forthright style, and spirit of Sytin in the original.

As for published accounts of Sytin, few are objectively neutral. *A Half-Century for the Book*, the six-hundred-page volume issued in 1916 by Sytin & Co. to mark Sytin's fiftieth year in publishing, puts only the best light on the *khoziain* (boss), as does the brief memoir contributed by Sytin. Then, in the 1920s, Sytin wrote an extended version of his memoirs, *A Life for the Book*. It finally appeared in 1960 minus three chapters, which still exist in typescript form at the Sytin Museum.

Assessments of Sytin in letters and memoirs by contemporaries have also been published, but these tend either to damn or eulogize the publisher. Of the several Soviet studies that have appeared on Sytin, none is a complete, sequential account.[8]

What emerges from all these sources is a publishing giant who preferred to be known as a simple man whose goal was to advance the well-being of the Russian people. Playing this role helped Sytin to attract leading literary talents to his side; and they, in turn, became one more essential element in his success. The story of how these many factors came together for this Russian entrepreneur is the substance of this book.

CHAPTER ONE

From Villager to Moscow Publisher

Outside, the wintry blasts of February 1917 made the wartime streets of Moscow all the bleaker, but inside the great auditorium of the Polytechnic Institute a thousand well-dressed celebrants applauded yet another message of congratulations, this one signed by the president of the French Chamber of Deputies. From his seat of honour on the stage, an imposing, well-tailored man in his sixties nodded a modest response. Multimillionaire Ivan Sytin was marking a half-century in the publishing industry. Just over fifty years before, he had arrived in Moscow, a provincial peasant boy of fifteen, to apprentice himself to a shopowner with a press.

Now Sytin headed the largest publishing company in Russia, if not the world. With his considerable backing, his daily *Russian Word* (*Russkoe Slovo*) had gained first place in circulation and an independent authority hitherto unknown under the autocracy. Along with huge profits, his trade had given him a wide audience; and today, as he had since early in the days when he first began printing on his own, Sytin was confidently proclaiming himself to be the pre-eminent edifier of the Russian people.

Sytin was also intent on buoying spirits. Despite misgovernment at home and defeats at the front, he was about to show his confidence in the future by announcing his most ambitious philanthropic venture: a non-profit publishing complex to benefit all the people. Instead, unwittingly, he would be sounding his last hurrah; for events set in motion within a fortnight would dissolve his immense wealth, his publishing empire, and his cherished *Russian Word*. On this day he had an excess of means for his grand project, but within the year he would be subject to rulers who abhorred private property and press freedom – the Bolsheviks he now opposed.

Through the impending Revolution and the nearly eighteen years to his natural death at eighty-three in 1934, Sytin would live on in Moscow by choice, but he would lose his holdings and never build his philanthropic publishing house. Under Lenin the new Soviet government would have some use for the adaptable old capitalist, but Lenin's successors forced him to retire. Thus, as Sytin could not foretell, his celebration of early 1917 marked both the fiftieth anniversary and the apex of his publishing career.

I

But Sytin had already earned his place in history. This man of lowly birth and little education, whose life spanned almost exactly the momentous years from the reforms of Alexander II to the purges of Stalin, ranks among the instigators of major change in Russia before the Revolution of 1917. Sytin matters for his solid accomplishments as an independent publisher under two tsars wary of opposition. He thrived on circumventing obstacles, including press controls, and he merits a place among those who fought successfully for a freer press.

Sytin's dogged determination was crucial to his success, but so was the declining authority of the imperial government. Despite clear evidence that Sytin could disturb the existing order, no official had the persuasive means or the legal grounds to keep him strictly in line.

Put another way, Sytin's expedience and elusiveness suited a time when the broadest commercial opportunities in publishing came to those who got along with both the government and its opposition. The government had some means for setting limits on publishing, and the opposition was the source of the best and most popular writers. Both camps found Sytin useful, and his ability to play the rustic "man of the people" enhanced his image. He could be many things to many men and still remain a loner during a period of intensely serious political alliances.

As a wealthy and increasingly influential publisher, Sytin came to know and deal with a wide range of notable persons, among them writers Leo Tolstoy, Anton Chekhov, Maksim Gorky, V.V. Rozanov, Vlas Doroshevich, Leonid Andreev, Dmitry Merezhkovsky, A.I. Ertel, and I.I. Gorbunov; artist Ilia Repin; attorney and politician F.N. Plevako; judicial scholar Maksim Kovalevsky; officials Constantine Pobedonostsev, Sergei Witte, Peter Stolypin, and Leo Kasso. He even managed to exchange words face to face with the last two reigning tsars and with the Soviet leader Vladimir Lenin. Generally speaking, this shrewd peasant and politically non-sectarian modernist valued others either for their professionalism or their influence, just as they valued him, as a man of the new age, for his commercial success.

At the same time, Sytin the traditionalist had a lifelong commitment to the Russian Orthodox Church and spoke of it movingly in the memoirs he published before the Revolution and in his notes about America, written after the Revolution but never published. Devotional works commonly appeared among his publications, and Sytin for a time included commentary by an Orthodox priest in his newspapers. In Russian fashion, he invited the local priest to preside at every company celebration, and he often turned to clerics for guidance. A regular worshipper at the Uspensky Cathedral in the Moscow Kremlin, he continued to believe profoundly in the faith of his childhood even after the ruling Soviets had labelled it rubbish. That constancy suggests genuine belief. Still, a hint of opportunism colours Sytin's piety.

Probably the truest measure of Sytin, however, is the complete record of what he published; and although he always insisted that benefiting the Russian reader was his prime concern, the catalogue of works from his presses seems to confirm that he put business interests first. Building a publishing empire was not, after all, a sin, especially when it could accelerate good works.

Sytin's start came with his unlikely apprenticeship far from home to a Moscow shopowner-printer who sold simple pictures and tales for peasants. When his benevolent master helped him set up his own print shop, Sytin expanded production to include livelier tales and, during the Russo-Turkish War of 1877–78, highly profitable battle pictures and maps. In 1884 he became the printer for the Mediator books; through the Tolstoyans who composed them, Sytin thus gained entrée to the intelligentsia and to publishing belle lettres and the "educational" books that became his mainstay. When, at Chekhov's urging, he entered the newspaper field, ostensibly to serve the public good, Sytin had lucratively diversified once again. In time his *Russian Word* earned profits beyond all other Moscow newspapers combined.

If what he published helps reveal Sytin's primary motives and character, how he published goes far to explain his phenomenal success. And he mainly borrowed his methods from the West. Sytin very early grasped the advantages of using the newest refinements in printing equipment, and the young printer from the forests of Kostroma bought a French press as his first investment. Later he would travel to Europe to find the best technological innovations – largely German – and then train his printers to use them. His own printing plant became a model of productivity in Russia, and his workers led all others in efficiency.

To streamline managerial and editorial tasks, Sytin likewise copied western organizational methods. For one thing, while largely retaining personal control, he imposed on his company a hierarchical system of management common in Europe but little practised in Russia, where firms were family-centred. Letting specialists run his departments – and he employed leaders in several fields – Sytin could concentrate on new ventures.

Once established as Moscow's leading publisher, Sytin enjoyed considerable influence. He had the wide audience of a first-rank publicist along with the power of a rich industrialist. Many sought him out or listened when he approached them, for Sytin was known to be venturesome and to take risks, even to the point of ruffling the government. He knew that his Mediator books advancing the Tolstoyan moral philosophy, for example, offended the procurator of the Holy Synod; and by collaborating with such radicals as Maksim Gorky, he provoked the attention of the tsarist secret police.

For the most part, Sytin leaned toward liberalism, although he deliberately avoided aligning with any political party. He usually backed his own editors and reporters when they decried misgovernment, and thereby helped to weaken the autocracy. Despite official frowns about his motives, he played a pioneering role in furthering literacy among the peasants. For his time, he was a progressive in labour relations; his employees, singly and collectively, were leaders in the workers' movement. Sytin, in sum, was a redoubtable agent of democratization in his native Russia.

As for his relationship with extremist revolutionaries, Sytin at no time gave them support, for the former villager feared a popular upheaval. Once the Bolsheviks had seized power, he stayed in place and selectively served, so far as he could, the new government. Lenin championed him, surprisingly enough, but his successors cast Sytin more and more into disfavour.

Six years after his death, the Soviet press printed yet another denunciation of Sytin. This time an old associate, I.R. Kugel, excoriated Sytin as an "entrepreneur in the American mould." The opportunistic Sytin, charged Kugel, had "published everything" – from "cheap popular prints" to "high quality literature" – just to feather his very pleasant nest. "When he felt dissatisfaction from on high ... pernicious [leftist] books are pushed aside and the sounds of patriotic bells ring for a time in the publishing house." Then, to revive "his kind of offering" to "dissident circles," they would as abruptly reappear. Moreover, concluded Kugel, this cheater who believed all men dishonest took great care to keep his own shady practices secret.[1]

Under Khrushchev, however, Ivan Sytin posthumously rose to an honoured place among Soviet heroes. His populism, peasantness, and industrious creativity made it possible. Despite the wealth he acquired, said his new canonizers, Sytin never lost his devotion to the people or his single-minded, innovative keenness to improve and advance publishing in Russia.

Sytin's rehabilitation began in 1960 with the appearance of *A Life for the Book*, a truncated version of the memoirs that the old publisher had finished in the 1920s but failed to publish in his lifetime.[2] Just as its title extolled a selfless publisher, at least one Soviet review of the book stressed the creative, not capitalistic, entrepreneurial focus in Sytin: "People who knew Ivan Dmitrievich, who observed him at work, spoke about his 'business-like' mind, not the mind of a merchant who had the single aim of profits, but one who had a creative capacity for putting to work what was new."[3]

In 1966, soon after Khrushchev's fall, *The Self-made Russian*, by Konstantin Konichev, appeared. Besides including incidents that discredit the Stalinist era, Konichev sets forth Sytin's impressive credentials as an enterprising folk hero. He uses the common licence of biographers to invent conversations and to flesh out characters, but main events in this case history, some of them footnoted, are verifiable and therefore trustworthy. Konichev spent a whole year with the surviving Sytin family to gather material for his book, an expanded second edition of which appeared in 1969.[4]

Two years later, in 1971, Sytin officially became a national hero when the Soviet government celebrated the 120th anniversary of his birth. Even more auspicious was the Moscow fête for the 125th anniversary in 1976, which also marked the one hundredth anniversary of Sytin's first printing plant. Put on display were some six hundred books from among the thousands Sytin had published. In that same year, moreover, a bibliographer at the Saltykov-Shchedrin Public Library in Leningrad called for an end to the "artificial division" of pre-revolutionary publishers into commendable "progressives" (those who favoured the Revolution) and despicable "capitalists" (those who opposed it). He mentioned Sytin in pointing out that many of the so-called capitalist publishers had done very good things for the Russian people.[5]

Sytin's goodwill and humanity came up for further praise in two memoirs, the first in 1973 by the writer Altaev, and the second in 1978 by former employee Motylkov.[6] In 1978, as well, appeared the second, still incomplete edition of Sytin's *A Life for the Book*. Its preface explains that the "Basic Directions for the Development of the National Economy of the U.S.S.R." presented at the Twenty-fifth Party Congress – in other words the five-year plan for 1976–80 – had put new emphasis on printing, publishing, and the book trade.

Sytin, the "self-made Russian" and battler for press freedom, emerged, then, as a useful symbol for a regime that was still censoring everything it printed. More recent proof of his rehabilitation is the salute to Sytin in February 1986 in *Book Review* (*Knizhnoe Obozrenie*) on the 135th anniversary of his birth,[7] and the decision by Kniga Press of

Moscow in 1989 to translate this book into Russian for publication in the USSR.

Sytin's last apartment at 12 Gorky Street, already marked as historically significant by an official plaque, will be officially dedicated as the Sytin Museum in 1991 on the 140th anniversary of Sytin's birth. And above Sytin's grave in Vvedensky cemetery in Moscow now stands an impressive memorial sculpted in marble. The memorial plaque at Sytin's biggest Moscow plant and what became the First Model Printing Plant, however, bears witness to the publisher's Achilles heel as a capitalist. That plaque honours the printers whose strike against Sytin helped touch off the revolution of 1905.

Still, in Marxist terms, Sytin innocently erred in becoming a capitalist, his times offering almost no other course for a simple man from the country with initiative, will, and vision. It is Sytin as the accomplished, benevolent commoner that the Soviets eulogize, and that idealization is the very one that Sytin favoured and furthered in his own lifetime. To a large degree it is true. Many of his contemporaries genuinely valued him for his simple manner, generosity, seemly modesty, buoyancy in adversity, and even for an oral incisiveness that seemed somehow sharpened by self-education.

Sytin certainly cultivated that image. He liked to call attention to his origins, to the schooling he sacrificed to help support his family, to his arrival in Moscow in peasant bark shoes. He never took pains to improve his almost illegible handwriting, and he often conducted business by haggling, as though he were still in his kiosk at the Nizhnii Novgorod fair. He exuded earthy honesty and decried the need for formal contracts between men who kept their word. More than once, however, bargainers discovered that Sytin's self-serving recollections of a deal differed from their own.

Sytin lost his wide berth for making deals in the October Revolution. Judged on his accomplishments before 1918, however, Sytin was the epitome of success as an entrepreneur in the most up-and-coming yet rapidly changing of all modern industries – mass communications. He started his phenomenal rise in the very years Russia began industrializing; and he ranks at the forefront of the capitalists of his time, a group of prime interest to scholars now assessing the degree to which modern technology had transformed Russia before the Revolution.

II

Ivan Dmitrievich Sytin was born on 24 January 1851 in Gnezdnikovo, a rural settlement three hundred miles or so northeast of Moscow in the province of Kostroma.[8] This province, along with those of

Moscow, Iaroslavl, Nizhnii Novgorod, Vladimir, Riazan, Kaluga (each with a capital bearing its name), lies in Old Russia, the ancestral homeland of the Great Russian people and of Russian Orthodoxy. Like the other central provinces, Kostroma then supported most of its population on lands claimed from the endless forests by slash-and-burn methods and tilled by ancient methods using animal power.

Most long-distance travel in Kostroma in 1851 was by inland waterways and especially the Volga River, beginning in the Valdai Hills southeast of St Petersburg (now Leningrad) and then across a southwest corner of the province and southward toward the Caspian Sea. Along that course, the port of Kostroma was a busy hub for trade and traffic and an important historical site. Within its Ipatiev Monastery – founded in the fourteenth century by a converted Tartar prince who began the famous Godunov family – Michael Romanov had received his summons from the *zemskii sobor* (assembly of the land) in 1613 to become the first of the dynasty that would rule Russia for 304 years. Another local hero, a Kostroma peasant named Ivan Susanin, had been immortalized in 1836 in Michael Glinka's patriotic opera *A Life for the Tsar* for sacrificing himself to save Tsar Michael from the invading Poles.[9]

Upriver from Kostroma was Iaroslavl, founded by the law-giving prince Iaroslav the Wise in the eleventh century. Downriver about twenty hours by steamboat was Nizhnii Novgorod (now Gorky), the rallying point in 1612 for the national army that expelled the Poles and, since the early nineteenth century, the site each summer of Russia's largest fair. Foreign travellers who left accounts of this river route in the nineteenth century all described a culture untouched by western Europe and a people proud of that fact. Here in the heartland of Old Russia, Sytin's lifelong nationalism and patriotism took root.

Sytin's birthplace of Gnezdnikovo ranked as a *selo*, a village one step above a *derevnia* because it boasted a church; and there the Sytins took pleasure in having risen a degree in status. In the first place, Dmitry Gerasimovich, Sytin's father, although of peasant stock, had been singled out as a bright boy in the village school to become a copier of official documents for the district. In addition, both he and his wife Olga Alexandrovna could read, a rare distinction for a peasant family in the middle of the nineteenth century, when only about one in every ten Russians was literate.

Materially, the family fared little better than the peasants around them who worked the land. Sytin remembers that he, his two sisters and younger brother got little attention from parents hard pressed to keep enough food on the table. An added problem was Dmitry Gerasimovich's "occasional bouts of melancholy" – that is, his weakness for vodka. (Sytin blamed that vice on the "misery of the times" and later prescribed literacy and good books as effective antidotes.) Dmitry Gerasimovich probably imbibed with the schoolmaster, a peer of sorts, since he must have been the only other male in the village with a modicum of learning. As a pupil, Sytin knew that same teacher to conduct his classes some mornings still showing the effects of alcohol.

Young Sytin stayed behind when the other village children set off with their parents for the fields. In 1861, the year of the emancipation of the serfs, he entered the one-room school run by the village administration. There the boy endured the haphazard teaching of Slavonic grammar, the Psalter, the Book of Hours, and elementary arithmetic. An unruly group of pupils resisted instruction, and the teacher tried, but failed, to maintain discipline by cuffing miscreants on the back of the head or sending them to a corner of the room to suffer punishment on their knees.

Upon the birth of his brother Sergei in 1863, Sytin quit his studies to help support his family, later admitting that he "left the school lazy and with an aversion to books, so loathsome had school become after three years of cramming by memorization." These were momentarily darker times for him in a decade that marked the first steps in the modernization of Russia. Two years earlier, the Emperor Alexander II had liberated privately owned serfs and, in 1863, had enabled the state peasants, bound to crown lands, to rent or purchase their plots. As a state peasant without land, however, Dmitry Gerasimovich had no prospect of securing a farmstead, and he may well have feared that the reforms in local government that would begin in 1864 threatened his modest job in the village.

During this time of national renewal, Sytin says, "everything collapsed" for his family as it spent its last savings. "Excruciating questions came up: what will happen, how will we live? Trips to saints and sorcerers only increased our deprivation, and we looked fearfully to the future. There was no time to think about the children."[10] The distracted Dmitry disappeared from home and work for an entire week, and although he returned somehow renewed – "alert, fresh, composed," says Sytin – this last of many truancies cost him his job. Fortunately the town of Galich, some fifty miles to the south, needed a clerk, and Dmitry successfully presented himself as a candidate. Moreover, in making the move with his family, he set an example for Ivan to go beyond the familiar to seize opportunity, a trait that would prove second nature in that eldest son.

Sytin made his first foray from home in his fourteenth year. That summer he travelled down the Volga to the Nizhnii Novgorod fair to work for an uncle who traded furs. At this crossroads for merchants from Europe and Asia, Sytin discovered the world of commerce.

He saw, among others, Armenians, Turks, Tartars, Chinese, English, Dutch, and the Siberians who never shed their furs no matter what the heat. Some, like him, had come down the Volga; others had come via Kazan on the Kama River steamers, or by way of Moscow on the Moscow-Oka riverway; still others had travelled overland on wagons or carts. In a babble of languages, they argued the worth of goods produced thousands of miles apart, whether to barter an exchange or set a price in a local or foreign currency. Besides getting along without standard rates of monetary exchange, they sometimes sealed agreements with just a handshake, deferring actual settlement until the next year's fair.

Commodities had to be portable, for buyers hauled their goods away. Nothing was traded for future deliveries. There were raisins, blankets, pictures of saints, leather goods, gold and silver work, Persian carpets, rice, glassware, porcelain, shawls, hides, and even carriages. Merchants selling particular items shared a designated area, and most lived on site with their merchandise, ready to do business at any time for the full six weeks of the July to September fair.

Some basic tenets of profit-making here became clear to Sytin: know the tastes of your buyers, sell in quantity, give credit. Sytin also learned to work long hours and to pay close attention to his employer's interests. For his summer's service he received the princely sum of twenty-five rubles. Matching that against the twenty-two rubles a month his father earned, Sytin caught sight of a goal common to budding entrepreneurs: he would outdo his father.

Young Ivan returned to Nizhnii the next summer to work not for his uncle but for a fur merchant from Kolomna. Taken by the boy's energy and seriousness, this new employer secured an apprenticeship for Sytin to begin the month after the fair with another fur trader – a modestly well-off Muscovite named P.N. Sharapov who happened, as a sideline, to print and sell simple pictures for the peasants.

Armed with a letter of introduction, on 14 September 1866 the sturdy fifteen-year-old Sytin presented himself at Sharapov's shop near Moscow's Ilinsky Gate, in the wall of the old Kitaigorod merchants' quarter near the Kremlin. Sytin says nothing about his first reactions to the sprawling city of four hundred thousand inhabitants; but, however grand his dreams, he could not have imagined that, as Moscow grew in the next forty years to include a million people, he would become the city's leading publisher. What he did record was the first advice he heard: "Well, brother, so you have come to serve. Serve, brother, diligently. Don't spare yourself but work; don't be lazy; get up earlier than the others and go to bed later. Don't be afraid of unpleasant tasks or assign credit to yourself. Wait to be evaluated. The market will name [your worth]."[11] In recalling this counsel, Sytin gave the credo that was to guide him for life.

Unlike St Petersburg, the westernized capital and leading city of the realm, Moscow was staunchly Russian in population, outlook, architecture, and business practices. When Sytin arrived, the pace of trade and transportation was quickening. Russia's first major railway line had linked Moscow to St Petersburg fifteen years earlier, and five more lines, then planned or begun, would be ready by the 1880s. Steam locomotion offered much faster, surer overland service than did horsepower on the eight dirt highways radiating from the city. For example, troika to Nizhnii Novgorod in good weather then took seven days; a one-horse wagon, ten days; and a bullock and cart, one month. New forms of energy were also changing the city itself. As cheap kerosene was lighting more and more streets in the 1860s, steam and electricity were mechanizing and increasing the production of textiles, sugar, and the like. In turn, larger buildings were rising in the city's centre.

One specialist has termed Moscow during this period a "revolving door," and most of the comings and goings were by peasants in search of livelihoods. The usual migrant was, like Sytin, a single male; but, unlike him, many supported families back in the villages, to whom they might return just for the growing season. In the city they sought work in factories and in cottage industries such as cobbling and sewing; in print shops; in vending and shopkeeping; in woodworking and construction; and in the food, hostelry, and tavern trades. Owning a horse and cart gave entry to the immense cartage business.[12]

Among those who did well, two who stand out sold liquor. In the 1850s P.D. Smirnov, a peasant, moved up from labourer to vodka producer and thus amassed a Moscow fortune, but he gave none of it – or so his obituary pointedly said – to charity. In turn, N.I. Pastukhov fled his lower-class background in Smolensk province for Moscow about 1861, rose to the rank of tavern-owner, started the *Moscow Newssheet* (*Moskovskii Listok*) in 1881, and died very well-to-do. Sytin, as a publisher, was to exceed both these men in accomplishments, but how many poor and lower-class migrants from the villages became rich in a lifetime and just how rich they became are questions still unanswered by scholars.[13]

Old wealth ruled the city, of course, and some two dozen industrial and commercial families had, by the second half of the nineteenth century, displaced even older gentry families as Moscow's financial and social elite. Their largest single interest was the textile mills that employed thousands of workers in Moscow's suburbs and in the surrounding central industrial region, and they also invested heavily in banking, railroads, chemicals, tobacco, and confections. These partisans of Russian values and dedicated patrons of Moscow's arts and charities deplored the collaboration of their St Petersburg counterparts with Europeans.[14] As conservatives chary of advanced technology, they left innovative industrialization to more venturesome enterprisers.

In the midst of a great transformation, then, Sytin started at the bottom, cleaning the boots of Sharapov and his workers, fetching water for their tea, and going regularly to church. Like many Russian merchants, Sharapov merged his business with his household and saw to both the material and moral well-being of his apprentices. His domestic and commercial establishment thus resembled the provincial life Sytin had left behind. Young Ivan was not thrust into an alien and impersonal sweatshop but into a homely enterprise with bed and board under the roof of a conscientious master.

When, not yet twenty, Sytin straggled home one night an hour before midnight, Sharapov awaited him at the gate with a lantern to let him through the locked door and to admonish him for his irresponsibility; for with no wife or children of his own, Sharapov took especial fatherly interest in his charges. As a devout Old Believer – a practitioner of the pre-reform church rite – he saw fit to advise them, "in your free time, for your soul, read good books," which meant doing so primarily "before going to sleep and on holidays."[15] Sytin says that the strong religious influence of Sharapov made a lasting impression on him, as did his own attendance at the Old Believers' services and prayers, "which were not always and not to everyone accessible."[16]

As Sharapov's confidence in Sytin grew, so did Sytin's responsibilities, and they came to include polishing household valuables and carrying a purse to the market to buy food. Sytin also began taking his turn at the hand-operated lithograph press. Quite by chance, he commenced to learn a trade that would make him a millionaire, just at the time when mechanized technology began to alter the production methods of the large Moscow printing shops.

Now, as later, rusticity helped Sytin by making him easy with the country folk who were Sharapov's customers. For them, the illiterate or barely literate, Sharapov printed pictures and little story books that sold for a copeck or two – a trade already hundreds of years old in Russia. Censorship still existed (the reformed press statute of 1865 forebade anything that undermined the church or state), but Sharapov, hardly the contentious sort, had no recorded run-ins with the censors.

Sytin became overseer for both the production and distribution of Sharapov's publications, all of them illustrated. Work began as he or a helper traced a line drawing on a piece of lime board and then gouged out the background with a chisel to produce a wood-based relief. This woodcut, along with any text set in moveable type, was secured on the bed of a simple hand press, liberally inked, and covered with a sheet of cheap, grey paper. Pressure leveraged downward from above imprinted the raised outline one page at a time, and by this slow process Sytin produced the thousands of copies his master wanted.

Next came the colouring of the printed sheets, for which a thriving cottage industry had sprung up in the Moscow suburb of Nikolsk. There peasant women haphazardly tinted hundreds of thousands of prints each winter, improvising their paints from such handy kitchen pigments as egg yolk. Sytin served as the solicitous courier to and from the homes of the Nikolsk colourists, and Konichev has described a likely exchange in a typical cottage. A mother and three daughters worked about a table, he writes, on which lay hundreds of copies of a village favourite: "How the Mice Buried the Cat." As she painted the trussed-up cat a verdant green and her daughters daubed the mice with blue and yellow, the mother cheerfully explained: "We don't have any other colours." But, certain that Sytin would accept her work, she freely went on to wonder, "How do those women live who don't have a trade?"[17]

Sytin also took great care to forge good relations with the buyers of Sharapov's pictures and little books. For the road-weary pedlars who came to Moscow each fall to buy the wares they carted or carried into the countryside, he provided a Russian version of the businessman's lunch, conducting them first to the public baths before inviting them to Sharapov's table. The meal that followed included plenty of vodka, though not so much as to dampen sales or delay buyers all too willing to hang about. To cultivate sales among stallkeepers, Sytin made regular circuits to outlying villages and fairs, conveying Sharapov's goods by horse and cart sometimes hundreds of miles into the provinces, even in the worst winter weather.

Probably the first summer of his apprenticeship, Sytin had returned to the Nizhnii fair as assistant manager of Sharapov's publications stall. When he cleverly took the initiative to recruit a peasant, Uncle Iakov, as an independent vendor strolling the fairgrounds, a new network of pedlars began. Over the next six years Uncle Iakov brought in one hundred others ready to buy books and pictures from the stocks at Sharapov's stall and then sell them in the countryside. In that same six-year period, Sharapov's turnover at the fair grew in worth from an initial four thousand rubles to a spectacular one hundred thousand. "My friendship with the master grew in proportion to the growth of the business," Sytin remarks.[18]

In all these dealings, the affable and quick-witted Sytin took careful stock of peasant tastes and interests, a commonsense method of market research that gave him grounds for urging Sharapov to forego certain pictures and books or to add new ones. Overall he must, as he claimed, have given long hours of hard work to his master's business, although surely with a mind to the possibilities for himself. He came to know Sharapov's relatively simple production and business methods inside and out as he worked in Moscow and travelled the countryside.

By 1876, a decade after joining the Moscow printer, Sytin decided that his own annual wages of 330 rubles were insufficient. The main reason for that conclusion was that he had, in his twenty-fifth year, acquired a wife.

Sytin admits that he first gave serious thought to marriage only shortly before he wed and that he did so then at Sharapov's urgings. What concerned the old man were the "temptations at the Nizhnii Novgorod fair," where "buyers, especially the Siberians, demanded that each transaction be marked by a celebration." Although he says nothing about his own behaviour at the fair, the few lines that Sytin devotes in his memoirs to the preliminaries of finding a wife do suggest that Sharapov had come to see marriage as the best means to fortify the will of his travelling salesman.[19]

The matchmaker was Sharapov's bookbinder, Goriachev, who knew an elderly, widowed pastry cook in search of a suitor for his daughter. With Sharapov's approval, Goriachev offered to take Sytin to call on the girl, whom Sytin had seen once before at Goriachev's own wedding two years before. There followed in that interview an awkward example of nineteenth-century Muscovite marriage brokering in which two elderly members of the minor merchantry fixed the future of a sixteen-year-old girl. Sharapov was present in his capacity as patriarch, although, through timidity or kindness, he did not arrive at the home on Taganka Street until Sytin and Goriachev had gained entrance. The father and daughter "received us very politely and without ceremony," Sytin recalls, but had no refreshments to offer "because they hadn't [then] expected us."

During the halting conversation that ensued, the young lady "silently gazed about the room" until Sytin addressed a question to her: "Have you been passing time pleasantly, Evdokia Ivanovna?" Her answer was that of a woman both dutiful and clear-eyed. "And how can it be pleasant? We work for others' pleasure at weddings and balls. My good times are when I go to church or to the theatre with Papa." She let Sytin know that he had no rivals. Then, Sytin continues, "the conversation got sticky. Sharapov was silent, like a little owl. The master of the house was silent. It was painful and awkward."

But, for all his discomfort, Sytin had found Evdokia to his liking. Before taking leave, he arranged to meet her alone a few days later in a public park. There he successfully proposed that a wedding take place in two weeks' time. Since Evdokia and her father expected the offer, she must have gone to the park to accept it. Arranged marriages were common in pre-revolutionary Russia, and this one was to last a lifetime. Sytin says almost nothing further in his memoirs about his married life, but he did take pride in having quickly negotiated both a worthy contract and a "typical merchant's wedding with music and dancing and many merry people."

Sytin had by now become shop director, and the couple moved into two rooms on the mezzanine of Sharapov's establishment. Evdokia, however, yearned for quarters of her own, since Sharapov's housekeeper seems not to have welcomed her. Equally restive, Sytin let Sharapov know that he needed one thousand rubles a year - a threefold increase in salary - and his own print shop. Sytin wanted to use more modern printing methods, and he knew that Sharapov would never agree. The master in turn admitted that he was too old to change his ways but said he would gladly defer to Sytin. Sharapov, with no direct heirs and with his thoughts turning more and more to the next life, consequently made a generous and mutually beneficial arrangement.

He would retire from printing but would remain officially as owner. Sytin would take over the printing side of the business but pay Sharapov a 10 per cent commission on every sale, an agreement that permitted the young assistant to acquire new premises. In the summer of his wedding year, 1876, Sytin established his first shop, with living quarters for himself and his bride, on Voronukhinaia Hill not far from the Dorogomilovskii Bridge. They would welcome a daughter, Maria, the next year.

Sytin had immediately taken steps to modernize. Using his wife's dowry of four thousand rubles and a loan of three thousand from Sharapov, he bought a hand-operated French lithograph press that could imprint colours faster, better, and cheaper than the ladies of Nikolsk. He could not yet afford the steam-powered equipment that had become standard in the large shops, but he could now handle every stage of production under his own roof.

Nor did his improvements stop there. As avid printers have done since the invention of moveable type, he visited other shops to discover better methods of production. He redoubled his efforts to cultivate the pedlars and added more dramatic, tale-telling prints and booklets to expand their purchases beyond "religious pictures and scenes from peasant life."[20] On many an evening he and Evdokia invited their employees for tea in their apartment and exchanged ideas on new projects for the shop.

Because his innovations required new skills, Sytin expanded his two-man print staff to include three lithograph artists, including M.T.

Soloviev, a future director of Sytin & Co. Their task was to draw directly on lithograph stones that had replaced the old woodcuts in the picture-printing process. Using lithographic crayons or lithographic pen and ink, they outlined the shaded illustrations on a stone specially treated to accept printer's ink only where their instruments had touched. To add a second colour, the artists had to draw, on a second stone, a set of shadings and lines that would "register" with the initial design. The pressmen then inked the new stone with the desired colour and over-printed each picture to add that colour.

In choosing these artists, Sytin almost certainly hired persons whose education exceeded his own, but differences of this sort would never deter him from acquiring the best technical, managerial, and creative personnel he could afford. This man from the country, still classified a peasant by legal estate, regularly followed his instincts, but always with due respect for the expertise of others. In this he was a typical entrepreneur.

All such maverick enterprisers also demand autonomy, and Sytin had been the one to insist on ending a long apprenticeship because the master was holding him back. Although he had necessarily given Sharapov a share in the new shop in exchange for start-up funds, Sytin would end thirteen years of dependent protégéship in 1879 by paying Sharapov back in full. After three years as master of his print shop on Voronukhinaia Hill, the twenty-seven-year-old Sytin would gain full independence and once again move up to bigger quarters.

During what proved to be the first third of his life, Sytin had schooled himself in the essentials of small-scale publishing and marketing and had acquired a print shop entirely his own. His obvious next steps were to expand his publications, his production, his markets, and his plant.

CHAPTER TWO

More Presses for the People

When Ivan Dmitrievich Sytin embarked on the choppy waters of independent publishing, he was intent on going far. A spirit of opportunism and the winds of change were with him, and by the turn of the century he would celebrate his fiftieth birthday in command of wealth, power, and a fleet of publishing ventures.

Success for Sytin came through a shrewd blend of idealism and opportunism. Old Sharapov had settled for publishing what the peasants wanted; Sytin set out to prove his social conscience and make his name and fortune by publishing what was good for them. Thus could he capitalize on populist ideals current among the intelligentsia; and thus, in 1877, he persuaded an accomplished graphic artist to help him uplift the benighted peasants through a joint publishing project.

I

A single surviving letter to Sytin in 1878 from the artist in question, M.O. Mikeshin of St Petersburg, documents, even epitomizes, the changing blend of self-interest and altruism that colours Sytin's long career. Like those who would later call Sytin a calculating hyprocrite, Mikeshin raises questions about the sincerity and reliability of the young publisher at the very start of his career.

In his letter, an aggrieved Mikeshin reminds Sytin: "I promised you that I would participate to the full extent of my artistic ability – not for money, of course, but for the disseminating through you of publications for the people containing the best examples of popular poetry and art. If I expected any advantage for myself, it would come later when our general endeavour bore fruit."[1]

The two had agreed to collaborate on an illustrated folk poem, "The Gypsy, the Peasant and the Mare," and Mikeshin was to receive one hundred rubles for drawings that required "weeks of full-time labour." A rate of pay that low, he continued, would eventually make him a beggar. Mikeshin restated the single condition he had set: excellent reproductions of his work. Thus, with Sytin's agreement, he had hired a St Petersburg lithographer, Rudometov, to make and send plates of the illustrations to Sytin's Moscow shop for photolithographic reproduction in colour. Before that order could be filled, however, Sytin had redirected Rudometov to etch the pictures on stone, the medium required by his lithographic press. Then he had refused the completed stones.

Mikeshin expressed strong dismay about that refusal and – as he had learned from an "unexpected letter" from Sytin – about the "temporary suspension of your payment [to me]." But Mikeshin was even more emphatic in his own refusal to entrust his drawings to Sytin's "experienced but not fully artistic" draftsmen. He had decided, therefore, to oversee the printing of the illustrations in St Petersburg. In addition, well before the final press run, Sytin was to send copies of the text set in type in Moscow to Mikeshin for proof-reading. Unless he had such control, Mikeshin would sever relations with Sytin.

On two counts – deferring the artist's fee and refusing to use Rudometov – Sytin had broken his agreement, and he had notified Mikeshin only about the first default. His pleas of financial difficulties could explain both lapses, but the reason could also simply have been Sytin's constant habit of trimming expenses. Not only had he arranged a low fee for Mikeshin but, in light of Mikeshin's saying that "any advantage for myself ... would come later," Sytin must also have kept to himself first claim on profits from their shared work.

Mikeshin's letter throws doubt, as well, on Sytin's claims to have acquired first-rate graphic artists. Mikeshin must have seen works by Sytin's staff, and in no way would he trust them with his illustrations. The final product, after all, depended on the lines and shadings fixed on the lithographic stones by the graphic artist. The defter he was, the better the printed picture; and copy skills were especially crucial in multicolour prints, which required a separate stone for each hue.

"The Gypsy, the Peasant and the Mare" made it to market in 1878, and Sytin later called it a great success.[2] That success was due, no doubt, to the quality insisted upon by Mikeshin in the face of Sytin's sharp tactics. Even before this venture with Mikeshin, however, Sytin had taken what he called his first step upward to commercial success by turning out highly profitable maps and battle scenes of the Russo-Turkish war.

Reports of Slavs suffering at the hands of the Turks had reached Russia in 1876, the year that Sytin began publishing on his own. The nationalistic Russian press had seized upon the issue, and intense public indignation followed. Some Russians had even volunteered to fight on behalf of the Serbs. So wide and strong a reaction forced a reluctant imperial government to declare war on the Turks in 1877.

Newspapers in general, and Michael Katkov's *Moscow News* in particular, fanned the nationalistic mood. Never before could reporters cover a Russian war so fully, for this was the first armed conflict to follow the censorship reform of 1865. This time correspondents could report directly from the battle zone, and at least two of them - G.D. Gradovsky and Vas. I. Nemirovich-Danchenko - won wide acclaim.

For the many Russians who could not read or afford newspapers, Sytin lithographed inexpensive prints illustrating the war. He considered it a risky venture. "I hired the best graphic artists and first class printers, did not bargain with them over wages, but demanded high quality work; finally, I followed the market and with the greatest effort studied people's preferences."[3] More accurately, Sytin had his workers copy maps from atlases and war sketches from one of the new illustrated newspapers, *The Universal Illustration*. From these he turned out prints showing battle sites and soldiers bravely serving the church, tsar, and fatherland. They sold well through the pedlar system and posed no problems with censors.

Sytin had collaborated with Mikeshin during the second year of the war, just before he became a fully independent publisher. In the next year, 1879, his first son, Nicholas, was born; he became official owner of his enterprise by buying out Sharapov's share; and he invested in a second press[4] and a building closer to the centre of the city. The new shop stood across the Moscow River from the Kremlin and about a mile down Piatnitskaia Street, a thoroughfare that runs through the old merchants' quarter and on into a manufacturing district. Here, where merchant and manufacturer met, Sytin suitably located his printing business; and here, for forty years, he would operate it, until its expropriation by the new Soviet state in May of 1919.

Commercial and industrial growth was stirring old Moscow in many quarters. The city itself was becoming the hub of the Russian railway system and the centre of cotton cloth manufacturing in the Empire. To promote additional development even as they displayed what Russia as a whole had accomplished, the city fathers helped stage the national exhibition in Moscow in 1882. Already disposed to fairs as a means of promotion, Sytin decided to take part.

Even though the assassination of Alexander II in 1881 cast a long shadow, that next spring the All-Russian Industrial and Artistic Exhibition of 1882 opened on schedule. From 20 May to 30 September over one and two-thirds million visitors viewed its wonders. Sytin managed to erect two of the exhibits and win a bronze medal. He felt he deserved better, but "peasants," he later explained, "could not receive gold medals."[5]

Preparations for the opening had been extensive in and around the huge building that housed the four-month exposition on Khodynskoe Field outside of Moscow. And to emphasize Moscow's importance to railroading, the government had commissioned the laying of train tracks from the city centre to a special station at the site. Fair organizers also provided another product of modern technology rapidly becoming commonplace in the large cities of Russia: a daily paper. For it and for a weighty catalogue that listed all exhibitors, the organizers bought distinctive type costing three thousand rubles. Then, to help defray costs, they sold space for advertisements in both publications, keeping their ad space discretely smaller than "our American colleagues" at the Philadelphia Exhibition of 1876 who, the Muscovites felt, had overplayed commerce.

Opening ceremonies on 20 May began with the arrival of Alexander III precisely at one o'clock. The Tsar heard words of welcome from Governor General Dolgorukov and praise to God for technology from Metropolitan Marcus, the ranking prelate in the capital. Mid-afternoon lunch came next with its mandatory toasts, hurrahs, and "God Save the Tsar"; and then the imperial entourage spent a good hour touring the exhibition building.

Half the hall housed the exhibits related to the arts. Their overseer, academician M.P. Botkin from Moscow University, had taken a liking to Sytin, and he personally steered Alexander to Sytin and his display of prints for the country folk so dear to this emperor. Moving on to the industrial displays, the imperial party again confronted Sytin. This time the young Moscow printer was demonstrating the "first printing machine manufactured in Russia," and he just happened to be printing pictures of the imperial family. Making a good impression could serve to advance his business.

II

Besides the new printing technology, however, what boosted Sytin's enterprise most was the great expansion of publishing in Russia in the last quarter of the nineteenth century. As railroads and industries grew, so did the need for business forms, catalogues, reports, and the like; and even greater was the increased demand for teaching and learning tools. The educational reforms of the 1860s provided new schools for the peasants, and the military started others after the mid-1870s for its unlettered conscripts. Literacy committees, responding to populist ideals, designed reading material for the people, including special texts to teach adults to read. Here were incomparable opportunities for a printer worth his salt.

Because pictures were at first his biggest stock in trade, Sytin at the start of the eighties set about selling bright, simple prints to the schools. He consulted educators such as A.V. Pogozheva, a leader in the Sunday school movement, about what was needed, and the results were "graphic aids in geography, ethnology, biology, history ... historical persons ... rivers, oceans, the Caucasus, dangerous fords, provincial cities, Petersburg, Moscow, notable buildings – all this we illustrated," recalled Sytin. Purchases by teachers during the decade, he said, helped raise his picture sales to fifty million copies annually. In the early nineties, Sytin's staff would innovate material to fit the elementary curriculum required by the minister of education. The first of these inexpensive albums illustrated "The Twelve Main Festivals of the Church and the Resurrection of Christ," and, over the next twenty years, another forty-nine would appear on subjects from art to zoology.[6]

Sytin had learned from Sharapov to print pamphlet-size books for the peasants, usually of sixteen pages.[7] Now, by adding a bookbinding shop, Sytin bravely, and fortuitously, branched into thicker spine-backed books for literate peasants, country clergy, and shopkeepers. These small books sold for two to five copecks each and fell into three categories: folk tales, severely abridged classics, and stories by local hack writers. Again consulting Pogozheva, Sytin added books suitable for children, many pirated from western writers such as Sir Walter Scott, Mark Twain, and Jules Verne.

For every new tale Sytin accepted, a local writer earned a meagre two to five rubles for sixteen pages, although star scribblers like Misha Evstigneev and Kolia Milenky could command twice that. To justify such low fees, Sytin expediently lumped his writers together as "dismissed seminarians, exiles from educational institutions, drinking officials, drunken priests, and failures of all kinds," implying that but for him they would have had no work. By a twist of Christian logic, he emerged a benefactor.

Sytin insisted that virtue triumph in every story, but he hired no one to edit his writers' rough prose. Confessing that his prime test for content was a quick survey by "touch and eye," he mainly riffled through submissions to gauge how long the book would be. Each purchase then went straight to the typesetters and on down the production line to the pedlars as quickly as possible. This slapdash rush into print was the work of Sytin the money-maker, not the Sytin who vowed that he cared most about printing works of merit for the masses. And his various books, like his pictures, sold in the millions of copies.

Among Sytin's authors was A.S. Prugavin, and from him comes a sample of Sytin's early publishing practices, purportedly in Sytin's own words.

I looked at the manuscript and I saw it was well put together, but the main thing was that it was terrifying. Such horrors simply made your hair stand on end. Well, I thought, this book will go well. I bought the manuscript, paid the writer five rubles, and sent it to the press. 30,000 copies were printed. And what do you think? It was a sensation. How they liked it! How they liked it! [But when] I ordered another 60,000 - the compositor suddenly came to me and said, "What are we doing here, Ivan Dmitrievich?" "What do you mean?" "Well, we have published Gogol without asking anybody - take a look." And he showed me Gogol's "The Terrible Sorcerer [actually, Vengeance]".[8]

Sytin read so little that such flagrant plagiarism could easily have escaped his notice, but it was also in character for him to dodge royalty payments. Probably even Sytin's censor had missed the need for a credit line to Gogol, but he skimmed over Sytin's manuscripts solely to find any seditious or heretical lines.

In 1882, his fifth year as an independent printer, Sytin borrowed five thousand rubles from Sharapov to open his first retail outlet, a bookstore at Ilinsky Gate, near where he had apprenticed. He still rolled up his sleeves every day, but having transformed his Piatnitskaia shop into a printing plant, Sytin was more and more the overseer who kept his hands free of ink.

By now both of Sytin's sisters had settled in Moscow, and the rising young publisher surely paid their dowries. One wed a merchant, I.I. Sokolov; in February 1883 he and two others, D.A. Varopaev and V.L. Nechaev, formed a partnership (*tovarishchestvo na vere*) with Sytin to found Sytin & Co., capitalized at seventy-five thousand rubles. [9]

For that outside backing Sytin accepted some fiscal advice as Sytin & Co. began, but he remained the undisputed publishing boss. By selling his bookstore and printing plant to the company for thirty-six thousand rubles, he had acquired 48 per cent of the stock and the title of chief executive. That December he bought from Chekhov the story rights for an estimable volume, *Tales and Stories*, which he would publish in late 1884.[10] Within two more years he would manage to have his firm "imperially authorized," a designation that gave it, among other privileges, a favoured position for commissions to do government printing. Perhaps the favour resulted from his cordial meeting with the Tsar at the exposition, but hostile critics would later contend, very plausibly, that Sytin paid a sizeable bribe.[11]

Not one to leave assets idle, Sytin opened a second bookstore in Moscow and bought out another printer, one Orlov, to acquire his five printing presses, type, and inventory. Best of all for his firm, Sytin in 1884 began marketing a new and lucrative item – the calendar he had had in mind for five years.

Calendars were a household staple for all who could afford them, their publication in Russia dating back at least to the sixteenth century.[12] Peter the Great had given the Academy of Sciences sole printing rights at the beginning of the eighteenth century, as a way to stamp out astrological calendars, opposed by the church as pagan, or any with dangerous political slants. An early nineteenth-century statute reconfirmed that monopoly, and the academy continued to print the only legal calendars in Russia until the 1865 censorship reform opened the field to private firms. Moscow publisher A. Gatsuk then became the dominant producer, with such book publishers as A.S. Suvorin printing calendars only as a sideline.

Sytin launched his calendar at his seventeenth Nizhnii Novgorod fair in the summer of 1884. Whereas Gatsuk and his competitors sold mainly to urbanites, Sytin aimed his innovative General Russian Calendar for 1885 at peasants, the buyers he knew best. The cover and an accompanying bonus picture were vivid colour reproductions meant for home display. The calendar's inside pages provided the numbered days of the year along with captioned coloured pictures of field work and rural landscapes.

This new item, like all Sytin's works so far, readily passed the censors. But now a wholly new venture was to bring Sytin under government scrutiny at the insistence of the Russian Orthodox Church and C.P. Pobedonostsev, the powerful ober-procurator of the Holy Synod. As a guardian of the faith, Pobedonostsev took strong exception to Leo Tolstoy (by now an outspoken critic of Orthodoxy and a proponent of what police reports termed "socialistic" beliefs) and his followers, the Tolstoyans. He and church officials found it alarming, then, when Sytin, with his broad access to common readers through the pedlars, began in 1885 to publish and market Tolstoyan books for the peasants.

Anyone seriously bent on spreading publications throughout the countryside needed a multitude of pedlars, and Sytin had by far the largest army of these brazen salesmen who walked or rode from remotest *izba* to *izba*.[13] They didn't knock on doors. Instead they bawled their spiels through windows: "books, icons, thread, buttons." Because they also brought a certain amount of news and gossip, they were usually welcome. By Easter, these trekkers headed back to their own plots for the tilling and planting seasons, a time when their customers spent daylight hours in the fields and had little spare change.

Sytin knew what kind of wares these independent vendors wanted. For one thing, they insisted on tales with bright and lively pictures, since many of their customers, like a good proportion of the pedlars themselves, could not read. Calendars and church books were also good items, but none could be bulky. Nor could they be costly. Since the peasant would pay only one to three copecks for a printed item and the pedlar insisted on a profit margin of 100 to 300 per cent, Sytin could charge the pedlars no more than about ninety-five copecks for one hundred copies of a sixteen-page book. And for flexibility in haggling, says Sytin, his pedlars wanted no prices printed on the books and calendars they carried.

Sytin tailored his *lubki*, or prints and simple books for the people, to meet these demands. From the outset he had specialized in emotive, iconographic pictures, and these became the standard for artwork on his calendars and *lubki* for the peasants. His artists took special care with book covers, usually placing a short arresting title above an eye-catching, even lurid picture. Merely by flashing a copy outside the window of the *izba*, the pedlar could often make a quick sale and so confirm a favourite truism of Sytin's - that the picture carried the book.

These little books attracted to reading untold numbers, young and old. The engraver I.N. Pavlov, who was later to work for Sytin, recalled his own childhood fascination with Sytin's *lubki* "with their many-coloured covers," each containing "the name of the fabulous publisher who so excited my passionate imagination." As an eight-year-old, he had loved going to a Sytin bookstore to buy "for 15 copecks a whole ten books, whatever the content."[14]

As literature or art, however, books for the people like Sytin's were usually slipshod, as one critic put it.[15] In some, the title had little to do with the contents, and the pictures might not relate to either. The sentences were often ungrammatical. Great gaps would appear in the text where the printer stretched out his type to fill the page. Because the paper was thin, soft, and absorbent, the impression made by the type tended to be blurred.

But what especially aroused intellectuals against these *lubki* was the "blood-stained action" that stirred coarse passions and fortified superstitions.[16] Tolstoy, for one, while lecturing the educated classes on their debt to the working poor, had been urging others to help him provide the peasants with simple, moral printed works of high quality. One zealous young Tolstoyan of some means, Vladimir Chertkov, had thus decided in 1884 to underwrite such publications himself, and Chertkov had turned to Sytin, the master pedlar of *lubki*.

III

For Sytin, the Tolstoyans meant entry into the world of respectable book publishers, a lucky fact he underscores in his memoirs. Referring to his marginal reputation at the time he formed Sytin & Co., the publisher recalled his frustration in aspiring to "make a connection with a world unattainable to us, of genuine writers and genuine literature." Then, through "chance ... everything turned out as in a magical tale. From Misha Evstigneev and Kolia Milenky, I stepped straight up to Leo Tolstoy and Korolenko."[17] Sytin was the only Russian publisher of folk printing - of whom about one hundred, like him, came from peasant stock - to gain literary respectability.[18]

Sytin began that transition in November 1884 when Chertkov stopped in at a Sytin bookstore to propose bringing him *lubki* pictures and text, paying for their publication, and then circulating them, at no profit to Chertkov, through Sytin's pedlars. Sytin listened especially closely at the mention of Tolstoy, whom Chertkov named as a collaborator.[19]

In his letter to Tolstoy about the meeting, Chertkov wrote that "Sytin requests text not only for pictures ... but also for books";[20] and books would prove to be the format of all Chertkov's publications. Neither now nor later did Sytin and Chertkov set down terms in a contract. Merely by informal agreement would Chertkov assume responsibility for layout, editing, and proof-reading (three stages that Sytin mainly omitted for his own *lubki*) and price his simple books at the level of Sytin's.

By February 1885 Sytin had given his censor the manuscripts of the first four books and surely smiled at the consternation he caused. Three were by Tolstoy ("What Men Live By," "A Prisoner of the Caucasus," and "God Sees the Truth but Waits") and one by N.S. Leskov ("Christ Visits the Peasant"). When all four came back approved, Sytin set in motion the remarkable Mediator (*Posrednik*) series, a name he claims to have chosen himself to denote his own modest role as intermediary between the intelligentsia and the popular market.

Suddenly Sytin was on the side of the good. Although his other ventures were commercial, he would remind his critics, "Mediator is like a prayer; it is for the soul."[21] To the extraordinarily pious Tolstoyan, Paul Biriukov, Sytin had become a "divine spark" in the "great business of enlightenment."[22]

This great business required the mundane energy of men and machines as well, and Sytin already had his presses going full tilt to fill ever larger orders for his own books, calendars, and posters. As was his habit, Sytin bought new equipment. He acquired a machine to make zinc electrotype engravings of typeset copy and illustrations because these durable forms were easy to store and reuse for later printings. And at the end of 1885 he added a press that could print fifty thousand books per day.

Chertkov, with more enthusiasm than accuracy, exulted to Tolstoy that December that the pedlars mainly wanted Mediator books and that demand exceeded supply, even though Sytin was "printing almost exclusively ours."[23] But Chertkov's expressed belief in the generosity and full-time dedication of Sytin was lost on Tolstoy, who had very recently met Mediator's publisher.[24] For Tolstoy, Sytin was just one more merchant-publisher intent on serving himself, not culture or his people. He expected problems over Mediator, as certainly as Sytin would demand his pay.

By the spring of 1887, it so happened, Chertkov had fallen far behind in his payments.[25] Once again through a merely informal agreement, Sytin regularized affairs by assuming all production costs and then selling the Mediator books to Chertkov, who resold them to the pedlars.[26] (This must be the point at which Sytin charged the price he quotes in his memoirs for printing the Mediator series – that is, eighty copecks for sixteen-page books in lots of one hundred.[27] He says he realized a fifteen-copeck profit on each lot, as would Chertkov in charging the usual wholesale price to pedlars of ninety-five copecks per one hundred books.)

It was this arrangement that Chertkov explained to V.G. Korolenko in 1891: "Initially Mediator required significant material means; at the present time all the major expenses are covered by the Sytin firm, which, society's belief to the contrary, does not make any money from these publications (over all the details of which we retain full and absolute control) although its expenses and labour are covered by small and fully legitimate mark-ups."[28]

Tolstoy would later chide Chertkov for praising Sytin for his charity when Mediator benefited Sytin & Co. so greatly in prestige.[29] But there is clear evidence that Mediator could not have survived without Sytin's intervention and generosity. Letters prove that Sytin not only paid all honoraria but also relinquished all related rights to Chertkov.[30]

Sytin, of course, agreed with Tolstoy about the great advantages to his company from the Mediator books, and he describes the series as his second crucial step upward. The prestige and contacts were invaluable.[31] How else could he have begun issuing the works of leading authors such as N.S. Leskov, G.I. Uspensky, A.I. Ertel, A.V. Grigorovich, Anton Chekhov, and Tolstoy? The admiration of the populist intelligentsia for them and for Mediator redounded very favourably on Sytin.

Church officials, in contrast, deplored Mediator precisely because of its links to Tolstoy. Since Tolstoy openly expounded views antithetical to Orthodoxy which Mediator would spread to the people, the weekly *Moscow Church News* campaigned in 1886 to have the series banned in its entirety, and an archpriest's brochure urged the clergy to obstruct sales of the books. In his report for 1887 as procurator, Pobedonostsev condemned Mediator by name, and later that year Sytin was complaining about slumping sales.

Knowing all along about Tolstoy's rift with the official church, Sytin had expected snags with the censorship over Mediator; and he dutifully answered summonses from Pobedonostsev about the series "more than once or twice."[32] All the same, he turned most of his attention in this period to his own publications and to new projects, his first love. With the help of professional educators, he brought out his first classroom textbook in 1887. This slim *Russian Grammar* was his unobtrusive first attempt at breaking into the lucrative schoolbook market.

Prodded by Ertel, he had even earlier begun to publish literate, illustrated, and exciting books of stories to engage young readers. The Victorians in England had led the way in the sixties with their lavishly illustrated, multi-coloured fantasy and adventure books,[33] but well into the seventies, Russian books for children "bore the heavy hand of the German pedagogue."[34] By handing over some of his own stories, Ertel pushed Sytin into publishing quality books for children in the Victorian mode but with Russian content.

Another independent venture into good books came in 1887 when, like several other publishers, Sytin seized the opportunity offered that year by the expiration of copyright restrictions on the works of Alexander Pushkin. Here were distinguished writings, fully edited, long since censored, and free for the taking; and Sytin set them forth in an undistinguished but inexpensive ten-volume edition. The complete works had before sold for five rubles. Sytin slashed his price to eighty copecks, followed that up with the writings of Gogol for only fifty copecks, and found that demand "exceeded my greatest expectations." The bold experiment was a runaway success and a notable innovation for Russian publishing.[35]

Sytin felt himself move one notch higher in respectability, for his cheap editions of Pushkin and Gogol allowed him to lay claim to spreading culture by his own careful design. With every multi-volume set he sold, he said, he had made it more likely that an ordinary Russian would pick up a copy, try a few lines, and find himself reading. A formula like this pleased Sytin and translated into profits.

His shift into weightier books did not go unnoticed by the Tolstoyans. "Sytin, who is more intelligent and farseeing than other popular publishers,'' one of them commented, ''has understood that the golden time for [*lubki*] has passed irrevocably.'' Sytin had consequently ''seized on Mediator as a sheet anchor so that, under its influence ... he would change little by little the character of his publications.''[36] More precisely, Sytin was diversifying, for he would continue to publish *lubki*. (Figures on annual sales of his *lubki* are not available, but one source does confirm that two thousand pedlars worked for Sytin through the 1890s.)[37]

Meanwhile, bookstores were becoming more and more important as outlets, and for their use Sytin in 1888 issued his first list of works in print. Entries in this *Catalogue of I.D. Sytin and Company's Books and Pictures* covered forty-six pages, and in one edition the educator N.V. Tulupov advised parents on the best books for different ages and interest levels.[38] Sytin made certain that libraries and reading rooms received copies, and he displayed them prominently in his growing number of bookstores in Moscow and beyond.[39]

That May the government came down hard on Mediator by forbidding further printings of nine of the dozen or so tales by Tolstoy it had earlier approved, and Sytin reacted to the ban by neglecting his Mediator production even more. By October Chertkov was trying to mollify Tolstoy over repeated delays. Sytin, he explained, ''does not now especially need such small books and is terribly slow in printing them''; moreover, so great was the disorder in his shops ''that some manuscripts are being mislaid and we have to replace them with our copies.'' Chertkov counselled against ''unpleasantness with Sytin, whom I like and in [whom] lies all the mechanical strength of our venture.'' Rather, he favoured ''gentle patience and unremitting insistence so that ... all the material provided by me will be printed, even if it should take a full year after I have received it from the author.''[40]

Sytin had earlier taxed the patience of Tolstoyans by using his connections with Mediator for commercial gains. Through Chertkov, Sytin had won permission to reissue some Mediator tales on his own and, in his so-called supplemental series, to publish stories that Chertkov had rejected but still considered worthy. On their covers could appear the red border used by Mediator but not its motto.[41] So strong were sales that Sytin had decided in mid-1887 to fill the distinctive covers with children's stories from his own files. In a letter to Tolstoy that fall, Chertkov says he necessarily intervened to save ''tens of thousands'' from reading ''trash.''[42]

At least by the time Tolstoy's stories were banned in May 1888, however, both Chertkov and Sytin had abandoned red-edged covers. Enough priests opposed to Mediator were warning their flocks against books bearing the devil's hue to make red borders a liability for pedlars.

By the end of 1888, which marked four years of collaboration between Sytin and the Tolstoyans, Tolstoy had all but ended his involvement. By then press runs of Mediator books had totalled an impressive twelve million copies.[43] The partnership would continue for another sixteen years and Sytin would list one hundred titles in the series by the end of the century, but his own publications always outnumbered and outsold Mediator books many times over.

Thus it was that in 1889 the thirty-eight-year-old Sytin bought a neighbouring building on Valovaia street (where it crosses Piatnitskaia) to house more bookbinding equipment. The next year he erected a new building at his complex, and a year later he installed a two-colour rotary press from Germany which could print ten thousand calendars a day. By 1893 his company's production of twenty-one million copies of fifteen different calendars would represent 70 per cent of the annual calendar production of the Empire.[44]

Having conquered the production of *lubki*, calendars, and books, Sytin decided early in the nineties to acquire a periodical, both to make money and to promote his other publications. Thus, on 22 June 1891, Sytin invested personal funds to speculate on an undistinguished weekly for urbanites called *Around the World* (*Vokrug Sveta*). Sytin brought in new editors and would nearly treble its circulation to twelve thousand the next year. Its readership would rise to forty-two thousand by 1897.[45]

Although censorship officials had readily approved Sytin's purchase of *Around the World*, early in 1892 the minister of the interior, I.N. Durnovo, warned E.M. Feoktistov, his subordinate and director of censorship (as head of the Chief Administration of Press Affairs), that Sytin was politically dangerous.

I have learned from someone in whose word I have confidence, that the head of the well-known Moscow publishing firm of popular books, I.D. Sytin & Co., has fallen completely under the influence of several persons, at the head of which stand Count L.N. Tolstoy and Vladimir Grigorievich Chertkov. These persons are striving, apparently, to undermine gradually in the popular consciousness the principles of Orthodoxy, and, by means of sectarianism in general and Stundism in particular, to instill in newly formed rational multitudes an understanding of Christian socialism – the latest passion of Count Tolstoy.[46]

Durnovo had become minister in 1889, the year after the censorship had banned the nine Mediator tales by Tolstoy, and Sytin and Chertkov seem not to have attracted his attention until his third year in office.

Because, said the minister, Sytin was "extraordinarily soft" and easily influenced, should Feoktistov find "it possible to call him in to point out the danger" of associating with the Tolstoyans, then Sytin would surely break with them. That done, "the circle ... will be deprived of its means to reach the people with dangerous ideas." Durnovo wrongly cast Sytin as a simple man, but he was correct in expecting the publisher to ponder carefully any new official signals against Mediator.

Feoktistov apparently never broached the matter with Sytin, but he forwarded Durnovo's letter to the Moscow censorship committee to alert them to the minister's concern; and on 15 March 1892 he secretly ordered censors to approve Mediator books "only with extreme caution."[47] He also required that each Mediator reprint be reset completely. No longer could Sytin save a lot of time and money by reusing the original stereotype plates.

Faced with this new production snag and a decline in pedlar sales during the terrible famine of 1891–92, Sytin proposed to Chertkov that they loosen their arrangements.[48] A former editor of Sytin's, I.I. Petrov, may have prepared the way. Earlier in 1892 he had fulminated to the Tolstoyans: "You in St. Petersburg are not as aware as we are of Sytin's relations to you." That collaboration fell outside the category of "business affairs," Petrov stressed, and Sytin had endured "a lot in order to get Mediator out, and he hasn't displayed any impatience."[49] Then had come Sytin's proposal for cutbacks. Ready for change himself, Chertkov had agreed midway through 1892 to pass the headship of Mediator to I.I. Gorbunov-Posadov.[50] Sytin continued to publish Mediator books, but as a less and less important sideline.

Restive for something new and promising, Sytin hit upon adding a weekly newspaper to his *Around the World*. In September he set off for St Petersburg to propose it to the censorship administration. Surprisingly, he took Gorbunov-Posadov with him, perhaps to make introductions and smooth relations. But the official he expected to charm was Feoktistov, who had been advised by the minister to tell Sytin in person to break with the Tolstoyans. Now the head of the Chief Administration found himself facing the "duped" publisher with a Tolstoyan at his elbow. Since the question at hand was the perennially sensitive one of starting a newspaper, Feoktistov flatly rejected the proposal – as he would again the next year.[51]

Sytin must have been taken aback, for never before had the government blocked an expansion of his. Still, he stayed on good terms with the Tolstoyans, so that Gorbunov-Posadov wrote Chertkov after the St Petersburg fiasco: "Despite everything he has endured in the name of Mediator, [Sytin] is very pleasant and even kind to us."[52]

The turndown of his news supplement cost Sytin nothing, and he had already another request of greater importance: government approval to transform his business into a joint-stock company (*tovarishchestvo na paiakh*), as four other publishing houses had done, to raise the huge capital needed to buy high-speed, western printing machines.[53] The decision depended on investigations at the close of 1892 by both the Department of Trade and Commerce and Durnovo's Ministry of the Interior about the commercial and political reliability of Sytin's company. Neither raised any objections.

From the Imperial Committee of Ministers on 1 January 1893 came the charter for the new Printing, Publishing, and Bookselling Company of I.D. Sytin (for brevity, here to remain "Sytin & Co.") capitalized at 350,000 rubles, nearly five times the worth of Sytin & Co. at its founding in 1884. Notably, insiders bought all the "new" shares (each worth one thousand rubles).[54]

Even though it would henceforth appear on the listings of the Moscow and St Petersburg stock exchanges, the stock of Sytin's company was never to vary in price and never to sell publicly because company rules gave first right of purchase to current stockholders and their friends and associates, who always snapped up any available shares at the set price. One ready buyer, moreover, was to be Sytin himself; for he was soon to discover that holding less than 51 per cent of the shares greatly eroded his corporate authority.

For now Sytin was still effectively in charge, and that same year he was to win his company a very profitable contract to publish the Kharkov Committee for Literacy's *Book for Adults*, ultimately three widely used volumes. The first and most popular would go through sixteen printings. Sytin, who had joined the Moscow Committee for Literacy in the late 1880s, was again mixing business with good works, but this time with a better return. By giving the committee part of the profit for each book sold, he motivated teachers connected with the Kharkov committee to urge their students to buy only his books.[55]

Thanks to generally brisk sales of all Sytin's publications, Sytin & Co. was to expand its capitalization by another 100,000 rubles at the start of 1895. In August of that year Sytin would get permission from Moscow officials to enlarge his main building on Piatnitskaia Street to accommodate his burgeoning workforce of four hundred.[56]

Meanwhile, the Tolstoyans had decided to publish a series of small, more literate books for urban readers. Sytin would have none of it. Bypassing Gorbunov-Posadov, he wrote Chertkov in October 1893: "I more and more think that Mediator ought to be independent with its intellectual publications, to have its own arrangements with printing plants." He wanted its "management to run itself reasonably and independently from us" – that is, without Sytin as philanthropic collaborator – to get its work done "more expeditiously."[57] The Tolstoyans took their new project elsewhere, and Gorbunov-Posadov would finally combine all his publications into a Mediator publishing firm independent of Sytin in 1904.[58]

As long as Sytin printed Mediator books, however, Minister Durnovo continued to lump him with those who published dangerous and "expertly concealed propaganda" which his censors were powerless to forbid. In a dispatch to I.D. Delianov, the minister of public education, in February 1894, he therefore insisted on close control over book outlets. A movement that had its roots in the populism of the 1870s, he said, was using bookstores, reading rooms, libraries, literacy societies, and the like to promote "revolutionary doctrines."[59] Durnovo thought of Sytin as a full participant.

A year later and three years to the day after informing Feoktistov that Sytin was a dupe of the Tolstoyans, Durnovo again assessed the publisher, this time for the newly crowned successor to Alexander III and last of the Romanovs, Nicholas II. Durnovo's "Memorandum on the widespread distribution among the people of harmful publications by the committees of literacy and by the publishing firms of Mediator, Sytin, and Ermakov," dated 12 February 1895, accused those named of subverting the existing order. Increased literacy, Durnovo told Nicholas, meant that more and more publications were reaching the people. Commoners, he continued, "draw from them with naive trust new views on religion, social life, and on relations among people"; and the end result – "the spiritual awakening of the popular mass" – would decide the "entire future of Russia."[60]

The government was remiss in circulating too few books, argued Durnovo; for only the Holy Synod had a strong publishing program, and its emphasis was entirely religious. Durnovo then contrasted the trickle of brochures from the Imperial Commission for the Organization of Popular Reading with the flood of books from private presses like Sytin's. Railing most against Tolstoy, the minister decried that writer's "false doctrines ... [that] have in recent times openly and without hindrance carried the most extreme socialism and anarchism under the banner of Christ." Tolstoy's military stories, moreover, taught that true Christians "stubbornly refuse" induction into the army. Durnovo closed by advising Nicholas II to appoint a publishing committee to produce cheap, right-minded books to divert the masses from the Tolstoyan lies published by Sytin.[61]

Still another internal government document, written a month before Durnovo's, linked Sytin to subversion. It was the report of the Moscow Okhranka (secret police) that led, very shortly, to the banning of the Moscow Committee for Literacy. The Okhranka declared that half the membership, 203 persons altogether, were "known for their political unreliability." They listed Sytin and two experts in teaching,

N.V. Tulupov and V.P. Vakhterov, who would both be working for Sytin within a year, along with such prominent Moscow liberals as Ertel, publisher V.A. Goltsev, and historian Paul Miliukov.[62]

Even as officials were sounding the alarm about Sytin, judges at the first All-Russian Exhibition of Printing in 1895 chose to give a gold medal to Sytin & Co. for its technical excellence; and this large, diversified publishing house, now distinguished by eminent collaborators, would win yet more awards in 1895 and 1896 for its books for primary schools and the general population.[63] The peasant who blamed his lowly birth for depriving him of a gold medal at the Exhibition of 1882 had since done very well.

Nor was he any longer a "peasant" by legal class. On an official document in 1894, Sytin listed himself as a "merchant of the second guild" - a legal rank in the merchant *soslovie* (estate) that bestowed special privileges and rights on Sytin and proved that he had risen spectacularly during his twenty-eight years in Moscow. Its entry requirements included wealth, position, and cultural contributions, and only "merchants of the first guild" and "honorary citizens" stood higher.[64]

On that same document Sytin also listed, by name and age, his six children at home: Nikolai (fifteen), Vasily (fourteen), Vladimir (twelve), Ivan (eight), Evdokia (four), and Peter (two). (Seventeen-year-old Maria was probably away at school.) In 1894 and 1895, moreover, Chekhov was figuring importantly in Sytin's life. As Sytin would hereafter seize every chance to tell, Chekhov was steering the ever-more-successful publisher into his next challenging and innovative project: a newspaper for the masses that would become a strong force for change in Russia.

The parents of I.D. Sytin, Dmitry Gerasimovich Sytin and Olga Alexandrovna. Sytin says little about them in his memoirs, *A Life for the Book*, but does suggest that the struggle to keep food on the table led them to neglect their family.

Handsome and debonair at twenty-two, Ivan Dmitrievich Sytin is still a bachelor but also the manager of the print shop in Moscow where he began as an apprentice seven years before.

Sytin at the turn of the century when he was about fifty with his wife, Evdokia Ivanovna. The occasion of the photograph may have been a wedding anniversary or the celebration in 1901 of Sytin's thirty-fifth year in the printing business.

Eldest sons Nicholas, on the left, and Vasily, in the uniforms typical of Russian students at the turn of the century. Because Sytin felt that they lacked judgment, his wife probably did not tell him about their consorting with political radicals in 1902. Later they held high positions at Sytin & Co.

Left: Daughter Maria and physician F.I. Blagov as newlyweds about 1897, the year that Blagov became business manager for *Russian Word*. Sytin finally won government approval to make Blagov official editor in 1901. *Right*: Youngest son Dmitry Ivanovich in the uniform of an imperial cadet. He was also to serve in the Red Army. After retirement, he started a collection of books published by his grandfather.

Sytin & Co.'s board of directors for 1904 in the frock coats and beards typical of the Moscow merchantry. Seated in ornate splendour from the left to right are M.D. Naumov, A.D. Stupin, N.I. Sviridov, and Sytin.

This studio photo, about 1912, of Sytin with his chauffeur, who remains unidentified, suggests a special camaraderie between the two men, one a multimillionaire head of Russia's largest printing enterprise, the other his frequent companion as driver of his elegant automobile.

The *Russian Word* building completed in 1904 on Tverskaia (now Gorky) Street in Moscow. It still stands, although the site of the building on the right is now an open square. Sytin lived here for many years in an apartment on the third floor.

Sytin gained respectability through these two men, Vladimir Chertkov and Leo Tolstoy. First came their close alliance with him to produce the Mediator series in the 1880s, which served to endorse Sytin among the intelligentsia. Other collaborations followed.

"Corn: how to cultivate it and the economic benefit to be gained from it" reads the title on this instructional book from Sytin & Co., one in its series "For the Peasants." The text, by a professional agronomist, ostensibly gives good advice on how to increase productivity and profits and serves Sytin's paired goals of enlightening the underclass and selling many books.

This cover on a bestselling classroom reader ("The World in Stories for Children") conveys the democratic spirit repeatedly promoted by Sytin. The illustration depicts a teacher in a country school surrounded by robust peasant boys, some actually attentive to the equation on the blackboard. This book from the third and fourth levels of the elementary school contains 416 illustrations and cost 85 copecks. Its twentieth edition in 1912 sold well over a million copies.

CHAPTER THREE

Conniving to Establish Russian Word

Sytin had long cast an envious eye at the daily newspapers of England and America that coupled broad domestic and world coverage with wide circulation: the so-called papers for the millions. Of particular appeal to him was their capacity to return huge profits. But how could he acquire one in autocratic Russia, where overseers of the press refused to license a "dirty liberal"? Here was an entrepreneurial challenge deserving his best wiles. He had only to gain somehow the command of a daily; then he could proceed, by deft stages, toward the boldness in print that western press barons thrived on.

I

Publishers of the vanguard mass papers in nineteenth-century Europe and America had aggressively bid for readers among the expanding and increasingly literate urban populations. They favoured a "new" journalism that injected emotionalism into reporting, even about affairs of state; and they sent reporters immense distances at great expense to find startling and often lurid exotica. Then, in tandem with generating demand for their papers, they had multiplied their production and distribution capacities through such new technology as high-speed presses, telegraph/telephone systems, and railway networks.

Among the American pioneers of the popular daily was a German immigrant, Joseph Pulitzer, who by 1878 had transformed two moribund dailies in St Louis into his own *Post-Dispatch*. In 1883 he bought the New York *World* where, by touching the "instincts of the largest numbers," he raised circulation ten times to 150,000 in two years time.

High readership gave Pulitzer multiple returns: big circulation profits, ready sale of advertising space at premium rates, significant influence over public opinion, and consequent social and political power. Because he claimed to serve the public good and speak for the masses, he could make a virtue of immense profits. In his modest summation, "money means independence."[1] By the end of the eighties, World had a circulation of 250,000, although its pre-eminence in New York would be challenged in the next decade by William Randolph Hearst's *Journal*.

Across the Atlantic, one English "penny" newspaper, the *Daily Telegraph*, beat Pulitzer's *World* to the quarter-million mark in readership. It did so in 1887 to stand first in the world in circulation. Cheapness was its hallmark, and, like many similar papers, it had emerged after the repeal in the 1850s of Britain's so-called taxes on knowledge – imposts on newsprint and the like that had kept publishing costs high.

An admirer and leading emulator of Pulitzer was Alfred Harmsworth (Lord Northcliffe), who acquired the London *Evening News* in 1894 and added the *Daily Mail* in 1896. After buying the *Daily Mirror* in 1903, he would take on the failing *Times* in 1908 and increase its readership from 31,000 to 318,000 in six years. One of his tactics to finance expansion was to sell stock in his papers to the public.

Northcliffe and his press peers, like Pulitzer, made a selling point of their independence and public spiritedness, a credo they could quote from a mid-nineteenth century *Times* editor. Writing in 1854, John Delane had described the newspaper press as England's "witness for justice and morality," a role he said the church had relinquished by entering politics. Since the government, in turn, was "purely practical" in conducting affairs, the press alone could meet the need of the people "not only to know what is done, but to be reminded and informed as to the principles and objects with which it is done."[2]

Since the sole restraints on published words were libel laws and the Official Secrets Act, journalists, often from the lower classes, had great latitude in citing wrongs at every social level. Their means was sensationalism – in the paper-hawking, emotive journalism favoured by Pulitzer – and one noted example was the crusade against child prostitution by W.T. Stead, the son of a poor clergyman.

Populist journalism came later to the European continent than it did in England and America. A major factor was the censorship that restrained privately owned newspapers in France, Germany, Italy, and elsewhere well into the second half of the nineteenth century. Only with the founding of the Third Republic in the 1870s did French dailies gain freedom from censorship, but there still remained another inhibitor of growth: factionalism. Most papers, all small in size, focused on a single interest, whether the theatre, sports, or a political party. Such papers proliferated, and Paris in 1900 would have 240, many of them dailies.

A few also generalized to win mass appeal, and *Le Petit Parisien* would emerge the undisputed leader in 1904 with a million-copy circulation. In Germany, where the new empire effectively continued censorship through its press law of 1874, newspapers in all the large cities reflected regional loyalties. To impose Prussian domination, Chancellor Bismarck used secret "reptile" funds to suborn private papers and gave a monopoly on information flow to the government-controlled Wolff Bureau.[3] The other leading continental paper was Italy's *Il Corriere della Sera* of Milan which would claim a circulation of 70,000 in 1900. Its readership centred in the Italian north.[4]

In Russia the relaxation of censorship by Tsar Alexander II in 1865 had lifted preliminary censorship from private papers in Moscow and St Petersburg, but the larger circulation papers that emerged there in the seventies and eighties fell mainly into the "boulevard," or apolitical and sensational, category. A paper that discussed serious issues could more easily provoke such costly sanctions as bans on street sales and advertising, subjection to preliminary censorship, or even closure.

Russia consequently had no popular mass paper of the sort published by Pulitzer or Northcliffe when Sytin came along in the nineties, and not even the bigger boulevard papers in the two capitals then exceeded five-figure circulations. Russia's most influential private daily, *New Times* of St Petersburg, would have just 60,000 readers by 1900; but so consistently supportive of the government was its publisher, A.S. Suvorin, that readers justly regarded *New Times* as semi-official.

Russian newspapers at this stage in Sytin's life, then, differed little in content and appearance from those of the sixties. Nor, by western standards, were they numerous. A survey of all the Russian papers circulating in October 1900 would show only eighty-eight daily, twice-weekly, or thrice-weekly papers in private hands, eleven of them in St Petersburg and seven in Moscow. It would list a few as "serious" but most as "unusual" or "of local interest."[5]

Classed in the latter category was a Moscow boulevard daily, *Russian Word*, with a circulation of nearly 30,000 – and Sytin as owner. As he would repeatedly explain, Anton Chekhov had convinced him that Russia needed an independent paper to counterbalance the semi-official *New Times* of Suvorin.

Chekhov knew Suvorin well. Having first broken into print in the boulevard papers, Chekhov had shifted to writing for Suvorin in 1886. The publisher paid well for printing Chekhov's short stories both in *New Times* and in book form, and the two men became business friends. In the company of Suvorin and his son, Chekhov visited western Europe early in 1891 and there marvelled at the high standard of living and cultural level of the people, as well as their freedom of expression.

His own commitment to Russia's downtrodden was deepening; as a doctor, Chekhov gave considerable time to fighting disease among the peasants on and near his estate at Melikhovo southwest of Moscow, and during the Russian famine of 1891–92 he attempted to organize private aid to supplement inadequate government assistance. Seeing grave need for liberal reform, he increasingly chafed at the anti-popular spirit of *New Times*. Thus he wrote Suvorin late in 1891 to criticize the paper's attacks on the radical philosopher Vladimir Soloviev.[6] The next year he visited Sakhalin Island to write an exposé of conditions at the penal colonies there, and he broke with *New Times* by publishing his account elsewhere. In an April 1893 letter to his brother, Chekhov railed against the *Times* editors: "To me, they are simply repulsive and I have already mentioned this to you repeatedly."[7]

Eight months later, on 16 December 1893, Chekhov met Ivan Sytin. As mentioned earlier, he agreed to sell him a collection of tales, and purportedly began his campaign for a paper to help make Russian life better – that is, to do what he had done through his Sakhalin account.[8] Chekhov, as a contributor to the Mediator series, already knew Sytin's qualifications for the populist paper he had in mind; and he himself was eminent enough to command Sytin's allegiance. A friendship began that would continue through the eleven years remaining in Chekhov's life – a period from which survive twenty-nine relevant letters from Sytin to Chekhov, merely four (one unsent) from Chekhov to Sytin, and several more by Chekhov giving his views on Sytin to others.[9]

Meetings between the two men convey a certain tenuous intimacy. Sytin was several times a guest at Chekhov's estate at Melikhovo, and Sytin more than once entertained the writer in return. When illness forced Chekhov to retire to his dacha in Yalta, Sytin visited him there.

All congeniality between Chekhov and Sytin might have ended in the fall of 1895 had Chekhov sent the Moscow publisher a message he framed on or about 4 October of that year. Chekhov filed away a pencilled draft of that acerbic letter but apparently never sent a copy to Sytin. He wrote it because Sytin had reneged on publishing *Surgery* (*Khirurgia*), a periodical of professional interest to Chekhov. The few peremptory lines began: "You for some reason refused and promised at one and the same time. Why?" Chekhov directed Sytin not to raise the matter again.[10]

Then, rather than send the letter, Chekhov tried another tack. He asked Suvorin to publish *Surgery* and got both his assent and his offer of a subsidy. When Chekhov in turn showed Suvorin's letter to Sytin, Sytin responded by matching that offer; and, with the deal closed, Chekhov expressed his thanks to Suvorin. "The matter suddenly caught fire," he wrote, and Sytin had agreed to "assume all expenses and will pay the editor two rubles for each subscriber, keeping the rest himself.''[11] Chekhov rightly guessed that Sytin would not let his St Petersburg rival get ahead of him.

Chekhov elsewhere says that he regarded Sytin as a shallow but still intelligent and intriguing character whose very real powers should be put to good use. That opinion underlay his advice to the writer I.I. Pavlovsky, when Pavlovsky was losing hope over getting Sytin to publish his works. ''With Sytin,'' wrote Chekhov, ''just get acquainted; about the publication of your works, I will speak of it when the occasion is appropriate. He is an interesting man. A great, but completely unlettered publisher, who came from the people. A bundle of energy together with slackness and purely Suvorinesque characterlessness.''[12]

All this said, Chekhov genuinely admired Sytin for having risen so far above his beginnings among the ''people'' and for establishing the only printing company ''where the Russian spirit reigned and where the peasant-purchaser was not pushed on his ear.''[13] This rough-hewn, uneducated man had acquired the means and machinery for accomplishing immense good but needed the guidance of cultivated minds to achieve it.

II

Within a year of their meeting, then, Sytin was saying that Chekhov had convinced him that the people needed a good newspaper. ''I didn't know the newspaper business and feared greatly its extraordinary complexity and difficulty. But A.P. Chekhov, whom I admired without reservation and deeply loved, almost at each meeting told me: 'Sytin ought to publish a paper.' ''[14]

Sytin may be name-dropping, however, in giving so much credit to Chekhov, since a letter of 1885 documents that, nine years earlier, Chertkov, Tolstoy, and Sytin were already discussing a newspaper for the people.[15] Moreover, before he had even met Chekhov, Sytin had twice applied for government permission to add a news section to *Around the World*. Chekhov surely encouraged Sytin, but Sytin may well have exaggerated Chekhov's involvement.

One certainty is that officials considered the publisher of Mediator to be, as a close associate of Sytin would later put it, a ''dirty liberal,''[16] and they opposed his owning so potent a shaper of public opinion as a newspaper. As a consequence, Sytin goes on to claim, Chekhov advised him to insinuate his way into ownership by quietly backing a properly conservative daily that he could transform into a liberal one. And Sytin took that course in 1894 to found *Russian Word*.

Confident of raising money enough to cover publishing costs and the mandatory five-thousand-ruble deposit to the government against possible fines, Sytin knew his main problem was finding a suitable "responsible editor" (the staff member required by law to face charges should the paper violate the press code). The man Sytin wanted had to be known to the government as a fervent patriot, and, again name-dropping, Sytin says that his acquaintance with Tolstoy led him to A.A. Alexandrov, then editor of the conservative journal, *Russian Review* (*Russkoe Obozrenie*).[17] The son of devout peasants, Alexandrov was bright, thoroughly conservative, and utterly disorganized. His slipshod attire and grooming made him look like a nihilist, the last sort of man he would consciously emulate.[18] After graduating from Moscow University in 1891 with top honours in Russian literature, he had joined his department as a *dotsent* (instructor), only to drop that post the next year when the publisher Boboroskin asked him to edit Moscow's "only conservative journal."[19]

At that juncture, the Chief Administration of Press Affairs had examined Alexandrov and found him "loyal" but too inexperienced. The "secret section," or investigative unit, of the Moscow governor general had agreed and had also questioned Alexandrov's sense of "mission."[20] Back came Alexandrov with a letter to the governor general promising – on behalf of himself, Muscovites, and the whole Russian people – "an excellent, healthy, truly Russian, truly conservative, literary-artistic, learned, and Orthodox-monarchical organ." He had been schooled, he said, by "the great patriot Katkov" who, right up to his death, "gave me signs of special favour."[21]

But an even more credible patron resided in St Petersburg: the Holy Synod's C.P. Pobedonostsev. The ober-procurator saw in Alexandrov a dutiful journalistic agent, and he surely figured in the Chief Administration of Press Affairs' reversing itself and permitting Alexandrov to assume the editor's chair at *Russian Review* on 1 January, 1893.[22]

Alexandrov would remain there until mid-1898, and letters during his tenure prove his friendly connections with Pobedonostsev and the Moscow Committee on Press Affairs. Pobedonostsev repeatedly gave advice on the *Review*'s contents, provided writings of his own, and arranged government subsidies to keep the journal going.[23] On one occasion an author sent Alexandrov his unsolicited article because, he said, Pobedonostsev had assured him it would be published.[24] Yet another sent his work through the head of the Moscow censorship, Prince N.V. Shakhovskoi, appending a note that Pobedonostsev had recommended the journal to him.[25] The hapless Alexandrov also received scores of letters (forty have survived) from authors complaining about broken promises and unpaid honoraria.

Alexandrov had just finished his first year of editing, then, when

Sytin decided that he would serve admirably as standard-bearer to win approval for an inexpensive daily in Moscow. Sytin had also learned that the overbearing, ambitious Mrs Alexandrov would favour another salary. Thus early in 1894 Sytin approached Alexandrov. In March he informed him that a backer, the merchant N.V. Reviakin, would soon arrive in Moscow.[26] Finally he had Alexandrov for tea.

In his memoirs Sytin sums up the wooing of Alexandrov in these words:

In the eighties, in the Moscow home of L.N. Tolstoy, I had met privat-dotsent Anatoly Alexandrovich Alexandrov, who was the tutor of the young son of the Tolstoys, Andrey Lvovich. Here was a chubby, awkward man 35 years old, lame, shaggy, ungainly. He was known for his closeness to Pobedonostsev and he published the reactionary *Russian Review* ... I concluded: there is only one man to whom Pobedonostsev without hesitation will permit the publication of an inexpensive popular paper - this is the editor of *Russian Review*, Anatoly Alexandrovich Alexandrov.

... I invited A.A. Alexandrov to tea, and with him I.L. Shcheglov [I.L. Leont'iev], the author of plays and a collaborator of journals, and G.P. Georgievsky, a teacher and writer known for his historical and philosophical articles.

Talking over tea, I carefully directed the conversation to the paper. "And why shouldn't we publish our own paper? You, Anatoly Alexandrovich are a personal friend of Pobedonostsev and, of course, he would never refuse you permission to publish a paper. He will even permit an inexpensive, uncensored and popular paper. ... Think how good it would be. The entire editorship is ready. You - editor; G.P. Georgievsky - lead writer; I.L. Shcheglov - feuilletonist; and I - your publisher. To strengthen the whole matter, it is possible to call on F.N. Plevako. Think about it, would it be so bad? Everyone will dance to our tune."

My ideas were greeted with approval by the entire company. "Yes, indeed, gentlemen. This is my idea: there is not a cheap paper in Moscow." Everyone began to discuss the future paper. Only Alexandrov was silent. "Well, how about you, Anatoly Alexandrovich, to be or not to be? Your turn to speak. Surely this is a worthy cause, and there will be work enough for all." ... I poured some wine in the glasses and proposed a toast to the future inexpensive paper. In order to strike while the iron was hot, I took from my pocket a 100 ruble note and put it on the table.

"Don't lose time, Anatoly Alexandrovich, here is some money for the road; go to St. Petersburg, to Granddaddy and he will do everything for you that is necessary."

Alexandrov agreed, "Well, why not? I am not against it. It may be worth trying. And what will the paper be called and what will its price be?"

"The price - five rubles a year," I said. "And the name depends on you. The editorship is ready, ... think up a name."

"And what if it is called *Russian Word*?" proposed Alexandrov. "Excellent. Superb. *Russian Word*." [This was a name made famous by a radical journal of the 1860s.]

Everyone agreed and a very happy, lively, jolly group broke up and went home. Several days passed. I was headed somewhere along Tverskaia. I saw Alexandrov with his wife Avdotiia Tarasovna in a cab. They saw me and stopped. His wife shouted from afar. "Congratulate us, Sytin! We have permission [from Pobedonostsev]."[27]

III

Validation of Pobedonostsev's permission took some time. The date of Alexandrov's formal application to publish and edit *Russian Word* is 10 May 1894. The interior minister gave his final approval on 16 October 1894.[28]

A letter on 29 June from Feoktistov, still head of the Chief Administration for Press Affairs, had in the meantime informed Alexandrov that consent was certain but awaited the five-thousand-ruble deposit required of all papers.[29] Payer of the deposit was a prominent attorney, F.N. Plevako, whom Sytin had mentioned over tea with Alexandrov as his counsel. Plevako was a friend of Sytin from his boyhood days in the shop of Sharapov and already a backer of Alexandrov on *Russian Review*. Sytin says he personally solicited his backing for *Word* only after Alexandrov's successful trip to St Petersburg.[30]

Besides Plevako and Sytin, others who helped provide the start-up capital of fifty thousand rubles were Reviakin, the Crimean landowner I.A. Verner, and the lithographer M.T. Soloviev. But Sytin saw to it that the only name to appear on official documents was that of Alexandrov both as publisher (meaning owner) and as responsible editor. Sytin also sensibly hired out the printing of *Word* to the government-owned press at the University of Moscow under V.A. Gringmunt, already publisher of the conservative *Moscow Bulletin*, a favourite paper of the autocracy.

Nothing in *Word*'s officially approved program suggested that the paper intended to break new ground.[31] Quite prosaically, *Word* had permission to print leading articles and telegrams; news from abroad, Moscow, and the provinces; articles from other papers; "expositions, interpretations, and elucidations of laws, regulations, and instructions" from the government; feuilletons of a "scientific and literary" character; and advertisements. In November the censorship gave *Word* the additional right to publish approved pictures of the imperial family and of prominent statesmen and gave it access to more readers by permitting it to lower its year-long subscription rate from five rubles to four.[32]

Word commenced in January 1895. Halfway through the previous month, as a truly spectacular promotion, Sytin had Alexandrov print 400,000 copies of a "specimen" issue dated 15 December for distribution throughout the country. But that extravagant effort failed to stir much interest. At a time when well-established dailies circulated 30,000 to 50,000 copies, *Word* started with about 10,000, and gave away one-third.[33] Regrettably, said Sytin, this new daily was an "echo of *Moscow Bulletin* [the conservative, nationalistic daily] ... for the simple people ... and unbearably vulgar."[34]

Word's inauspicious start worried Sytin. "In a state of melancholy and depression," he claims, "I took some of my usual medicine – I went to talk to A.P. Chekhov." Chekhov reassured him: "This editorial staff is not permanent. ... It is necessary only to await its natural death and to substitute another. And patiently await your hour." The first goal was "to secure the right to an uncensored paper." Then Sytin must hope for a "more enlightened time and the possibility of reforming" his new daily.[35]

Word lost a great deal of money in its first year. As early as March Sytin had begun to warn Alexandrov that he was spending at an unacceptable rate: "The only thing left is to go bankrupt and this will happen quickly."[36] By December nothing remained of the initial fifty thousand rubles that he had raised.[37] Plevako also had sharp words for Alexandrov. "The paper obviously has not found its road and gets along with cliches ... the idea that it satisfies its readers is clearly illusory."[38]

In desperation, Alexandrov asked for aid through the Grand Duke Sergei Alexandrovich, the governor general of Moscow, who endorsed the request and sent it on to his brother, Nicholas II. On 19 April 1896, Nicholas granted *Word* ten thousand rubles and on 5 June added another twenty-five thousand. Alexandrov managed to increase the press run by giving away more papers, but by the following December he reckoned an annual loss of twenty thousand rubles. In the new year Alexandrov asked the grand duke for another subsidy, describing his need as one of state importance.[39] (In Sytin's account, the grand duke was the one who responded with thirty-five thousand rubles in 1896, and the Tsar matched that figure in 1897.[40] But official records that have come to light so far confirm only that Nicholas II granted thirty-five thousand rubles in 1896.)

Perhaps on the insistence of unpaid landlords, Alexandrov had moved the offices of *Word* three times in the first year before settling on Tverskoi Boulevard near the Pushkin monument. That building had a mezzanine floor which struck his wife as a good place to set up housekeeping, and Avdotiia Tarasovna at once made her considerable presence felt. As staff member N.P. Bocharov put it: "The frequent hullabaloo which penetrated the editorial office down an interior stairway shattered the calm mood of the writers and hampered their work."[41] In the spring of 1897 Avdotiia Tarasovna – who could barely read, write, or calculate – installed herself as business manager. That Easter, after telling writers who asked for their wages that the money was needed elsewhere, she and Alexandrov tripped off to the neighbourhood of a favourite monastery to buy a cottage. A few months later, in August, Gringmunt refused to publish another copy of *Word* or *Review* until a bill amounting to several thousand rubles was paid.[42]

By this time Alexandrov and Sytin had had enough of their original agreement, and Sytin was ready to buy Alexandrov's sham title as publisher. To get the government approval he needed, Sytin paid Alexandrov yet more rubles on the condition that he tell officials that the "sale" of *Word* was his one means to keep *Russian Review* alive. On 28 August the two men signed an agreement requiring Alexandrov to go immediately to St Petersburg to petition for the transfer of *Word* to Sytin as both publisher and responsible editor. Should Sytin be unacceptable as editor, Alexandrov was to stay on in that role. Completion of at least the proprietary transfer would obligate Sytin to pay Alexandrov fifteen thousand rubles,[43] and probably neither expected Sytin's implausible candidacy as editor to succeed.

Sytin accompanied Alexandrov on his mission to the capital, and they went straight to the ober-procurator. They were received "ironically, but all the same graciously," says Sytin, and Pobedonostsev approved Sytin's becoming publisher (but not, evidently, editor). Thus armed, the pair approached M.P. Soloviev, the newly appointed and archly conservative head of the Chief Administration of Press Affairs, who had earlier written for *Word*. After hearing them out, Soloviev insisted on consulting the grand duke before he made a final decision.[44]

Confident that the grand duke would fall in line with Pobedonostsev, Sytin returned to Moscow and claims to have rushed to tell Chekhov the news. By Sytin's account, Chekhov first offered his congratulations and then his old advice "to change the editor and the matter will be in the bag." And part of what Chekhov had in mind, interjects Sytin, was the promotion of reading. Sytin quotes him as saying, "A newspaper reader ought to grow into a book reader. From where else will he learn about new books ... which book to buy."[45]

In recounting this advice many years later, Sytin justified on cultural grounds the many columns of advertisements in *Word* and *Around the World* that promoted Sytin's books. By invoking Chekhov, Sytin blunted charges like those by two journalists in the nineties (and many others later) that he kept *Word* going for strictly self-promotional reasons.[46] Not so, Sytin always contended. His first calling was his mission from Chekhov to edify the Russian people.

To underscore Chekhov's involvement, Sytin went on to recount that Chekhov held a party to endorse him as publisher of *Word* before a dozen Moscow journalists. The very evening of their informal talk, he says, "Chekhov arranged a small, very friendly meeting in the great Moscow Hotel" with twelve men from *Russian Bulletin* and *Russian Thought* (*Russkaia Mysl*). "Charming and affectionate as always, Chekhov asked his literary friends to support and help me."[47] But the reliable *Chronicle* of his life places Chekhov in Moscow only in February during 1897. As part of that February visit, Chekhov did entertain journalists at dinner two successive nights in the hotel Sytin speaks of; and Sytin was present with several others for the first affair.[48] Sytin thus misremembered or intentionally misreported being congratulated and then fêted by Chekhov just after seeing Pobedonostsev.

While the grand duke was pondering the sale of *Word*, Sytin and Alexandrov wrote to Soloviev on 2 September 1897 with a new request. Apparently assuming that Sytin would be rejected as editor, they asked that Alexandrov stay as responsible editor only until Sytin found a successor for him. Exactly a week later, Sytin sent off another missive, this time to request the official title of "second editor" for his newly appointed business manager at *Word*, F.I. Blagov, a practising physician who had married Sytin's first-born, Maria.[49]

Uncertainties over *Word*'s future set Sytin on edge. On 7 October he wrote to Chekhov despairingly. "Our money is being entirely plundered. This *Russian Word* gave us huge, unproductive losses, now a simply awful panic has befallen me. I don't know where to go now. One thinks that everything is lost."[50]

One week later the grand duke finally gave Soloviev his views. "The merchant Sytin (known to the Department of Police as the publisher of various brochures of a tendentious character)," he wrote, "proposes to change completely the staff [of *Word*] by recruiting persons who are politically unreliable." He understood that Sytin hoped soon to install as editor someone who had been under police surveillance.[51] If, regrettably, Alexandrov had to sell *Word* to save the *Russian Review*, he should do so only if he remained as *Word*'s editor. Such "close ties ... undoubtedly ought to reflect favourably on [Sytin's] publishing activity." Should Alexandrov leave, dictated the grand duke, Soloviev must close *Word* immediately.[52]

The head of the Moscow police reported similar concerns on 20 October. Although his investigation had uncovered nothing against Sytin's son-in-law, he suspected that the naming of Blagov was a first step toward turning *Word* in a "populist direction" under persons of "liberal orientation."[53]

In line with all this advice, Soloviev ruled that Sytin could publish

Word so long as he kept Alexandrov as editor, and he rejected Blagov as "second editor." Sytin and Alexandrov consequently went again in November to the censorship office in St Petersburg, and there Sytin signed a document making it "an absolute condition" of his publishing *Word* that he "maintain exclusive management and full responsibility in the hands of A.A. Alexandrov."[54] The Chief Administration officially approved the transfer on 3 December, and the first issue with Sytin as publisher came out nine days later.

That "first" issue came exactly four years after Chekhov's advice about starting a paper for the people and just three years after Sytin's first sample copies of *Word*. Sytin, moreover, had fathered his daily along with the last of his ten offspring: Dmitry (1895), Anna (1896), and Olga (1897).

With ample funds in the bank and so many under his roof, Sytin was gladly providing his wife Evdokia Ivanovna, the cook's daughter, with household help. He had also parted with fifty thousand rubles in late 1896 to buy for his family the Bersenevka estate of Prince Sviazhsky to the north of Moscow. There his children could freely roam the small acreage, use the larger of the two ponds for swimming or skating, and stretch out in the large, two-storied, multi-windowed manor house with its big closed-in front porch. Chekhov had at once remarked on the purchase and the price to Suvorin, surely to convey how well Sytin was doing.[55]

Now openly a newspaper publisher, Sytin proceeded to cut production costs by setting up his own plant for printing *Word* in a remodelled building on Strastnaia Square, separate in all ways from his publishing company. That February of 1898, he and Alexandrov petitioned to supplement *Word* with a weekly illustrated magazine, but Soloviev rejected the proposal.[56]

Three months later, having given up on *Russian Review*, Alexandrov notified the Chief Administration of Press Affairs that he was leaving *Word*. But the closure of *Word* required by the six-month-old transfer agreement did not take place. As Alexandrov and Sytin well knew, laws required the government publicly to justify every closure; and, given *Word*'s exuberant loyalty, Soloviev could hardly base the paper's termination on the mere departure of its editor. Instead he approved Sytin's replacement for Alexandrov – E.N. Kiselev, already editor of *Around the World*; and, sometime between September and year's end, Soloviev added Alexandrov to the Ministry of the Interior payroll as one of his censorship functionaries.[57] Kiselev, who assumed his duties at *Word* on 8 September 1898, inherited Alexandrov's principal writers, but Sytin could now see his way clear to shift gradually to journalists of a livelier stamp.[58]

One of the writers Sytin added in 1899 was the titled journalist, Prince B.A. Shchetinin, who would later publish an exposé of how and why his "sanguine" rags-to-riches employer started *Word*. Shchetinin contends that Sytin's motive for publishing a paper was quite simply "to rake in mountains of gold" and that Sytin typically complained about his poor lot to conceal how well he was doing.[59] Thus Shchetinin found Sytin's initial greeting to him contrived: "You will pity us, our paper is a poor one." After all, the circulation was by then nearing 18,000 under de facto editor Aksel Karl Germonius, newly hired away from the lurid street sheet *Petersburg Gazette*. Kiselev, officially the responsible editor, merely blue-pencilled any libellous or otherwise illegal material, says Shchetinin, who ranked *Word* at this stage among the worst of the "petty street papers."[60] While still keeping *Word* politically conservative, Sytin had transformed his paper from staid to sensational as a means to increase its sales.

But *Word* was still losing money. Early in 1899 Sytin told Chekhov that he was spending his personal savings to keep the paper afloat. "All the money accumulated in stocks ... has been squandered on *Russian Word*," he lamented.[61]

To get an outsider's opinion, Chekhov asked E.Z. Konovitser, owner of a rival paper, about the financial condition of *Word*. Konovitser replied that he would by then himself have owned *Word* if Sytin were not such a "difficult fellow." To acquire both the paper and its subscription income, he and his colleagues had offered Sytin stock in *Word* plus two deferred ten thousand ruble payments. Konovitser considered these terms "favourable, given the position of the paper, but [Sytin] refused, demanding twice as much."[62]

Sytin, after all, had Sytin & Co. to fall back on. Besides giving him ample earnings to gamble on private projects like *Word*, Sytin & Co. paid Sytin well for large ads in *Word* to promote its publications. So, too, the company treasury helped Sytin to gain some manoeuvring room with Soloviev. That is, he had the company hire Alexandrov to edit "popular publications" at ten rubles a printer's signature and then contrived to pay him triple that rate. To company officials who objected, Sytin pointed out the value of cultivating a friend in Soloviev's hire.[63]

Any publisher the least liberal was finding Soloviev a force to reckon with. This "Ignatius Loyola of the censorship," put in place as Pobedonostsev's ally in mid-1897, was an "exceptional despot" determined to make everything in print conform to his political, cultural, and religious orthodoxy.[64] He therefore abhorred all works that were commonplace (that is, popular) and once specifically said that no mere capitalist or "casual hack," as Soloviev surely deemed Sytin, should run a periodical.[65] As an administrator, moreover, this "ill, hysterical, peevish man ... completely discredited his department.''[66] He was, in sum, an obstructionist.

Sytin had carefully deferred to Soloviev and the procurator to gain open control of *Russian Word*, and he would keep his paper thoroughly orthodox, if basely commonplace, all through Soloviev's tenure. Meanwhile, at his well-established company he had continued his liberal direction; and toward that end, in 1897 he had hired a Mediator contact - N.V. Rubakin, a bibliographer and popularizer favouring leftist causes - to launch five ambitious series, or ''Libraries,'' for readers with at least a primary education, as well as a more advanced ''Library for Self Education.'' Frustrations caused by Soloviev are probably the main reason for Rubakin's staying only until 1899.[67]

From the outset Rubakin expected censors' objections to the books he published, among them E. Dementiev's *The Factory: What It Gives the Population and What It Takes From It* and Charles Le Tournier's *The Evolution of Slavery*. His headstrong expediency did not help. In July 1897, just as Soloviev took office, for instance, Rubakin had decided to circumvent troublesome censors in Moscow by sending the final, more controversial part of Le Tournier's book for typesetting and censoring in St Petersburg. At Sytin's behest, someone at the company with the initials ''N.I.'' intervened, ruling that the censor in the capital would recognize the ploy and ''cause great unpleasantness both for us and for [the St Petersburg printer].''[68]

At this very time, Sytin was still manoeuvring to become official publisher of *Word*. He had already found it wise to have his company back away from the Mediator series, his main point of friction with the censorship. He did not want Rubakin to cause new and unnecessary acrimony.

IV

Doubt among officials about the trustworthiness of Sytin never disappeared, of course, and questions about his acquisition of *Word*, given the almost immediate loss of Alexandrov, had cast the publisher in more bad light. To his further discredit, in 1898 Sytin faced charges, this time from the police, of subversive machinations through a bookstore that happened to share a building with a printing plant of the Holy Synod.

The police held that the store violated prescribed ''boundaries'' by featuring Sytin's Popular School Libraries, a series begun in 1896 for the popular educational market and edited by Tulupov. More important, they classified as politically and morally ''unreliable'' the stock company formed in September 1898 to back the store - namely, designated-owner I.V. Tulupov (the brother of Sytin's editor), F.I. Blagov (Sytin's son-in-law), Barbara Morozova (the wealthy Muscovite with a penchant for radical causes), and Vakhterov (another of Sytin's book editors). These same persons, argued the police, had ties with the Moscow Society for Literacy, allegedly a new version of the banned Committee for Literacy. Finally, citing Sytin as the "principal creditor," the police described Tulupov as merely a "fictitious owner."[69]

All these data convinced the police of a conspiracy by Sytin and his associates to spread subversive books to the people; thus at the end of 1898, with the approval of the Ministry of the Interior and the Moscow governor general, the police closed the store.[70] When Tulupov pleaded to sell to new owners, the police refused, agreeing with the governor general that such a "sale" would undoubtedly leave Sytin in control as before. Besides, according to police calculations, the stockholders would lose only about four hundred rubles each.

What troubled Sytin most about the bookstore closure in 1898 was its likely dampening of his chances to publish the Sunday supplement he still hoped to add to *Word*. In January 1899 he again sent Chekhov his gloomy thoughts about selling *Word*, evidently about the time that Soloviev had, for the second time, rejected the proposed free supplement. Soloviev had termed it "premature" and an innovation that would "promote the distribution of the paper" - Sytin's precise objective, of course[71] - even though the year before Soloviev had somehow seen fit to let Sytin & Co. at last add a news supplement to *Around the World*.

Even more disheartening was the recommendation that spring by a Moscow censor to prohibit the illustrated section already appearing each Sunday in *Word*. Learning of the threat, on 4 May Sytin implored Alexandrov, still an insider in the Ministry of the Interior, to intervene. In a follow-up letter the next week, Sytin wrote that the "angry" censor, S.I. Sokolov, "is mauling *Word* as much as he can and all that is left is to simply close it down." In yet another letter, Sytin implied that he was ready to pay to "avert a blow and to propitiate Soloviev not to destroy us."[72] Thanks to bribery or not, *Word* suffered no cutback.

Finally, late in 1899 Sytin won approval for an illustrated weekly called *Sparks* (*Iskry*),[73] but readers would have to subscribe to it alone or, at a higher price, in conjunction with *Word*. Soloviev, who was ill and on the verge of stepping down, stood firm in refusing to approve a free Sunday premium that would boost *Word*'s readership.

On Sytin's orders, the designers of *Sparks* spent the next twelve months readying a rotogravure like the popular *Illustrated London News* and *The Graphic* of London, *L'Illustration* of Paris, and *Illustratione Italiane* of Rome.

Sytin knew that he had to win readers away from a formidable rival, *Tilled Field* (*Niva*), the respected St Petersburg magazine of the Marks Publishing Co. that circulated about 250,000 copies in and well beyond the capital. *Sparks* would compete head-on with *Tilled Field* for the same audience of general readers in the central provinces.

Eclectic in every way, *Sparks* provided fiction, popular science, social and political commentary, theatrical criticism, line and prose sketches of public figures, advice on what to read, cartoons, travelogues, a report on judicial events, sporting stories, music with words for home sing-alongs, and reproductions of art – often of beautiful women. There was always something frivolous, like the sixteen drawings of shoes in the specimen issue of 1 December 1900 – one pair "running from the police" and from a victim and a knife in a pool of blood, the "feet of authority" in the jackboots of the gendarmerie, and "naughty feet," one masculine shoe, one feminine, suggestively paired.

Much later and well after his death, Leo Tolstoy would be named by Sytin's publicists as a mentor of *Sparks*. That is, the jubilee book about Sytin in 1916 would claim that Tolstoy had personally given the "fatherly advice that [*Sparks*] should publish exactly in the Russian spirit to foster love of the fatherland, its life, its leaders, its workers." Special issues over the years did, in any case, commemorate such icons as Pushkin, Turgenev, Gogol, Chekhov, and the emancipation of 1861.[74]

In December 1900 when he perused his first issue of *Sparks*, Sytin had been in charge of *Russian Word* exactly three years. Now, in this month of annual subscription campaigns, his desk was surely covered with advertising copy for both periodicals. Once again the inveterate promoter was offering free calendars from Sytin & Co., a premium he had begun at *Word* three years before to net 13,200 subscribers; then 18,700 in 1899; and 28,400 in the year just ending. Sytin regretted that *Word* had yet to make a profit, but he rightly expected it to break even and then some in 1901.

Meanwhile, Sytin was breathing easier because the head of the Moscow censorship committee, Prince N.V. Shakhovskoi, had moved up to succeed Soloviev in 1900. This friendlier overseer had, for example, immediately granted Sytin's request to publish a lithograph based on "Makar's Dream," a Siberian tale by Korolenko, even though five lesser officials had rejected it for depicting angels in heaven. Shakhovskoi would also approve Blagov as *Word*'s "responsible editor" in May 1901, perhaps in part because Sytin made a place at Sytin & Co. for the director's lady love – or, more accurately, added her name to the payroll. But even more persuasive was Sytin's appointment of a bona fide reactionary, Iu. M. Aderkas, as *Word*'s de facto editor that same May, a tactical manoeuvre by Sytin that would last five and one half months.[75]

Shakhovskoi in turn tried to exploit his rapport with Sytin. As Sytin tells it, the new director of press affairs ''proposed that I publish 'popular' books in St. Petersburg parallel to Mediator'' but under the sponsorship of ''the celebrated Society of Alexander III, which [officials] dreamed of substituting for the banned Committee for Literacy.'' Sytin says that he recognized this request as ''a simple attempt on the part of Prince Shakhovskoi to engage me in the government orbit and to make Sytin a semi-official publisher.''[76]

As a follow-up some time in 1900 or 1901, the president of the ''celebrated Society,'' Count S.D. Sheremetev, bid Sytin call on him in his splendid palace in St Petersburg; and Sytin may have made his way there in the sleek, black, chauffeur-driven motor car that was one of his few concessions to grandeur. When the count received him in the drawing-room adorned like an ancient Muscovite prince, Sytin claims to have felt no more than bemused concern lest his fabulously wealthy host break into an aria from *Prince Igor*.[77] Nor would he become his lackey publisher. Sytin too well appreciated the marketability of ''progressivism'' and knew that closeting with the autocracy would cost him his liberal collaborators from the intelligentsia.

Sytin said no to Shakhovskoi and Sheremetev, even as he revelled in the growing respect he sensed from the government. Now that he commanded so large a share of Russia's publishing industry, some officials were coming round to the notion that winning Sytin as an ally made more sense than attempting to control him by administrative, judicial, or policing means.

Sytin, after all, was genuinely nationalistic and honestly contemptuous of radicals bent on violence. But neither trait prevented his being a friend of populists and reformers, especially since possible change was on everyone's mind as the twentieth century began. Not surprisingly, then, this publisher who championed the masses was about to experience in his own plant the stirrings of the workers' movement that would lead to the revolution of 1905.

CHAPTER FOUR

Strikes, Politicized Sons, and Profits

Sytin had plenty to boast about as he forged into the twentieth century, his many presses running full ahead; so he hosted a big affair in 1901 and rallied guests who would extoll his good works and advertise his company. Critics could label him an opportunist and poseur, but no one could deny his success in large-scale production and profits. Figures continued to prove it. From 1900 through 1904 he was to increase the circulation of his *Russian Word* by well over four times and put its ledgers solidly in the black; and the separate records of Sytin & Co. for the five fiscal years in this same period were to show a better than doubling of profits.

I

Sytin's first party for self-congratulation had been a spur-of-the-moment affair in September 1896. Long-time friend Nicholas Teleshov, a writer published by Sytin, saved the invitation, which read: "I will observe on September 14 the thirtieth anniversary of my service to publishing. Thirty years ago I arrived from the Kostroma forests and at Ilinsky Gate embarked upon publishing. Not having prepared anything and not having put any thought into it, I only yesterday evening considered the matter and, in order not to pass this day in ordinary fashion, decided to ask over for the evening my closest friends."[1] The gathering included relatives, senior workers from the printing plant, and a few from what Teleshov termed Sytin's "small number of social contacts."

The much grander party for Sytin's thirty-fifth anniversary took place on 1 October 1901. A priest opened the celebration in typical Russian fashion at an afternoon service in the printing plant. The gala banquet, a full-dress affair at the Hermitage restaurant in Moscow, followed at 5 o'clock and centred wholly on Sytin. Among the noted persons who sent greetings in absentia was Chekhov, whose repeated success at the Moscow Art Theatre since 1898 had made him the city's leading celebrity. Teleshov gave a tribute in person, as did the artist V.V. Vereshchagin.

Sytin told his guests that they had helped him accomplish a great deal, but there was more to be done. His enterprises still lacked a central, guiding publication. His long-held dream, he explained, was to acquire the premier Russian illustrated magazine, *Tilled Field*, with its "rich assemblage of Russian authors." Just such "spiritual forces," said Sytin, will "help us with the great building that is so necessary and important to Russia" – that is, the advancement of literacy, education, industriousness, and self-confidence in the Russian people.[2]

To less sympathetic ears, however, such a plan smacked of monopoly. When Sytin later approached the publisher Marks about merging their enterprises, says one contemporary, Marks concluded that his Moscow rival was a "dangerous man" who wanted to control the book trade.[3]

From a late 1901 issue of *Messenger of the Booksellers* (*Vestnik Knigoprodavtsev*), meanwhile, came a far different summation of the thirty-five-year publisher. It praised Sytin for his multitude of publications that had "penetrated to all corners of our vast fatherland spreading useful and necessary knowledge to the people." Fortunately, continued the trade journal, "the creation of one of the greatest book publishing enterprises has not exhausted your many-sided talents." But such grandiose phrases could be expected from the *Messenger* because Sytin partly owned it and had helped to found the sponsoring Society of Booksellers.[4]

Some doubters also had their say. Leonid Andreev, just beginning his notable career, ridiculed the anniversary celebration in the journal *Courier* (*Kurier*). He scoffed in particular at the banquet remarks of Vlas Doroshevich – of whom more in a moment – and his naming Sytin as the "real minister of public education" in Russia.[5] However, Andreev had private cause to toss barbs.

It seems that the previous year Sytin had promised Andreev a flat 350 rubles with no advance for a first edition of his stories and had then dawdled over production, despite Andreev's being ill and in desperate need of money for his family. Here entered a rival publisher and rising literary star, Maksim Gorky. Learning of his fellow writer's plight early in 1901, Gorky wrote Andreev: "[Sytin] is a swindler and a son-of-a-bitch, for he has cleaned you out shamelessly, ruthlessly. My friends behave that way only at nights, on lonely streets ... because they want to eat; but your publisher is sated [Gorky used the adjective "syt," a play on Sytin's name]. He has become a robber by nature, that's for sure." Gorky proposed that Andreev instead commission Znanie (Knowledge), the publishing house in which he was a partner. "Don't you want to sell your stories to me? I will give you all the profit from them and 500 rubles now."[6]

Gorky promptly wrote the director of Znanie, K.P. Piatnitsky: "I wired Andreev that he is a blockhead and promised him right away 500 rubles plus the entire profit on the sale. He agreed. He is ill and is now in a clinic."[7] A grateful Andreev later summed up the deal to a friend: "I cannot expect anything but good from Piatnitsky. He and Gorky extracted me from the claws of Sytin – who had bought my book for 350 rubles! (And from Znanie I received 6,000 rubles [in 1901].) Without them I would have perished under heavy newspaper work."[8]

In his defence, Sytin probably had no notion of the literary worth of Andreev's stories and merely offered the terms he gave to all non-established writers. But that lack of discernment let Gorky easily dismiss Sytin's claims of being a publisher serious about raising the literary tastes of Russian readers. Later Gorky would place a higher value on Sytin, but another of his letters in 1901 confirms his early and partly expedient scorn for the rival publisher. That December, once again recruiting for Znanie, he sent a bid to Sytin's friend Teleshov: "Go ahead with Znanie ... the main thing is the firm. It is important that [it] not be swallowed by various bookselling crocodiles such as Sytin & Co. If your book is published with Znanie, I guarantee that it will be circulated in the country through the *zemstvo* bookstores and it will not serve as a source of income for those booksellers who are currently planning to crush the *zemstvo* stores with the weight of their heavy purses."[9]

Gorky thought Sytin had the wrong goals of getting rich and of boosting capitalism and the autocracy. And the same month he wrote to Teleshov, Gorky railed to Andreev about the chauvinism of Sytin's *Russian Word*, especially in the articles of Father Gregory Petrov, who signed himself "The Russian." It was the "Russians of *Russian Word* and other people of pious spirit," he wrote, "who can simply be called scum for Christ's sake, not a genuine Christ but only a Church-police Christ, who have recommended the rendering to God and the Tsar equally." Gorky wanted revolutionary change and hated the "plasterers who smear over the cracks of the old structure of our life."[10]

Sytin, who would never agree with Gorky on politics, did share Gorky's reservations about the quality of *Russian Word* and had already taken steps to change it. He had, after all, long been seeking a new overall editor to steer *Word* in a liberal direction and to increase its readership – someone experienced, ambitious, right-thinking, and excellent.

One prime candidate, I.I. Iasinsky, then editor of the successful *Stock Market Bulletin* (*Birzhevye Vedomosti*) in St Petersburg, says that Sytin offered him the job for twenty thousand rubles a year and big money for published editions of his works. He quotes Sytin as proposing to draw readers from *Bulletin* to *Word* "as wine is poured from one glass to another" and ends the story with his turning Sytin down.[11]

By mid-1901 Sytin had markedly raised his offer to secure someone else from St Petersburg. He was the thirty-seven-year-old Vlas Doroshevich, a seasoned journalist who commanded wide attention and high pay. His early writings had appeared alongside Chekhov's in a satirical boulevard paper in Moscow called *Alarm Clock* (*Budilnik*), so Chekhov may have endorsed him; but when first Sytin made a bid in the late 1890s, Doroshevich had bluntly said that he cost more than Sytin could afford. Sytin had since become desperate enough about revitalizing *Word* to meet Doroshevich's price.

II

Doroshevich was the most successful among the aggressive corps of journalists who, with Sytin, changed news coverage in Russia during the two decades before the 1917 revolution.[12] He was born in the decade of the "Great Reforms," grew up in the seventies when thousands of young students "went to the people," and began writing in the eighties under the conservative Tsar Alexander III. He learned early to fend for himself and to scoff at conventions and the established order. But, in contrast to the grimly serious radicals and populists who were his contemporaries, Doroshevich joked about a creaky system and flawed human beings and thereby won a vast audience.

In choosing to be a journalist, Doroshevich followed in the footsteps of his mother, Anna Ivanovna Sokolova. She was already a widow when she gave birth to her son on 15 April 1864, and then left him in the care of a Belorussian named Michael Doroshevich so that she could resume writing full time for the popular press. This stand-in father gave the youngster his surname and dubbed him "Vlas." Sokolova regained custody through the courts in 1874, but six years later Vlas left her to start out on his own.[13]

With both his mother and his good marks in school to recommend him, Doroshevich first caught on as a proof-reader at *Moscow Newssheet* (*Moskovskii Listok*) shortly before the assassination of Alexander II in 1881. The number of papers in all of Russia would surge to eighty-three that year, up from the sixty-two registered in 1880, as special interest, satirical, and boulevard papers for the common reader cropped up alongside the staid dailies and official government sheets.

Moscow Newssheet fell into the boulevard category, and its founder, the peasant-born, Moscow tavern-owner N.I. Pastukhov, had a penchant for reporters with initiative and brashness. His best was V.A. Giliarovsky, who managed a major scoop in July 1882 by rushing to the scene of a train disaster on the Moscow-Kursk line to wire back a graphic account for the next day's paper. This story and follow-ups raised *Newssheet* sales "by the thousands" and set an aggressive standard soon to be the norm.[14] At about this same time Doroshevich became a *Newssheet* reporter.

Once an experienced writer, Doroshevich in the mid-eighties became a peer of Chekhov at *Alarm Clock*. Like other papers specializing in satire, *Alarm Clock* lampooned stuffy officials through caricatures bordering on the libellous. It was here that Doroshevich made a name for himself.[15]

In 1883 Doroshevich left Moscow to join the *Odessa Newssheet* (*Odesskii Listok*), which sent him to learn from the great dailies of western Europe. In Paris he discovered how the French styled their feuilletons - brief essays, familiar in tone and catholic in subject - and he returned home to replicate their short, simple sentences liberally sprinkled with dashes. It was as a writer of chatty but elegant feuilletons, then, that Doroshevich gained fame for his "galloping thoughts" and "staccato style" to become Russia's most emulated journalist.[16]

In 1897 Doroshevich set out as an investigative reporter for *Newssheet* aboard a Russian prison ship bound for prison camps near Japan on Sakhalin Island. Six years before, Chekhov had created an enormous stir with his eye-witness critique of life there. Doroshevich presented his own observations more impressionistically in a series of articles, which Sytin would later publish, with great success, as a book.[17]

Within months of his return to Odessa, Doroshevich had rebuffed Sytin only to accept an offer from G.P. Sazonov to join his projected St Petersburg daily, *Russia* (*Rossia*). Its goal, under the banner of journalistic objectivity, was to find and expose hidden wrongs in order to promote reforms. ("Muckraking" journalism, though not yet so named, was well under way in America, where far fewer restrictions bedevilled editors determined to condemn wrong-doing.) Doroshevich and the equally renowned A.V. Amfiteatrov agreed to help forge a daily entirely new to Russia, and even ten years later, Amfiteatrov would tell Sytin that no other paper, past or present, could compare.[18]

With provocative irony, these writers skirted the permissible to win 45,000 subscribers for *Russia* when the daily began in 1901, compared with roughly 31,000 that same year at Sytin's *Word*. When Doroshevich wrote his "Eastern Stories" about the foibles and follies of Turkish viziers and Persian satraps, readers easily saw the mirror image of their own administrators. During this "happy time," Doroshevich was to recall, the "enemy was as obvious as serfdom [once had been]; now it was the bureaucracy."[19]

But as the second year of *Russia* began, Amfiteatrov went too far by sharply satirizing the Romanovs. In his irreverent description of "The Obmanov Gentlemen," which appeared on 13 January 1902, no one could miss the links with the ruling family. Some homely household details came straight from the palace of Nicholas II.

Because the criminal code forbade ridicule of the imperial family, closure of *Russia* would certainly have resulted from legal prosecution. But Nicholas used his own authority on 16 January to impose that penalty immediately. In addition, he personally exiled Amfiteatrov to the village of Minusinsk. The Tsar acted against the advice of Count S.I. Witte, his finance minister, and Shakhovskoi, still censorship director, both of whom preferred judicial action as less arbitrary.[20]

Russia's closure did not discommode Doroshevich because he had already, the summer before, agreed to "general supervision of the editing" of Sytin's *Russian Word*. On 16 July 1901 after only six months at *Russia*, Doroshevich had signed an irresistible three-year contract with Sytin to become the best-paid journalist in Russia.[21] Sytin gave him complete control over *Word*'s content and an unprecedented 20 per cent of the net profit. Doroshevich in turn promised to write an article about Moscow for each Sunday edition (for six thousand rubles annually) and no fewer than fifty-two additional pieces each year on "current questions of social life" (at five copecks per printed line). As general supervisor, Doroshevich could be in and out of Moscow at will so long as he always showed up within three days of a summons.

The contract took effect that September, but Doroshevich – except for stepping forward to praise Sytin at the anniversary celebration travelled and stayed behind the scenes until 1902. A trip in the interim to western Europe, along with six thousand rubles, came to him from Sytin as payment for the book version of his Sakhalin stories.

The closure of *Russia* early in 1902 gave Doroshevich an unexpected windfall, for he signed up at least ten writers from the defunct paper, Amfiteatrov among them. Out of the ashes of *Russia*, said Doroshevich, "was created the present *Russian Word*" implying the consignment to the ashes, as well, of the paper that Sytin had published before 1902.[22]

Chekhov seems not to have known about the contract between Doroshevich and Sytin for a long while, since five months after its signing, he wrote to his brother that Doroshevich must surely be unhappy at *Russia* serving the "giftless" Sazonov, adding that he would likely move only for better terms.[23] Chekhov had apparently failed to hear a word about Doroshevich's new post during his extended visit to Moscow to see his new wife just after Sytin's October fête. Chekhov was then still reasonably well; and, even though obligations to his wife would have kept him busy, two dear friends and close allies at *Word* would surely have found time to talk about their long-term project for a liberal daily. Here is further reason to doubt the claims of Sytin in his memoirs that Chekhov was his close adviser.

In those same memoirs, Sytin also misstates when and how he hired Doroshevich; as he tells it, he approached Doroshevich only after *Russia*'s demise. He said he had then given Doroshevich ten thousand rubles for his Sakhalin stories, urged him to revive his spirits in Europe, and promised him a job when he returned.[24] The terms and signing of the contract in July 1901 are certain, however, because Doroshevich's daughter saved the original copy. And an unpublished history of *Russian Word* says that Doroshevich first wrote for the paper on 15 September 1901.[25]

Spurred on in part by his share of the profits, Doroshevich rigorously enlivened and upgraded *Word*. He extended its network of correspondents in Russia and abroad, required full use of phone lines night and day, and gave greater emphasis to the St Petersburg bureau and its reports on the imperial government. Emulating what he had seen in Europe, Doroshevich divided the news staff under section editors titled with their speciality: "military editor," "Moscow editor," "provincial editor," and the like;[26] and he required each correspondent to be "familiar with public issues, careful and scrupulous in his verification of reported facts, adept in journalistic work, keen, responsive, ... able to catch fire with the necessity of speed."[27]

The intensified coverage caught the attention of readers and officials alike, and in August 1902 the censor V. Nazhevsky detected a "liberal orientation" in *Word*. The cause, he said, was "undoubtedly ... the move of a number of writers from the Petersburg daily *Russia* (closed) and the editorship of *Russian Word* by Doroshevich."[28]

Sytin, of course, was the head man at *Word* who had hired Doroshevich, both to steer a liberal course and to run a tight ship. And he often dropped in when his chief editor met each morning with section heads, under a life-size portrait of Chekhov, to plan the next 4 a.m. edition. By ten in the evening, when page layouts began, most stories had been set in type; but compositers on the night shift added late-breaking news right up to press time. With strict adherence to deadlines, the first papers were ready for loading onto the earliest trains out of Moscow.

Such a pace struck the staff as foreign. Doroshevich's arrival each day, recalled V.A. Giliarovsky, signalled everyone to fall silently to work until the day's edition went to press.[29] A.R. Kugel agreed that the editorial rooms were a marvel, lacking any "sign of bohemianism, of disorder, of familiarity."[30] Doroshevich himself worked in a private office and stationed a *dezhurnaia* ("woman on duty") outside his door to prevent interruptions.[31] The newsmen indulged their penchant for conviviality only after work in nearby restaurants, and Doroshevich often led the way (three bowls of borscht were a starter for him). On the job, however, seriousness reigned.

Doroshevich demanded the same high seriousness during his absences, which were frequent, through letters of very specific instructions. One missive of over twenty pages from early 1903, written on hotel stationery in Italy, went to N.V. Turkin, then heading the staff in Moscow.

Of prime importance, wrote Doroshevich, Turkin was not to permit "Sytin or anyone else" to interfere with editorial policy. If pressed, he was to "show the steel" behind the "velvet curtain" of tact to make clear that Doroshevich alone gave orders.[32] Among other things, Turkin must expunge the "inanities and vulgarisms" from *Sparks*; and, because "high-sounding nonsense ... about the divine origins of credit ... compromises the paper," he must turn away a protégé of "our nice Fr. Petrov." Counter-demands, whether from the owner, the business manager, government officials, or advertisers, were impermissible.[33] "Independence ... is my only strength," wrote Doroshevich.

Doroshevich laid out here, as well, his main strategy for building readership. This was "the year of our attack on the provinces," he wrote, because from them one day would come "half or three-fourths of *Word*'s business." Turkin must therefore demand the best from *Word*'s "Cossacks, our light cavalry" – that is, from the provincial correspondents who alone could "seize the high ground" by enticing provincials to read about themselves.

Like Sytin, Doroshevich intended to make *Word* as big as the biggest dailies in the West. The challenge of capturing readers had inspired a battle metaphor in his letter to Turkin; but later, once he had made *Word* the runaway bestselling and most widely read daily in Russia, he would describe his tactics in homelier terms. He would say that under him *Word* had become an "informative and entertaining friend with whom one would like to spend a pleasant half-hour over tea,"[34] just as his typical feuilleton was a "story concerning you."[35] Through such person-to-person journalism, Doroshevich won the mass audience and loyal following that justified his high salary. When later he ceased to edit and merely wrote for *Word*, Doroshevich would still command a high figure from Sytin.

On the strength of that popularity, Sytin would make the mistake in 1906 of having Sytin & Co. publish Doroshevich's varied journalistic writings in a nine-volume collection. Because the stuff of daily columns quickly becomes dated and bogs down in concentrated form, the work got poor reviews and sold badly. One literary critic applied the adjectives "kind, pleasant, and accommodating" to Doroshevich's book and advised reading it in snatches "on the tram, [or] between dinner and coffee."[36]

As for other arbiters of taste, the poetess Zinaida Hippius labelled Doroshevich a success in catching the attention of "the unsophisticated provincial," but scoffed at his having any literary merit.[37] In his *History of Russian Literature*, on the other hand, D.S. Mirsky, without documentation, says that Tolstoy ranked Doroshevich as second only to Chekhov among contemporary writers.[38]

The ambivalent position of Doroshevich as a writer is reflected in the story about him repeated in Moscow salons. When he first arrived in St Petersburg to join *Russia*, Doroshevich paid a visit to the Philosophical Circle, a group organized for serious discussion by Nicholas Berdiaev and others. There the writer Dmitry Merezhkovsky informed Doroshevich that he wrote well but had few ideas. Doroshevich's answer, the story goes, provoked laughter all around: "I have one new idea every day; do you call that few?"[39]

Sytin, in any case, understood that Doroshevich had talent and he gave his editor a free hand to use it. They would work together, with good results and some disharmony, for fifteen years.

Just after hiring Doroshevich, Sytin gave his paper another boost by planning and constructing a new building for *Word* on Strastnaia Square facing Tverskaia street. When it opened during the rising tide of revolution in May 1905 it replicated a "great Paris daily," says Giliarovsky, something "unheard of in Moscow."[40] Long corridors with offices for the major writers made it possible for them to work undisturbed. There, in Old Russian fashion, Sytin installed his own spacious apartment on the third floor but still in close proximity to the newsrooms and presses.

There, too, in the main editorial office on the second floor, he placed the life-size memorial portrait of Chekhov that commanded the editors of *Word*; for Chekhov had died on 2 July 1904 in Berlin.[41] Six weeks before that day, on 19 May, Sytin had called on the playwright to welcome him back to Moscow.[42] When, the previous May, Chekhov had also been in Moscow and was thinking of remaining there through the winter, Sytin had offered him the use of his estate.[43] Instead Chekhov had returned that July to Yalta, where he had stayed until spring except for a visit to Moscow for rehearsals and opening night of *The Cherry Orchard*, his final play.

Now Sytin was free to claim openly that Chekhov was the instigator of *Russian Word*. The portrait helped him to make that statement. And, standing before it, Sytin could the more dramatically exhort his staff to be a credit to Chekhov.

Without question, *Word* took centre stage for entrepreneur Sytin in his mid-fifties, and its immense potential made it a project exactly to his liking. For Sytin thrived, as son-in-law Blagov put it, on "innovative business affairs, fresh pangs of the organizer, a new boiling point, anxieties, sleepless nights given to thought about the matter at hand, its perils and its risks to established enterprises."[44] Therefore he also applied to *Word* his "law of the preservation of energy and economic strength."[45] That is, to avoid any risk to his incorporated company, Sytin was building up his daily as a strictly personal project until it certainly succeeded.

As his new building for *Word* took shape, Sytin committed Sytin & Co. to an expansion of its own that changed the Moscow skyline: a block-long, four-storey building designed by A.E. Erikson for the publishing complex on Piatnitskaia Street. At its 1904 opening Sytin inaugurated new letter and lithographic presses and a steam-generating plant beneath the adjacent courtyard. (He also added the thirteen presses and services of M.T. Soloviev, an early employee who had built up a rival business and would now, as head of the lithographic/artistic section, acquire enough stock to become a company director.) Approached during regular night shifts, this vast structure resembled a great ocean liner ploughing through dark seas with engines rumbling and lights ablaze.

Sytin set up both of these new plants as models of modernity; and, as the revolutionary year of 1905 ended, his crews were operating 40 per cent (or nine out of twenty-three) of the complicated new typesetting machines then in use in Moscow. Astute since his early shop days about the mechanics of printing, Sytin now kept up with every advance by visiting the pace-setters of Europe. On one such trip, he would decide to buy a new colour-printing rotary press the moment he saw it perform in Germany.[46]

III

In the same year that Doroshevich took over at *Word*, Sytin got the first inkling of the labour trouble that lay ahead, almost all of it in the publishing complex on Piatnitskaia Street. Despite his own benevolence as an employer, the large size of his book plant served to concentrate discontent at a time when workers in general were restive. Wages at the turn of the century were lagging as inflation sent prices upward. In addition, Sytin's reputation for "liberalism" invited his employees to demand better pay and terms of work and to use the pressure tactics of western European industrial workers.

Despite their illegality, strikes had been taking place sporadically in Russia since the 1890s. Sytin faced his first one on 12 February 1902 when 124 bookbinders refused to work unless they got a 15 per cent pay raise.[47] As piece-rate workers, they shared the grievance with many others in the plant of having no fixed wage; but because none of their peers supported them, they returned to their benches, defeated.

Leaving the regular police to handle such routine unrest, the Okhranka meanwhile searched out radicals who might stir workers' discontent into revolutionary activity. Their archives for 1902 record suspicious activities in Sytin's book plant and at *Russian Word*.[48] Beginning in June, the Moscow Okhranka opened the first of a series of unsigned letters from Europe addressed to *Word*'s editorial office and to persons designated only by their initials. That fall the police finally identified the writer as P.I. Nechaev, a twenty-four-year-old graphic artist who had left Russia after taking part in student demonstrations. By then they had also intercepted letters dispatched from *Russian Word* to Nechaev.

In his letter of 29 May to "N" and to "V.I." - Sytin's elder sons, Nicholas and Vasily - Nechaev mentions that his address could be had from "any of the graphic artists in the Sytin company." The police consequently added eight from the book plant to the two young Sytins on their roster of suspicious persons, and they confirmed from other passages that Nechaev had gone to Europe to study democracy, constitutions, and human rights.[49]

A letter of 27 October from Vasily ("I have worked in the editorial office of *Russian Word* for half a year") advises Nechaev: "You ask of [Blagov] a business card in your name; this of course he cannot do for you because, as a person, he is too cautious and he does not know you. With respect to your correspondence, he agreed." Thus Blagov is implicated as the conduit. "Put my initials larger," continues Vasily, "or the letters will be held up because [the mail sorters] will not understand at once."[50]

Another letter a month later reveals that Vasily has detailed knowledge about young radicals. He tells that two of the "Siberians" have fled to Switzerland. He deplores the use of patently false testimony by authorities at a recent trial of student demonstrators in Saratov, and notes that the Okhranka has established special agents to monitor activities at Moscow University. Because the local treasury of the Social Democratic Party is empty, he cannot send money at the moment, but could Nechaev obtain for him copies of the illegal emigré publications "Zh," "O," and "I" (that is, Posse's *Zhizn* (*Life*), Struve's *Osvobozhdenie* (*Liberation*), and Lenin's *Iskra*).[51] Finally, outgoing letters toward the end of 1902 show that Sytin's wife ("mother" and "Avdotiia" in the correspondence) had learned of the letter channel at *Russian Word* and had put a stop to it.

When Nechaev returned to Moscow in 1903, the police subjected him to a search, found no incriminating materials, and took no other measures. His correspondence had mentioned the outlawed Social Democratic Party led by Lenin and others, but the letters in themselves provided no grounds for charging anyone with criminal acts. The police chose merely to continue surveillance. Using weak evidence against a publisher's sons and their friends might cause a barrage of unfavourable publicity. Besides, "Avdotiia" appeared to have the matter in hand.

Beyond their implications for the police, the letters provide some rare insight into the Sytin family. For one thing, they show that two of the sons were consorting with leftist workers and, going well beyond their father's populism, had taken up with a revolutionary party. The part played by Blagov confirms only that he was an easy-going man, not that he had radical views himself. As for Evdokia Ivanovna, she emerges as a mother who could take decisive action, even as she would appear to have kept a serious family-related matter from Sytin. The mention of her intervention only, with no reference to Sytin, suggests that he so far knew nothing about the letters and their implications. He is on record in later years complaining about his sons' lack of discipline, and he would certainly have been both furious and despairing to have learned at this point about their involvement with radicals. (Sytin, according to one associate, "did not think too highly of his sons" and never delegated full authority to them in business matters.)[52]

Sytin would soon learn, however, that his publishing plant harboured a great many such agents of change. As the police would pointedly record, the employees of Sytin at the Piatnitskaia complex – the "Sytintsy," as they were known in Moscow – would figure significantly in the city-wide printers' strike in 1903 and in the revolution of 1905 as well.

According to the imperial census of 1897, 4 per cent of the city's industrial labor force, or eleven thousand persons, were "printing" employees – that is, workers involved with printing anything from brochures to wallpaper. Well over half were in newspaper and book plants. The overall total had increased to twelve thousand in the census of 1902, when Sytin himself employed over one thousand.[53] Many, like Sytin, were peasants from the countryside; nevertheless, among all industrial workers, printers ranked as the most literate and best educated group, making their sector easier than most to inform and to organize.

At least by early 1903, activists from Sytin & Co. and from print shops across Moscow had broken Russian law to organize the Union of Moscow Typographical Workers. Print workers at each affiliated shop informally chose deputies to represent them at the *soviet* (council) of deputies, which in turn advised the small executive committee at the top. This three-tiered organizational form became the prototype not only for the subsequent, openly proclaimed Soviet of Printers and for other industrial unions, but also for the city-wide soviets of all workers in both Moscow and St Petersburg during the revolution of 1905. To elude the police, the fledgling soviet met infrequently in the spring of 1903 but conveyed all executive decisions through its deputies to the rank and file. Early that summer it relayed plans for a strike in October or November, the peak production period of the year, when Sytin and his fellow publishers would be most under pressure to reach a settlement.[54]

When the police began arresting some members of the executive committee in July, the leaders still free decided to move the strike ahead to 9 September.[55] Their followers agreed. By noon of the appointed day, most of the Sytintsy were among some three thousand print shop workers who had walked off the job. They were demanding better pay and a nine-hour, rather than an eleven-hour, work day. As directed by their leaders, union-aligned printers at Sytin & Co. had reported for work as usual, declared a strike, then prodded their co-workers to join them. Flying squads of strikers moved to other shops with the same mission. The disruptive walkout ended on the fourth day when Sytin and the other members of the Society of Operators of Printing Plants agreed to raise wages and to cut daytime work shifts to ten hours and night shifts to nine. Sytin honoured his decision, but some publishers reneged because, they said, the strike had been illegal.

In the aftermath, the police arrested no fewer than 446 alleged strike leaders. Eventually, they ordered 286 of them back to their home villages and kept the rest under surveillance. The few remaining adherents of the illegal union, a number in the Sytintsy, covertly declared themselves the Moscow Typographical Workers for the Struggle to Improve Working Conditions, allied with the Menshevik faction of the outlawed Social Democratic Party, and bided their time. Printers could and did meanwhile join the legal Russian Workers' Assembly, but the Sytin plant remained a centre of illegal union activity for the next several years.

As for the city-wide dimensions of the September walkout, the Moscow chief of police estimated that 76 per cent of the letter press and lithographic printers took part (6,599 of 8,233) and that 60 per cent of all printing establishments were closed (89 of 149). The Okhranka, which painstakingly compiled its own figures, counted 703

Sytintsy among the militant strikers.[56] In contrast, none of the printers at *Russian Word* appear to have joined the strike.

IV

Five months after the September strike the Japanese declared war with their surprise attack of 27 January 1904 on the Russian base at Port Arthur. By the end of the twenty-month conflict, Sytin would own the largest newspaper in all of the Empire, and no other pre-revolutionary Russian daily would ever catch up or come close. The highest press run in 1903 had been 43,000 copies; by December 1904, *Word* was circulating 117,000 copies daily. Because expenses during the first year of the war rose sharply (telephone and telegraph fees climbed 353 per cent and editorial costs 133 per cent),[57] Sytin raised advertising and subscription rates in 1904, the latter to seven rubles. The net result was his first year of substantial profits as a newspaper publisher.

Nemirovich-Danchenko was one of twenty *Word* correspondents who covered the war, and he sent back 350 dispatches in the first year alone. *Word* extolled him as always out front, always under fire, viewing the positions.[58] Reports also came in from correspondents in such outposts as Shanghai, Vladivostok, Chi-Fu, Singapore, Colombo, and San Francisco.

Through one intrepid writer, V.E. Kraevsky, *Word* accomplished a dazzling journalistic raid behind enemy lines; travelling with a counterfeit British passport in the name of Percy Palmer, he toured Japan to conduct interviews in English in the last months of 1904. On 3 January 1905, *Word* made this surprising but understated announcement: "Yesterday V.E. Kraevsky returned to Moscow. He gathered a mass of material in Japan. After an uninterrupted journey from Yokohama to Moscow, [he will have] one day of rest, and the day after tomorrow the feuilletons will appear about Japan at the present minute." The editors timed the series to coincide with the annual campaign for subscriptions, promising extended revelations about "The Country of the Enemy in the Time of War," their general title for the series.

Thirteen articles by Kraevsky appeared from January through May. They are remarkable in refuting shibboleths about Japan made current in Russia by official and unofficial propagandists,[59] for Kraevsky showed the Japanese as intelligent, prosperous, and, but for their cruel treatment of prisoners, civilized. For one thing, they had plenty to eat. Wrote Kraevsky, "I know well a Chinese crowd, but what a difference in Japan. Here there are no emaciated persons resembling squeezed out lemons." Further to show the prevailing normalcy, Kraevsky said that he had concluded from his lengthy talks with Japanese bankers that commerce and industry in Japan were on "full course."[60]

Kraevsky described drinking claret with a decorated young Japanese major on the terrace of the Grand Hotel in Tokyo. There, in fluent English, the major accurately predicted that the Japanese would defeat the Russians at Mukden in southern Manchuria. He attributed the superiority of the Japanese to, among other things, their cleanliness and their frank discussions of politics. "Aren't such discussions dangerous?" asked the ingenuous Kraevsky. "Not at all," he quoted the major, because debate sharpened their determination to fight.[61]

Just as the "Percy Palmer" series put government propaganda about the Japanese in a bad light, the news columns of Sytin's *Word* caused readers to view with scepticism official stories on the war. In close proximity, sometimes side by side, appeared government versions of events and off-setting reports from *Word* correspondents and foreign papers. In 1905 *Word* reporters began to count and report the number of wounded daily arriving in Moscow hospitals and to identify them in long columns of names. They also visited the wards to talk with convalescents and then reported both their valour and their humiliating losses.

Word's guiding principle, Sytin would have said, was strict honesty, and he approved such forthright coverage on a mass scale because it effectively stymied government officials. Since his daily was not subject to preliminary censorship, thousands of readers had access to it as soon as members of the Moscow press committee. And should that committee cite *Word* for dangerous content after the fact, they risked making the government appear to fear the truth. Similarly, any time a government prosecutor considered charging *Word* before the courts with an act of criminal publishing, he had to weigh the value of a conviction – an unpredictable result – against the extent to which a public trial could discredit the government.

Despite the difficulty of deciding when disciplinary measures against *Russian Word* did more harm than good, the minister of the interior, V.K. Plehve, had slapped Sytin with a severe punishment in October 1904. Because his daily had advocated expanded powers for local government and was making insinuations against officials, Plehve suspended Sytin's street sales of the paper from 14 October to 13 December.[62] *Word* continued to reach its subscribers, of course, and they still constituted the bulk of its readers.

By January, when Kraevsky's series began, press control was made even more problematical by a new crisis: the volatility of public feelings after "Bloody Sunday." On that day, 9 January 1905, guards at the Winter Palace in St Petersburg killed well over one hundred unarmed people marching with Father George Gapon, an Orthodox priest, to present economic and political demands to the Tsar.

Acting before *Russian Word* or any other paper could report the tragedy, the government forbade the publication of any accounts but its own. Doroshevich had to comply. His issue of 9 January, printed before the St Petersburg confrontation, mentioned deepening unrest among workers in the capital and unusual numbers on the streets. The next day he ran only a background story on Father Gapon, making no mention of the Sunday march. A day later, on 11 January he published an official communiqué describing how revolutionaries among the St Petersburg Society of Factory Workers had forced troops, in their own defence, to kill 76 persons and wound 203. On 12 January he reprinted from *Government Messenger*, an official paper, a description of the capital returned to normal.

News of the deaths in St Petersburg spread throughout Moscow on 10 January anyway, and before the end of the day the Sytintsy and other workers began walking off their jobs in protest. The police estimated that four thousand persons, including twenty-five hundred printers, joined the impromptu strike.[63] They also recorded that all twelve hundred persons employed by Sytin at his book plant "stopped work at 5 o'clock in the afternoon – two hours earlier than usual – and walked along Small and Great Serpukhovskaia streets and around Serpukhovskaia Square."[64] Among all the large publishers, Sytin alone suffered a complete shutdown.

Both day and night shifts of Sytintsy stayed away on 11 January, and all but the typesetters and bookbinders returned the next day. By 13 January, all walkouts across the city had ended (and at no time had the printers at *Word* left their posts). On 22 January, the police predicted more trouble from the Sytintsy: "Sytin's workers, as more enterprising and readier to give in to dangerous influences, have more than once rebelled on their own initiative; they do not offer a future guarantee of stability."[65]

At some point during the protest over Bloody Sunday, these same enterprising Sytintsy had seized the moment to present Sytin & Co. with shop-related demands. The surviving members of the Union of Moscow Typographical Workers from the 1903 strike had kept their list intact: an eight-hour day, pay increases, no overtime, and an arbitration panel (half labour and half management) to hear grievances and to ratify the hiring and firing of workers. To these were added six more demands: pay-cheques twice a month, no searches, no fines for tardiness, a fund to aid ill and disabled workers, election of elders to speak for workers, and a boiler to heat water for tea.[66]

Sytin and his fellow board members immediately replied that they would consider the changes but could act only in concert with other publishers. When next the Society of Operators met, the majority easily rejected the strike as the work of "outside agitators" and refused to go beyond the wage and hour settlement of September 1903.[67]

Meanwhile, defeats in the war added to social unrest. In February, as Kraevsky's Japanese major had predicted, the Russians lost at Mukden. That same month, a feuilleton in *Word* alluded to lives wasted at Port Arthur before its fall the previous December and asked why the government had courted disaster by keeping forces in that doomed outpost.[68] Necessarily choosing words with care, staff writers were nonetheless coming close to sharp criticism of the authorities. On 17 May, *Word* published the first fragmentary reports on the destruction during the three previous days of the Russian fleet in the Strait of Tsushima. Two days later the paper had nearly five columns on the disaster, including accounts from survivors who reached Vladivostok. On 25 May, it carried a correspondent's description of the battle and a sketch of ship positions provided by a secretary at the Japanese embassy in Vienna.

All through the first half of 1905 Sytin's *Word* also described domestic unrest. Because one story accused an unnamed village constable of assaulting peasants, the Moscow vice-governor asked Blagov early in April to identify the official so that he could be prosecuted. When Blagov applied the principle of press freedom to answer that he had no "right" to provide that information, the governor pointed out that vague accounts of injustice, being unresolvable, served only to encourage violence.[69]

Midway through May the paper described the first meeting of the Union of Unions, a liberal political action group formed to co-ordinate the reformist activities of fourteen professional unions, all still banned by law. *Word* explained the democratic principles of this umbrella group and its sympathies for workers bent on organizing. Labour coverage in *Word* during the next ten days included two columns summarizing strikes around the country, and that round-up gave importance to scattered events that otherwise would have escaped public notice.[70] To the dismay of officials, Sytin had equipped *Word* with the technical capacity to gather news of scattered disturbances and concentrate them into a single compelling story.

On 26 May, a story headed "Above the Law" reported that the Doukhobors and certain other sectarians had proclaimed a new, free civic order in Russia; on the same day Sokolov, the press official long critical of *Word*, filed a report charging that repeated stories about illegal protests in Sytin's daily, "undoubtedly more than in other papers, act to encourage [uprisings and strikes]." He further complained that Sytin had been publishing these provocations for two years and the government was not taking necessary steps against them.[71]

Acting on Sokolov's report, the Moscow committee on 9 June

informed the editors that *Word*'s contents showed a dangerous tendency. It cited, as a typical quote, these lines: ''We know that the country cannot prepare itself for an electoral campaign [*Word* had taken a stand for elections] when the press is subject to censorship, when society is deprived of the right of assembly, when every day people are persecuted for their social ideas.''[72] A week later the Chief Administration of Press Affairs sent an official warning to Blagov, formally charging *Word* with printing ''tendentious and incorrect news'' and ''systematically seeking to undermine ... faith ... in the measures undertaken by the government.'' It again suspended the street sales of the paper, but the distributors of *Word* seem largely to have ignored that order.[73] If *Word* got three such warnings, Sytin would suffer the suspension or closure of his paper.[74] But he and Doroshevich knew that it was one thing for the government to shut down a small paper and quite another to interrupt a daily with a circulation of over 150,000 copies and close to a million readers. Stopping *Word* would be like closing the switch on an essential public utility, and it would certainly cause a public outcry. Because its own authority had faded everywhere in 1905, the government was unlikely to confront Sytin with a third warning unless his daily advocated revolution.

Word had become especially prodigious because its readership crossed over several classes,[75] and that broad following impressed not only the government but also local merchandisers. Sytin's daily thus led all Russian newspapers in advertising content and revenues. A typical issue of six pages – like the one for 3 May 1905, for example – devoted the entire front ''cover'' and most of the back to ads. On this particular front page, next to the subscription rates for *Sparks* and *Word* and book promotions from Sytin & Co., paid notices announce a cattle auction, an exhibition of paintings, several concerts, and the annual meeting of the board of directors of the Moscow First City Hospital. Private schools and kindergartens invite enrolment. Offered for sale in display ads are horses, Swedish matches ''at the old price,'' koumiss, photographic equipment, dachas near Moscow, ''Straw'' cigarettes (claimed to be ''original, convenient, and hygienic''), Oldsmobiles from America, and plumbing fixtures from England. In one column, S.F. Maikov's clinic offers hydropathic, electrical, and light therapy, along with the Zabludovsky method of massage and x-rays. In another, a cleaning company touts its use of chemicals on rugs and curtains and of steam on feather beds.

On the back cover classified ads fill five of the seven columns. There dentists advertise gold or porcelain fillings and painless treatment, while eight different drug stores promise cures for syphilis. Tutors list their qualifications. Rooms and apartments are advertised and sought, and job openings for mechanics, paper-hangers, and flower-arrangers appear among bids for work by domestics, governesses, man-servants, and grooms. Inside, on pages four and five, are yet more ads.

Only five years before this May issue appeared, Sytin had been despairing to Chekhov over *Word*'s losses. Now, in the fiscal year for 1904 just ending, he celebrated net profits for himself as *Word*'s sole owner that amounted to the considerable sum of 32,374 rubles. Sytin & Co. was also completing a very good fiscal year that May, recording profits of 188,300 rubles – well over twice the 1900 figure of 85,000 rubles. During this same month, at the stockholders' meeting of the publishing house he dominated, Sytin sold 80 per cent of *Word*, along with *Sparks* and an inconsequential daily he had started in 1904 called *Russian Truth* (*Russkaia Pravda*),[76] to Sytin & Co. for 200,000 rubles. The shift apparently gave both him and his company worthwhile tax and other financial advantages.

Under the sales agreement,[77] Sytin & Co. made its acquisitions for nothing. The terms specified that its first payment to Sytin was the entire profits of the three publications for 1904 – that is, earnings that were already Sytin's whether he "sold" the publications or not. In 1905 and each subsequent year until the purchase price was met, the company was to give him half the publications' profits. (Despite the failure of *Russian Truth* in 1906, the company would complete its obligation in 1910.)[78] Also spelled out in the 1905 contract was the continuing role of Sytin as president of Sytin & Co. and his authority as chief executive officer of *Word*. The latter included his right to hire *Word*'s editors, writers, correspondents, and office personnel.

Just as the revolution of 1905 deepened in the summer of that tumultuous year, so Sytin recorded high profits and consolidated his expanding holdings. The time of war and civil unrest had been good for the publishing business, a fact not lost on the printers. The Sytintsy had been staying on the job in the book publishing plant since the brief strike of January, but activists there were continuing to organize what amounted to a union. A strike was on their agenda, and this time the printers at *Word* would join in. So would nearly all the workers of Moscow.

CHAPTER FIVE

Weathering the Revolution of 1905 and Its Aftermath

The revolution of 1905 gave headlines to *Russian Word* along with headaches to Sytin & Co., its new owner. Work and transportation stoppages interrupted the flow of power and materials into Sytin's plants, crimped production, and hurt the circulation of works that did make it through the presses. Armed strife that December would impose an even heavier toll on Sytin by igniting a disastrous fire in his new book publishing plant on Piatnitskaia Street.

With far-reaching implications, the upheaval also made very clear where Sytin and his editors stood politically. Many safely conservative works still came from the book plant, but so did many that were sympathetic to the revolution; and officials could have no doubts about the liberal bias of *Russian Word*. Small wonder officials would conclude that the Sytintsy were leaders in the workers' movement; and how just, some felt, that flames set off during the December uprising should reduce the work place and earnings of the Sytintsy and their boss.

I

As the police had predicted in January, more would be heard from the workers in Sytin's immense plant on Piatnitskaia Street, where, early in August, police investigators detected a resurgence of the illegal Union of Moscow Typographical Workers (UMTW). At a meeting on 11 August, about four hundred Sytintsy voted in favour of four union demands: regular shifts of nine hours but of only eight hours before a holiday; sick leave at half pay and maternity leave at full pay; elections for representatives immune from dismissal, and pay increases of 30 per cent for workers earning a mere nine to twenty rubles per month; 20 per cent for those earning twenty-one to thirty rubles; 15 per cent for those earning thirty-one to forty-five rubles; and 10 per cent for those earning over forty-five rubles.

Although the spokesmen who delivered this list to Sytin & Co. demanded an answer within two days,[1] the Sytintsy complied when the company asked to delay its response until mid-September. Several directors were out of town – including, evidently, company president Sytin – and the financial results of the Nizhnii Novgorod fair were unknown.

Precisely as promised, Sytin and his fellow directors replied on 13 September. They met the demands about one-third of the way, arguing that full agreement would cost 100,000 rubles, or more than the company could afford. Without conferring with the owners' group, the board granted the nine-hour regular work day and improved sick-leave benefits (full pay for one week and then half-pay for up to two months). Estimating that earlier increases to wage-rated workers had put them 10 per cent above their peers in other plants and was costing the company 35,000 rubles annually, the directors gave only one additional concession: a 5 per cent increase in the piecework pay for typesetters, who comprised perhaps 15 to 20 per cent of the Sytintsy.

All other pieceworkers suffered a net loss in earnings because of the 10 per cent cut in working hours. Besides refusing paid maternity leave, the board said that government rules precluded the election of representatives by specifying the appointment of so-called elders. Finally, Sytin and his board reminded workers of the special benefits they already enjoyed: a kitchen, a library, a pharmacy dispensing free medicine, and a school for graphic artists. Declaring the terms effective 1 October, they considered the matter closed.

The pieceworkers felt betrayed. Already the lowest on the scale with respect to earnings, education, and skills, they had just sunk lower in pay. Moreover, they saw diminished prospects ahead with every new purchase by Sytin of labour-saving technology. Not surprisingly, on the morning of 19 September, many of them remained in the yard of the plant and refused to work.[2] Before the day's end, most of the Sytintsy had joined them. At this juncture, plant members of the illegal UMTW, seeing a new opportunity in the mood of the workers, advanced twenty demands on behalf of the Sytintsy, who fell in behind them.

Insisting again on elected deputies immune from dismissal, the UMTW added that these deputies must comprise a workers' soviet within the plant under a formal "factory constitution" – a document setting forth certain collective workers' rights that would restrict the authority of management. The soviet, which would replicate the middle level of the three-tiered Moscow printers' organization of 1903, would have a crucial say on hirings and firings, health and safety standards, apprenticeship assignments, and working conditions.[3]

This time the Sytintsy stayed off the job while management framed a reply. To draw in more printers, the UMTW members carried their demands to other Moscow shops, including that of *Russian Word* on Tverskaia Street. When sympathetic typesetters at the newspaper followed them out, the stoppage of *Word* on 24 September put added pressure on Sytin and his board to make concessions.

UMTW members were also calling for a new city-wide soviet of printers' deputies, and enough shops had named deputies for it to cause authorities to take the body seriously. Consequently, on 23 September the Moscow chief of police gave legitimacy to the fledgling Moscow Soviet of Printers' Deputies (MSPD) by granting it permission to meet two days later in a school building he provided. Forbidding the meeting, he contended, would only drive the printers underground.[4]

At this stage, worried officials hoped to contain the anger of idled workers by showing reasonableness. But sputtering street demonstrations became especially disruptive on 24 September, and police on patrol, who had to duck rocks, claimed to have heard two gunshots. Lest "local revolutionary groups" force shutdowns everywhere, they took alleged troublemakers into custody - 197 persons during 22-24 September, with three-quarters of them, or 144, under the age of eighteen.[5]

When the MSPD met on 25 September, the register showed 110 deputies from thirty-four plants (the tenth and last meeting six weeks later would attract 264 deputies from 110 enterprises).[6] Confirming their solidarity, they voted to negotiate a single agreement with all shop-owners and approved a general meeting of all city printers for the next day in the Georgian National House.[7] Each deputy then returned to his plant to notify his co-workers. Whether the chief of police had approved the general meeting is unclear, but he sent his men to turn away the some two thousand printers who gathered in front of the Georgian National House at the appointed time. The printers left peacefully but with new resentments that bound them closer to the MSPD and to those who favoured confrontation.

Commenting on the aborted meeting in a leaflet, one activist would sarcastically thank the chief of police "for a lesson we will not forget: a peaceful struggle by workers for their interests can never be legal in the eyes of authority. Accordingly, the struggle of the workers is a political struggle."[8] But despite this and all other attempts to turn the printers' movement against the government, the MSPD, which superseded and absorbed the old underground UMTW, dealt solely with trade union issues during its existence. It did so because that was what most printers wanted.

By the end of September only Sytin & Co. and one other firm had agreed to the MSPD's offer of talks.[9] Faced with that stalemate and aware that the strikers' resolve was stronger than ever, Sytin and his board of directors on 30 September voted to send their own workers a much more generous version of their mid-month offer. The company also notified the district police that it was closing its courtyard on Piatnitskaia Street, where workers had repeatedly met, because "outside agitators" were stirring excitement "to a stronger degree"; and it asked that a detachment of Cossacks enforce the closure.[10]

Threats of violence aside, it was unquestionably the solidarity of the Moscow printers that had moved Sytin and his fellow directors. That solidarity was bolstered further on 2 October, when a delegation from the MSPD took part in a police-approved meeting of printers in St Petersburg. Quite unexpectedly, that assembly of about two thousand printers voted to stage a three-day strike in the capital in support of the Moscow printers.

Agreement between the Sytintsy and Sytin & Co. came on 4 October with the announcement of new, more generous terms - a settlement that won Sytin some credit among his printers and set a standard for the other large publishers.[11] Since it also effectively ruled out an all-city agreement, the MSPD gave up that hopeless goal and, on the very day of the Sytintsy settlement, directed its members to return to work wherever management made acceptable concessions. One day later *Russian Word* reappeared.

Besides holding to the nine-hour day, Sytin and his board granted all the Sytintsy more generous pay, with increases of 7½ per cent to the wage-rated workers. Typesetters received an additional two copecks for each thousand characters they set, and bookbinders got a 5 per cent raise in their piece rate. Strikers would receive half of their back pay for the period of their walkout and suffer no reprisals. All body searches would end. The company flatly excluded the so-called factory constitution and its system of representatives. No mention was made of paid maternity leave, which surely made no sense to Sytin.

What the MSPD had struck for was strictly labour-related. Political reform, however, was central to the demands emanating from the much wider workers' movement, directed in Moscow, as in St Petersburg, by the all-city workers' soviet of deputies from many trades. When, by 14 October, scattered walkouts in various places had escalated into a general strike across Russia, Nicholas II could no longer ignore the ultimatums for change. On 17 October he issued his Manifesto promising broad concessions, including freedom of expression. *Word* celebrated it in bold headlines the next day.

II

Word's unreserved welcome of the October Manifesto came as no surprise, for Sytin's paper had played a major part in spreading arguments for a liberal solution to the political crisis through all the earlier months of social discontent. On 16 September, for example, it had given full publicity to the *zemstvo* congress in Moscow and publicized the causes endorsed there: more freedom for the minority peoples of the Empire, free professional unions, the right to strike, and a standard eight-hour day. Sytin saw to it, however, that *Word* aligned with no single faction even as it mainly backed liberal political views like those to be espoused by the Constitutional Democratic Party, or Kadets.

Word published the Manifesto, in which Nicholas II promised limited political rights and elections for a new legislative assembly, on 18 October, the morning after its release in St Petersburg. Beside it, under the heading "Renewal," Sytin's editors gave their commentary on this immensely important political document. After exulting that for the first time they wrote freed from censorship strictures, they blamed the government for the long, unnecessary delay in granting change. Officials had consequently caused great "shocks": communications breakdowns, factory closings, fusillades, barricades, and the flow of blood. Taking a position dear to Sytin, *Word* credited the people, especially the workers and the students, for "self-confidently, courageously, and selflessly" attaining their own freedom.

On the following day Sytin's paper stressed again the democratic roots of the Manifesto. "The Russian people have shown to humanity a new means of struggle," and since the Manifesto had legitimized their fight, the government should release all persons arrested during the revolutionary period for political reasons. The next logical step was to organize full popular participation in building a new order through meetings, unions, and press discussion. Sytin stood committed to westernization, as his paper called for a universal, equal, direct, and secret ballot by the people to elect an assembly to frame a constitution.

Word could present and discuss the Manifesto only because Sytin's workers, so recently returned from their September walkout, had not joined the general strike. That October strike did, however, interrupt the rail service Sytin needed to carry *Word* into the provinces and the electricity he needed to run his newspaper presses. He had solved the latter problem by printing *Word* at his book plant, which was powered by his own generators, even though his editors had had to shrink their news pages to fit the smaller book presses.[12]

Although the Manifesto, as intended, quickly put an end to the general strike, Sytin faced more labour agitation as the Sytintsy and most Moscow printers took advantage of the freedom of association promised by Nicholas II. In no mood to await government rules defining that principle, the MSPD called a meeting on 19 October to reorganize their thirty-five hundred members as a trade union to be known as the Moscow Union of Print Workers (MUPW). An estimated eight thousand persons showed up. The next day, to mark the funeral of Nicholas Bauman (a Bolshevik shot down by a Black Hundred sympathizer), some one hundred thousand demonstrators flooded the streets, Sytintsy among them. Ten days later, another out-sized assembly of the new MUPW managed to pass resolutions calling for a city-wide agreement with the Union (formerly Society) of Operators guaranteeing an eight-hour day and a factory constitution in all plants – demands that Sytin and all the other owners would reject out of hand.[13]

Acting on their own, the Sytintsy had meanwhile shown that they still had differences with management. When Sytin sent a priest into his plant during a day shift in October to lead prayers of thanks for the Manifesto, some workers openly and loudly mocked the cleric, who trimmed his words and made a quick retreat. Still others in November refused to set type for the *Kremlin*, a paper not owned by Sytin but printed in his plant. Although its editor, Ilovaisky, tried to negotiate with them, they flatly refused any part in what they saw as a right-wing "Black Hundred" paper.[14]

Then, allegedly to fend off Black Hundred reprisals, Sytin gave his workers a two thousand ruble defence fund, which his son Nicholas used to buy fifty revolvers to arm a "fighting detachment" in the plant.[15] He also involuntarily donated one thousand rubles to the MUPW. That is, he gave his workers that sum for a banquet to celebrate the Manifesto, and they had diverted it to their union the very next day for the fight against tsarism.[16]

These various moves by Sytin, however well intended, provoked government officials already angry with the liberal political line of *Russian Word*. To their added annoyance, a three-part series of articles appeared in *Word* that November by Professor M.M. Kovalevsky, a respected scholar recently returned from European exile who was shortly to help found the Party of Democratic Reform. Kovalevsky extolled western countries as political models and argued from English history that true constitutional order would follow only when Russia introduced laws guaranteeing human rights.[17]

Press freedom was one of those rights. At the time of Kovalevsky's articles, Sytin and his editors at *Word* and the book plant were further at odds with the government by ignoring the Tsar's clarification, on 19 October, that the Manifesto had merely promised, not decreed, a fully free press. In what was a major political mistake, Nicholas had had the Chief Administration of Press Affairs announce that the old system would stay in effect until new press laws were ready. In angry response, the MSPD had followed the lead of its counterpart in St Petersburg by declaring on 7 November that publishers must cut all ties with "censors" or suffer printers' walkouts and other reprisals. When Sytin and most large publishers in both cities complied, the new prime minister, S.I. Witte, accused them of having been revolutionized by cowardice.[18]

In the case of *Word*, Sytin had merely let Blagov stop a mandatory free subscription. One of the 1865 regulations still in effect required *Word*, and all uncensored periodicals and newspapers, promptly to submit each just-circulated issue to the local Press Affairs Committee, who could, upon finding objectionable content, initiate judicial prosecution or such administrative sanctions as warnings leading to closure. By not complying, Blagov forced the committee to rush to patronize a just-supplied newsstand to obtain the earliest daily copies of *Word*.

Then, just thirty-eight days after the Tsar's Manifesto, a government ukaze of 24 November gave effect to the promised regulations that granted full press freedom to *Russian Word* and every other paper in Russia. No longer could the government impose administrative sanctions as an ordinary measure. It could merely cite published words as grounds for criminal proceedings against such publishers as Sytin, and against his editors and authors. And only if judges found the cited words illegal under clearly defined laws could the court mete out penalties, also defined by law.

Within days, those new rules enabled the government to check the revolution of 1905 because eight capital dailies had published the "Financial Manifesto" of the St Petersburg Soviet of Workers' Deputies. That document urged readers to withhold all tax payments to wrest still more concessions from the Tsar. Despite their having printed it under ultimatums from their printers, the newspaper publishers were guilty in the eyes of the government of circulating seditious words. So was the collective that authored the Manifesto. On Sunday, 4 December, the police consequently arrested the executive committee and 233 members of the St Petersburg Soviet.

III

News of the arrests galvanized the Soviet of Workers' Deputies in Moscow to call for both a protest strike and an armed uprising on

Wednesday, 7 December. The strike took effect on schedule all across Moscow, but full-scale fighting centred only in one area, well away from Sytin's printing plants. That same day the printers at Sytin's daily worked long enough to publish the 7 December issue of *Word* and to include in it Soviet directives for the strike and for a ban on all but revolutionary papers – criminal content from the government's viewpoint. They then began a strike that would last eleven days.

By noon all of the Sytintsy at the Piatnitskaia plant had also walked out, and some attempted, in vain, to recruit soldiers stationed nearby to join their rebellion.[19] That evening, at what proved to be their last mass meeting, the printers' trade union endorsed the strike and learned that the first issue of the Moscow soviet's *Izvestiia* had been printed that afternoon in Sytin's book plant on Piatnitskaia Street. The Workers' Soviet had ordered a flying squad of printers and a bodyguard of armed workers to use Sytin's idled plant to inaugurate its revolutionary newspaper. The invading printers commandeered type, paper, ink, and the necessary typesetting machines and presses, without inflicting any damage.

Learning of the invasion, Sytin had gone to the press room along with Doroshevich, Blagov, and Petrov, and all four found themselves under "honourable" arrest in the name of the soviet. To Sytin's protests that he had absolute authority as owner of the plant, the intruders replied, "No, we are the bosses here when you are under arrest." The confrontation ended with the completed press run, and Sytin stayed away when a second crew came three days later, seemingly helped by his son Vasily.[20]

Sytin's book-printing plant had become a focus of revolutionary activity. It stood squarely in the centre of the Zamoskvoreche section where workers were ringing the inner city with barricades. On 11 December soldiers and workers exchanged sporadic gunfire there, and that night, while Sytin was on the train to St Petersburg, flames destroyed almost all of the main four-storey building in the complex, including press and composing rooms and part of the bookbindery. Sytin charged that someone in authority ordered troops to set the blaze or, at the least, directed firemen not to fight it. "I cannot deny that the workers of our company took part in all the greatest events of the revolution of 1905," wrote Sytin. "This is unarguable. But why Admiral F.V. Dubasov, who was at the time the head of the Moscow city administration, decided to punish the company and destroy the building I cannot grasp to this day."[21]

Government complicity seems likely, at least at a lower level, since many officials agreed with police claims that the Sytintsy were deeply involved in labour agitation. One highly placed military officer told

Sytin so on the very night of the fire. Sytin was at that time, and by his own admission, removing himself from Moscow lest he suffer "arrest or murder" – presumably at the hands of right-wing Black Hundred terrorists; and he chanced to encounter an assistant to Dubasov, General P.M. Baranov, on the overnight train to St Petersburg. Baranov, who was on his way to the capital to report on Moscow's troubles, bluntly told Sytin that he regarded the Sytintsy as "the leading gang of the whole Moscow mess." When Sytin replied that all Moscow workers were alike in their feelings, Baranov rejoined: "No – not so. Yours are especially rebellious; at the Bauman funeral they were in the lead."[22] By implication, Sytin's management was at fault to some degree.

When the train reached St Petersburg, five reporters were awaiting Sytin at the station. After they broke the news of the fire and asked his reaction, Sytin called his wife for details. Then, seemingly jubilant, he invited the reporters to go with him to Palkin's restaurant for a "binge." He openly celebrated, insisting that the publicity value would be enormous.

Three days later Sytin returned to Moscow and the scene of the fire. Sobered by the charred walls and the rubble of "my cherished presses, my pride," he would later relate in his memoirs, he deplored that "only several days before ... presses were humming, machines running, and workers were swarming around like ants."[23]

Sytin at once set about seeking payments from his insurance coverage, and several accounts of the events leading up to the fire come from the transcripts of the judicial inquiry into Sytin's claims.[24] One witness quoted there was Ivan Telkov, a policeman whose apartment window happened to face the plant. He testified that about two hundred persons arrived at the plant at 8 a.m. on Sunday, 11 December, and that he recognized some as Sytin's printers and office workers. At 2 p.m. they dispersed, only to return with bricks and boards enough to build four barricades, with which, in effect, they sealed off street access to the plant. Troops arrived at 3 or 4 o'clock, continued Telkov, and he thought that apprentices at that time fired about five shots from the factory courtyard and from neighbouring buildings. The soldiers returned the fire over a period of fifteen minutes and then removed the barricades, remaining in the area until 2 a.m. on Monday morning. Telkov also testified that not until 4 a.m. did firemen enter the courtyard of the burning building.[25]

How the fire actually began was crucial, and three witnesses friendly to Sytin claimed to have seen soldiers act as arsonists. One was a plant watchman, N.A. Zakrevsky, who said that he and Sytin's brother Sergei had spent twenty minutes trying to extinguish the flames;[26] and the second was seventeen-year-old N.S. Semenov, apparently an apprentice.[27] The most precise was one P. Egorov, who recounted that soldiers had used a telegraph pole to break windows for entry into the plant. Once inside, he said, they had torched the lower floors of the plant. Firemen arrived more than once in the night but told Egorov they had orders to do nothing.[28]

Corroboration came from the chief of one of the fire brigades, Colonel Eduard Lund. He had arrived at the Sytin plant about 8 p.m. to find a small fire at the main entrance and three idle fire brigades, but because the head of the military detachment had given a "signal - do not put it out," Lund had directed his brigade to leave. When the fire became a big one during the night, continued Lund, the chief of police forbade countermeasures unless neighbouring buildings were endangered. Only later were there "instructions to put out the fire."[29] (Firemen certainly went to work at some point, for the water from their hoses caused some of the destruction in the plant.)

In a collection of recollections by members of the Sytintsy, N.I. Miretsky blames the fire on soldiers angered by the *druzhinniki* (volunteer defenders) who were shooting at them from the plant. These snipers, he says, were apprentices who fled after each fusillade through the tunnel connecting the plant with their dormitory. Although these same workers found and put out the first flames, "the soldiers, together with the firemen on the scene, took control, and the huge building burst into flames."[30] Another witness tells the same story and says that the troops made three unsuccessful attempts to catch the snipers.[31]

In a report to the minister of war just after the fire, the commander of the Moscow military district gave the cryptic, official version of events. He tells that two companies of soldiers and fifty Cossacks were sent to the plant on 11 December. "They were met with strong fire from armed defenders that called forth volleys from the besiegers, and a fire destroyed the printing plant."[32] He gives no reason for the fire.

A story in the liberal newspaper *Law* (*Pravo*) speculated that the fire resulted from artillery shells or from arson by workers who wished to keep the plant out of the authorities' hands because "documents of the [Printers'] Soviet had been stored" there.[33] The latter assumption may have been shared by officials.

At the actual trials in 1908 the courts upheld the insurance company's refusal to pay any part of the more than 600,000 ruble value of the destroyed property on the grounds that civil disturbances and/or official military activity had set off the fire. Sytin's lawyers had vainly countered that the plant had been quiet during the revolutionary agitation. It was several armed, drunken, undisciplined men who happened to be in military uniforms, they held, who broke into the plant and set the blaze, and a confused and intimidated fire brigade who allowed the blaze to become a conflagration. The lawyers for Sytin would have preferred to argue that persons in authority had ordered the plant destroyed or that their deliberate actions at the scene had ensured its destruction, but they lacked evidence.[34] Later Sytin said he understood the decision of the Moscow Circuit Court, upheld in the Moscow Court of Appeals. Claiming never to have expected compensation, Sytin says he pressed his claim of ''administrative arson'' in the safe forum of the court only to air the affair publicly.[35] He would insist to his dying day, however, that the government had conspired to strike a blow against him, an assumption he had leaped to the moment he heard about the fire.

In any event, showing his predominant optimism in the face of adversity, from the moment he saw the charred ruins Sytin began to plan his recovery. Relying almost entirely on the internal resources of his company, he immediately set to work to replace the building and its contents under terms that raised his credit rating. He mobilized his school of graphic artists to replace drawings and lithographic stones. He made a deal with suppliers to pay their bills in full if they gave him three months' grace and charged no interest, and he refused any further concessions. When the paper supplier Hans-Frank Marck, for example, offered to reduce Sytin's bill by half a million rubles, Sytin declined. Word of such fiscal resilience spread, and Sytin found ''that our credit ... with all banks and suppliers ... became almost unlimited.'' After six months, said the publisher, he was back in full operation, stronger than ever.[36] However, 1906 figures show that his company's share of publishing profits had fallen sharply (see appendix 5, figure 3).

On the labour front, workers everywhere had returned to their jobs, wearied of conflict and loss of pay. Thus the government could once again enforce its ban on unions; in March 1906 it had limited worker organizations to ''societies'' with no role in plant administration and no right to strike. Workers could elect ''representatives'' solely to collect dues and keep membership rolls.

IV

New regulations governing the publication of books came in April 1906 to complete the reform granting a free press; but when he read them, Sytin could still see troublesome limits. For one thing, the April rules retained the pre-circulation waiting period for short books (the usual format of dangerous tracts). If the government found grounds in that period to file suit, the police could confiscate the contested book and keep it from circulating pending trial; if the court in turn banned the work as criminal, no copies ever reached the public. Longer works could also be cited and seized but, like periodicals, only after they had gone on sale.

Prosecution as a means to control both books and periodicals had been, of course, a weapon available to the government since the censorship reform of 1865; but now, except for "emergencies," prosecution had become the only weapon. Thus, even with a losing case, government prosecutors could and would purposefully embroil Sytin, his editors, and his authors in costly, time-consuming litigation.

Officials wanted to use the same tactic against Sytin's daily, and records show that the local Press Affairs committee requested the Moscow prosecutor to lay charges based on content in *Russian Word* twice in late 1905 and thirteen times in 1906.[37] Some of the charges rested on verbatim quotations from legally convened assemblies, even though existing laws permitted that coverage. But since incendiary speeches could easily erupt at such meetings, officials sought to establish the precedent that publishing any and all seditious words was a criminal act.

Of special concern, for example, was press coverage of the 1905 All-Russian Peasant Congress, and that November Governor Osorgin of Tula province had wired a warning to the minister of the interior that news stories in Sytin's *Word* were inciting peasants to break the law. "If the newspaper *Russian Word*, which is widely circulated among the country population, will not be prosecuted for printing reports of sessions of the peasant congresses ... which invite open robbery in the speeches of self-appointed delegates, then the provincial authority has no possibility and justification to explain to the peasants that chopping down landowners' forests is illegal, which is happening more and more."[38]

Upon investigation, the Chief Administration of Press Affairs took issue with several quotations from the congress in *Word*. One was the threat that if officials failed to "give us land this winter, we will take it in the spring," while another, from a speaker arguing that only bloodshed would secure peasant rights, was clearly a call to arms. Still another called for emulating the civil disobedience of Sytin and his newspaper peers: "Look, how did the papers secure press freedom? They got together and decided, 'We will send nothing more to the censorship.'" Labelling these quotations criminal, the Moscow Press Affairs committee asked the government prosecutor to charge that their appearance in *Word* served to undermine private property.[39] The prosecutor refused, however, because the criminal code permitted Sytin to publish anything legally in the public domain.

Of the thirteen times the committee cited *Word* to the prosecutor in

1906, evidence of two indictments has come to light. One authorized the confiscation of *Word* on 9 June; but, because the seizure order reached the plant when only 24,355 papers remained of the 95,000 printed and because the police could recover only 22,413 more, well over half the copies for that day circulated as usual.[40] There is also evidence that a court ruling in 1906 against *Word* stopped a series of articles on 1905 by Doroshevich called "Whirlwind."[41]

To the relief of Sytin and the annoyance of officials, prosecutors and judges generally found *Word* in compliance with Russian law after 1905. Made painfully aware of that fact in 1906, the Moscow committee would request indictments with respect to *Word* only six times in all of the next five years, and would seemingly fail each time. As a countermeasure, Nicholas II would use his emergency powers in 1907 to reinstate administrative fines against outspoken papers; and his officials would levy substantial, but far from debilitating, fines against *Word* in the years that followed.[42]

Meanwhile in 1906, as newspapers in general proliferated,[43] Sytin launched two new dailies, his own *God's Truth* (*Pravda Bozhiia*) and his company's *Duma*; but the police and then politics closed each in turn. With respect to *God's Truth*, the police acted against a journalist who had worn out his welcome at *Word*, the able but outspoken priest and Kadet, Father Gregory Petrov.[44]

Sytin seems to have started *God's Truth* in January 1906 out of loyalty to Petrov, whose support had been crucial to *Word*'s survival in the nineties. Doroshevich had inherited Petrov, only to find him less and less suitable to his own secular, non-party editorial stance. Sytin had therefore opened a religious/socialist daily where Petrov, as editor, could freely continue his longtime career of Christian agitation.

Born, like Sytin, into an impoverished family, Petrov had gained entrance in his teens to St Petersburg seminary and had become a priest in 1891. Unlike his peers, he began attracting attention by discussing social questions, science, art, and even political issues in his sermons. The young called him the "modern father" because of his progressive ideas, and in 1893 the twenty-five-year-old Petrov became chaplain to the Mikhailovsky Artillery Officers' School in St Petersburg and later professor of theology at the St Petersburg Polytechnical Institute. By 1896 he was writing for *Word* – his submissions signed "The Russian" had elicited Gorky's scorn – and making monthly trips to Moscow to keep it going.

When the Russian Orthodox Church excommunicated Tolstoy in 1901, Petrov openly denounced this assault on freedom of conscience. For this impertinence, the church barred Petrov from public lectures and his chaplaincy and briefly exiled him to a monastery. During the

Russo-Japanese war he won public attention through articles in *Word* that challenged traditional ideas of patriotism and argued that Christians must extend brotherhood to all men, even the enemy.

This irrepressible priest took on his new role as editor of *God's Truth* just as candidates were campaigning for seats in Russia's first Duma and the Tsar was reasserting his authority following the revolutionary events of 1905. When the long-awaited Duma opened in April, Sytin branched out to St Petersburg with company funds to start his daily *Duma*. He hired the prestigious liberal publicist Peter Struve as editor and directed him to focus wholly on Russia's first legislative body.

As tension between the Duma and Nicholas mounted, the Moscow chief of police used emergency powers on 6 June to close *God's Truth* after 132 issues because it was "dangerous." This same month, and perhaps just before the confiscation of *Word* on 9 June, Sytin learned first-hand in the capital of the intense hostility by high officials toward *Word*. He hurriedly wrote to Blagov: "Change the paper. Trouble is at hand. For Christ's sake, save the business." A few hours later, having recovered his equanimity, he sent a second missive ordering Blagov to maintain course.[45]

Early in July, after a prolonged political crisis, Nicholas's dissolution of the Duma also ended its namesake paper. Sytin thus had losses from three very different dailies that failed in 1906: *Duma*, *God's Truth*, and the earlier mentioned *Russian Truth*. Sytin valued his company's flagship daily all the more for its strong potential. Although it would fall some 24 per cent below its record 1905 profits of 53,015 rubles, *Word* would still net a respectable 40,000 rubles in 1906. As for its 38 per cent decline in circulation from 1905 (157,000) to 1906 (98,100), *Word*'s editors mainly blamed the new allegiance of the politicized public to party papers.[46] In the face of disappointing numbers, Sytin responded quickly.

Midway in 1906 Sytin took the cost-saving measure of stopping Monday editions of *Word* by acceding to his typesetters' demands for no work on Sundays. He thereby cut out over fifty issues a year without lowering subscription prices. He also installed in all his plants, but especially at *Word*, more of the typesetting machines that produced lines of type faster and one-third cheaper than hand-setting them. No formal complaints about the displacement of workers came from the Sytintsy, although they would illegally stage a number of small strikes related to other grievances over the next several years.

Business aside, Sytin was very saddened and distracted this year by the death of his daughter Maria, the first of his ten children, who had wed Blagov twelve years before. He would lose only one other of his offspring during his lifetime, his son Vladimir, a casualty in 1915 of the war.

V

At the end of 1906 Sytin heard from some of the section editors at *Word* that he should elevate both the readership level and the subscription price of his daily, but Doroshevich and Petrov opposed them. "Really, do we want only 30 to 50 thousand readers?" asked Petrov. The paper should stay with Sytin's mass audience formula and aim for readers with interests no "higher than those of a non-commissioned officer."[47] Sytin held the price at seven rubles (where it would stay until 1913) and *Word* remained Russia's least expensive major daily.

Under the new laws of November 1905 the government could no longer ban street sales of newspapers, so Sytin made a concerted effort from 1906 onward to push single-copy sales of *Word* at stalls and stores - his metropolitan pedlar system.[48] He continuously negotiated more sites for street sales and in September 1906 opened one more company outlet, his new Bookstore of the Russian Word in his Tverskaia Street building.

Sytin also insisted on more aggressive coverage of political affairs in St Petersburg. To head his news bureau there, Sytin in 1906 appointed journalist A.V. Rumanov, whose many contacts in the social and governmental circles of St Petersburg included especially useful ones at the French and British embassies.[49] Because he also got on very well with Sytin, Rumanov often served as the publisher's stand-in in St Petersburg. Although he was known for the slight affectation of pronouncing his surname to make it sound "just like that of the reigning dynasty,"[50] respect for his even-handedness as a journalist won Rumanov important interviews and inside stories.

But Sytin outdid even Rumanov with a spectacular journalistic scoop on his own late in 1906. Thanks to his good relations with Chertkov, the former head of Mediator who had since become the literary agent of Leo Tolstoy, Sytin obtained for *Word* an unpublished and controversial work by Tolstoy, "Shakespeare and the Drama." This critique, which classes the English playwright as neither a great genius nor "even an average one," appeared in *Word* in November as a six-part series and aroused enormous public interest.

Tolstoy had written the piece in 1902 and had said that he would not publish it in his lifetime. How he felt about its appearance in *Word* is not entirely clear. When Gorbunov-Posadov, Chertkov's successor as the head of Mediator books, immediately asked Tolstoy for permission to reprint the articles as a single Mediator title, Tolstoy sent approval in a letter which included these words: "I absolutely don't understand how this article got to Sytin and I very much regret it."[51] Tolstoy may simply have regretted that his essay had appeared anywhere or he may have especially deplored its appearing in a newspaper owned by Sytin. In any case, there seem to have been no grounds for Tolstoy to contest *Word*'s serialization of "Shakespeare and the Drama," and Sytin is certain to have paid a good price for it.

From 1905 through 1907 Sytin made no change in *Word*'s advertising rates, although, since the charge was by column line, he had effectively raised them late in 1905 by narrowing ad-page columns. He charged seventy copecks for each column line of eight-point type on the front page and half that price elsewhere, and his year-to-year rise in advertising revenue was 34 per cent in 1906 and 20 per cent in 1907.

Production and editorial costs had meanwhile risen almost enough to wipe out profits and more than enough to dismay Sytin's fellow directors. They called an extraordinary meeting of shareholders on 26 September 1907 to propose that Sytin & Co. extricate itself from *Word* by refinancing the daily as a separate stock company. The nineteen shareholders agreed, and, once the government had given its approval on 4 October, the new stock - six hundred shares at one thousand rubles each - went up for sale.[52] Newspapers were chancy, however, and by Christmas the stock offering would be withdrawn for lack of buyers.[53]

In 1908, claims grandson Dmitry Ivanovich, the directors took a hard line by refusing to subsidize any shortfalls at *Word* that fiscal year. Crediting his grandmother with a "definite role" in Sytin's business affairs, Dmitry goes on to say that at some point in 1908, Evdokia Ivanovna wrote the staff to reassure them that Sytin would certainly keep *Word* going, even if his support meant that the two of them had to "become beggars."[54] Rather than dig into his own pocket, however, Sytin had instead raised ad rates at *Word* by nearly 15 per cent (to eighty and forty copecks) to increase ad revenues in 1908 by a heartening 64 per cent.[55] He did so, moreover, because his fellow directors had imposed that solution on him.

Gradually over the fifteen years since his publishing house had become a joint stock company, Sytin had discovered his vulnerability in the board room; and each loss of face there made him angry. After his risk-taking and hard work had established this publishing giant, why should those who had belatedly bought into his going concern hold the deciding seats on the directorship? His own principal share of stock and the block held by loyal family and friends did guarantee him a permanent seat (for it was the stockholders, casting one vote for each share owned, who chose the directors). But only a majority shareholder had both the votes and the moral right to control the board.

No mere principal shareholder, he'd already been told, should even try to tilt the board in his own favour. For Sytin, it seems, had already shown a streak of the crafty muzhik at a stockholder meeting in March 1906 by contriving the last-minute nomination of his twenty-seven-year-old son Nicholas for the board. By also lining up enough votes to elect him, Sytin had provoked a condescending letter from Ertel. "How," demanded Ertel, "is it possible for one to harmonize broad plans and projects and then behave like a petty shopkeeper?" Not only had the election been "completely rigged," but Sytin's nepotism and sneakiness had also lacked – "excuse me" – tact and intelligence. For all Sytin's "stories about 'discord' on the board," fumed Ertel, he found strange his colleagues' eagerness to "rush to please him [Sytin]."[56]

Board constraints on Sytin were often just, even though no full-fledged entrepreneur ever wants to share power over his enterprises. So far all his losses had been by three-to-one votes on the four-man board; but the number of directors and Sytin's degree of frustration were bound to go up. His solution, reckoned a very determined Sytin, was to acquire a majority share of the stock; for, as of 1907, he owned only 27 per cent.[57]

For all their differences, Sytin and his fellow directors did have many points of agreement, and one of them was *Word*'s independence from party politics. Doroshevich was therefore regularly making a point of criticizing the Constitutional Democrats, the party with views most like those of *Word*. Thus, since *Word* also advocated a constitution, Doroshevich had mockingly insisted early in 1907 that the Kadets assumed a constitution would "cure everything – syphilis, drunkenness – and will take care of the filling in of rivers. To cure consumption – a constitution. To kill cockroaches – a constitution."[58] As 1907 came to a close, he charged them on 6 November with being pompous: "Already the press has no love for the Kadets." Through jibes like these, Doroshevich signalled that *Word* was singularly unaligned.

An editor of the rival *Voice of Russia (Golos Rossii)* agreed that *Word* stood apart from all other leading Russian dailies in its independence. He described his own paper as the voice of the left wing of the Moscow merchant class and *Moscow Newssheet* as "solidly bourgeois." Sytin instead succeeded "to a greater degree" in making *Word* "a paper outside of party, outside of class, and well-informed, with a great press run and great influence."[59]

In its annual report for 1907, the Moscow Press Affairs Committee concurred by finding no "ideological line" in *Word* nor a precise political category to place it in. While seeming closest to the Constitutional Democratic Party in viewpoint, it frequently backed positions favoured by the left. The main fault of *Russian Word*, said these particularly attentive readers, was its tendency to cater to what the public wanted in a newspaper and to publish what the government did not.[60]

Earlier in 1907 Sytin had helped instigate and gain official approval for a stock company very different from his own, one comparable to what today is called a non-profit, philanthropic foundation. The success of Sytin & Co. had already brought considerable attention to the peasant-born publisher. He was now undertaking a new venture meant to heighten his reputation as a man of good works.

CHAPTER SIX

The Targeter Becomes Target

Sytin endlessly set his sights on new goals. In the three years before 1910 two broad targets of his were to gain more public esteem for himself and to re-establish Sytin & Co. in the first place among the publishing houses in Moscow. To do both, he set in motion a high-minded scheme to help gain him entry into the lucrative marketing of textbooks to schools, a sales area that he claimed a few insiders wrongly monopolized. But even as he took aim, Sytin became the target for others. The government would take him to court for publishing criminal words, and two papers would charge him with profiteering.

I

In the first dozen years of Mediator books, Sytin had merely dabbled in school texts, and he described the ten that he published before 1896 as "completely accidental" in character. They evolved because experts he met through the Tolstoyans and the literacy committees had gravitated into collaborating with him. But with the hiring of N.V. Tulupov, the former *zemstvo* school teacher, in 1896, Sytin had added to his company a department for designing pedagogical books; and from it, from the next year on, had come specialized texts and the Popular Schools Library series. In 1897 Chekhov had remarked approvingly about the "brisk sales" of "Sytin's new grey-covered self-teaching manuals based on English models" and the "tremendous demand in the provinces for serious scientific literature."[1]

But Sytin did not easily get these books into classrooms because teachers could adopt only the ones ranked as "approved" or "permitted" by the Ministry of Public Education. Repeatedly the ministry turned down books submitted by Sytin for consideration; and those it rejected, said Sytin, simply "died."

While "permitted" books could win substantial sales, the higher endorsement of "approved" guaranteed wide adoptions. Sytin charged that that higher rating went solely to what he called "a syndicate, an organized monopoly of book publishers and privileged authors of text books." As proof, he named publishers and several authors whose publications repeatedly made the preferred lists. One author even sat on the appraisal committee; and although he withdrew from votes that involved his own works, this "kinsman" always won committee backing. What resulted was a discriminating "tax on knowledge," argued Sytin, because monopolists of the top ratings could extract prices so unfairly high as to be prohibitive to the "poor, forgotten, ... half-hungry peasant" struggling to learn.[2]

The appraisal system that troubled Sytin included six official committees, the highest and most important of which was the ministry's Learning Committee. But teachers were the final judges. Selecting the more expensive "approved" books was their safest course but, since students bore the costs, many teachers opted for the cheapest permitted texts. The Russian primer by Vakhterov that Sytin published in 1897, for example, was just such a book. Its annual sales neared one million copies, and it would go through 118 editions. Tulupov's readers for classrooms also sold widely.[3]

Sytin used his book catalogues and strongly competitive prices to woo teachers, listing in a separate section all of his books accepted by the government. The catalogue for 1905 offered forty such titles, including one book that had won the approved rating the year before. The list in 1906 had grown to sixty-five titles - an auspicious start.[4]

Without citing specific years or figures, Sytin boasts in his memoirs that his "texts began to be sold in unheard of numbers and the first break in the monopoly of text books had been made." What made it possible, he claimed, was the "general grumbling in the press and in society" that forced the "favoured publishers and, so to speak, the first born of the Ministry ... to make room so that the tightly sealed door of the Ministry little by little opened to all the others."[5] Sytin says he made "personal agreements" to have notable educators such as N.V. Chekhov, E.A. Zviagintsev, and A.A. Stakhovich write texts that the ministry could hardly reject.

Evidence suggests that Sytin greatly exaggerated the monopoly he split apart. For one thing, given the 1896 approval of Vakhterov's primer, the break Sytin speaks of could have come no later than the first year he seriously entered the textbook market. For another, the 60 per cent approval rate for all the textbooks Sytin's editors designed from 1887 to 1915 suggests more than marginal success, especially in light of other figures from 1901 to 1916 showing that, from all the submissions by Sytin & Co., the ministry approved eleven hundred different books. By 1910 Sytin & Co. would be publishing 22 per cent of all domestic textbooks in Russian.[6]

The scheme that Sytin launched in 1907, then, to enhance himself and his educational publishing, came squarely midway in the twenty-year period when he actively pursued the textbook market. His method was to declare his dissatisfaction with schools in Russia and to step outside his company to organize a reform project.

Sytin recruited four public figures as co-sponsors. One was Professor Maxim M. Kovalevsky, the Duma member and law professor who had contributed liberal commentary to *Word* in 1905. The second and third were old allies of Sytin on the Moscow Literacy Committee: the wealthy, well-placed Barbara A. Morozova, who hosted leading intellectuals in her Moscow salon and already funded educational projects and her husband's liberal daily, *Russian Bulletin*; and A.I. Ertel, the writer much admired by Tolstoy who had worked with Sytin on the Mediator series. The last was V.I. Kovalevsky, a wealthy mine-owner of liberal bent and president of the Russian Imperial Technical Society who in 1905 had favoured a national manufacturers' political party. Kovalevsky had formerly headed the Ministry of Trade and Industry, which would shortly have to approve this stock company.

Not only must Sytin have found their liberal bias congenial, but the four co-sponsors must also have felt comfortable with him. Perhaps with the purest of motives, Sytin was hob-nobbing with aristocrats who had brains, money, and gilt-edged social credentials. Teaming up with these patricians showed just how far he had risen above his beginnings. And he could challenge the best of them to match his generosity, since their project – a non-profit joint stock company to be called the School and Knowledge Society – rested on the sale of 250 shares at four thousand rubles each. Only persons of means could manage donations on that scale, and Sytin agreed to invest fifty thousand rubles straight away.

In their application for government approval, Sytin and his four co-sponsors decried Russia's lagging behind every leading country of the world in basic schooling for the masses.[7] With cavalier frankness, they argued that the government could not adequately respond, even if it were to "change fundamentally its relationship to popular education" – that is, if it were to spend lavishly to provide the facilities, teachers, and materials needed. Thus, since "all the economic resources of Russia" had to be marshalled, the new society would raise private capital and enlist experts to put those funds to work.

Sytin and his partners set the colossal overall goal of one hundred thousand new school buildings and three hundred thousand new teachers. The society would itself help provide study aids, and do so with a cost-cutting efficiency the government should emulate. And here, surely, emerges the prime concern of Sytin, who had used mass production and other economies of scale to such good effect in his publishing house. Such western methods as long press runs could benefit the schools, said the founders, by cutting book costs in half.[8] The prices for texts charged by insiders in the schoolbook trade would appear ridiculously high in comparison.

Sytin later described School and Knowledge as an "exclusively educational" venture with "no commercial aims": a school-related version of Mediator. He had earlier helped the Tolstoyans promote literacy in the countryside; now he would accomplish even more. His society would supply needy classrooms with essential printed works; but he left unsaid that Sytin & Co. would be the publisher.

Posing a threat to other publishers, however, was just one of several liabilities for the founders. They had belittled the Ministry of Public Education and set goals that seemed almost laughable; and their methods recalled those of the committees for literacy which had already put Sytin, Ertel, and Barbara Morozova in the bad books of the police. Finally, the prime founder, Sytin, was soon to stand trial for criminal publications.

But, by strategic design, Sytin had set up the novel non-profit stock company under the province of a proven ally, the Ministry of Trade and Industry. To assist an industrialist whose prowess was helping to modernize Russia, its officials had already approved several of his reincorporations. In May 1907 they unhesitatingly gave their approval for Sytin's School and Knowledge Society.

Recruiting stockholders went forward quickly, as such matters can among the very rich. Early subscribers included land-owners who had been active in the *zemstvo* movement and had since become Kadets or Octobrists; a leader of the latter was M.A. Stakhovich, while the Kadets included Prince G.E. Lvov, N.N. Shchepkin, and Prince D.I. Shakhovskoi.[9]

Within a year, however, Sytin had abandoned School and Knowledge. For one thing, the powerful Moscow governor general had gone on record to predict dire consequences if the state's absolute controls over educational books were breached by a private group, especially one with so obvious a "liberal" and "democratic" bias. Then in 1908 had come two more severe setbacks: in the state Duma an influential conservative deputy, V.M. Purishkevich, had publicly denounced the program of School and Knowledge as an assault on both the government and the Holy Synod; and a crucial sponsor, Ertel, had died.[10]

Judicial troubles must have been another reason for Sytin to have backed away from School and Knowledge. In the same year as Ertel's death, Sytin received summonses for two trials and indictments for three more, all with respect to his being responsible for allegedly criminal publications. This blitz of charges strongly suggests a government campaign to restrain the man who – both to the judiciary and to the general public – was *the* publisher at Sytin & Co. enterprises.

II

Whenever the government based a prosecution on the contents of a book or brochure, the person legally identified as the publisher automatically faced charges of criminal responsibility. (In cases against periodicals, only the "responsible editor" was indicted.) The number of press-related trials had soared during the post-1905 years as the government used the court system to try to put limits on publishing,[11] and although the burden of proof lay heavily on the prosecutors, a defendant such as Sytin had a lot at stake. Convictions could bring serious penalties, and the prolonged litigation, commonly running for two years, was costly and distracting. These judicial inquiries were not mere cat-and-mouse games, and they caused Sytin and everyone else in publishing to look closely at their projects.

Not surprisingly for someone with no literary interests and many deals to manage, Sytin did not read the works that issued from his presses – and he thereby gained a solid defence against responsibility for their content. He was to use this argument, formulated in more elaborate fashion by his attorney S.I. Varshavsky, in five trials; and although all the cited works would be found criminal, the judges would acquit Sytin each time.

Court decisions against three of his publications but not against Sytin came down in a single trial in 1908. Dealt with there were three brochures that had appeared in 1905 as "volumes" in the Religious-Social Library: *On Self-Government* by A. Elchaninov; *What Do the Peasants Need?* by V. Sventsitsky; and *The Position of the Jews in Russia* by V. Markov. Censors had rejected all three as manuscripts before 1905, but Sytin's editor, V. Ern, had gone ahead with them during the anarchic revolutionary year.[12]

Sytin next appeared and won exoneration in court in 1908 for publishing, three years earlier, a book called *Fantastic Truths* that approvingly described the revolution of 1905. Tried and convicted in absentia was its author, A.V. Amfiteatrov, whose satire on the Romanovs had caused the closure of *Russia*. When, in 1906 or later, the prosecutor had first indicted Sytin for his role in spreading falsehoods "which incited society" through this work, Amfiteatrov had already gone into voluntary exile abroad.[13]

The criminal judgments in 1908 against all four books required their destruction, but the financial loss to Sytin & Co. was negligible, especially since there were so few unsold copies. Two other interrelated cases launched in 1908 against Sytin put nine thousand unsold copies at stake.

Nothing had initially happened when the six thousand copies of *Yearbook of Popular Schools* were published by Sytin in November 1907, at one ruble, fifty copecks each. V.I. Charnolussky, a radical of sorts who had belonged to the St Petersburg Soviet in 1905, had edited this collection of pedagogical documents and added an essay, "Teaching Organizations in Russia." What proved criminal were the resolutions favouring political activity that had come from the All-Russian Teachers' Conference at the close of 1905 in Finland.[14] In his essay, Charnolussky chose to repeat the most radical ones calling for a constituent assembly, boycott of Duma elections, and the division of land among the peasants – issues much discussed by everyone in 1905.

One month after *Yearbook* appeared, Sytin & Co. printed three thousand copies of *Teachers' Organizations in Russia*, a sixty-copeck brochure comprised only of Charnolussky's essay and the resolutions from Finland. This shorter, less expensive version was much more likely to circulate widely, so the Moscow Committee for Press Affairs found it subversive, required its confiscation, and summoned the government prosecutor. His indictments of 27 April 1908 held Sytin and Charnolussky criminally responsible for producing *Teachers' Organizations*.

As soon as he had learned of the committee's actions, Sytin had himself withdrawn all copies of the longer *Yearbook* from his bookstores and had destroyed the five thousand copies in his inventory. (About five hundred copies had by then reached the public.) But the Moscow Committee on Press Affairs did not ask the government prosecutor to indict Sytin and Charnolussky for the *Yearbook* until December 1908, because the Moscow governor general had wanted to use his own emergency powers to destroy the *Yearbook* without a trial, and the committee had had to await a ruling from St Petersburg against that administrative short cut.

Sytin would answer the charges based on *Teachers' Organizations* before a panel of judges of the Moscow Court of Appeals in the fall of 1909; on 24 October the court would find the book criminal but acquit him and Charnolussky. The same result would come from the *Yearbook* trial in 1910 when Sytin would argue in his own defence: "Can I be held responsible for a book which was approved by the press committee, by the *Government Messenger* [which had published a favourable review of it], and which I myself destroyed before receiving orders from authority?"[15]

With an excess of melodrama, Sytin's attorney would describe the tension for Sytin "waiting hours for the verdict" because persons "in the conference room ... were demanding heavy criminal penalties for him."[16] In fact, the prime target, once again, was the indicted material.

Finally, the seventh book to embroil Sytin in a court case was one the government apparently had difficulty in tracing to his company: a radical dictionary that had surfaced just after the revolution of 1905 with no reference to its source. The indictment against it before the Moscow Court of Appeals on 18 November 1908 shows that the author was then still not known to the prosecutor, for charges of responsibility were directed only against Sytin as publisher and Tulupov as editor.[17]

During the pre-indictment investigation both men denied having seen the contents of the dictionary before its publication, but they agreed that the book had come from Sytin's presses as part of Tulupov's Contemporary Library series. The dictionary in question, *The Modern Social-Political and Economic Dictionary*, was a lexicon of contemporary political terms to supplement *The Complete Dictionary of Foreign Words Used in the Russian Language*.

No fault could be found with the *Complete Dictionary*, stated the indictment, but the supplement listed Karl Marx as a "great teacher," his *Communist Manifesto* as a compendium of "timeless" ideas, and a number of his predictions as historically inevitable – all the while defining "autocracy" as "uncontrolled bureaucratism." Very possibly the original source to link Sytin & Co. with the anonymous dictionary was N.A. Skvortsov, a former employee who testified against Sytin and Tulupov when the trial over the book took place in 1910. During those hearings Skvortsov swore that both Sytin and Tulupov had read the manuscript in January 1906, and that Tulupov had edited it as well.[18]

S.R. Nazaretskaia, the secretary of the editorial board, countered for the defence that she remembered receiving the finished manuscript directly from the author, sending it at once to the typesetters, and then having the author proof-read the galleys. The author had, seemingly by this time, been identified as P.G. Sennikovsky, a graduate student at Moscow University, but his belated indictment would defer his testimony and the judges' verdict until the next year.

Meanwhile in the 1910 hearing Tulupov described Skvortsov as a biased witness, inasmuch as Sytin had recently fired him. Indeed, Skvortsov was then personally suing Sytin & Co. for three thousand rubles allegedly due him for reprints of stories of his that were first published while he was secretary of the editorial staff for children's books and journals.[19] Relying on his usual defence, Sytin had his lawyers interject statistics on the hundreds of manuscripts handled yearly at his book plant to show why he had to delegate them entirely to others.[20]

As for the third and primary defendant, Sennikovsky took all blame for the cited words and convinced the judges the following May that neither Sytin nor Tulupov had known about his radical dictionary before publication. Thus the decision on 3 May 1911 went only so far as to ban the book and sentence Sennikovsky to a year in jail and a fine of one thousand rubles.

Documents show that Sytin himself paid the fine, and he probably also arranged Sennikovsky's appeal to the Senate, which shortened the jail term by two months. Sytin must have felt some obligation, especially since the curious course of the anonymous dictionary strongly implicates his son Nicholas, who then supervised all the typesetters and pressmen. Sytin had manoeuvred his eldest son not only onto the 1906 company board but also into this very responsible post. Nicholas, with his leftist sympathies, could easily have rushed the manuscript into print and then diverted the finished copies into underground sales channels. The books surely did not go on sale in Sytin's bookstores, or authorities would not have taken two years to identify the publisher.

Still other books from Sytin's presses struck the Moscow Committee on Press Affairs, but not the prosecutor, as criminal. Judicial records for 1907 give an example: a book by a French socialist, T. Hervé, entitled *Socialism and Patriotism*.[21] In the three-day waiting period after Sytin & Co. had printed four thousand copies priced at forty copecks, the committee found criminal content in the claim by Hervé that the proletarians of the world had no fatherland and would be ''swindled fools'' to die on behalf of one. That statement, the committee argued, was a call to Russian soldiers to abandon their posts. The prosecutor, in contrast, found the entire book strictly theoretical and freed it to circulate.

Five known court cases over books that implicated Sytin sputtered along over the five years from 1907 to 1911 but inflicted little damage on him or his company. Public dishonour was negligible and the financial loss was slight. More to the point, the occasional indictment showed liberals that Sytin was a publisher willing to take some risks to test the limits of the permissible.

Russian Word, in this same period, annoyed officials but mainly stayed out of trouble. Sytin and Doroshevich agreed, first, that nothing appear in their daily that could put *Word* at risk of peremptory closure; and secondly, they effectively relied on their two-edged sword of *glasnost* (lawful publicity), made especially hefty by *Word*'s wide readership, to fend off arbitrary autocratic controls.[22] Thus the Tsar's officials who chose to discipline *Word* with their administrative (non-judicial) arrest and jailing of responsible editor Blagov in October 1910 learned the folly of ''emergency'' penalties against *Word*.

Cause for the arrest was a ''completely accurate'' news account of police brutality during demonstrations in the streets after the funeral of S.A. Muromtsev, the president of the Duma,[23] and Sytin was furious when the government ordered Blagov to serve three months in jail. In the immediate outcry from Moscow papers, Sytin's *Word* on 16 October labelled the punishment too severe for the alleged crime and scorned the absence of judicial procedures. When Blagov's release came in only two weeks, Sytin could claim that the protests from *Word* and other papers had given the press another victory on behalf of free speech.

III

Both court cases and fines had peaked for Sytin & Co. in 1908, but the public image of Sytin remained bright. The publisher won a seat that year on the Moscow Duma (city council) and was gaining notice as a philanthropist.[24] In 1909, however, Sytin for the first time faced a punishing public assault against his good name. His assailants were two rival papers and the charge was profiteering.

In a three-part series called ''Secrets of the Sytin Publishing Company,'' the weekly *Capital Talk* (*Stolichnaia Molva*) specifically cited Sytin for miscalculating royalties.[25] According to an unnamed informant on the company staff, Sytin based his payments to an author on the number of books that he had agreed in advance to print even though he secretly printed more.[26] The oversight was deliberate theft, *Talk* insisted.

Another deceptive practice described by *Talk* involved Sytin's transforming works from his periodicals into books without paying additional fees. In one example, an author had proposed that the stories he wrote for *Little Bee* also appear in book form, only to be told that Sytin & Co. no longer reprinted works that required royalty payments. When the author had then discovered a bound volume of his stories while browsing in a bookstore in 1907, he had demanded payment. Company spokesmen insisted that the books were merely pages from unsold copies of *Little Bee* bound in new covers, but the author cited the renumbered pages and launched a suit for restitution. The company directors, continued *Talk*, responded with a conciliatory letter in *Russian Word* and then apparently paid the author enough to persuade him to drop his suit.

Yet another example of alleged trimming concerned two translators. They, too, had discovered their work for Sytin's magazines reappearing in book form. The directors dismissed their claims for new fees by claiming that translations became the property of the company in the initial transaction, but they also seemed to admit wrong-doing by offering token payments of one hundred rubles. According to *Talk*, one of the translations, a Jules Verne novel, sold a very substantial ten thousand copies at sixty copecks each.

Sytin, concluded *Talk*, had an odds-on chance of getting away with unfair practices. A writer or translator might never know he had been short-changed; but once he did, he had to accept whatever additional pay Sytin would begrudge him or face a costly court battle that had to start within two years of the day the disputed publication appeared. Finally, any author or translator who looked ahead would prefer to stay on good terms with Sytin rather than jeopardize all chance of again working for him.

Questions of fair play were partly the fault of the loose Russian copyright law which favoured the publishers (as did Russia's not being a signatory of the international convention until 1911). But still more to blame was the free-wheeling expediency that Russian businessmen took for granted. Maybe his struggles upward from peasant status had made Sytin wilier than most, but he was not alone in falsifying figures for his own benefit.

Talk's long, detailed series must have stung Sytin sharply because it mocked his cherished claims of being, above all else, the people's benefactor. Moreover, just a month before, *Moscow* (*Moskva*) had done the same by impugning a speech that Sytin had delivered in early July. The occasion had been a banquet in St Petersburg for the first All-Russian Congress of Booksellers and Publishers.[27] Speaking through a haze of cigar smoke and post-prandial good feeling, Sytin may not have had the most attentive audience, but at least the reporter from *Moscow* had listened closely. Sensing a story, he took note of Sytin's assertion that only when all Russian publishers chose to meet the reading needs of the muzhik would Russia become a literate country. He also jotted down Sytin's claim of labouring for over thirty years "to spread good, necessary and useful books" among the villages, and Sytin's boast of providing more than four thousand pedlars with such popular Russian folk tales as "Bova Korolevich."

In *Moscow*, within days, that same reporter asked his readers just how the bloody medieval tale of Bova might be "good and useful." The answer, he continued, was that such tales enabled Sytin to build printing plants and enrich himself. In the next lines he made a charge that was levelled against Sytin again and again:[28] "Building your career, you were always able to adapt yourself to the demands of the minute. When people demanded 'Bova Korolevich,' you gave them 'Bova Korolevich.' When in your view it was time to be unctuous and support Black Hundred causes in your paper, you were unctuous and a Black Hundred. Another wind blew and you began to publish the latest red brochures. In a word, you are always and primarily a merchant and above all study the mood and demands of the market."[29] Sytin the expedient profiteer, he concluded, was parading as the altruistic evangelist for literacy for the common people. "Ah, Mr. Sytin! Do you have to be not only a bookseller but also a Pharisee?"

IV

Two months before the attack in *Moscow*, Sytin had had to deal directly with the private complaint of another critic, his long-time collaborator Gregory Petrov. In May 1909 Petrov had written letters to both Blagov and Sytin from abroad demanding that *Word* print his articles. To Blagov he grumbled: "As you know, I send my articles not just for the typesetter but for the reader."[30] His plaint to Sytin challenged the publisher's sincerity. "You have assured me of your devotion and respect over many long years, in the sense that you understand and feel in yourself the [loyalty] that I have shown to *Russian Word* ... Not long ago with tears in your eyes you convinced me that you are indignant at the editors' treatment of me."[31]

To side-step Petrov's complaint, Sytin replied that June with anguish of his own: "Be generous to me although I rarely write, [given] all the various internal petty and silly misunderstandings, which simply cloud like dust the minds of people ... Doroshevich is living in Moscow and after two months of uninterrupted night work on the paper has fallen ill. He has been at home in bed for three weeks. There are complications in some misunderstandings among the writers. This was always the case, one has to go from one to the other, to talk them around ... Ah, how very strange all this is, I simply with each year am becoming more tangled in my thinking, and I wonder where truth lies and who is right." Sytin then spoke of Ertel, the novelist and co-sponsor of School and Knowledge who had died in 1908, and quoted Peter Struve's remarks that Ertel's renunciation of literature to become a farm labourer had been full of religious meaning. "If Struve is right," Sytin continued, "then again confusion in the head, [and] I would in my heart of hearts like to explore all these matters with you. I am thinking of leaving Russia for a time, for a rest, but I can do it only after my case [on *Teachers' Organizations*] is heard in court."[32]

Sytin meant Petrov to understand that editor staff relations were in such delicate balance that he could not intervene on his behalf. Sytin takes some of the blame, suggests his own heavy burdens, and longs for Petrov's counsel. But he probably did not assuage Petrov, who would eventually threaten to take Sytin to court for keeping him out of the columns of *Word*. Sytin was at least honest in saying that he could not possibly visit Petrov before the trial over *Teachers' Organizations* ended, and he had the same reason, among others, for declining that summer to visit another author abroad – Maksim Gorky, the radical writer in exile, whom Sytin very much wanted to publish.

V

For some months now, Sytin had known that he might have an inroad to the once-hostile Gorky and his circle because Gorky was facing financial shortfalls with his own publishing company, Znanie, and his literary miscellany of the same name. Government confiscations and the slumping book market had cut profits; and in contrast to the bright noon of his public acclaim at the start of the century, Gorky's celebrity as a writer had faded. In 1901 Gorky had scorned Sytin; in 1909 he needed his backing. From his self-exile on Capri, Gorky had asked Ivan Bunin, one of Znanie's leading writers, to sound out Sytin.

Even though Gorky had backed the armed rebellion in Moscow in 1905 and had left during the reactionary aftermath of 1906, Sytin had a very high regard for this writer approved by Chekhov. He also knew that Petrov had come away from a 1905 meeting with Gorky favourably impressed.[33] Both Sytin and Gorky had, as well, risen from the "lower depths." Most important, Gorky and his circle could enormously enhance *Russian Word* and Sytin's book list.

Bunin had managed to see Sytin in April 1909 and found himself of first interest to the publisher. "It seems I could be tremendously rich," Bunin at once wrote Gorky. Sytin, he explained, had asked him to edit one or more periodicals because he had the right style to "attract the young." And, to enhance his offer, Sytin mentioned lining up sales outlets at some three hundred railroad stations. "But how this will end I don't know," mused Bunin. "I am afraid of perishing, of getting in over my head."[34]

Even before hearing from Bunin, Gorky had written to I.P. Ladyzhnikov, his director of Znanie, about the projects he hoped Sytin would finance. "We are dreaming about a lot: that [Sytin & Co.] give us 50,000 rubles for a journal and 20,000 for an encyclopedia. There are even other proposals. Please keep in mind the following: it is very likely that Sytin or Teleshov [a mutual friend] will come here this summer, and I will ask you to visit also to work out an agreement with these people."[35]

Gorky was naively optimistic about Sytin's readiness to deal and to do so on Gorky's terms. For one thing, Sytin did not passively invest in other men's companies. With Sytin's capital went Sytin's control and dovetailing of projects. For another, Sytin mainly wanted Gorky and his confederates to write for him. In his meeting with Bunin, Sytin therefore promised nothing, making clear that he had to deal with Gorky face to face in Capri, when he could get there.

In May Bunin agreed to become editor of a foundering literary journal, *Northern Lights* (*Severnoe Siianie*), printed by Sytin & Co. at less than cost and subsidized, as well, by the publisher, Countess V.N. Bobrynskaia. It had begun in November 1908 and bogged down after its third issue that January. Abetted by friends from Znanie, Bunin produced in June what proved to be the last issue, for Sytin's fellow directors still saw no hope of the journal's succeeding and cut off any further support.

Since *Northern Lights* was part of a series envisioned by Sytin especially for travellers, Sytin might have won a reprieve for the journal had he at that time succeeded in negotiating a ten-year contract for railroad kiosks. But because outlets at train stops accounted for most single-copy periodical sales in the provinces and were much sought after, the railway directors would commit themselves only to a contract renegotiable in three years.[36]

Sytin at least had the satisfaction of having Bunin agree at this point to write for *Russian Word*. This acclaimed writer, who would win admission in November to the prestigious Russian Academy,[37] became a prized addition to Sytin's daily, along with another noted novelist, Dmitry Merezhkovsky, who had already signed on.

That September Bunin informed Gorky that his proposed dealings with Sytin were still stalemated. "I have seen Ladyzhnikov and Sytin," he wrote. "Ladyzhnikov is in a gloomy mood over having little hope of finding a monied person. And Sytin is up to his neck in work. With great delight, he showed interest in your plans, but definitely said one thing: 'It is necessary to go to Capri, absolutely necessary, but it is possible no earlier than the holiday [Christmas].' "[38]

Gorky from Capri in the meantime tried to attract backing from Sytin for a multi-volume encyclopedia on Siberia, a somewhat esoteric project that was necessary, Gorky argued, to promote the development of a neglected but important region. He got no more satisfaction than did Bunin, but neither did Sytin say no. The elusive publisher would yet go to Capri to lay out his own proposals, but not until 1911.

Sytin had no need to hurry or to go hat in hand. Five years after the revolution of 1905, his business was booming again. Sytin & Co. had continuously ranked among the five largest printing firms in Moscow since the turn of the century; once more it was the undisputed leader. Profits of 236,800 rubles in 1910 exceeded the earlier top figure of 188,300 reached in 1904 – just as the press runs of *Word* in 1910 at 198,000 outdid all previous years (see appendix 5, figures 3 and 6, pages 207, 210).

Reflecting the quickening economic pace in Russia, long columns of ads about typewriters, autos, stoves, bonds, patent medicines, jobs, and services added to *Word*'s profits. Dividend payments on the stock of Sytin & Co., which had fallen from consistent 10 to 11 per cent levels to a low of 5 per cent in 1905 and then rebounded to 8 per cent in 1908, had climbed back to 10 per cent in 1910. Another gauge of success is the comparative performance of Sytin & Co. against the other four top publishing houses (see figure 3). As its portion of their combined profits, Sytin's company realized about a 20 per cent share in each of the first three years of the century, followed by 29 per cent in 1903, 37 per cent in 1904, and a peak of 41.3 per cent in 1905. Following the 1905 book-plant fire, its 1906 profit share fell to 7 per cent, only to return to roughly the 20 per cent level in 1907 and 1908.[39] The figure for 1909 rose to just under 32 per cent and to a solid 36 per cent in 1910.

As for comparative increments, five-year profits from 1900 through 1904 for Sytin & Co. more than doubled, against a gain of only 5 per cent for Sytin's top four competitors. In strike-ridden 1905, Sytin & Co.'s annual profits fell about 6 per cent; that of the other four, about 21 per cent. Those same competitors enjoyed a windfall of work and an annual profit rise of 160 per cent in 1906 because Sytin's company, while rebuilding its book-plant, suffered production losses and repair costs that cut its profits by 82 per cent. From 1907 through 1910 Sytin increased his company's net earnings nearly sevenfold, in contrast to an end-of-decade combined profit for the four just below him that was only slightly higher than their total for 1906.

The principal source of profits for Sytin's company continued to be publishing "for the people." For the first decade of the century as a whole, Sytin's three bestselling categories had been calendars, popular literature, and pictures of religious content, which together numbered nearly 100 million copies. In fourth place were belles lettres, or works for relatively sophisticated readers. In fifth place were more pictures, of "varied content" (see appendix 2 for the complete figures). Sytin's "educational" publishing was just becoming significant.

Sytin had been a driving force behind the recovery of his company; as the first decade of the twentieth century ended, he enjoyed a reputation well beyond Moscow as a man of prodigious energy and means. Neither the fire at his book plant nor labour disruptions could deter him. Although he was a target of press and governmental barbs, he had won over a former critic, Gorky. The reason again was his commanding lead in publishing. Not only did it represent immense resources, expertise, and access to the people, but it also enabled the Moscow publisher to push freedom of expression beyond the limits favoured by the government.

VI

As an ordinary mortal, Sytin also felt the aches and pains of someone nearly sixty, especially in his hands and feet. Extreme obesity had become a nagging problem for his wife, Evdokia Ivanovna, or Buka, as he called her. Thus, rather than visit Gorky in Capri in the summer of 1910, Sytin took Buka that June to spend three weeks at the spa in Karlsbad.

Three letters survive that Sytin wrote home to Blagov, and in the first one, he sounds the long-suffering husband and worried father. "Today at 9 o'clock we finally arrived in Karlsbad. The end of our first ordeal. The wife has to look on things as a foreigner. A genuine foreigner, even understands foreign words and expressions, speaks a little German with the chambermaid ... Tomorrow we will get into the correct drinking [of the water] and the routine of the pension ... Write me about the paper ... It has already been ten days since I have seen the paper. Little result from the trip, got to know [some] people. Don't know if I'll have enough patience to keep up the treatment. My health except for my hands and foot is good. *Be a good chap and look after the fellows* [his sons]. *Don't let them lose discipline.* They already look upon everything too lightly. Just as well [I] found out. I tried to explain, whether it was understood I don't know ..."[40]

Sytin wrote the second letter, the only one he dated, on 11 June, and Gregory Petrov had just turned up at the spa. Here was the chance for the two men to come to an understanding about *Word*'s not publishing Petrov's articles. What Sytin writes home, however, confirms that he has all along been less than honest with Petrov. "I am climbing everything with Petrov and I am feeling good and walking and she sleeps and takes the cure for fat and obesity in bed. It is a good thing that they give her massages here. Petrov is terribly upset that nothing of his is printed in [*Russian Word*]. If possible do me a favour and print something, but without violating conditions of censorship [Sytin uses this word loosely, since there were no censors] or the interests of the paper. He has very leftist views."

Sytin finds Karlsbad "so-so" and less pleasant than Bersenevka, his estate north of Moscow. The disciplined hours for rising, sleeping and meals he finds appalling: "Whoever is the boss here devised a bastardly regime of the Devil."[41] His mind on home, he asks Blagov to look after "the tires of the automobile so that it will run until Christmas without repairs."

By letter number three, perhaps about the end of the second week, Sytin is thoroughly restive. "We are," he writes, "bad Germans. We don't get much joy out of foreign watering places. It is hard to adapt to foreign ways. It is not like our own, like the wide-open Caucasus. It was a stupid thing to come here. Although this is my personal opinion. I have not asked Buka about it ... She sits, grumbles, drinks water, and takes massages. Well, it keeps her busy all day. I am taking mud baths every other day and drink water. We don't fight much and mostly glower at one another." Next follows a request for a guidebook of Europe because Sytin wants "to return through Prague and through Odessa." He concedes that "travel is all right, but it is better at home."

Sytin closes with a query about two of his fellow directors - "How are our enemies in the persons of Rozenhagen and Soloviev?"[42] - a reference to the problems Sytin faced in holding just one vote on the directorship of the company he founded. Even stronger differences were to arise at board meetings in the next two years, in part because of Leo Tolstoy, whose final days would, that fall, provide sensational copy for *Russian Word*.

CHAPTER SEVEN

Leaning to the Left

Contradictory impulses were at work in Ivan Sytin from 1910 to 1913. Through constant expansion and mass production he had acquired wealth, influence, and upper-class standing, along with nagging doubts about their worth. The death of Leo Tolstoy in 1910 made him all the more open to such Tolstoyan preachings as common cause with the humble, and Sytin would shortly make possible, probably at considerable personal expense, the great writer's bequests to the peasants of Iasnaia Poliana and to the public domain.

But even as he wondered if piety and charity should be his first concerns, Sytin remained the consummate entrepreneur. He knew that to keep his ideals and drives in harmony he should concentrate his efforts on popular but worthy publications – the kind favoured by Chekhov and Tolstoy. Since *Russian Word* was far and away his company's leading publication to serve the common good and its own treasury, Sytin would single-mindedly set about to place at *Word*'s helm a committedly "democratic" editor.

I

A matter of unfinished business for Sytin when he returned to Moscow in the fall of 1910 was volume four of a series from Tolstoy entitled *Circle of Reading*. It was, to be precise, the revised edition of a book originally issued by Mediator, the publishing house set up by the Tolstoyans when their collaboration with Sytin had fallen off early in the century.

Chertkov, still Tolstoy's literary agent, had persuaded Tolstoy to engage Sytin for the book, even though Tolstoy had never abandoned his earlier impression of Sytin as a mercenary that no artist could fully count on. (Tolstoy's wife likewise cast Sytin among the "unscrupulous businessmen" she knew.)[1] Sytin had agreed to the project only to find grave problems in *Circle of Reading*. This compilation of inspirational thoughts excerpted by Tolstoy from many different writers contained themes, pacificism in particular, unacceptable to the government. Sytin had consequently slowed the typesetting of the text.

Fully a year earlier, in 1909, Tolstoy had sent Chertkov a terse order: "Take back from Sytin the second edition of *Circle of Reading*. This book is very dear to me and it is evident that it has no hope of appearing."[2] On a rare stopover in Moscow that September, Tolstoy more directly relayed his impatience to Sytin, using as his messenger a reporter from *Word* who had approached him for an interview at the Kursk railway station. Sytin had at once urged Chertkov to hurry with his reading of the galley proofs. "It is terrible to think," he wrote, "that I distressed Leo Nicholaevich by this delay and fear of the censor. A rabbit-like cowardice is to blame."[3]

The book was still incomplete when Sytin came home from Karlsbad, but outside circumstances would give him a reprieve. On 7 November 1910 the death of Tolstoy forced the shelving of *Circle of Reading* until the literary estate could be settled. That protracted business, which closely involved Sytin, would take two years.

The death itself occasioned extensive coverage and increased circulation at *Russian Word* because the circumstances surrounding Tolstoy's final days were so bizarre. The writer had fled in secret from his wife and fallen ill at an out-of-the-way railway station at Astapovo. Newsmen swarmed there from around the world, and *Word* reporter K.V. Orlov (in a wire requesting an interview) had been the first to inform the frantic Sonia (Sofia Andreevna) about her missing husband's whereabouts.[4] When the funeral took place at Iasnaia Poliana on 9 November, *Word* was among the Russian papers to criticize the government by reporting that officials had forbidden any role by the Russian Orthodox Church in services for the excommunicated Tolstoy.

It then followed that Sytin helped to smooth a family rift over property rights. He learned that, years before, Tolstoy had grudgingly given to Sonia ownership of all that he had published in Russia with censorship approval before 1881, and she never gave up seeking more. In 1901, as Sonia had reason to fear, Tolstoy had abrogated even this limited agreement by secretly willing his life works to his daughter Sasha (Alexandra Lvovna). His landed estate was still to go to his wife and children, but he directed Sasha to buy it back for allotment to his peasants. He named Chertkov as co-executor with Sasha and informed them both that he wanted his complete works to enter the public domain.

When she finally heard the will in November 1910, Sonia seemed ready to contest it, and Sasha and Chertkov consequently enlisted a four-man committee to help devise a settlement.[5] Their goal was to sell, by contract, short-term publishing rights to Tolstoy's complete works to raise money, in part to reimburse Sonia for her pre-1881 rights and the rest to buy back Tolstoy's lands. At the contract's expiration, all the works would enter the public domain.

One of the four arbiters was Sytin, an expert in publishing but hardly a disinterested party.[6] As early as 1907 he had approached the Tolstoyans about publishing some of Tolstoy's works in a joint venture with the émigré publishing house, the Free Word (Svobodnoe Slovo). He had long since figured the commercial worth of the posthumous works, now up for bids. Offering them as a supplement to *Around the World*, he knew, would boost *World*'s circulation; and once the works had been set in type, he could print further editions much more cheaply.

Directors of the prestigious A.F. Marks Co. of St Petersburg, who became Sytin's lone rival for the rights, had the same double use in mind. After all, many editions of Tolstoy were already available. Adding the unpublished manuscripts would attract some owners of earlier collections, but the prime potential customers – and the ones targeted by Sasha and Chertkov – were common readers. Knowing, like Sytin, that premiums attracted many more subscribers and that a very large readership increased advertising revenues, the Marks directors wanted to promote their own *Tilled Field*, already the leading weekly in Russia, by offering subscribers the complete works of Tolstoy for a few extra rubles.[7]

After both publishers had declared themselves contenders, Sytin vainly negotiated with the Marks Co. through most of 1911 about dividing the works and purchase costs. By December, complaining that "*Field* is giving up very little [to *Around the World*]," Sytin proposed to go it alone. He would pay the estate 250,000 rubles for the complete package, stipulating that 50,000 of that amount go to Sonia for rights to the pre-1881 works that she felt belonged to her.[8]

Only after raising Sonia's portion to 100,000 rubles in January 1912 did Sytin get his fellow advisers and Sonia to agree to his terms, but Sasha had meanwhile found that she needed 300,000 rubles to buy back Tolstoy's lands. Chertkov consequently persuaded the Marks Co. to make a higher independent bid. On 28 January Marks' offer of 300,000 rubles arrived from St Petersburg.[9]

When Sytin immediately matched that bid, Chertkov made a new proposal for splitting the rights at a total price of 400,000 rubles. Under the terms put forward on 16 February, the Marks Co. would publish the complete works solely as a supplement to *Field* (at the price of twelve rubles), while Sytin would issue an inexpensive edition (at twenty or twenty-two rubles) and an expensive one (at thirty-five rubles). Both companies were to pay 200,000 rubles.

The very next day, Sytin backed out of this decidedly lopsided deal, since he would be paying the same price as the Marks Co. for the least marketable editions and forfeiting all link-ups with his periodical.[10] In other words, Sytin still primarily wanted the works as a premium to bolster *World*, for how else could he convince his directors to buy short-term publishing rights at so high a price? He agreed with the Tolstoyans that the rich should be philanthropic, but that credo was worthless in board-room debates.

The Marks Co. at once revived its independent bid of 300,000 rubles, and Chertkov held out for more. Early in April G.V. Filatev informed Chertkov that, on Sasha's behalf, he was still pursuing a joint agreement. Sytin then travelled alone to St Petersburg to see Chertkov. Although there is no record of what price he offered to pay, this time he got Chertkov to back Sytin & Co. as sole publisher. Sytin accepted certain conditions, Chertkov would later obliquely explain, that the Marks Co. had rejected.

What Chertkov could not publicly say, lest he shame the family by revealing Tolstoy's perfidy, was that during April 1912 Sytin had handed over to Sonia 100,000 rubles for literary rights that were justly, but not legally, hers. Confirmation comes from the diary entry that Sonia made on 21 April 1912: "I completed the business with Sytin today. I received 100,000 for the books [published before 1881] and sent the money round to my sons."[11] Sonia's claims aside, this payment purchased nothing; and, even though it seems to have persuaded Chertkov to favour Sytin & Co., Sytin's gift to Sonia lay outside the bidding competition between the two publishing houses. Sytin's fellow committee members, in any case, chose to oppose Chertkov's recommendation that Sytin & Co. receive exclusive short-term rights for 300,000 rubles, the price that was now acceptable to Sasha. They still wanted to divide the rights so that both companies would publish the complete works.

Near the end of 1912 Sytin & Co. consequently informed Sasha "that we now agree to the acquisition of rights jointly with Marks." Again the two sides dickered. Because the Marks Co. held out for supplementing its weekly *Field*, Sytin explored the feasibility of supplementing his daily *Russian Word*. And, since he expected Marks's magazine to outstrip his newspaper in selling multi-volume premiums, Sytin insisted that, once *Field*'s subscription list reached 250,000, Marks was to pay him a percentage of each subscription above that number. When the Marks Co. again temporized, Sytin sent Chertkov a confidential bid for exclusive rights, in which he offered to share any profits with Chertkov and the others who were fulfilling Tolstoy's wishes. "Percentages on your behalf will be clear only after the complete liquidation of the publications." Only if sales were strong, he cautioned, "will there be profit."[12]

At this point the Marks Co. bowed out because it could not or would not meet the committee's conditions. The final result early in 1913 was a two-year contract for Sytin & Co. to publish Tolstoy's complete works. Sytin had gained rights for a singularly inexpensive edition – twenty-four volumes in 100,000 sets at ten rubles each – as twice-monthly premiums for *Russian Word* and *Around the World*, and an elegant twenty-volume edition of 10,000 sets at fifty rubles each.

Although documents verify the bargaining just described, Sytin gives an elided and slightly different version in his memoirs.[13] As he tells it, the committee formed following the death of Tolstoy set a price of 300,000 rubles on the literary rights and proposed that the Sytin and Marks companies each pay half. Marks would publish a complete edition to supplement *Field* while Sytin would bring out either an expensive or inexpensive edition for sale through bookstores. Disagreement arose because Sytin wanted to market editions at both price levels and the directors of Marks insisted he sell only the costly one.

When the committee next asked that one company alone buy the rights for 300,000 rubles, Chertkov picked Marks, continues Sytin, because the drawing power of *Field*, as the most popular magazine in Russia, would attract the widest possible readership and thereby meet Tolstoy's prime goal. (Sytin probably here explains one of the reasons why his committee colleagues and the co-executors courted Marks for so long. For them, *Field* was a better bet than *Around the World*.) Sytin says flatly that the Marks Co. could not raise 300,000 rubles and, as a result, that he met the obligatory price to enable Sasha to repurchase Tolstoy's country estate. Thus she could keep her promise to her father to give his lands to the peasants, as his will dictated.

In citing the 300,000-ruble figure, Sytin refers only to the sum contractually paid by his company, a fee that matched exactly what Sasha had to pay for Tolstoy's lands. Like Chertkov and the others, Sytin kept in confidence the additional 100,000 rubles that compensated Sonia for her lost rights, a payment that almost certainly came from Sytin's own pocket.

As the drawn-out negotiations show, 300,000 rubles was the most that either Marks or Sytin & Co. could justify on business grounds as payment for exclusive short-term rights. When Sasha, in deference to Sonia, insisted on 400,000 rubles, the two firms could find no way to split the rights between them at 200,000 rubles each. In the end, it was Sytin's April payment to Sonia that enabled Sasha to fall back on Sytin & Co.'s 300,000-ruble bid. Because his board resisted going even that high, Sytin surely did not meet Sonia's demands with company funds. Rather, given his ample riches and sense of debt to Tolstoy and his circle, he must have paid Sonia himself. Sytin, then, seemingly by his own secret charity, not only made possible Tolstoy's tangled bequest of land and literature, but also secured a gratifying package for his company.

"Of course," Sytin says about the settlement, "our publishing company made no profit."[14] And taking into account the works alone, he may have been right. The great benefits were the prestige for Sytin & Co. and the boost in circulation for *Around the World*. In October 1913 Sytin would write to company stockholders about the "colossal flow of subscribers to *World*." He would announce a tripling of subscriptions, thanks to the Tolstoy supplements, to make *World* one of the bestselling magazines in Russia. He would also predict that advertising in *World* "will bring greater results than all Russian journals taken together."[15]

The Tolstoy premium would also have a considerable effect on Sytin's flagship daily. Readership in 1913, when the premiums began, would rise a respectable 13 per cent, in the wake of the much larger surge of 31 per cent in 1912 during *Word*'s coverage of the Balkan wars and the election of the fourth Duma.[16]

II

Readership was up as well, because industrial expansion was providing more and more Russians with pocket money for newspapers. Buying a daily had come to mean keeping pace with modernity and the Europeans, and Sytin's *Russian Word* – cheap and up to the minute with news and trends – fitted well into that image.

Word also won more buyers with its special editions, some nationalistic and safely conservative, others tending toward the left. In the first category were its 1910 edition honouring Sytin's revered Chekhov on the fiftieth anniversary of his birth, the nine-page encomium in 1911 to Alexander II for giving birth to "modern Russia" through his emancipation proclamation fifty years before, and the centennial issue in 1912 hailing Russian courage at the battle of Borodino. Left-tending were editorial salutes to two radical writers of the 1840s: in 1911 to Vissarion Belinsky, whose outspoken commentary through literary criticism would have landed him in prison but for his illness and death from tuberculosis in 1848; and in 1912 to Alexander Herzen, a "state criminal" whose writings and very name were barred from print until the 1860s.

Sytin was negotiating over Tolstoy's estate through most of these editions, but he still kept constantly in touch with the operations and personnel of the daily he had founded. Single-mindedly intent on improvements, he tended to weigh in with his authority as chief executive; and his indirect but nagging interference had caused Doroshevich, some time in 1910, to leave for St Petersburg, where he made his home. Doroshevich may have hoped to command the capital version of *Word* that Sytin had decided to start that year, but his break-away led instead to Sytin's rethinking the editorship and orientation of his Moscow daily.

N. Valentinov (born N.V. Volsky), the first-rate Marxist journalist and economist whom Sytin finally put in command in mid-1912, summarized the prelude to his hiring in a memoir. He there describes Sytin as a "nearly illiterate man, a self-made organizer, with amazing scope and persistence" who did not "directly interfere in the running of [*Word*]." Rather, Sytin dominated his son-in-law and business manager, Blagov, who had the official rank of "responsible" editor, while Doroshevich was editor in fact. Doroshevich, he continues, constantly quarrelled with Sytin and altogether ignored Blagov. "'The relationship among these people had gotten so strained in 1910 that Doroshevich had had to abandon the editorial office. Sytin, superstitiously figuring that the circulation of the paper would drop without Doroshevich, proposed to him [not until 1912, in actual fact] ... an increase in salary to 48,000 rubles a year (a huge sum!) but under rather strange conditions. Doroshevich, who lived in St. Petersburg, would have to return to Moscow only several times a year (for five months [actually three] in all) 'to straighten out' the newspaper, 'to enliven' it, 'to make it more interesting,' 'to put something new in it.' "[17]

What next influenced the direction of *Word* has already been discussed: Sytin's repeated exposure to Tolstoyan thinking in 1911 and 1912. The last wishes of Tolstoy and persistent arguments for them by Sasha and Chertkov appear to have prodded Sytin into donating 100,000 rubles to carry them out. It was in this same period that Sytin decided to make *Word* decisively "democratic" and to do it through his hiring authority as *Word*'s chief executive.

Until late 1911 Sytin put greater emphasis on literary qualifications than on political leanings in his hirings at *Word*. He bought a skilled writer, not a polemicist, when he signed on the novelist Bunin in 1910, and the same was true when he began publishing Gorky in 1911. Not so that November when he asked the notorious mocker of the Romanovs, A.V. Amfiteatrov, to write feuilletons for *Word*. Amfiteatrov's last work for Sytin had been the book on the 1905 revolution that the courts had ruled criminal, and this author, like Gorky, had fled Russia for self-exile abroad to avoid being charged. Sytin sent his offer by wire to Italy, and Amfiteatrov wrote back on 9 December to request specifics about politics and salary.

Amfiteatrov wanted Sytin to understand that because a ''minority'' of *Word*'s collaborators were ''of such a clearly right-wing character ... I at first considered it quite impossible to join the company.'' He had since decided ''that your very turning to me is indication of your intention to move the paper leftward and set it on a leftward course more firmly and decisively than it has been up to this time. Of course, only under such conditions could I join the paper and for this I would need certain guarantees.'' Being so far from Moscow, he had neither the wish nor possibility of shaping editorial policy, but he found it ''necessary to clear up jointly the boundary of our ideological contact and to specify the conditions for a long and solid program.''

As for recompense, Amfiteatrov understood that Doroshevich had been receiving thirty-two thousand rubles per year plus a percentage of the paper's profits. ''I could never hope to deserve such a sum,'' he wrote. ''Not because I want to disparage [Doroshevich] ... but because I simply do not understand what a writer can do for a paper in the form of literary work to be worth 32,000 a year.''[18] Amfiteatrov, probably aware that Doroshevich was at this time doing nothing at all for *Word*, must have assumed that Sytin was about to replace his lead feuilletonist. Reaching the same conclusion, Sytin's fellow directors at Sytin & Co. called an extraordinary meeting on 12 December to demand that the indispensable Doroshevich remain under contract, and they may by then have received Doroshevich's formal resignation. For the sake of readers, the board majority insisted, Sytin must keep an institution like Doroshevich firmly in place.[19]

Negotiations would not be easy, and the irrepressible Sytin meanwhile sought on his own to hire a new de facto editor who would direct the paper as Blagov could not and Doroshevich would not. He offered the post to the well-known political liberal, Peter Struve, the former Marxist who had edited Sytin's short-lived *Duma* in 1906 and who had since become editor of *Russian Thought* (*Russkaia Mysl*), a leading journal for intellectuals. Struve had opened the pages of *Thought* to a variety of viewpoints on cultural and literary topics but had kept its political articles in line with his own principles of western constitutionalism and democracy. Struve liked Sytin's proposal, and on 19 December he sent a positive reply.[20]

Consternation must have reigned among the directors, but the lone documented protest came from Gregory Petrov. His letter began diplomatically: ''I have nothing against the editorship of Struve. I will welcome his participation.'' Then Petrov raised his objection: ''I am afraid only for the paper, for the sake of your interests. You have built for a long time, and you could destroy it in a minute. I am speaking not only for myself but also for Fedor Ivanovich [Blagov].'' Put another way, *Word* must not become or seem to become a party paper. It would do so under Struve because he was linked with a moderate liberal group of Moscow businessmen called the Faction for Peaceful Renewal. Struve had also participated in the faction's controversial ''Economic Dialogues.'' An editor with such obvious connections to a political group would have been a complete departure for *Word*, and Petrov was therefore urging Sytin to reconsider.[21]

By early January 1912 the out-voted Sytin had abandoned Struve and backed off from Amfiteatrov. No record remains of what he wrote to either man, but the response from Amfiteatrov that month suggests that Sytin had made an excuse about starting a daily in St Petersburg. In his reply Amfiteatrov doubted that a new paper could prosper in the capital and regretted having to send elsewhere the three pieces he had composed for *Word*.[22]

Having lost out on hiring his first choices because of their political reputations, Sytin decided to recruit a journalist from the hinterland who was on the left but less well known. He invited I.R. Kugel of *Kievan Thought* (*Kievskaia Mysl*) to talk with him, and this time he included Blagov in the negotiations. During two evenings early in January the three men bargained to a fifteen-thousand-ruble-a-year agreement over dinner at the Praga, one of Moscow's finest restaurants.[23]

Kugel later described a crucial private exchange in which Sytin told him: ''What is needed is to ... transform [*Word*] into a red paper. The reader has outgrown the paper. Now is the time when the paper must become more democratic in accordance with the growing opposition of the country. A mass paper like *Russian Word* cannot stand on the sidelines and repeat stale news because ... it will lose subscribers.''[24] To make that change, Sytin said he needed Kugel, and Kugel wanted his reader to understand that he signed on only because Sytin vowed to move *Word* sharply to the left.

As it turned out, Kugel did not make the move to Moscow from Kiev. As soon as enough key persons learned of his appointment another censure came. To quote Valentinov again: ''For reasons that would take too long to explain, the agreement with Kugel was broken, he did not even show up to work, and a big forfeit was made to him.''[25] In his version, Kugel blames Petrov and *Word*'s war expert, Nemirovich-Danchenko, but says that the only explanation he got was a ''pleasant'' letter from Sytin about ''dark forces'' having ganged up on them. He declined Sytin's invitation to go to Moscow anyway, saying he had no taste for ''unpleasant surprises.''[26]

In alluding to surprises, Kugel would have known about another

January reversal at *Word* because it involved his brother, A.R. Kugel, the director of the Moscow theatre, the Crooked Mirror. This broken agreement between Blagov and L.N. Andreev, the playwright and writer, also had political overtones, and it helps show why Sytin wanted to relieve Blagov of editorial authority.

As part of his push to publish leading literary figures in *Word*, Sytin had reached a one-year agreement with Andreev early in 1911, thus regaining the writer he had lost several years before to Gorky. For one thousand rubles Andreev agreed to provide six short stories to *Word* and nothing to other papers. He also received the discretionary right, like Doroshevich, to require *Word* to print whatever additional belles lettres he submitted. Then, during the staging in St Petersburg of his new play, *The Sabine Women*, Andreev got Rumanov to ask Blagov about publishing the playscript in *Word*. Blagov said yes.[27]

Blagov received the play in time to print it on opening day in Moscow but failed to do so, probably because he found the political satire too biting. (In it Andreev chides the Kadets for futile liberal posturing and the government for constant law-breaking.)[28] After several performances had gone by, Blagov advised Andreev that the play was by then too familiar to Moscow audiences to appear in *Word*. In his reply of 18 February 1912 Andreev reminded Blagov that he had had ample opportunity to publish the play as it premiered, in keeping with established custom. Moreover, *Word* was bound to accept everything that he submitted. Andreev announced that he would submit this "crude and dishonourable" episode to an arbitration tribunal. "Of course, under present conditions, I consider my further collaboration with *Russian Word* impossible."[29]

The next day Andreev told Rumanov what had happened. "I very much want to think," he wrote, "that [Sytin] is not involved." All the same, he concluded, "you and I have become a sacrifice to the complete and inveterate boorishness of what is indeed a street paper."[30] Art and politics had been wasted on the vulgar and timid Blagov. At Rumanov's insistence, Andreev would spell out his grievance to Sytin in April. Sytin in turn would ask Rumanov to placate Andreev but would not agree that December to the large amount of money Andreev demanded to return to *Word*. There the matter would end.[31]

Sytin had meanwhile gone again to *Kievan Thought* to find an editor to take over from Blagov, and Valentinov continues that story. "In place of Kugel," he writes, "I was invited in the capacity of assistant to Blagov, that is, assistant to the [responsible] editor." But Valentinov makes clear that he assumed the role of de facto editor by saying that Blagov "was not a journalist" and "could not write even a simple, little article." Even Doroshevich, whose heralded return on 1 March as lead feuilletonist predated Valentinov's arrival by several months, conceded editorial authority for all except his own writings to the new man.[32] Although the ex-editor at first treated him almost as an enemy, says Valentinov, "our relations improved so much that Doroshevich declared to me, 'It is time for me to fade and for you to bloom. I give you the keys to the editorial office and all my rights.' "[33] Doroshevich then mainly stayed away from Moscow to serve Sytin as a writer and adviser under the terms of his new, more lucrative contract.[34]

Perhaps the make-up of the board had made it easier for Sytin finally to get confirmation of the editor he wanted, for the shareholders may have just slanted the board in his favour. Company records show that in May 1914 about 55 per cent of the stock collectively belonged to Sytin and to relatives and friends presumably loyal to him, so a pro-Sytin majority could have emerged by 1912.[35] Whether such a group ever chose to seat directors who would permit Sytin to rule the board and how soon they might have consolidated his power are open questions, however, since the directors (now probably numbering more than four) may have served staggered terms of two or more years.

Sytin, who would not himself hold the majority of shares until 1915, clearly did not control the board early in 1912. From mid-1912 onward he seems to have had things more his own way. Perhaps he first predominantly held the upper hand when he asked the board, as *Word*'s chief executive, to confirm the hiring of Valentinov in mid-1912.

III

Not long after hiring Valentinov, however, Sytin had to accept defeat in his two-year effort to start a daily *Russian Word* in St Petersburg. That September the project abruptly fell apart because he had neglected one seemingly trivial detail.

Sytin had cleared his first hurdle by getting the expansion approved by his fellow directors in 1910. His argument for opening a new market had convinced them. *Word* had by then won relatively few readers in St Petersburg, having a mere 5 per cent of all its subscribers there, because it reached the capital too late to compete with local papers distributed hours earlier. A capital version of *Word* also fitted into Sytin's even grander scheme for a national network of papers linked by his own telephone and telegraph lines, provisioned by his own paper and machine factories, and supplied with world news by a syndicated wire service that he would organize with foreign publishers. (Rumanov, giving no dates, describes Sytin negotiating with a German telegraph agency, with *Le Matin* of Paris, *Corriere della Sera* of Rome, and with Lord Northcliffe of the London *Times* about a European wire service.

He alludes, as well, to a vertical trust that was to make Sytin & Co. self-sufficient in every essential for publishing, from trees for paper pulp to ink for its presses. Sytin was surprised, says Rumanov, to learn that such "trusts" and "combines" already existed in America.)[36]

A first step, then, was adding a paper in St Petersburg, and Sytin's old friend Petrov again had had advice to offer. He suggested – perhaps sarcastically, as developments much later will show – that Doroshevich sound out the president of the Council of Ministers, or prime minister, P.A. Stolypin.[37] Doroshevich refused, but Sytin himself paid a call on Stolypin mid-way through 1911. As Sytin tells it, he arranged the session through A.A. Makarov, the assistant minister of the interior, after learning from that acquaintance that Stolypin was displeased with him. At their meeting, continues Sytin, Stolypin muttered first about the obligations incumbent on a publisher for the people "not to corrupt the Russian soul"; and then he lashed out at *Russian Word* for criticizing as too narrow his program to break up the communes and thereby create a strong class of independent farmers. Agreeing that the plan would benefit the "entire economy," Sytin expressed his own support.[38] But he also sensed that Stolypin wanted unconditional backing from *Word* like that of *New Times*, Suvorin's capital daily. By extension, Sytin realized that he could never expect Stolypin to favour a capital version of *Russian Word* because it would lure far too many readers from *New Times*.

Sytin would nonetheless push ahead, in part because he had already arranged lines of credit for up to 500,000 rubles from several banks to finance his projected daily.[39] At some point in 1911 he also secured for it 150,000 rubles in backing from the son of Suvorin himself and another 150,000 from A.I. Putilov, the administrative president of the Russo-Asiatic Bank.[40]

Consumed though he was by this project and by staff problems at *Word*, Sytin remained as habitually, even obsessively, attentive to the small daily details of his business – so much so that a friend took pen in hand, in July of 1912, to advise Sytin that he direly needed a rest. The writer, P.A. Sergeenko, deplored the "sad impression of my last meeting with you." Because Sytin's extreme nervous tension could cause a breakdown, "you should protect yourself, at least temporarily, from petty details, from trifles." One should not, he warned, "chip splinters from a Stradivarius violin for kindling."[41] Then, aware that the advice would go unheeded, Sergeenko filed his letter away unsent.

Ironically, two months later Sytin was lamenting that his neglect of a petty detail had enabled officials and one M.P. Zaikin effectively to stop his capital version of *Russian Word*. In a letter dated 17 September 1912 Zaikin had broken the news to Sytin that he had pre-empted him on name rights by requesting and receiving official permission to publish a St Petersburg paper called *Russian Word*. He was offering to sell Sytin those rights, with no mention of price but with the condition that Sytin make him editor; and he demanded a reply by 22 September - that is, within five days. Even though he valued the name too much to proceed under any other, Sytin could not even consider such outrageous terms; and Zaikin has to have been either a thoroughly naive opportunist or, more likely, an agent to frustrate the Moscow entrepreneur. His family name and middle initial suggest he was the son of P.D. Zaikin, editor of the mass-circulation St Petersburg daily *Copeck Newspaper* (*Gazeta-kopeika*), whose publishers issued a Moscow version as well. These business rivals would not have welcomed Sytin in the capital.[42]

As for the government, although Stolypin had been assassinated the previous September, just after his talk with Sytin, other officials opposed to the capital daily that Sytin had planned could easily have blocked his naming it *Russian Word*. That possibility is very strong, given the notice that appeared in the government periodical, *Journal of the Post and Telegraph Administration*, on 20 October. There the Administration offered subscriptions for a capital newspaper under its jurisdiction to be named *Russian Word*. In response, Sytin & Co. strongly protested to the Chief Administration of Press Affairs over unfair and confusing appropriation of the name of its Moscow daily.[43] Although no government version of *Russian Word* ever materialized, the October offer surely confirmed that Sytin could not publish *Russian Word* in St Petersburg. Should he try, the government could simply resurrect its prior rights to that name.

This débâcle over name rights served as one more setback for a man widely seen as a master manipulator. In the twelve months before October 1912 Sytin had suffered the blows of three vetoes against journalists he had invited to *Word* and now he had been outflanked in St Petersburg. By way of historical record, however, the charge later made by Natalia, the disgruntled daughter of Doroshevich, that about this time her father kept Sytin from selling his Moscow *Russian Word* to the Kadets is without supporting evidence.[44]

Sytin's frenetic attempts in a short space of time both to hire journalists of more leftist persuasion for key roles at *Word* in Moscow and to start a separate *Russian Word* in the capital had much to do with the elections in the fall of 1912 for the fourth Duma, which would convene that November. The third Duma, which lasted from late 1907 to early 1911, had accomplished some substantial legislation (Sytin especially approved their creating an extensive system of elementary and secondary schools), and the publisher of *Word* wanted to encourage more reforms in the next session. In Valentinov he got an editor intent on the same goal and bold enough to hit campaign issues hard.

Valentinov and "two assistants covered the electoral campaign as much as possible," the new editor was to recall, and at least once they were too bold even for Sytin. In this instance, says Valentinov, "telegrams were coming in from all corners of the country about the shady role of priests on the political scene. I combined all this material and gave it a 7-column heading, 'The Shady Host of V.K. Sabler [procurator of the Holy Synod].' I.D. Sytin ... reacted in horror to this headline. F.I. Blagov also became fearful and agitated. 'Wasn't it too controversial?' I insisted on the headline and it was repeated in several editions ... The editors expected a fine of 5,000 rubles; there wasn't one (it seems it came later)."[45] Disagreements over how to treat priests aside, Sytin valued Valentinov as a competent and necessarily strong-willed leftist editor bent on making *Word* thoroughly "democratic."

Meanwhile Sytin had committed personal funds to back another democratic daily, *Day* (*Den*), which would begin in St Petersburg that fall with Kugel as editor. Aside from the likelihood of profits, here was a means to help compensate Kugel for the contract that Sytin & Co. had broken in February, and Sytin seems to have become involved in *Day* even before Zaikin's September letter ruled out a capital version of *Russian Word*.

When Sytin sought backing for *Day* from Sytin & Co., the board refused any part in a "Jew organ" - a rebuff that Kugel had then learned about and angrily denounced to outsiders. Spelling out these details to Rumanov, who may also have invested in *Day*, Sytin regretted that Kugel "still wants to be chummy with us." Sytin preferred "to stand aside," but he urged staying the course "to avoid any possible harm that can come to us" should *Day* succeed. "We have enough enemies already."[46]

Kugel, in his account, tells that Sytin invested sixty thousand rubles but "concealed himself" behind others. That is, the Trading Company of F.I. Mareev, I.R. Kugel, and M.T. Soloviev became the official owner of *Day*, with Sytin as a silent partner.[47] Although no corroboration from Sytin or anyone else has turned up, Kugel says that at this point he and Sytin specifically agreed to make *Day* a strong democratic voice in the capital. *Day*'s first issue appeared on 2 October, or about six weeks before the fourth Duma began. The predominantly critical attitude of Kugel toward Sytin casts some doubt on Kugel's appraisal of Sytin's behaviour, but the company and the newspaper are verified facts. Moreover, since Soloviev, the long-time director of Sytin & Co., almost certainly would not have launched the project himself, there is good reason to believe that Soloviev served as Sytin's stand-in.

Kugel says that his next crucial meeting with Sytin came near the end of the year, when his erstwhile Moscow backer arrived in St Petersburg to request a meeting at the Cuba Restaurant. There, once the two men were seated, Sytin allegedly took the publisher's arm in friendly fashion and, keeping his voice low, asked Kugel to release him from *Day*. Kugel says that Sytin went on to condemn a turn that was "not his fault but mine: the gathering at *Day* of the most leftwing journalists to create an intolerable paper which served rebellion and anarchy." Sytin complained that its direction – pro-Jewish, for one thing – had been "commented upon in the Chief Administration of Press Affairs."

"Permit me, Ivan Dmitrievich," Kugel claims to have replied, "but did we not together work out the anarchistic program which *Day* has followed?" When Sytin insisted not, Kugel pursued the matter all the same and wondered if Sytin's about-face was a result of attacks on *Day* by the "philistines" at *Russian Word*. Kugel sarcastically promised never to reveal "that I.D. Sytin was the author of an anarchistic program."

The next thing Kugel says he learned was that Sytin had sold his interest in *Day* to the banking house of G.D. Lesin for about the cost of the rotary press: ten thousand rubles.[48] At their next encounter, when Kugel wondered at so cheap a price, Sytin replied in high good humour that he was in a hurry. As for the new owner, Kugel contends that Lesin bought the paper "out of a sense of obligation to his Jewish brothers," that period being one of intense anti-semitism in Russia.

Sytin apparently had caved in to his fellow directors at Sytin & Co., who must have objected to Soloviev's open sponsorship of *Day*. At the end of 1912 the board also had some leverage over Sytin because he then needed their approval and 300,000 rubles from the company to commit Sytin & Co. to buying the rights to Tolstoy's works.[49]

IV

In Moscow, in the meantime, the assured and decisive Valentinov had been putting his stamp on *Russian Word*. Politically, he said, it had been "limping on both legs." His goal was "to make *Russian Word* ... a democratic paper."[50]

Despite his youthfulness, Valentinov already had the firm will of a seasoned activist. In 1898, as a nineteen-year-old, he had joined the outlawed Russian Social Democratic Party (as Sytin's sons seem to have done in 1902); then, for actively supporting the Bolsheviks who split off in 1903, he had landed in jail in Kiev. Upon his release in 1904 Valentinov had fled to Lenin in Switzerland; but within a year he had returned home to the rival Mensheviks, who favoured party democracy, electoral politics, and independent thought. (He was still nominally a Menshevik in 1912.)

Valentinov had since become a journalist-economist who cogently argued that Russia must industrialize; and he thus was an editor of whom Sytin's fellow directors approved. After the Revolution, he would serve the Soviets nearly ten years as editor of the *Commercial and Industrial Gazette*, the newspaper of the Supreme Council of the National Economy. He would emigrate to Paris in 1928, where he wrote *Encounters with Lenin*, one of the best studies of its kind. He died in Paris in 1964 at the age of eighty-five.

A letter written by Valentinov in September 1913 helps convey the journalistic approach of the young editor, for here he answers implicitly critical questions from Rumanov about editorial policy. In reply to the query about his daily choice of leading articles, Valentinov says that he aimed for one on foreign policy, one to give "business propaganda" (i.e., to argue that production and marketing growth were good for Russia), and one to air a current political topic. As for a reporter's fear that the paper agreed too closely with the Ministry of Foreign Affairs, Valentinov describes *Word* as an "independent, oppositional paper." *Word* would never commit the "directly criminal" sin of being a conduit for the government, even though it did quite reasonably agree with the government on some things. Then, claiming for himself the credo of an independent journalist ("I know no other"), he favours promoting "peace, culture, and international social-economic relationships" and makes a virtue of teamwork: "We both love [*Word*]," he reminds Rumanov, "and this love is a great force."[51]

These generalizations on democratic journalism by Valentinov may today sound prosaic, but they fitted well with the objectives of Sytin for his paper. Both men sought to make *Word* "democratic"; and both wanted something new and rare in Russia – an honest investigative paper of high standards that spoke for the people and not for the government or any faction.[52] To many, and especially to conservatives, not speaking for the government meant speaking against it; to these people, Sytin seemed to be growing more and more subversive. Not only did these critics condemn his *Russian Word*, but they also began to attack his books for Russia's classrooms. Through these texts, they warned, Sytin was deliberately undermining loyalty and obedience to the autocracy.

At risk from the attacks was a prime source of Sytin's profits, for, as Valentinov noted in summing up the "particular" speciality of Sytin & Co. when he joined it in 1912, this "largest publishing house in Russia mainly produced books for schools and pupils." Valentinov exaggerated by overlooking Sytin's many *lubki* and calendars, but he was correct with respect to the bulk of Sytin's bound books. A company catalogue for 1911, after all, contains 250 pages of "Text Books, Text Aids and

Visual aids for the Lower, Middle, and Higher Educational Institutions of all Departments and Also for Self Education.''[53]

The first public censure in 1913 of Sytin's classroom publishing came on 6 March when thirty-two members in the State Council roundly condemned *Virgin Soil* (*Nov*), a textbook from Sytin & Co. that the Ministry of Public Education had approved in 1910. This book of readings for the elementary classroom, they contended, showed only the ''dark'' side of Russian history, especially the horrors of war, and sowed the ''spirit of doubt'' in children ''whom it will be necessary to summon to military duty.''[54] During debate on the resolution, some members defended the book as balanced, rather than one-sided – in showing, for example, how the upbringing of Ivan IV had led to the terrors of his reign. Yet more deplored the ''utilitarian morality'' and ''materialistic world view'' that was typical, one speaker argued, in Sytin's school texts. The final speaker carried the day. Nothing in *Virgin Soil* was dangerous, he said, but its discussing evil as well as good confused and distressed elementary students. When the chair proposed to require the ministry to account for having approved the book, the motion passed, ninety-two to fifty-nine.[55]

At issue was the role of education at a time of increased social disruption. A massive strike movement had begun the previous year after soldiers killed and wounded over one hundred workers at the Lena River gold fields in central Siberia. The signers of the resolution argued that subversives were exploiting the growing unrest to destroy the Russian state from within and that ministry-approved texts like *Virgin Soil* were helping them.

On 24 April the State Council received the response from the Ministry of Public Education about *Virgin Soil*. The statement from the minister, L.A. Kasso, explained that two experts had reviewed the book favourably, but since there was ''reason to be cautious'' about its source, the committee had stamped the book ''permitted'' rather than ''approved.'' He went on to note that opponents of the book had not cited a single mistake in it, nor could he find ''party-mindedness'' or ''partiality'' in the report of the Learning Committee. In closing, Kasso promised another review of *Virgin Soil*.[56]

Next came condemnation in the Duma from V.M. Purishkevich, Sytin's critic in 1908. At the end of May this right-wing deputy from Kursk took the rostrum in the lower house to rail against purveyors of materialistic texts, including the ''revolutionary Sytin.''[57] In a two-session diatribe, Purishkevich echoed his tract of a year earlier, *School Preparation for the Second Russian Revolution*, which crudely likened subversive texts to ''one massive, gigantic, malignant boil'' that would burst into fire to set off a revolution far worse than 1905, thanks to

"Judeo-masonic leaders" and criminal publishers.[58] And he had singled out Sytin in that tract, too, as founder of the "revolutionary" School and Knowledge society.

Sytin would ruefully mention the attacks of Purishkevich during a scandal about School and Knowledge early the next year, but his immediate reaction went unrecorded. The Duma episode, in any case, took place about the time Sytin had gone abroad and then decided to have a second round of talks with Maksim Gorky on Capri.

V

At the initial encounter between Sytin and Gorky two years earlier, in March 1911, each publisher had taken the other's measure. Sytin recalls that there was time for tea and snacks and talk about enlightening the Russian masses while sitting on Gorky's terrace,[59] but Gorky wrote to his wife at the end of the two days that he had worn himself out "snarling uninterruptedly like a borzoi on the hunt."[60]

On hand in 1911 with Gorky to seek funds for Znanie were the other two principals, Piatnitsky and Ladyzhnikov, and they had heard with surprise Sytin's proposal to restructure their publishing house as a stock company. Sytin had offered ten thousand rubles to become principal stockholder and director of the "practical side of the business," leaving the editorial side unchanged. He had also demanded a share of profits on works already in print.

Piatnitsky had refused, insisting "we need money and only money"; and, despite much more talk, no deal was struck.[61] Gorky, again recounting to his wife what had happened, described the Sytin he encountered as best kept at arm's length, for "if one falls into the hands of such a *muzhik*, he will quickly extort from you all the living spirit, crystallizing it in the form of rubles and books, and you will be tossed into a dark corner as something useless."[62] That said, Gorky was still expecting to bring about his proposed Siberian encyclopedia through Sytin. Moreover, he had agreed to publish literary works in *Word*.

In the intervening year of 1912, Sytin had proposed by letter that Gorky send everything he wrote to *Word* but, to Gorky's disappointment, had done nothing about the encyclopedia of Siberia. "This idea," Gorky had told a friend, "very much appealed to Sytin, and, were I in Russia, would most likely be realized gradually, with the resources of Tomsk University and the Siberian intelligentsia. But since Sytin very much dissipates his energies ... the Siberian [work], obviously, has been put aside."[63]

Gorky was ready with a new proposal when he hosted Sytin on his spur-of-the-moment return visit in May 1913. Having long hoped to organize a radical-democratic party in Russia positioned between the centrist Constitutional Democrats and the extreme left-wing socialists, Gorky had decided he needed a newspaper. He now proposed to begin a St Petersburg daily to be called *Ray* (*Luch*) with Sytin as his backer and publisher.[64] The one firm agreement reached, however, was a coup for Sytin; Gorky agreed to accept twelve thousand rubles for the serializing in *Word*, in 1913–14, of his just-completed *Childhood*, plus another fifteen hundred rubles for the book version.[65] Cordiality prevailed, and whether the invitation came now or later, Gorky would stay for a time on Sytin's estate, Bersenevka, near Moscow, when he returned to Russia that December.

During Sytin's trip to Capri, Valentinov was laying the groundwork for another probing series of articles in *Word*, this one to show outsiders' misappropriating a basic resource; and, as May ended, he called on Rumanov to help him investigate the "*behind-the-scenes state* [his emphasis] of oil speculation." The man to contact in St Petersburg, he wrote, was "Naum Gavrilovich Glasberg (tel. 40-29) ... a smart operator and ... the head of a company competing with Nobel." Glasberg might know the "secrets of Nobel's speculations." A week later Valentinov printed the first of three articles that exposed Nobel's purchase of oil fields in Baku through figureheads and the involvement of the Russo-Asiatic Bank in plans to sell Russian oil interests to a British syndicate.[66]

Far more provocative was *Word*'s extended coverage this same year on Mendel Beilis, a Jew charged late in 1911 with having ritually murdered a Christian boy. His trial finally began in Kiev in October 1913, and Valentinov published in full – with Sytin's approval – the opposing attorneys' speeches and eye-witness reports from the courtroom. Especially gratifying to Sytin was the commentary in *Word* from such prestigious foreigners as Anatole France, Clemenceau, Maeterlinck, and D'Annunzio, all of it criticizing the government's handling of Russia's Dreyfuss case.[67] *Word*'s own correspondent in Kiev was Brazul-Brushkovsky, the journalist who defied the local police to show that others, not Beilis, had committed the murder.

Public interest in the trial's outcome – a verdict of not guilty – pushed *Word*'s press run to the year's high of 325,700 papers on 26 October. Three days later Doroshevich openly expressed in *Word* his scepticism about government motives and integrity. How, he asked, could the jury deduce from the evidence that Beilis was innocent but that a ritual murder had occurred? He implied that the prosecutor had manipulated underlying anti-semitic feelings among the jurors, who, lacking grounds to convict Beilis, had yet slandered Jews in general. On the next day *Word* editorially declared that "progressive society" was unanimous in applauding the acquittal and in condemning the government for letting the trial take place.

It was in this same year of outspoken criticism of the government that Sytin offered, as a supplement to *Word*, the complete works of the best-known critic of the regime, Leo Tolstoy.[68] Through Sasha, he had in turn arranged for *Word* to print excerpts from Tolstoy's private diaries, even though the diaries, which were not a part of the "complete works," had caused a contentious public dispute between Sasha and her mother.[69] Finally, as another exclusive in 1913, Sytin acquired for *Word* the memoirs of Tolstoy's son, Ilia. From Sytin's publishing house had also finally come the edition of *Circle of Reading* that had been delayed by Tolstoy's death.[70] But because the Moscow Committee on Press Affairs found in it indictable content - words against war in particular - Sytin, as publisher, would go on trial that December.

The cumulative effect of the aggressive editorial policy of his *Russian Word* and the controversial content of his books served to place Sytin in November 1913 seemingly more at odds with the imperial government than he had ever been. In *Word*, in particular, he had brought about an editorial policy that was deliberately "democratic" - that is, independently oppositional. That December, however, Sytin would lose Valentinov at *Russian Word* over a tribute to the Romanov dynasty, even as he openly welcomed the leftist Gorky back home to Russia.

An artist's view of the front porch of the house at Bersenevka, Sytin's country estate north of Moscow.

Above: The resilient Gregory Petrov about 1916, when Sytin had returned him to full status as a writer for *Russian Word*. A mainstay of the daily when it started, the onetime priest and liberal politician made threats in 1909 and 1912 against Sytin over repeated rejections of his articles in *Word*.

Left: To credit Anton Chekhov with instigating *Russian Word*, Sytin hung his portrait in the office where the morning editorial conference was held. Seated in the forefront is Vlas Doroshevich, *Word*'s leading writer and peripatetic de facto editor. At his right hand is official editor F.I. Blagov.

Here shown in 1922 during a trip to Germany sponsored by Lenin's government, the seventy-one-year-old Sytin has changed little in appearance since posing with his chauffeur a decade before. This picture records a reunion with two of his children, Evdokia and Peter, and conveys a confident deal-maker whose talks with German industrialists about investing sums in the Russian Soviet Federated Socialist Republic have gone well.

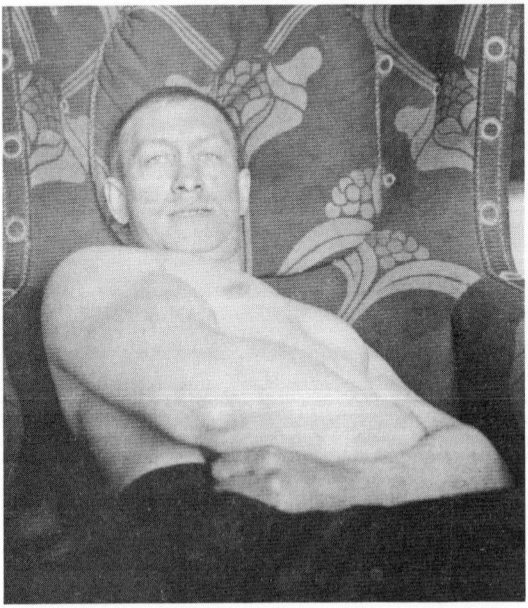

N.V. Valentinov, a Social Democrat and onetime acolyte of Lenin who was Sytin's choice as de facto editor in 1912 to make *Russian Word* more independently democratic. Valentinov resigned at the end of 1913, a good two years before striking this casual but self-confident pose in Moscow in 1916. Published by permission of Oxford University Press.

"Your Grandpa looks younger," Sytin wrote home in 1924 at the time of this New York photograph. As co-promoter of the Soviet art exhibit and sale, he looks especially fit among his fellow delegates, left to right, T. Zakharov, S. Somov, Sytin, I. Grabar, I. Troianovsky (the other co-promoter), and S. Vinogradoff.

Octogenarian Sytin in the early 1930s, when age and politics had idled him and he was wholly out of favour. Officials had required him to move to his last apartment on Gorky Street.

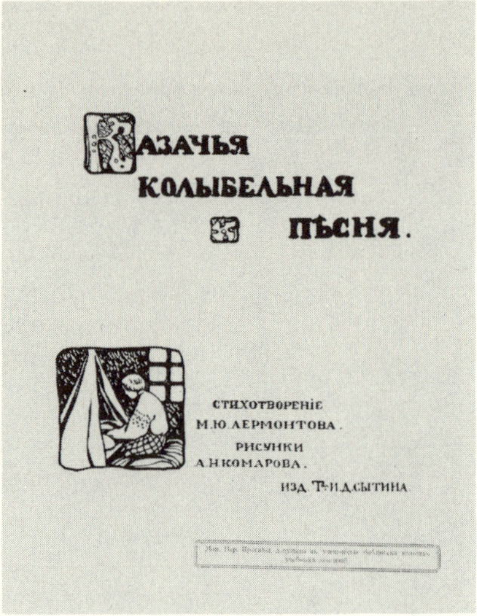

The cover and title page for "Cossack Lullaby" by the early nineteenth century poet and writer, M. Iu. Lermontov. The legend at the bottom right of the title page announces that the "Ministry of Popular Education has approved this book for the libraries of elementary schools." Because such ministry approvals helped sales, Sytin & Co. published catalogs listing approved books.

The Tsar-Bell, a famous Russian monument in the Moscow Kremlin, is an eye-catching frontispiece for "The Tsar-Bell Illustrated Calendar Almanac for 1913," priced at 60 copecks. As the leading publisher of annual compendiums of information like this one – an essential in nearly every household – Sytin & Co. offered the calendar-almanacs on every imaginable subject.

Left: This volume of "lively readings" from the "Library for Discussion, in Class and Outside" features a company logo, the initials "IDS," in the lower left-hand corner. Evidently, Sytin & Co. had become enough of a household word that no more explicit identification was necessary. The Company had achieved what might now be called "instant brand name recognition." *Right*: The cover of this "Illustrated Calendar" shows a Russian scene, a characteristic of many Sytin publications. Such covers, Sytin felt, acquainted Russians with their vast and varied country. This one pictures "Yalta and the Yalta Roadstead."

Left: Traditional Russian decorative art serves as the background for this cover on a Sytin book, *The History of Russian Art*. *Right*: An illustrated title page for a Sytin publication of Ivan Turgenev's "Perepelka" ("The Quail"), a short story describing how a boy loses his taste for hunting when his father shoots a mother quail with chicks. The boy is pictured burying the quail and marking its grave with a cross.

Grandson Aleksei Vasilievich Sytin, who was born at Sytin's country estate, during a visit to the Sytin Museum, Moscow, in 1989. Aleksei Vasilievich appears several times in these pages as the author of a memoir about his grandfather.

The staff members of the Sytin museum in Moscow with the author in June 1989. From the left are N.N. Aleshina, I.E. Matveeva, C.A. Ruud, L.I. Maksimova, and V.V. Kirillov. The portraits are of N.I. Sytin, Sytin's oldest son (left); Evdokia Ivanovna, Sytin's wife; and N.V. Tulupov, one of Sytin's leading editors and an author and compiler of classroom texts.

CHAPTER EIGHT

The Dilemmas of Overreach and Expansion

Along with vacillating between good business and good works, Sytin in the years just before 1914 wavered in his political course. Given the growing strike movement and spreading discontent in the countryside, Sytin could not decide with certainty whether to support the autocracy or to press it to share power. Outwardly he seemed a reformer, a label that had won him enemies in government and conservative circles. Within Sytin & Co. in these same years, however, editorial and business conflicts were partly a cause and partly an effect of Sytin's political uncertainties.

But he was still the entrepreneur. Even as his enterprises recorded high profits, Sytin planned new projects and cut new deals, both on his own and through his company. A series of setbacks was to suggest, however, that he was overextending himself.

I

During all the years he was in command, Sytin frequented the offices and newsrooms of *Russian Word*, but he left behind few comments – but for his 1909 letter to Petrov – about divisive clashes among the staff. The sketchy accounts in the memoirs and letters of principals on the staff, however, suggest that Sytin had to contend with especially contentious differences at *Word* in 1913 during Valentinov's tenure.

As the newspaper itself proves, Valentinov exercised firm editorial authority to make *Word* aggressively more liberal during his tenure. Taking exactly the stand of Doroshevich before him, he termed it his most important right that "not a single political article be run without my approval, not a single journalist be hired." By extension, he could overrule the objections of Sytin or Blagov to stories he favoured and get rid of writers he disliked.

"I joined the editorial staff of *Russian Word* not because I sought a large salary," Valentinov said further; "at the time I already had an attractive job and decent earnings." And, since his main goal was to produce a democratic daily, "I had to insist on the dismissal of three notable writers, whose articles compromised the paper."

Valentinov omits names, but the trio cannot have included one conspicuous conservative, V.V. Rozanov, whom Sytin himself had dismissed in November 1911 on the eve of asking Struve to edit *Word*. Rozanov, a philosopher and an outstanding prose stylist, used the pseudonym V. Varvarin at *Russian Word* because he also contributed to Suvorin's *New Times*, a connection that in itself, Sytin knew, made Rozanov intolerable to liberals.[1]

Very likely one of the three to whom Valentinov alluded was Gregory Petrov, whose expectations of a directing role at *Word* had come to nothing with the hiring of Valentinov. In the second half of 1912 Petrov had once again been reduced to waiting in vain for articles of his to appear in print. The ex-priest consequently wrote another bitter letter in December 1912 threatening to take Sytin and the editors of *Word* before an arbitration tribunal for ignoring his submissions. He addressed it not to Sytin but to company director Soloviev and to Sytin's third son, Vladimir, then well placed in the company and very likely serving as a director.

Petrov spoke of repeated humiliations "over the past four years." When *Word* began, he fumed, he had been indispensable. Back then, Sytin "literally [fell] on his knees, begging me not to leave the paper, to save it." An indefatigable contributor from 1896 to 1905, he wrote two, three, and sometimes five articles for a single issue.

Although, continued Petrov, Doroshevich had recently lapsed into long spells of idleness with no loss of favour or exorbitant pay, "I, being overly considerate, and working for years, now receive mockery." He had "shattered" his life for the paper. "And what is the result? When the paper has prospered on our bones, our blood, I have to wait months for the publication of my articles."

Then comes the curious charge that Petrov vowed to relate to the tribunal. Sytin, he said, had written to him "three years ago" (late 1909) about moving *Word* to St Petersburg and about Doroshevich's going to Stolypin to "come to an agreement with him on how the paper should be run. I protested in a letter to Sytin that this would be a new *Azeffshchina* [Azeff was a notorious double agent serving both the secret police and the revolutionaries]." Since he and Sytin had together "created" the paper for the people, "not for secret service to Stolypin,"

Petrov declared it his proprietary right to "publish the whole story." This exposure threat, the ex-priest concludes, had made his position at *Word* worse than ever.[2]

Exposure threat or not, his denunciation here of links with Stolypin supports the likelihood, already mentioned, that another letter of Petrov's (about 1911) was facetious in advising that Doroshevich consult the first minister about starting a second *Russian Word*. It was out of character for Petrov to propose any such collaboration. As to why his writings were not appearing in *Word*, the reason seems mainly to have been his advocacy of a radically Christian, communal populism. Sytin, as quoted before, found Petrov's writings too "leftist."

Petrov, after all, had given the police cause in 1906 to close *God's Truth*, the religious daily he edited. In turn, he had become a spokesman for the Kadets as one of their successful candidates for the Duma of 1907. Because his church superiors had by then forbidden him to write for any periodical, he had left the priesthood to concentrate on preaching in print. When he resumed submitting articles to *Word* in 1908, Petrov had chafed at the cool reception he received. The paper which owed him so much now had a readership in six figures and denied him that audience. No matter that Sytin faithfully sent him a monthly stipend of two thousand rubles and swore he knew no better man, Petrov cared most about being heard.

Because his complaint in 1912 about having no voice in *Word* comes during Valentinov's tenure, Petrov is very likely one of the three writers Valentinov insisted on excluding. That leaves two others, and one of them was certainly Alexander Blok, a leading Symbolist poet, whom Rumanov had set about recruiting six months before Valentinov arrived at *Word*. Rumanov had taken the initiative with Blok after receiving a letter from Sytin early in December 1911 about the necessity of printing "good belles lettres ... every day ... in succession: novels, stories, tales - having finished one begin another."[3] Fine writers would enliven and elevate *Word* - and promote sales of their longer works in editions from Sytin's presses. Among the notables Sytin had already signed up was novelist-philosopher Merezhkovsky, who had joined *Word* about 1910. Merezhkovsky had since had reason to hope that his wife, the poetess Zinaida Hippius, might edit the literary section for the daily, and, in angling for that appointment, he had been the first to try to recruit Blok for *Word*.

Blok very soon learned that Rumanov was about to approach him. On 24 December he jotted in his diary "everything essential" for deciding whether or not to collaborate with *Word*. He noted on the plus side that, unlike any other major daily in Russia, the editorial board was "entirely Russian," that is, "without Jews." On the minus side were "internal contradictions" and "patriarchal sluggishness," but, all the same, this "conservative paper might become progressive."[4]

Once Rumanov had approached him on 30 December, Blok confided the terms he had heard to V. Piast, a friend already working for *Word* but a lesser poet who would never rate a byline. Surprisingly, says Piast, Blok was to discuss social issues in prose articles and feuilletons in the manner of a "passionate publicist" and "an heir to Katkov."[5] In that role, he was "partly to replace one writer" who had just been dismissed "at the insistence of the liberals" – a reference by Piast to Rozanov.[6]

Blok felt strong reservations, but his diary entry of 31 December again spells out offsetting attractions. For one thing, *Word*'s audience was awesome, and Blok estimated that at least ten persons read each of the 224,000 papers that circulated daily. For another, the paper was richly endowed, thanks to the "miracle of Ivan Dmitrievich Sytin ... who is not fussy about the means he employs." Still, continues Blok, a complacent "note of peace and mildness" in *Word* "sometimes hardens into contented philistinism" and that was something that "Sytin himself worries about."[7] Blok finally gave his assent to Rumanov in June 1912, just as Valentinov joined *Word*. Part of the inducement was a promise from Sytin's second son, Vasily, then overseer of juvenile books at Sytin & Co., to issue two collections of Blok's poetry for children.[8]

Once aware of the offer, Valentinov blocked an actual contract. "When I learned that someone," he writes, "bypassing me, wished to enlist Blok as a permanent writer (I didn't know it was Rumanov), I reared up. Attempts to recruit others as permanent collaborators had already taken place more than once, and ... if I gave in on Blok ... nothing would remain of my protecting the paper from other undesirable persons." Sytin, Valentinov points out, had been known to hire a favourite of the minister of education or the procurator of the Holy Synod to help get his books approved for the state- and church-run schools.[9]

Valentinov says he further learned that Blok was "not to write verses but articles of a sensational character, and his writing in prose literally nauseated me, especially after such a 'masterpiece' as the article, 'On the Current State of Russian Symbolism.' This was undoubtedly combined with – I will not hide it – my revulsion for Blok in general, as a man." Valentinov said he got "stubborn pressure" about a contract for Blok "from all sides"; and the second time Blagov proposed it, Valentinov retorted that Blok's works "undoubtedly will be useful to *Russian Word* when I leave the paper." That "threatening hint" ended the subject between them, but it also turned out to be an accurate prediction.

When no contract materialized during the rest of 1912 and well through 1913, Blok wrongly blamed Rumanov, who was doing everything he could to open the doors for him. "I slammed them shut," says Valentinov, "and while I was on the paper not one article of Blok's appeared in it. But when I left, there appeared (on 25 December 1913) not an article but a poem, 'New America.' And let me affirm - why should I lie? - that if this poem had come into my hands when I was in fact editor of *Russian Word*, ... I would have sent it to the typesetter." Blok's poem was a paean to the promising industrialization of Russia that would make it a "New America" - just the economic optimism that Valentinov sought to spread.[10]

Valentinov also gives his reason for leaving *Word*. He tells that, because December 1913 marked the three hundredth anniversary of the Romanov dynasty, he presided that month over a special commemorative edition. When Doroshevich provided, as the lead article, what Valentinov called a "fawning account" of Romanov virtues and accomplishments, a "sharp skirmish" resulted between him and the one staff member he could not edit. Doroshevich pulled rank, and Valentinov chose to leave. The era of the single, commanding de facto editor thus came to an end; authority over policy and content would henceforth rest with a collective, or editorial "committee," intermittently dominated by Doroshevich.[11]

Whether he wrote his Romanov tribute from conviction or to offset his harsh criticism of the government's prosecution of Beilis, Doroshevich must have expected to clash with Valentinov about the piece. He knew, after all, that Valentinov would reject any words that seemed to seek favour in St Petersburg and would balk at anything less than complete control over *Word*'s political content. Doroshevich may therefore have deliberately forced a showdown, perhaps in collusion with Sytin's fellow directors or even with Sytin himself.

Sytin, in turn, might have preferred to keep Valentinov only to be outmanoeuvred by Doroshevich, whose contract gave him the right to insist on the publication of his Romanov piece. Most likely, however, Sytin seems to have decided to temper *Word*'s policy toward the autocracy with a more even balance of confrontation and conciliation. That stand would still be appropriate to a liberal, non-party daily, and would still win readers and good writers.

Mixing *Word*'s criticism of the government with kind words for the Romanovs would also help the book publishing side of Sytin's business. Because he was angling for a bigger share of the market for school texts, Sytin could see some value in blunting the detrimental charges that he was undermining the existing order. So far in 1913 there had been attacks of just this sort not only in the State Council, the Duma, and in Purishkevich's book, but also in the Moscow Court of Appeals, where judges had singled out criminally subversive content in four of his publications.

II

After the last of an earlier series of government prosecutions had been resolved at the start of 1911, Sytin had enjoyed a respite from courtroom harassment by the state. But the nature and timing of the four trials in 1913 (they coincided with Valentinov's tenure at *Word* and came just after officials had blocked a second *Russian Word* in St Petersburg) suggest a new concerted drive by the government to push Sytin to the right.

The first trial, in March, concerned a brochure that Sytin & Co. had published back in 1905. Even at this late date, the author, P. Senatorov, was sent to prison to serve two months. His "Wake Up, Archbishops! A Letter to the Metropolitan Antonio of St. Petersburg and Other Bishops" was criminal, ruled the court, because of its "callous disrespect for the Supreme Authority [the Tsar]" and "censure of the fundamental laws." Sytin again denied any personal involvement. Although one judge entered his doubts into the record, the panel found no proof of criminal intent and acquitted him.[12]

The next case concerned a translation of "The Contemporary Proletariat" by P. Kampfmeier, a German Social Democrat of revisionist views, that had cleared the Moscow Press Affairs Committee before Sytin & Co. had circulated it in 1907. When the committee had ruled the same work impermissible for another publisher in 1910, Sytin had immediately pulped the four thousand copies still held in his warehouse from the five thousand printed. But the initial printing still provided grounds in 1913 for the government to indict publisher Sytin and editor A.P. Semenko. At their April trial the court exonerated both defendants but found the Marxist arguments of the work subversive and ordered all copies destroyed.[13]

When the third trial took place in September, the government may have had a larger point to make by posthumously convicting Tolstoy just as his works were appearing as bi-weekly supplements to *Russian Word* and *Around the World*. Grounds for this trial came from a pamphlet containing Tolstoy's "The Great Sin," which Sytin & Co. had reprinted from a 1905 issue of *Russian Thought* (*Russkaia Mysl*). Tolstoy's endorsement there of the single-tax ideas of Henry George as a corrective to the endemic poverty of the Russian peasants, the prosecutor charged, was an illegal call for the abolition of private property. Although Sytin's defence attorney pointed out that no less than the Chief Administration of Press Affairs had approved the original article in 1905, the prosecutor countered that the court should correct past mistakes. The judges upheld him on 19 September by ruling the pamphlet illegal, but they also acquitted the defendants as not directly responsible.[14]

The final trial, in December, is remarkable for taking place so soon after the appearance of the cited work, *Circle of Reading*, which Sytin had finally published earlier that same year. As Sytin had feared back in 1909, the prosecutor sought a ban on its numerous pacifistic passages. Agreeing that words against war and bearing arms harmed government authority, the judges ruled the cited lines illegal and ordered the destruction of all unsold copies. To reissue the book, Sytin's editors would replace the banned sentiments with acceptable ones.[15] Sytin had to tally up a considerable loss, however, from having to destroy *Circle of Reading* and the other extant books banned by the courts in 1913.

In this or any other year, all of them hectic, Sytin saw little of his family, for he often slept and ate in hotels and on trains. When he did arrive home, he would retreat to his study, recall Mikhail and Aleksei, sons of Vasily Ivanovich; and Grandmother Evdokia Ivanova, who ran a strictly regulated household, would admonish all at hand: "Quiet! Himself has come!" The order applied to young and old alike, says Aleksei, who goes on to describe his grandfather as "strict, very busy, taciturn, rather frightening even to adults," and inclined to "pace the corridor, his hands behind his back." Aleksei and his cousin Dmitry, Ivan Ivanovich's son, would sometimes fall in step behind to mimick him. "Grandfather would not notice, or perhaps he noticed but paid no attention to us [thinking]: 'Let them amuse themselves.' " On one occasion, however, Sytin had "abruptly and unexpectedly turned to us and ... commanded, although in friendly fashion: 'Scat!' "

When he saw his grandfather, mostly at midday meals, Mikhail recalls that Sytin had little to say to him other than the usual questions about school. Dmitry remembers that twelve usually sat down precisely at 1 p.m. for a "very simple" meal of *shchi* or another soup followed by kasha or *kotlety* and then compote or *kissel* for dessert. "A small bottle of vodka," continues Aleksei, "appeared from time to time with tiny vodka glasses at each place. But to take some without permission was not allowed. Grandfather himself drank none and was strict with liquor, for all his ostensible easy-goingness."

Nor was his assignment of seats democratic. Sytin presided at the head with his sons to his left and the womenfolk and children to the right, each at a place already set with cutlery and a napkin in a bone ring. No one so much as walked to his chair until Sytin had entered the room and invited the rest to join him. Aleksei admits to childishly naive recollections of his grandfather but confirms the stereotype of him as wholly devoted to business. "He thought about work constantly, had no time for rest, and he had no energy left for activities with his family." Sytin, remembers Mikhail, occasionally did join the family at the estate outside of Moscow for a dip in the pond and there would solemnly "cross himself, splash three times ... but did not swim."[16]

Sytin concentrated on work mainly because he preferred to, partly because he had to. But even this dedicated man had felt the need for a reprieve midway through 1913 when business and courtroom pressures, combined with a gloomy international outlook, had sorely tried him in the year before the outbreak of the world war. As Sytin wrote later, "Everything was falling apart. I wanted to run from it." He said that "in those terrible years when everyone waited the catastrophe, even I was tormented by depression. I looked for a way out, a place where I could flee from myself." Sytin had consequently set off for western Europe and then, on the road, decided to turn to Italy to visit Gorky on Capri and to feel the Italian sun. Not even on this escapist venture, of course, had Sytin held back from talking business on Gorky's terrace.

En route to Capri, moreover, Sytin had once again encountered a disturbing undercurrent in western Europe that made him prefer the Russia from which he had fled. He found it this time in Naples, the day before he took the ferry to Capri, as he walked alone on the deserted beach. "Suddenly there fell on me an army of shabby young heroes – ten little boys in men's rags. They surrounded me and demanded something 'for macaroni.'" When the change from his pockets did not satisfy them, "I quickly thrust my purse at them and tried to run ... [but one] threw himself at me and grabbed my legs. [As] I fell down ... another rushed up and grabbed my wallet. He ran and the others after him." For all the majestic beauty that nature had endowed on Italy, Sytin was to reflect, "a dark, evil force reigns and far from everything is in order." When Sytin reported the incident at his hotel, the staff expressed surprise that the thieves had spared him his overcoat.[17]

Once back in Russia in mid-1913, the restless publisher had then proceeded to stir up even more difficulties for himself by designing and initiating a project that very soon backfired. His long-standing tendency to go it alone would again create trouble.

III

During the charge-laden year of 1913, says Sytin, textbook profits for Sytin & Co. fell by fifteen thousand rubles. As a countermove, Sytin claims that he first resorted to price cutting, only to have other publishers accuse him of unfair tactics. Resourceful as ever, he next set about marketing more books by resurrecting School and Knowledge, the society that he described as "independent of Sytin & Co." which he had started in 1907 and had since "marked with a cross." He would claim this time to organize the society to pool talent rather than the rubles of the rich; and, in the defence he was impelled to write early in 1914, he chose to describe its members as pedagogues and text writers working together to engender good cheap books for Russian classrooms.[18] But Sytin omitted two crucial facts: the close involvement both of the Ministry of Education and of his publishing house. Two of the pedagogical experts in the society happened to be Ministry of Education officials. In turn, Sytin & Co. happened to be the society's sole publisher. Rivals who had discovered this cosy arrangement had been understandably quick to expose it as a public scandal.

Here, again, no one can know the prime motive of Sytin. He typically presented himself as a crusader for enlightenment, as can any serious publisher, and he did undertake idealistic projects at considerable cost to himself. His revived School and Knowledge, however, strongly suggests that Sytin combined altruism with plans to expand his business by taking advantage of inside influence in the ministry. Sytin himself later admits as much in describing his visit to Leo Kasso, minister of public education, in late 1912 or early 1913. He says that he had then bluntly declared: "I would like your help to overcome the chaos in my publishing work." That is, would Kasso please intervene so that Sytin could sell more texts to "all our schools - elementary, secondary, and university ... of course with the preliminary approval of the Ministry." The means that Sytin proposed was for Kasso to reform the book selection process which then enabled a reviewer to reject a book for even one questionable page. Kasso should instead give the author a chance to correct any such minor flaws while the work was still a manuscript.

Kasso, Sytin says, eventually gave his assent to the proposal while stressing that the ministry would continue to make the final selection of books for the schools. Even though Sytin goes on to claim that "I took this matter up not for myself but for everyone, and there could be no talk about a monopoly," the lone publisher who benefited from this "reform" in 1913 was Sytin.[19] As for what Kasso had to gain, one credible observer contends that the minister's willingness to accommodate Sytin constituted an attempt "from the realm" to soften the critical, liberal stance that *Word* had taken under Valentinov.[20] The School and Knowledge committee began functioning late in 1913, and Valentinov's departure from *Word* came that very December.

Notably, just after the newspapers charging Sytin and Kasso with collusion would have reached him in Germany, Valentinov wrote Sytin a letter deploring both Russia's preoccupation with "politicking (we have not politics, only politicking)'' and ''our spiritual emptiness, our lack of energy'' - very likely jibes at Sytin for comporting with the government just as his daily became lethargic about criticizing it. He closes by stressing that never again ''would I be able to work on *Russian Word*''; for the School and Knowledge exposé must have caused Valentinov, too, to link *Word*'s moderation with Sytin's self-interested quest to sell more textbooks.[21]

By Valentinov's standards, another highly self-interested, ''politicking'' publisher - Sytin's rival in St Petersburg, A.S. Suvorin - was the one who exposed the School and Knowledge arrangement. It was Suvorin's *New Times*, on 21 January 1914, that first protested Kasso's having given ''one nimble Moscow publishing firm [Sytin & Co.] a privileged position in marketing school texts.'' Then followed a long question: ''Is it known to the Ministry, that behind the School and Knowledge Committee ... stands the well-known Moscow book firm Sytin & Co., which is skilfully flooding the schools and popular reading rooms with books, 75 per cent of which have been rejected by the same Ministry because of propaganda on behalf of atheism, antipatriotism, and anti-militarism?'' (The true overall rejection rate, documented earlier, was about 40 per cent.)

Kasso, charged *New Times*, had ordered E.L. Radlov and V.A. Semeka of the ministry's Learning Committee to become members of School and Knowledge. The ministry would be naive, the paper continued, to assume that it could influence the publishing policy of the Sytin ''book factory'' through ''two aged officials'' who received sums originating from Sytin. Instead, the ministry was covertly helping Sytin to gain a monopoly over textbook publishing. By its own self-evident readiness to approve books submitted through School and Knowledge, the ministry was causing authors to join Sytin's society. These same authors then necessarily signed with Sytin for the printing of their texts because he was his society's sole publisher.[22] The Moscow daily, *Morning of Russia* (*Utro Rossii*), followed up three days later with a two-part article entitled ''The State Monopoly of Text Books.'' The revelations about Radlov and Semeka, it said, had provoked a strong written protest from Moscow and St Petersburg publishers against the ''unprecedented advantage'' the minister of public education had given Sytin. It further stated that others on the Learning Committee saw the dual roles of Radlov and Semeka as an ''unexpected humiliation.''[23]

When indignant writers joined the protest by telling Sytin they would bypass his firm so long as it collaborated with the government and Leo Kasso, Sytin understood that he was in the midst of both a business and public relations disaster. He appealed urgently to Rumanov to advise him how to answer the charges in print in such a way as to ''draw a veil over the existence of our [School and Knowledge] committee." A sharp refutation was needed, he felt, to prevent boycotts of Sytin & Co. both by writers and by teachers choosing class texts.[24] What resulted was a series of open letters.

To "defend his name," Radlov gave his side of the story in *Morning of Russia* on 25 January. He denied receiving any pay or granting any favours. The ministry had asked him to join the School and Knowledge Committee solely to engender good textbooks. Insisting that the Learning Committee had not and would not accept inferior works, he debunked any contrived monopoly for Sytin's company. As proof, he repeated *New Times*'s misstatement that, from all Sytin's submissions over the years, the Learning Committee had rejected three-fourths.[25]

That same day Sytin used the columns of *Russian Word* to issue his own defence. "I will carry on the struggle for the book to the end," he vowed. "My dream is that the people will have inexpensive, understandable, wholesome, useful books." For years, he said, other publishers and their authors had held a monopoly on textbooks through certain government committees. Because this combine had kept book costs for students disgracefully high, he had founded the non-profit School and Knowledge Society back in 1907 to introduce competitiveness. But after the assaults of Purishkevich, the society, as originally conceived, "could not, of course, take a step," and his own school texts met insurmountable obstacles in the ministry.

At this point, continued Sytin, he had decided on a new measure "independent" of his company. Then followed this passage which would later be quoted verbatim in *A Half Century for the Book* and in his memoirs:

> Not intending to gain any guarantees and certainly not a monopoly, I decided to try to rescue the textbook from that complete uncertainty and defencelessness in which it found itself outside the hands of the monopolists. Valuing the connection [of School and Knowledge] with the schools, I proposed to invite experienced and knowledgeable pedagogues to collaborate with us on behalf of the schools, hoping that their familiarity with the criteria for textbook approval would help [writers] in their work, especially those living in the provinces who did not have "connections" in St Petersburg.

His prime aim, Sytin insisted, was "to lift the burden of tax from the needy pupil." His only acknowledgment, if any, to links with the ministry was his euphemistic reference to a "connection with the schools." And by alluding to pedagogues, he used a term that was broad enough to include Radlov and Semeka.[26]

A letter from the board of directors of Sytin & Co. appeared the next day, 26 January, in *Russian Messenger*, the daily identified with Moscow's liberal intellectuals. The signatories, like Sytin, insisted that the School and Knowledge project had merely been a response to the capricious favouritism of the Learning Committee. In defending Sytin, the directors insisted that he had acted on his own and regretted that, "by a strange irony," his public-spirited efforts to end a monopoly had been seen as an attempt to gain a monopoly of his own.[27]

In this same issue, however, S.P. Melgunov – a company stockholder, liberal politician, and editor and publisher of *Voice of the Past* (*Golos Minuvshego*) – criticized Sytin.[28] For all Sytin's avowed good intentions, Melgunov complained, the publisher had not explained his ties with the ministry. He should do so at once. But, having made independence from the government a company virtue, no spokesman for Sytin & Co. would ever admit to ties of any sort with St Petersburg. In no company history or personal sketch that he published, for example, did Sytin ever refer to an even closer collaboration with officials in 1912: his publishing nearly three million peasant-directed books and pamphlets, all tailored to government standards, under contract with an official newspaper of the Ministry of the Interior.[29] Sytin therefore issued no further statements on School and Knowledge, preferring to let stand his claim that he had merely been fighting monopolists in the cause of helping writers and schools.

Not even to Kasso had Sytin fully spelled out his primary aim: to cut his own commercial losses by getting texts approved while still in manuscript form. Because the ministry reviewed only published texts, those it rejected became virtually worthless to the publisher and Sytin could recoup their cost only by raising prices on other books. Through School and Knowledge, his writers could revise their manuscripts under ministry insiders to meet government standards before Sytin published them, and the resulting books would almost certainly pass the formal ministry review.

Somehow *New Times* had learned how the newly contrived School and Knowledge worked and Sytin's critics relished the exposé. Purishkevich, for one, felt vindicated by the uproar, which was still echoing when his second vitriolic book, *Before the Storm: the Government and Russian Schools*, circulated sometime in 1914. In it Purishkevich again targeted Sytin's authors and editors – Vakhterov, Tulupov, and others – and this time aimed, as well, at Sytin's educational journal, *For the People's Teacher* (*Dlia narodnogo uchitelia*).[30] From a "class of unique, half-Jewish and thoroughly disreputable 'intelligentsia,'" harangued Purishkevich, had come the self-appointed "new enlighteners" of Russia with their three-part plan for anarchy. They sought to use school texts to subvert the church and state, incite class hatred, and mislead the young into pessimism and pacifism; to use the "left-wing daily press," which had "multiplied incredibly since 1905," to discredit their opponents and further spread lies and filth; and, third, to infuse teachers' congresses with their contemptible "spirit of protest."[31]

Sytin says in his memoirs that he could not fathom Purishkevich's motives but suspected that "this personal hatred for the Sytin publishing house had political and even commercial motivations because Purishkevich wanted to establish his own publishing house to issue textbooks." This was, he continues, the All-Russian Filaret Society for Popular Education that stood squarely against the "progressive orientation" of Sytin and his associates.[32] Sytin casts the debate in terms still familiar today: disagreement between the modernists and the traditionalists about the right books for the impressionable young. But it was also a struggle for influence and profits.

In defending himself in *Word*, Sytin contended that his company had been suffering heavy, unwarranted losses from school texts, but profit figures from Sytin & Co. belittle that complaint. The steadily upward annual earnings had risen impressively in 1911 and 1912.[33] Thus the profits for 1911 showed a strong 25 per cent rise over 1910, while the 1912 increment was an unprecedented 35 per cent. (see appendix 5, figure 3). As already stated, the circulation of *Word* in these same years went up by 11 per cent in 1911 and during the Duma elections, the Balkans war, and Valentinov's stint as editor by 31 per cent in 1912. In 1913, the year of the fifteen-thousand-ruble decline in textbook earnings, dividends fell to 8 per cent as company profits as a whole plunged by 21 per cent;[34] but this was also the year that Sytin & Co. made two purchases: the Moscow Trading House of E.I. Konovalova, which then stood fourth in the production of popular books and calendars, and the children's magazine *Path* (*Tropinka*).[35]

Stockholders clearly felt no misgivings about business trends, for the next year they nearly doubled company capitalization from 1.8 million rubles to 3.4 million by voting, at their meeting of 23 May 1914, to issue 1,600 new shares. As always, insiders got it all. Just over half, or 850 shares, were handed outright to Sytin in exchange for what was then his 15 per cent ownership of *Russian Word*. By purchasing some of the remaining 750 shares, Sytin emerged with a resounding 61.3 per cent overall interest and, at last the single, dominant power of majority shareholder.[36] Ironically, in only six more weeks the fatal spiral of war and revolution would disallow absolutely his expansive plans for a verticle trust and vast network of papers.

The stock settlement that Sytin got from his company as a final payment for *Word* was another artful, but legal, transfer; and the Ministry of Trade and Industry consequently approved the recapitalization. But when Sytin claimed that over 170,000 rubles of the transaction should escape taxation as being merely a redistribution of his holdings, the Revenue Department countered that all of Sytin's gains from the 1914 transfer of his 15 per cent ownership must be treated as profits because Sytin had continuously run the paper even after "selling" most of it in 1905. This dispute would be resolved in Sytin's favour in November 1916.[37]

Not that Sytin would have had any trouble paying the taxes in full. He simply had better uses for his money: his projected paper manufacturing company, for one.

IV

To end his dependency on imported paper, Sytin had first taken steps to start a paper plant in 1910 by exploring possibilities in Russian Karelia. He had paid a technical assistant one thousand rubles a month for two years to assess the resources just inland from the White Sea near the town of Kem on the river of the same name. A waterfall there, he learned, could produce 20,000 horsepower, and the surrounding forest, unexploited and owned by the state, could easily provide the required wood pulp.

Estimating that he needed nine million rubles in start-up capital, Sytin went to Germany to get help from the German industrialist Hugo Stinnes, whom the press called "the richest man in Germany." Stinnes, however, got no further than favouring the project in principle, no doubt put off by the anti-German stance of *Russian Word* and the deteriorating relations between Germany and Russia. Stymied by equal disinterest at home, Sytin would once more grumble about the unwillingness of Russians to support their own vitally important publishing industry.

By 1913 Sytin had lowered his sights. Thus, to acquire and expand the small St Petersburg paper plant of N.V. Pechatkin, he had joined with E.F. Davydov, a director of the Orenburg Forest Products and Trading Society, to organize and direct a joint stock company capitalized at 4.5 million rubles. Sytin, Rumanov, and Soloviev had emerged as the major shareholders of the new Russian Writing Paper Manufacturing Factory, and Sytin & Co. immediately signed a ten-year contract to buy paper at discount. But because he still had to buy imported paper, Sytin was to confront shortages and steeply rising prices once war began in 1914. By 1916 his publications would need 7,000 poods (252,000 pounds) every 24 hours – 30 per cent of that for *Word* alone, but all the Russian factories together could not have provided that amount.[38]

Sytin's acquisition of the paper plant with Davydov led to an incident that provides another example of the shady business practices that must have been commonplace. The conspirers against Sytin were Pechatkin, Davydov, and banker G.D. Lesin. It seems that Davydov transferred some of his own forested land to Lesin and then, with Pechatkin, arranged for the paper plant to purchase it at an inflated price. Together the trio pocketed 643,894 rubles. When he uncovered this trick by insiders, Sytin felt both betrayed and humiliated. He wrote Rumanov that he reeled from a sense of "falling into an abyss" because the "smart dealers operating behind my back ... have spit into my soul disgracefully and nastily" as though he were "nothingness." Sytin asked Rumanov, his trusted agent, to demand 200,000 rubles from each of his tormenters, seemingly for charity, but there is no record of any resolution.[39]

Sytin, meanwhile, was cheerfully losing money on a project that involved him with the military. It was the immense and distinguished *Military Encyclopedia* that his company published from 1911 through 1915 and that proved to be the single most important work on the Russian armed forces before the Revolution. A group of officers, the so-called "Young Turks," had first proposed the encyclopedia to Sytin in 1910 because they expected eventual war between Russia and Austro-German forces and wanted to show the superior readiness of the other side in order to stimulate Russian preparedness.[40] The minister of war, V.A. Sukhomlinov, disapproved the project by the young "liberals" but seems not to have interfered. Endorsement came, however, from the minister of naval affairs, Admiral I.K. Grigorovich, who got on well with Sytin. Indeed, during the Balkan wars, Grigorovich had permitted *Word* correspondents to radio dispatches to Moscow uncensored from a Russian cruiser in the Black Sea, and his backing would help Sytin rise in civic rank to honorary citizen in 1914.[41]

One of the officers instrumental in the project, V.A. Apushkin, rented special editorial offices in St Petersburg within walking distance of the Imperial General Staff quarters and the Admiralty. The military personnel granted leave to work there apparently received maintenance allowances and salaries from Sytin. To expedite their work, Sytin also provided a graphic artists' workshop, a typesetting shop, and a plant to produce matrices. The page matrices then went to Moscow for casting and printing in Sytin's book plant.[42] The editorial staff assembled all of the projected twenty-one volumes, but war shortages kept Sytin & Co. from publishing beyond volume eighteen in 1915. Ironically, "Port Arthur" – the first major defeat for Russia in the Russo-Japanese war – was the final entry.

From early on, slow sales and high costs portended losses, and the jealously observant Gorky, anxious that Sytin invest with him, had expressed regret in late 1912 that Sytin "dissipates his energies" on so "unwieldy" a publication.[43] Cumulative losses would reach three million rubles. In comparison, the combined profits of Sytin & Co. for 1911, 1912, and 1913 - the last years for which figures are available - were just over one million rubles.

In itself, the *Encyclopedia* appealed to Sytin because it was monumental, unprecedented, and historically significant. It had also given him reason to open typesetting operations in St Petersburg just as he committed his company to starting a daily there. Thinking big, Sytin back in 1910 had taken on the *Encyclopedia*, explored papermaking in Kem, and sought backers for a St Petersburg *Word*. Plenty of complications had plagued him in the three years since then.

V

But whatever the consequences, Sytin's compulsive drive to improve his business was apparent to everyone, even his errand boys; and one of them in his St Petersburg bookstore, Motylkov by name, recalls how much Sytin relished the "organizing role of the boss" and direct "personal supervision over his huge business." Consequently, this "very mobile man ... spent more nights in a sleeping car than at home."[44] Arriving early in the morning at the St Petersburg station, Sytin would go directly to his store on one corner along Nevsky, co-opt the office of the manager, and send Motylkov for tea and a flaky pastry. Motylkov recalls Sytin alone and soberly absorbed in his affairs. "I never once saw him smile or heard a joke from him."

This no-nonsense Sytin, continues Motylkov, had an "expressive, intelligent face, a quick, shrewd glance," and an abrupt severity. In his modest but flawless attire, there "was not the smallest sign of disorder." Aware of his brusqueness, Sytin would sometimes apologize for speaking too sharply or make a point of generosity. Besides paying wages above the norm, he was known to give cash advances to employees that were to be repaid over several months and then, in a few weeks' time, to forgive the loan entirely, says Motylkov. With managers, Sytin's generosity gave way to brusqueness rather than the reverse. I.N. Pavlov, one of his leading engravers, remembers that Sytin entertained all his foremen each Easter at a dinner for about 150 in his apartment. He would greet each guest at the door with the traditional triple kiss and then, often as not, confront him with his shortcomings. Pavlov heard him scold his bindery foreman, for example, for the excess of refuse under his machines. "How can you take pride in this?" Sytin had demanded. Pavlov also recalls Sytin severely counselling the head of his drawing school to forget about donning the "frock coat" of a company director (as had the head of the mechanical section) because his "half-penny" abilities fell far short of the "scope that I insist upon." But, however abrupt Sytin could be, says Pavlov, his élan and imagination in running his business on "the level of progressive European enterprises" outweighed the impatient outbursts that went with them.[45]

From associates of a higher rank come descriptions of the merchant affability of Sytin, especially when they met him in one of the fine restaurants he frequented; and Chekhov told his brother in 1902 that he had found it best to set proposals before the publisher over lunch at Moscow's Slavianskii Bazaar.[46] Altaev, for another, recalls Sytin's "cherished table" in a corner near the entrance of the elegant Moscow dining room of the Metropolitan Hotel, where he would daily sit "for an hour or so" and expansively talk business.[47] Sytin had few close friends outside publishing, even by 1914; but since business was his first love, his favourite socializing was to talk shop over good food. And to engender warm feelings all around, he was known to make informal commitments that came to little or nothing later on.

Gorky was among the accomplished people, then, who gladly socialized with Sytin in hope of forging deals with him, even as they knew Sytin's elusiveness. Thus Gorky had told an associate after entertaining Sytin in May 1913 that "nothing is certain ... although a proposition has been put forth." After quoting a grandiose pledge by Sytin – "Do what you want, with whomever you want; I will give you whatever means you want" – Gorky had emphasized that Sytin's promise was so far only words.[48] In September Gorky repeated to Ladyzhnikov his tentative hopes of getting direly needed funds for Znanie from Sytin.[49]

When, that December, on the occasion of the three hundredth Romanov anniversary, Nicholas II pardoned many persons charged with political crimes, Gorky made his planned return to Russia and, accepting a long-extended invitation, arrived on 19 January 1914 at Sytin's country estate. The Okhranka took careful note of his three-month stay, and since the press reported Gorky's every movement, the public knew about it too – including Gorky's visit on 8 February to Sytin's Moscow printing plant.

One recent historian described the relationship of the two men in 1914 in these terms: "On his return to his homeland, Gorky found a new strong man to admire and to work with ... a self-made man like Gorky himself, with the same belief in man as man, the same deep instinctive love of Russia, the same autodidact's reverence for culture in all its forms and all its works. The publishing giant I.D. Sytin was the owner of a great empire he had built himself ... with unlimited funds and unlimited faith and good will to put at Gorky's disposal for nothing less than the general enlightenment of mankind.''[50]

This tribute, however, overstates Sytin's generosity and omits commercial and political considerations. Sytin was helpful but did not put his wealth at Gorky's disposal. Rather, Sytin informed Gorky almost at once that he would not finance the history of Russia they had been discussing and proposed instead to pay 200,000 rubles for Gorky's collected works in an edition of forty thousand copies. As provisos, he insisted on reimbursing Gorky in instalments to 1918 and on holding the right to deduct fifty thousand rubles if the works had grossed less than 200,000 rubles by 1 January 1917.[51] Sytin also wanted Gorky to guarantee *Word* first rights on all his future writings. These stringent terms suggest that Sytin was underscoring that he had limited capital to invest. He was also fending off joint projects such as Gorky's proposed newspaper, *Ray* (*Luch*), where volatile politics would enter in. Sytin preferred to keep his dealings with Gorky strictly literary – as in reaching an agreement to publish in *Word* a second memoir of Gorky's impoverished youth, *My Apprenticeship*, which Gorky would write during the first year of his return.[52]

Each man appreciated the other as a sharp bargainer, and in mid-May Gorky wrote to Ladyzhnikov: ''Sytin has a good head; he very quickly and surely understands what others would have to ponder for a year.''[53] Within three weeks he wrote again: ''Sytin is dragging out negotiations [on *Ray*], hindering me from beginning the matter with other people. I am determined to have a decisive explanation from him.''[54]

Whatever Sytin replied, *Ray* remained in the planning stage. However, a literary review edited by Gorky seemed to Sytin not only to merit support but also to make sense as a supplement to *Word*. When Doroshevich and Blagov roundly disagreed on political grounds, Sytin provided the funds that alone enabled Gorky to start *Chronicle* (*Letopis*). That review would last from 1915 to 1917; but because it would attract only eight thousand subscribers, Sytin ultimately lost fifty thousand rubles on it.[55] In his memoirs, Sytin tersely says: ''We published *Chronicle* with [Gorky], but this publication had to stop.''[56] Sytin would also hire Gorky for several editorial jobs and back his new publishing house, Sail (*Parus*).[57]

The return of Gorky to Russia made a great difference in Sytin's willingness to deal with him, but Gorky came home just before the onset of war made publishing far chancier for everyone concerned. Although he would get far less than he asked for, Gorky would still do well financially from knowing Sytin. He would, at the same time, value Sytin the more as a benefactor and exemplar for the people. Like Chekhov, Gorky felt that backward, lethargic Russia sorely needed hard workers and enlighteners, and into both categories he put Sytin with himself.

Gorky was negotiating with Sytin over his complete works and his projected daily paper when the assassination of the Austrian Archduke Ferdinand on 15 June 1914 suddenly opened the door to war. Several of Sytin's children had gone off to Germany despite the tension among the powers, and once fighting broke out, Sytin had enormous difficulty getting all but one of them home. That done, Sytin was forced to ponder just how the contingencies of war would affect his publishing and his politics.

CHAPTER NINE

A Publisher Goes to War

Russian defeats in the first two years of the First World War were to bring to the forefront Sytin's sturdy nationalism. Unlike in 1904, Sytin was now to help the autocracy by promoting hatred of the enemy and blunting the worst of the news from the front. In addition, as heavy losses in the battles against Germany and Austria caused political disarray in the capital (now Russianized to Petrograd) and mounting shortages, despair, and criticism everywhere, Sytin saw to it that *Russian Word* muted its criticism of the beleaguered government. The new essential was the good of Russia in trying times. Even as military censorship and shrinking paper supplies put limits on publishing, Sytin himself felt he should temper his Chekhovian principle of giving the people the complete truth.

I

Germany's declaration of war on 19 July 1914 genuinely surprised Sytin and Russians at every level, despite the Germans' casting blame on Nicholas II and his government for mobilizing to support the Serbians against the Austrians. Still, Sytin did not expect the conflict to last very long, and his editors at *Word* geared up to cover battles and strategies as objectively as they had during the Russo-Japanese war. The government, in turn, especially fearful of enemy propaganda and domestic criticism, imposed strict military censorship and alerted its censors to watch *Word* closely. Besides being Russia's most-read newspaper, Sytin's daily penetrated the countryside to an unusual degree, and it was the villages that provided most of the conscripts for the Tsar's army.

That September the head of the Chief Administration of Press Affairs summoned Rumanov to his office in the capital, showed him orders from the Russian High Command on press policy, and directed him to convey their sense to Sytin and the editors at *Russian Word*.[1] In only two months, he complained, *Word*'s reporting had aided the enemy. He was a "friend of the paper," but unless it changed, he would clamp down hard. There was no excuse for advance information about military operations, and henceforth no stories could predate the relevant official communiqués.

By October the military censorship had imposed still stricter rules and singled out Sytin's *Word* for more criticism. Two censors would now read the military commentaries and everything else in the paper related to the war. They were also to weigh the effect of stories on the civilian population and to reject anything that seemed "depressing." With respect to naval matters, *Word* was henceforth strictly to confine itself to official releases.[2]

Back came complaints from the editors of *Word*. Clearance of stories by the Moscow military censorship, they said, sometimes took hours, and often came too late to permit publication the same day. Now that the press run had climbed over 500,000, they faced even earlier deadlines. Why, they asked, must dispatches undergo censorship both in the field and in Moscow?[3] (Local censors attached to the Moscow Telegraph Agency [MTA] reviewed each dispatch as it arrived by wire.) Since some of the fault for delay and flawed copies of the news wires lay with MTA itself, Sytin had his editors complain to telegraph officials too.[4] They also resubmitted his request, first made in 1913, for a telegraph line directly into his newsrooms, but the government barred any changes in its censorship arrangements. *Word* would not get a direct line until 1917, when the Provisional Government took power,[5] so Sytin meanwhile hired his own courier to and from the MTA office: a rider on a white horse whose galloping rounds reminded Muscovites that his daily went to extra lengths to keep them immediately informed.

As Russia suffered defeat after defeat to the seventy German divisions at the front, government efforts to control the news became more intrusive, and in July 1915, Sytin's editors received a copy of a telegram from the General Staff at the Supreme High Command to the minister of the interior (whose responsibilities included the press): "It is necessary that unofficial articles be widely circulated in the press to prepare public opinion for a possible [German] offensive ... in the Warsaw military district."[6] An example of what *Word* should print came in August when the General Staff asked all papers to publish the saga of the heroic death in combat of peasant Stephen Veremchuk.[7]

By as early as June 1915, however, Sytin's editors had already begun to slant war coverage in an optimistic, even a misleading way.[8] To outsiders the shift was too slight to detect, and a military censor would still complain to his superior in August that Sytin's *Word* was "playing into the hands of German propagandists, who seek by all means to lower popular morale in Russia."[9] But morale could hardly be high as the predicted German offensive drove the Russian army out of Galicia and western Poland. In 1915 alone the Russian army suffered two million casualties. Late that year a grief-stricken Sytin received word that one of them was his son Vladimir.[10] His two older sons, Nikolai and Vasily, were past the age of serving, but namesake Ivan, aged twenty-nine, must have helped the war effort in some capacity. Sytin had mixed feelings that Peter, then twenty-two, had remained abroad in the land of the enemy (where he had gone in 1913), but he rightly expected his only other son, twenty-year-old Dmitry, to enter the imperial army (as he would in 1916). To make a personal sacrifice of his own, Sytin gave his country estate to the Red Cross for use as a hospital.[11]

Sytin had strong private reasons, then, for rallying behind the flag. And in September of 1915, whether at his specific direction or not, two reporters and an illustrator from *Word* went to the front to focus wholly on the bravery of Russian soldiers. The objective of the entire staff, Blagov told the minister of war, was to build "popular morale and the highest patriotism" by emphasizing the "heroic feats" of Russia's fighting men.[12] In turn he stressed to the Moscow Press Committee that *Word* stood first among Moscow newspapers in its compliance to military censorship.[13]

Only a month later, however, Doroshevich wrote a series of articles for *Word* that implicitly laid blame for the desperate suffering of civilians in the Western territories on both Russia's foes and Russia's leaders. To report the most compelling story of his career, Doroshevich had travelled from Moscow in his own automobile to meet the tide of humanity forced eastward by the guns of the enemy and by the misguided scorched-earth policy of imperial officers. He told how these millions had disastrously overtaxed what little the government had to offer of food and shelter. An English translation of the articles would appear in New York and London the next year as a book, *The Way of the Cross*. Its introduction summarizes what Doroshevich had seen and reported to *Word*: "At first he met sparse survivors and first comers, those who were furthest ahead in the procession; afterwards they came thicker and thicker till they were a great moving wall. He tells how they camped in forests, how they died by the way, how they put up their crosses by the side of the road, how they sold their horses and abandoned their carts, how they starved, how they suffered. The words speak for themselves."[14]

II

Meanwhile at his book plant, Sytin had been churning out propaganda on behalf of the war effort since the start of the conflict. He was, after all, an old hand at turning a profit on war-related broadsheets. In 1914, using the illustrations of N.I. Roerich and others, he had issued the first of what would be millions of patriotic posters – a prime example being Roerich's most widely circulated drawing, "The Enemy of the Family of Man," which portrayed the German Emperor William II as a scaley, reptilian creature holding a skull in each hand next to the names of cities that his army had conquered.[15] In predictable contrast, Sytin graphically idealized Nicholas II and his devout subjects, and one such poster shows the calm, wise Tsar of Russia surrounded by leaders of the other Entente countries, all in small scale. In another, a regimental priest proved that God was on Russia's side: armed only with the icon of the Miraculous Saviour, he was persuading some Austrians to lay down their guns.

From illustrator D. Moor, Sytin bought depictions of real acts of Russian heroism. Moor's poster of a soldier bearing a wounded officer to the Red Cross dressing station, for one, depicts the heroic four-mile trek of "Private David Vyzhimok under strong enemy fire"; and "Women at War" shows Nurse Korokina attending the wounded while gunfire from Germans in the distance riddles the Red Cross flag overhead.

But in "German Atrocities," also by Moor, Sytin spread classic propaganda with all its emotive excesses. Here Moor portrays the Germans as methodic sadists who wanted "new colonies both for the profit of their trade and for the distribution of excess population." The text then goes on to excoriate the enemy's arrogant "conviction that 'Germany is over all,' that only Germans are truly cultured people, that other peoples are merely trash, not deserving notice. And so the Germans ... torture and shoot peaceful inhabitants, carry men into captivity, dishonor women, rob, send property to Germany, and destroy the masterworks of art." In vivid colour, German soldiers are shown as barbarians, one impaling an infant on a bayonet and another shooting a priest.

Besides this propagandistic support, Sytin in 1914 showed the government another co-operative sign by not contesting its suit against one of his publications – the only such instance on record. The book was Kornei Chukovsky's *The Poetry of the Future Democracy: Walt Whitman*, which, like Tolstoy's *Circle of Reading*, contained pacifistic ideas. By not sending a company lawyer to the 1914 trial, Sytin conveyed tacit agreement that the book should be destroyed, as the Moscow Court of Appeals was to rule.[16]

III

At *Word* Sytin and his editors had been in agreement all along about backing courageous soldiers and civilians. Although they stopped short of printing nothing but praise for the Tsar and his government, they did restrain their criticism of the autocracy in these initial years of the war. Unstinting support is what officials most wanted from *Word*, however, and the highest in rank among them tried a new form of pressure early in 1916. Thus it was that Sytin, for at least the second time in his life, found himself face to face with the reigning Tsar of Russia.

Sytin visited the Tsar in Minsk, White Russia, where Nicholas was headquartered after assuming the post of commander-in-chief of the army in September 1915. Sytin arrived there on 12 February 1916 for his audience two days later. In the memoirs he intended for publication by the Soviets, Sytin gives two reasons for his trip. First, before his own death, he wanted to see the man who had sent millions of Russians to theirs. He had to act quickly, he suggests, because he knew that Nicholas would not be ruling much longer. Saying he believed at the time that a great popular upheaval was in the offing, Sytin considered it "evident to the experienced eye ... [that] this bloody insanity ... would not end with good result, that exasperation was growing among the people and that all the state fastenings of the old monarchy were giving way and could not hold."[17] As his second reason, Sytin said he hoped to enlist Nicholas's support to help advance his old dream of improving education for the Russian people.

Sytin also tells that, as he boarded the train for Minsk, he encountered an old acquaintance, Father George Shavelsky, chaplain of the forces. After justifying his trip as a way "to find out what the Tsar is thinking and how he looks upon matters," Sytin says he got the impression that Shavelsky thought him a nuisance to pester Nicholas so needlessly. Then, for the second time in this account for Soviet eyes, Sytin implies that it was he who instigated the journey: he credits Boris Sturmer, the prime minister since January, with getting him the necessary clearance - but merely in response to Sytin's casual request.

When, at last, he stood waiting in the appointed room to meet Nicholas, Sytin says he felt only trepidation.

> The door opposite opened quietly and the Tsar walked in. In a conventional officer's uniform ... in high boots ... his hair already touched with grey.
>
> I said something confusedly and indistinctly. My speech was so strange I heard

> my own words with surprise, words I somehow managed to blurt out, and I awaited a reply, awaited the words that were as necessary to throw to me as if they were a life preserver. But there were no words. The Tsar stood, listened, and was silent.

Sytin ventured more words: "My business, your majesty, is the publication of books for the people." Then, as the Tsar remained mute, he plunged on to tell that he had much earlier approached both Pobedonostsev and Witte with a plan for educating the people, but neither would help. He quotes Nicholas's reply: "This is a great pity, I do not agree with Pobedonostsev or Witte. I will check on it ..." At this point, continues Sytin, the Tsar extended his hand and ended the audience, and Sytin claims to have left the room perplexed. Except for those few final words, "Why so long, so agonizingly long, had [the Tsar] remained silent?"[18]

Father Shavelsky left an account of the same trip. His recollections square with Sytin's in fundamental details: the advance interview with Sturmer, the meeting of Sytin and Shavelsky on the train, and the Tsar's approval of Sytin's wish to advance education. But Shavelsky adds a great deal more.[19] Well before Sytin's trip, states Shavelsky, Sturmer had decided to fight mounting criticism of the government through a new propaganda agency and, with five million rubles in hand from the Tsar, he had asked Sytin to head it. The chaplain continues:

> However flattering it was for Sytin to have the friendly attention and confidence of the President of the Council of Ministers, cautious reasoning dominated his feelings. Sytin understood that to join Sturmer would mean the death knell of his business and would mean giving up everything he had worked all his life to achieve. Sytin, however, did not wish to give an outright refusal and thereby sunder his relations with Sturmer.

When the publisher hedged, recalls Shavelsky, "Sturmer understood this subterfuge of Sytin, just as he also understood that for all his liberalism Sytin was fully a Russian *muzhik* for whom one tsarist word was sufficient and he would fulfill any command." Informing Sytin only after the fact, Sturmer arranged the meeting with the Tsar, along with a compartment in an official railway car and a first-class hotel room in Minsk. Thus it was, says Shavelsky, that he and Sytin met aboard the train.

In conversation, Sytin confessed his problem with Sturmer and said that he would have to give the Tsar a refusal. Shavelsky says he protested: "What if the Tsar upon greeting you requests that you take the matter in hand, or says that your agreement has been reported to him and thanks you. What will you do then?"

Shavelsky offered a way out. He promised to see the Tsar at once and put in a "good word" - that is, tell Nicholas that Sytin would agree to fund a new school at the imperial palace outside St Petersburg to instill religion and patriotism in Russia's future leaders. Because he did so, claims Shavelsky, Sytin heard not a word about a new propaganda agency but, rather, got a school that he had wanted, and Nicholas had congratulated himself on shaking funds loose from one of Russia's millionaires.

A third account comes from M.K. Lemke, who was then serving at military headquarters as a censor. It appears in his book, *250 Days at Military Headquarters*, as an entry for 14 February 1916 and begins:

> Today at 10 a.m. Sytin presented himself to the Tsar. He received him in his study, standing, ... [and] the entire reception lasted 15 minutes. The Tsar said he knew of his work as publisher of *Russian Word* and he hoped that he would continue to "work on behalf of God, Tsar, and Fatherland." Sytin answered as one usually does in such cases but added that he was happy that the Sovereign fully sympathized with enlightenment.[20]

Lemke officially timed the interview and either listened in as part of his duties or jotted down what he learned from Sytin or Nicholas. His account continues that Sytin told the ruler that he felt it pointless to produce books for the people in the old Slavonic language; the Tsar agreed but thought, on the other hand, that the educational ideas of Leo Tolstoy went too far in a populist direction. Lemke concludes: "Sytin was in a frock coat. Voeikov [the Imperial adjutant] had recommended tails to him, but the cunning fox did not want to be taken for a member of the intelligentsia [for whom Nicholas had a well-known dislike]."

While Lemke says the Tsar asked that *Russian Word* back the regime, Sytin, in his very different version of the interview, emphasizes that Nicholas uttered only a single sentence that in no way suborned the publisher. Nor does Sytin mention that *Word* continued to reserve harsh judgment about the autocracy for another eight months, although it did so for many more reasons than any direct appeal from the Tsar.

By far the biggest worry was getting enough paper, and well before seeing the Tsar, Sytin had expressed fears of "paper hunger."[21] The soaring price - up four-fold in recent years - reflected the short supply, and Lemke, just after describing the meeting of the Tsar and Sytin, goes on to remark on the advantage of this very shortage to the government. "It is curious that the restrained tone of the great papers, especially *Russian Word*, with its 600,000 subscribers [619,500 in 1914; 655,300 in 1915; 739,000 in 1916], depends on the fear that the government will subject it to paper starvation – by surreptitiously holding up the delivery of paper from Finland." *Russian Word*, he noted, "follows its [non-antagonistic] line very discretely."[22]

Not surprisingly, only two months later, on 16 April, Sytin carefully chose his words when speaking to some thirty business leaders because he would rightly have assumed that an informant for the Okhranka was present. The group he addressed was the War Industries Committee (WIC) organized by businessmen in Moscow, as in a number of cities, to help the foundering government to manage the war-ravaged economy. Officials distrusted the WICs, fearing that they would use the war crisis to bring in constitutional government, a goal that many of them held.

Sytin favoured a larger role for able businessmen in politics and government, but on this day he warned his audience against an alliance with the "intelligentsia-politician theoreticians" who styled themselves as leaders of the workers' movement. These activists, once the war was won, would go "hand-in-hand with the workers and the revolutionaries" toward a goal fatal to businessmen. To level living costs they "will begin to determine prices, to dictate obligations, to introduce a new order of things" – in other words, "brew the stew" of socialism that "one will never get out of." Because Sytin must have known that persons in the room had for two years sought to find common ground with left-wing parties, his words help to confirm that he had no sympathies for such collaboration.[23]

Having just been elected in February as a director of the Russian Union of Trade and Industry, Sytin spoke with authority, and foremost on his mind was rallying his colleagues into independent rather than dependent political activism. Their business skills, he felt, especially equipped them for dealing with affairs of state. As he later wrote, "among the merchants, it seemed to me, were more creativity and more administrative elasticity than in the gentry, and it had long since been time for this fresh, new force to be more involved in political affairs." Sytin wanted the younger men in the ranks to do what he for many reasons had never done: rise to positions of power within the government.

Among those from his class who should have been national leaders of stature, he thought, was A.V. Krivoshein, who had married into the wealthy Morozov family and enjoyed its political support. Krivoshein, who had favoured negotiations with the liberals in the Duma to establish a "ministry of confidence" in 1915, had been passed over the previous year for the post of prime minister when the Tsar chose old bureaucratic loyalist I.I. Goremykin. He had then stayed on as minister of agriculture until running afoul of Rasputin in November 1915.

Much earlier Sytin had had high hopes for a businessman a decade younger than himself: the heir to the Morozov industrial empire, Savva T. Morozov. Lacking the "powerful black earth strength" of his father and grandfather, however, Savva had "passed his short life warming himself at [the] fires" of artists he admired.[24]

Later in 1916 Sytin threw down the gauntlet himself by trying to prod the Moscow merchants into volunteering 10 per cent of their profits to provide millions of rubles for an Army of National Salvation to beat back the Germans. At a meeting of the Moscow Merchants' Society, he summoned the "children of Mother-Moscow" to make genuine sacrifices, "in the name of the Lord God, Justice, atonement and witness," to replicate the heroic national effort of 1812 when every Russian devoted his energies to expelling Napoleon's army. But Sytin wholly failed with his extravagant, religious-like crusade, despite starting off with a 100,000-ruble donation of his own.[25]

These patriotic appeals, undoubtedly genuine, would not have hurt Sytin at a time when he was seeking not only more newsprint but also a smaller tax bill from the government. His bid for reduced taxes in 1916 stemmed from the government's estimate that Sytin's book inventory was worth 2.25 million rubles at the close of 1915. Sytin set a much lower figure. For years, he pointed out, he had been storing all his unsold books and many had sharply depreciated in value. Nicholas Sytin and M.T. Soloviev, in a company brief, argued that the war "upsets all calculations" - an open admission that neither side could set figures accurately.[26]

IV

About ninety days after Sytin's chat with Nicholas II, the editors of *Russian Word* proposed an orchestrated propaganda plan somewhat like the one the government was already urging. On 7 May they sent V.V. Filatov to military headquarters to recommend that *New Times*, *Stock Market Bulletin*, *Speech*, *Russian Bulletin*, and *Russian Word*, the papers most closely read in Russia and western Europe, conspire together to mislead both the Russian people and the Central Powers. Through their co-ordinated publication of false stories, Filatov explained, the papers could divert enemy troops from points targeted for attack and also "calm the mood of Russian society." Then emerged the one term that makes the whole proposal, which was considered and then rejected at high levels, seem an audacious ploy: the requirement that Russian military leaders keep the conspiring papers fully informed on the true state of military affairs.[27] Sytin's editors had set an impossible price in asking the government to share state secrets with the press.

Later in May the commander of the Moscow Military District would question the motives of these same editors when he read about Rasputin in *Russian Word.* Censorship rules clearly forbade any mention of this Siberian peasant so widely disliked for his links with the Tsarina Alexandra Fedorovna, but here was a story chronicling his movements under a heading, "Rasputin's Trip." On 2 June the commander ordered that not even the name of Rasputin appear in print because of its adverse effect on morale.[28]

As public respect for the imperial family fell, it so happened that Sytin was tasting international acclaim, first through a story that June on the pages of the *New York Times* in connection with his fiftieth year in publishing. *Times* correspondent Montgomery Schuyler described Sytin as a "typical Moscow businessman, selfmade, shrewd, and wide awake with only a limited education."[29] Although he must have used a translator, Schuyler also praised Sytin's "speech of the people" – "crisp, sharp sentences, each full of thought and epigrammatic, with the shrewd native wit of the real Russian."

During their conversation Schuyler asked Sytin to jot down whatever he would most like to say to Americans, and a translation of that message provided the last paragraphs of Schuyler's article. Here Sytin told how Russian peasants had won their freedom fifty years before, only to sink lower. On cheap vodka, he explained, "... they drank themselves into insensibility, without ever sleeping it off, flinging away all their earnings. The village grew wild and poor ... life passed in scuffling and ugliness. The school played no role, gave no real learning; children of from nine to twelve scarcely learned to read at all. [Some] books were proscribed, making reading a dangerous matter." Sytin said that his firm had consequently organized six thousand pedlars to get good books into the villages, but, now that Russia was "on the eve of a complete reconstruction, ... we call on the United States." American investors should, for one thing, help fund a paper-manufacturing plant. "If cultured and skilled America will join hands in common work ... it will perform a great and worthy undertaking." Books were for Sytin the instrument of real liberation, and to him the major issue of the day, after the war, was the education of the peasants.

Views like these were meanwhile being readied for Russian readers by Sytin in a special 1916 volume to mark his fifty years in publishing – *A Half-Century for the Book*, which he would distribute during his jubilee celebrations of February 1917. The lavish, 610-page work served in itself to demonstrate the technical accomplishments of Sytin & Co. and to convey his reverence for books. Despite material and labour shortages, Sytin had it printed on the finest stock and ordered photographs of everyone of some importance, along with multi-coloured lithographs of paintings and drawings, many pasted in by hand. Alongside tributes from associates and persons of renown, he entered a memoir of his own. One clear purpose was to answer all those who had called him a monopolist or an opportunist - or worse.[30]

V

What Sytin had built from nothing in fifty years was a publishing enterprise that constituted a major presence in Russia. On the eve of the February revolution, a full quarter of all the books printed in the tsarist empire came from presses owned by Sytin. No other newspaper in the country came close to his *Russian Word* in readership.

Classic formulas of capitalism had furthered Sytin's success. First of all, he had persistently reinvested his earnings, trimmed his outlays, met essential obligations, and earned excellent credit ratings. More funds in turn had become readily available from Russia's leading banks, and even from the bankers themselves. Secondly, Sytin made "protective" expansions into such related manufactures as paper and oil in order to gain sure sources of essential supplies. Thirdly, Sytin revelled in taking risks, launching new projects, aiming high - all the while confident of the rightness of his course. He believed what he said about enlightening Russia.

Across the heart of Moscow lay the axis of Sytin's publishing empire. At one end stood the five-storey printing plant of *Russian Word* built in 1904 on Tverskaia Street at Strastnaia Square within sight of the Kremlin. Marking the other end, at a point across the Moscow River to the south of the Kremlin and about equidistant from the centre of the city was his great book publishing plant on Piatnitskaia Street. (Both sites are focal points of Soviet printing and publishing today.)

With its jumble of large and small structures, Sytin's book publishing plant was a Moscow landmark. It straddled the line between two commercial sectors: the industrial region still farther to the south, and the merchant district along and near Piatnitskaia Street, an old, curving thoroughfare densely lined with square shop buildings and an occasional church or courtyard to break the monotony.

Eleven years after moving to the Piatnitskaia site in 1879 Sytin had built what came to be known as the "old building." Architect A.E. Erikson designed the next two important structures: the great four-storey "factory" which was partly gutted by fire in 1905 and the more compact five-storey building facing Valovaia. Near the back of the property stood the two-storey machine shop and a four-storey warehouse mainly for paper. Facing the factory, well enough away to form a courtyard, were a three-storey apartment building for personnel and a house for the company's technical director. Several smaller buildings housed a dispensary, library, and cafeteria - all run by the workers.

Beneath the courtyard was a large generating room containing three boilers to produce steam for electricity. Underground tunnels connected the buildings to expedite the moving of paper from the warehouse to the presses and of finished publications to the cutting, binding, packing, and shipping areas. On a property slightly removed from Piatnitskaia Street was a storehouse, formed from two buildings acquired in 1914, which housed a stable for horses, a garage for company automobiles, and rooms for the drivers needed night and day. Sytin had also before the war erected a large new building on Maroseika Street near the centre of Moscow to add a bookstore, business offices, and more warehouse space.

Workers and clerical staff at the complex levelled off at a peak of 1,725 each year from 1913 through 1915. War conditions and production cuts lowered their number in 1916 by 432, or better than 25 per cent, but just over one hundred would be restored to the payroll in 1917. The printers at Piatnitskaia were the famous Sytintsy, the militant vanguard of the Moscow workers' movement that grew and solidified in the industrial district where the plant stood.

Printers at the newspaper plant on Tverskaia, in contrast, saw themselves less as industrial workers and more as necessary adjuncts to the editorial staff of *Word*. Part of the reason was their wholly different milieu, a good distance from the Piatnitskaia plant in a district of urbane theatres, restaurants, and speciality shops, the perfect setting for reporters and editors addicted to food and drink once the paper was in bed.

In another corner of the city Sytin employed three hundred inmates of the Moscow City Jail in a bookbinding shop overseen by the jail administration. Whether the shop was a philanthropic effort to rehabilitate criminals or a source of cheap labour, Sytin, ever the Russian modernizer, made a point of installing the very latest technology.

Equipment in all his shops usually met that standard, and Sytin professed great pride in his workers' quickness to adapt to the West's most advanced machinery, mainly German made.[31] Of the twenty-three rotary presses in his plants in 1916, fifteen came from the German firm of Koenig and Bauer, three from Marinoni, the premier French manufacturer, and two from Albert & Co. of England. His typesetting machines included twenty German-made typographs (six at his book plant and fourteen at *Russian Word*), seventeen American-made linotypes (all at *Word*), and six English-made monotypes.[32] Sytin dreamt of one day manufacturing such devices himself, but in the meantime he shopped in the world's most advanced market. Paralleling his mechanical improvements, Sytin upgraded his workers. He singled out one of his best stereotypers, V.P. Frolov, for example, to train at the advanced printing plant in St Petersburg where the government printed its own documents. Frolov later became head of the mechanical operations at the Piatnitskaia plant.[33]

Across Moscow and beyond, the company owned a number of sales outlets for its publications. In its home city, besides a dozen scattered shops and stalls, it operated four large stores: at Ilinsky Gate, on Nikolskaia Street, on Maroseika Street, and at the offices of *Russian Word*. Still other company bookstores served Petrograd, Kiev, Warsaw, Kharkov, Ekaterinburg, Rostov-on-Don, Odessa, Voronezh, Irkutsk, and Sofia, Bulgaria.

Expanding its interests well beyond the Piatnitskaia-Tverskaia axis continued to be company policy right through the war, a time when Sytin & Co. used capital to buy into other, probably faltering publishing companies. The value of outside shares grew from 19,000 rubles in 1914 to 2,193,000 rubles by the end of the 1916 fiscal year.[34] In 1916 Sytin bought the Moscow Company for Publishing and the Press from N.L. Kaznetsky and became chairman of its board and co-publisher of its *Early Morning* (*Rannoe utro*) and *Evening News* (*Vechernye novosti*).

Also in 1916, about October, Sytin made his biggest penetration into Petrograd with the purchase of a controlling interest in the A.F. Marks Company, his old competitor for the posthumous edition of Tolstoy's works. Sytin acquired 308 out of 400 outstanding shares, installed himself as chairman of the board, and made directors of two of his own men, Rumanov and Frolov. For making financial arrangements, the Russo-Asiatic Bank charged Sytin a commission of 15,000 rubles and then discounted the promissory note he needed. At the end of the 1916 fiscal year, Sytin & Co. had bank loans for 1,650,000 rubles at 6 per cent annual interest.[35]

Shortly before he signed the Marks deal, Sytin wrote Rumanov about the expected purchase and his hopes for the postwar era. The "reconstruction of all primary education" would create "demands for tens of millions of school and library books and teaching aids." He wanted not only the Marks Company but also two other eminent firms: Enlightenment, and Brockhaus & Efron.[36] In addition, vowed Sytin, the company would open "a great political paper in Petrograd and from here will develop papers in all the most important cities of Russia." Offering familiar phrases, he swore that his was "the greatest moral happiness and spiritual joy to see, to feel, to serve the great popular awakening from brutish darkness to enlightened understanding of the joy of life."[37]

In buying the Marks Company, Sytin was once again buying prestige. For all the charges of philistinism and superficiality against him, no one could question the immensity of his operations, and, four months after the *New York Times* story, Sytin was singled out in *The Times* of London as "the greatest publisher in Russia and one of the greatest in the world."[38] That comment appeared in a special supplement about Russia on 28 October 1916 and was written by correspondent R. Wilton, an Englishman who had grown up in Russia and become a friend of Sytin.

VI

This same Wilton, during one of their encounters about this time, urged Sytin to pay a call on Rasputin, whom he considered "an extraordinarily original man." Claiming already to know enough peasants, Sytin initially denied any interest, but then reconsidered and asked Rumanov to arrange a meeting. In Rasputin Sytin encountered a Russian peasant gone to seed: "A white shirt worn outside his trousers, blue trousers, felt boots ... Hair combed in peasant fashion, with a part in the middle, pasted down by grease. A large man, shaggy, with a black beard, a belt around his stomach. General impression: a *muzhik* holidaying from work, a loafer well-satisfied with prosperity and manor house delicacies."[39]

When Rasputin asked why he had come, Sytin replied, "Brother, I merely wanted to take a look at you ... to see an intelligent and important *muzhik*." But when Sytin asked Rasputin if he truly had the "persuasive power" in "affairs of importance" often ascribed to him, Rasputin had protested sharply: "You are all fools and nothing more. What do you want from me?" Then, with grudging pride, he added: "Well, various women folk, cunning bureaucrats, and even ministers come to see me." Rasputin ended the conversation by offering to drop in on Sytin in Moscow. Sytin declined and departed, dismayed at the influence of this cunning countryman, a type he knew well among his pedlars.

Perhaps Rasputin, as is widely believed, had a hand in an appointment that September that affected Sytin – the naming of a member of the Duma from the Octobrist party, A.D. Protopopov, as minister of the interior. Nicholas mainly wished to make a conciliatory gesture to the Duma, by appointing one of its own. Protopopov, in turn, wanted to succeed where Sturmer had failed, in getting Sytin's help with pro-government propaganda. Protopopov's means was a new daily newspaper of "progressive orientation" named *Russian Will* (*Russkaia Volia*), backed by Russia's top bankers and the government and edited to promote imperial policies.[40] To gain credibility the paper ostensibly would be independent.

M.M. Gakkebush (Gorelov), the conservative who had edited *Russian Truth* for Sytin in 1904–6, took on the editorship of *Russian Will* and began to line up well-known writers, Ivan Bunin and A.V. Amfiteatrov among them. Leonid Andreev agreed to edit the literary, critical, and theatrical departments of the paper, fully convinced, because no one interfered with his sections, that the daily was an independent organ.

Gorky, who deplored Andreev's participation and who announced publicly that he would have nothing to do with the paper, reported in October that Gakkebush had "embarrassed" Sytin by asking him to collaborate with Protopopov. "According to rumours, [Gakkebush] is very apprehensive over the success of the future paper. He is promising Sytin the earth - up to 20 millions." Gorky noted that Sytin had kept his distance and was warning off others. "Sytin, it seems, is undertaking his own paper in Petrograd." Gorky understood that Sytin wanted him for the planned daily but rightly doubted it would ever materialize.[41]

Gorky had never given up starting his own Petrograd daily, and when the first issues of *Russian Will* appeared that November, he redoubled his efforts to round up backing. Near the end of the month he thought he was about to sign a deal with Sytin and some others when Sytin suddenly doomed the venture by dropping out. As Gorky told his wife: "It seemed that everything was ready, and suddenly everything went to pieces. That damned Sytin does not let himself get caught, like a fish."[42] Gorky would finally start a daily called *New Life* (*Novaia Zhizn*) five months later, and it would be one of only two private papers that Lenin would briefly tolerate after the October Revolution.

Economic and political factors had probably caused Sytin to withdraw his support for *Ray*. He had just paid a high price for majority interest in the Marks company (thereby acquiring the rights to Gorky's complete works) and for its *Tilled Field*, the weekly he had wanted since 1901.[43] Even more reason for backing away from a firebrand daily, however, was the ominous confrontation then going on between the Duma and the government that was making Nicholas II appear fatally incompetent. Although he consistently refused to back extremist factionalism like Gorky's, Sytin had already permitted *Russian Word*, earlier that fall, to align with the so-called Progressive Bloc, a coalition of moderate and centrist parties who were pressing the government to share power with the then-recessed Duma. *Word* endorsed the Bloc's call for constitutional concessions and full recognition of the Duma as the people's legitimate representative body.

As principal strategist for the Bloc and leader of the Constitutional Democratic Party, Paul Miliukov had some hope for the Duma when it reconvened in mid-October, but he also feared that the deepening popular discontent, mainly directed against the tsarist government, could rebound against the assembly. Therefore on 1 November he sought to distance the Duma from the government in what is known as his "stupidity or treason" speech. Indicting mismanagement in high places, he even implicated the Tsarina and Rasputin by quoting in German (to avoid the chair's ruling him out of order) critical reports from the Austrian press.[44] When military censors forbade publication of the speech, *Word*'s major writers – Doroshevich, S.V. Iablonovsky, B. Veselovsky, and Petrov (reinstated as a correspondent when the war depleted the staff) – still conveyed the substance of the chamber speeches against tsarist ineptness. Other writers chronicled the crisis in stories about breakdowns in the city's generating system, shortages of food and fuel, and transportation snarls that kept supplies from reaching major cities.

After the Miliukov speech, Nicholas replaced Sturmer on 10 November with another conservative bureaucrat, A.F. Trepov, who would only briefly serve as first minister. Two weeks later, on 24 November, an unsigned commentary in Sytin's *Word*, "The Voice of the Land," blamed Russia's "dangerous internal crisis" on a "total collapse of authority," but hailed the "genuine renewal ... in the State Duma, which accurately expresses the mood of all Russia." On 14 December *Word* again charged that the "bureaucracy is cracking up completely" and "no one is running the country."

Precise measurement of a newspaper's influence on political events is never possible, but through *Russian Word* Sytin unquestionably played a major role in spreading disaffection with the imperial regime. His daily amplified to millions of readers the idea, widely held among politicians and government leaders, that the autocracy had lost all effectiveness. *Word* also openly demanded the introduction of liberal political institutions – a change that Sytin had favoured, with varying degrees of fervour, for more than a dozen years.

On 17 December Rasputin died at the hands of assassins, and *Word*, among others, gave his demise banner headlines, defying the censors' ban. When Nicholas immediately named the inexperienced Prince N.D. Golitsyn as prime minister, *Word* was to score the change as a "new and natural step in the mournful disintegration of authority."[45] In a long account of the conspiracy against Rasputin, *Word* reported on 20 December that, although no one had yet been arrested, some who took part were "from the highest aristocratic families." Evidence suggested that the scene of the crime was the Petrograd palace of Prince Felix Iusupov, although the assassins had moved the body to the river by automobile. The next day *Word* printed the prosecutor's report, rumours of arrests, six columns about the final days of Rasputin, and samples of his handwriting.

The murder of the Tsarina's seer and confidant was a story tailor-made for a publisher like Sytin – wholly unexpected, sensational, and genuinely important; and Sytin used his daily press runs of *Word*, amounting to well over 700,000 copies, to print every shred of information his multitude of reporters could find. In all of Sytin's fifty years of publishing and two decades of *Russian Word* nothing quite matched it, not even the last days of Tolstoy. And although the death of the palace villain seemed a good thing, the assassination would not restore popular confidence in the government. The stormy revolutionary year lay just ahead, and so did shattering changes for Sytin.

CHAPTER TEN

"Naked I Will Depart"

Just as he marked fifty years of hard work and savoured world rank as a publisher, Ivan Sytin faced the uncertainties of 1917. Russia's costly, inept war with Germany had shattered the economy and further discredited the autocracy, and discontent was unravelling the remnants of order. Sytin celebrated his jubilee anyway and then became witness to two revolutions. The first would dethrone the Tsar; but the second, by foreclosing private business and press freedom, would force Sytin to give up, one by one, all his enterprises. In the radical imposition of socialism, Lenin would have some uses for an old capitalist like Sytin; his successors, none at all.

I

Moments after midnight, on 19 February 1917, a tsarist emissary rang the bell of Sytin's apartment. He brought congratulations from Nicholas II timed to be the first to reach Sytin on the day celebrating his fiftieth year in publishing. And thus began an extravagant jubilee in the midst of strikes and riots over food shortages and general despair over the war.

Tulupov and a seven-man commission had spent a year on arrangements, even to the point of clearing them with unnamed personages in St Petersburg.[1] Now had come the appointed day, chosen to coincide with the fifty-sixth anniversary of the emancipation and to approximate the fiftieth anniversary of Sytin's introduction to the printing press in Sharapov's shop. Although he must have felt some qualms, Sytin could justify so lavish a wartime event both as a confident expression of optimism about the immediate recovery of his country once the war was over, and as a rousing celebration of a first-rate Russian accomplishment – a publishing company built by a penniless, unlettered peasant into one of the largest in the world. Besides, December had brought encouraging peace feelers from the Germans and the death of Rasputin. It was time to look ahead.

That afternoon, accordingly, one thousand guests filled every seat in the great auditorium of the Polytechnic Institute in Moscow. As at all Sytin's observances, a brief program of worship came first, and the cleric's words and prayers praised the courage of stalwart Russia in such troubled times. Seated on stage with the officiating priest were members of the Jubilee Commission; Tulupov, as chairman, invited Sytin and his wife to join them. When the "thunderous applause" that greeted them stopped, Tulupov began the formal tributes.[2]

"Without exaggeration," he said, "in no Russian home, in no school, in no peasant hut is there a corner without some publication issued by Sytin." This entrepreneur of "singular, extraordinarily valuable personal quality" had made the enlightenment of the masses his life work; and, as of that day, Tulupov announced, Sytin was founding a new institution, the Society for Co-operation in the Development of Book Publishing in Russia. Its purpose, he said, was to help "prepare for the time when the agony is over" – a clear reference both to the wracking internal upheaval and to the war. The society, a purely philanthropic venture, was to build a dual-purpose House of the Book (*Dom knigi*), the first of its kind in the world. Its school would teach printers basic through advanced skills, and its shops and laboratories would develop better inks, paper, presses, typesetting machines, and the like.[3] Sytin intended to end the "stagnation and backwardness" of the Russian printing industry. His exemplar was America, whose technical expertise and book production Sytin thought unrivalled anywhere.

Sergei Varshavsky, the attorney who regularly defended Sytin in press cases and who also wrote for *Word*, spoke next. He praised the "colossal energy, intellect, Russian acuity, and great strength" of Sytin, whose production far exceeded that of the two leading German publishers together. In 1913, when Meier had issued 85 million publications and Brockhaus some 60 million, said the attorney, Sytin had published 225 million books and periodicals (this figure did not include newspapers).

After similar words from V.G. Mikhailovsky, the spokesman for the *Word* staff, Tulupov read telegrams from such dignitaries as M.V. Rodzianko, president of the State Duma, who called Sytin "the first citizen of the Russian land"; Paul Deschanel, president of the Chamber of Deputies of France, Russia's ally in the war; and G.E. Lvov, the Kadet politician who would, two weeks later, be named prime minister of the new Provisional Government.[4] Still others personally delivered congratulations.[5]

The guests next assembled at the Praga restaurant, one of the largest and finest in Moscow, for more tributes and a banquet. This time the speakers included Ivan Bunin and the London *Times* correspondent, R. Wilton. Their praise and much else that was said during the fête would reach an even wider audience through *Russian Word*, which, the next morning, circulated a special edition that devoted its principal news pages to the jubilee. Similar coverage filled the next six issues.

Because of its blunt criticism of the autocracy, the most extravagant tribute of all had appeared in *Word* the morning of the celebration without a byline. Its author deplored that the "potential popular power so evident in Sytin, the former *muzhik*, still languishes in a condition of repression under the weight of the prevailing governmental regime." Nonetheless, through "striking persistence" and an "unquenchable thirst for creativity," this "American with a Russian soul" had still done wonders. Sytin had single-handedly introduced the Russian peasant to printed works while the intelligentsia were still pondering the task.

In his own oration to climax the day, Sytin announced at the dinner a second project to accompany his House of the Book. "All my life," he confessed, "has been spent in very large, deliberately commercial work. Much was idealistic, but this idealism accompanied commercial aims." Now having "sufficient means" from fifty years of "capitalistic" work, duty required him to found a "purely altruistic publishing house." Perhaps inspired by the rich American who was loaning his people good books through Carnegie libraries, Sytin was about to transform the Marks publishing house, recently acquired in Petrograd, into a public institution to provide his own fellow Russians with good books.[6]

What Sytin told his evening guests complemented two short autobiographical pieces in *Word* that morning. In one, "From My Past," reprinted from *A Half-Century for the Book*, Sytin professed his deep religious convictions. He there reveres the words spoken by his late friend, F.N. Plevako, when they had worshipped at the Moscow Kremlin as young men. Plevako had then predicted that "the happiest moments of our life we will pass here in this great, holy, and ancient cathedral ... All the rest will be vanity of vanities." In the other, "The Three Stages of Life," Sytin describes his first commercial success during the Russo-Turkish war, his introduction to altruistic publishing through the Tolstoyans and Mediator, and his coming to a fuller understanding of serving the people through his founding of *Russian Word* under the guidance of Chekhov. The illness and death of Chekhov, he said, "was extraordinarily painful, because the relationship with Chekhov was something special. Everything that he proposed, counselled, and told me was sacred. His advice played an enormous role in my life. And now, looking back on my past life, I can say only one thing: 'Forgive me, dear spirit of A.P. [Anton Pavlovich] if I have in any way sinned before you.' ''

Inordinate wealth and the approach of death troubled this believer of low birth at a time when hardships afflicted so many fellow Russians, and – in a trinitarian cast of mind – Sytin was planning yet another benevolent project. He spoke of it to his friend Teleshov in a private conversation just after the jubilee. His one remaining dream was to provide a country retreat for his workers, at no cost to them.[7] He would include a home, school, hospital, theatre, and park. ''You have known me all your life,'' Teleshov quotes Sytin, ''and you know that I came to Moscow, as it were, naked. I don't need anything. Everything is vanity. I have seen the fruits of my work and life, and it is enough for me. I came naked and naked I will depart.'' Then came a confidential vow, both Tolstoyan and Chekhovian: ''I am leaving everything. I am going to a monastery.''[8]

History stalemated Sytin, for all his good intentions. On 27 February his newspaper stopped publishing speeches from the jubilee to report the uprisings in Petrograd, where the army and police had lost control. Three days later Nicholas II abdicated.

After its long but steady decline, the autocracy had failed; but now Sytin was to witness and deplore the continuing breakdown of social stability under the Provisional Government. Rumours, he would later recall, sapped what morale was left: ''From the front, as if an omen to a storm, an unending series of panicky stories spread, each more cheerless than the last.'' Throngs of angry people crowded the streets in search of bread. Supplies fell even further; prices rose yet more. As an ugly hostility against the ''boorzhui'' erupted, hungry citizens resorted to stealing ''fur coats, jackets, even trousers ... Senseless and purposeless shooting occurred on the streets, as though rifles and revolvers started firing on their own with the approach of darkness. The customary foundations of life began to crumble and a grey, dull, evil chaos came to replace order ... With each day the crowds at the shops grew and the faces of the women were angrier and more ominous.''

Convinced that food was the first need of the people, Sytin had once more undertaken a grandiose project: raising three hundred million rubles to buy food in Siberia to feed the hungry of Moscow. Pledging six million of his own, Sytin had next recruited fellow millionaire N.A. Vtorov to help him approach their still-wealthy acquaintances; but, as one more evil sign of the times, his collaborator was shortly murdered by his illegitimate son in a dispute over money. The rest of the Moscow merchantry, on whom he was placing his hopes for the last time, would fail Sytin as well. So lacking were they in ''genuine sympathy and broad decisiveness,'' he would recall, that ''not even brute fear, even the approaching, awful, undoubted danger could force these people to undo their tight purses voluntarily.''[9]

II

Meanwhile, as the press run of his daily approached the million mark Sytin had long sought, *Word*'s editors focused on the politics of the new era. On 3 March, the day after the Tsar abdicated, they exhorted the people to accept the new Provisional Government under Prince G. Lvov. In their opinion, the State Duma (still the fourth one, elected in 1912) had just established, ''in close agreement with the [Petrograd] Soviet of Workers' Deputies, ... the first cabinet [of ministers] invested with the confidence of the country.'' There was hope that the new order just sprung from the people would ensure a stable government.

One day later *Word* detailed the legality of the transition of power. The Tsar had yielded to his brother, the Grand Duke Michael, who had then abdicated to the Provisional Government. The Grand Duke was quoted as saying that the new government could meet the challenges ahead better than he and that a constituent assembly, elected by the people, would reform justly the ''basic law of the land.''

Word in turn printed frequent interviews with officials, with exiles still abroad or just returned to Russia, and with common soldiers and workers, even those aligned with the newly revived soviet of Moscow and its counterparts in outlying cities and towns. (Some of these soviets nonetheless ordered boycotts of Sytin's paper as a ''bourgeois'' organ.) Besides sampling opinion to confirm that most citizens wanted the Constituent Assembly to meet in Moscow, *Word* reporters discredited the old order by digging out secrets from the Okhranka files – among them that the former assistant head of *Word*'s St Petersburg bureau, I.I. Drilikh, had been a police agent.[10]

As *Word* recorded the growing anarchy through spring and summer, the initial optimism on its pages became as blurred as the often illegible words imprinted there, the consequence of unskilled workers and ersatz ink. Another downturn for *Word* was the departure in June of Doroshevich, whose contract had expired in March. He would move to the south the next year on the orders of his doctor.

The new government meanwhile granted press freedom to all factions, including the Bolsheviks, and persisted in the war; but a failed offensive against the Austrians and Germans in July led to Lvov's resignation. The new prime minister, Alexander Kerensky of the Socialist

Revolutionaries, named General Lavr Kornilov as army commander, only to order him arrested in August for leading an aborted military assault on Petrograd to forestall a Bolshevik attempt to seize power.

Lenin, who had returned to Russia from Switzerland in April, had since withdrawn to Finland to avoid arrest. From there he advised the Central Committee of the Bolshevik Party to urge the workers to close "bourgeois" papers that championed the government,[11] and he would several times single out Sytin's *Russian Word* as a prime target. *Word* now had a press run hovering at the million mark, while all the Bolshevik papers together were mounting a daily circulation of about 600,000.

In the long term Lenin planned the "nationalization" of publishing, as of the entire economy, but he made few advance pronouncements about it. In September, however, he did envision that the post-revolutionary state would "seize *all* printing plants and *all* paper and distribute it justly."[12] He also published his misleadingly titled article, "How to Assure the Survival of the Constituent Assembly" (subtitle: "On Freedom of the Press"), there declaring that bourgeois press freedom was freedom only for the wealthy. Private advertisements made such papers succeed - as *Russian Word*, he said, clearly showed.[13]

Concurrently Sytin's *Russian Word* published commentary both supportive and critical of the Provisional Government. On the one hand it backed government goals: "the renewal of order inside the country and of the fighting capacity of the army, and the summoning of the Constituent Assembly." On the other hand it deplored that Russia had "almost no government at all." By seeking to appease the left the new government foolishly allowed the Bolsheviks to circulate propaganda which "undermines the ability of the army and the confidence of our allies in us." Amidst turmoil, the many new local soviets were able to harass, censor, and even to confiscate papers not to their liking, and they had even resurrected licensing.[14]

About this time, in a joint letter to the leaders of the Petrograd and Moscow Soviets, Lenin argued that, "by seizing power and taking over the banks, the factories, and *Russian Word*, the Moscow Soviet would secure a strong foundation and enormous strength."[15] When he elaborated this idea in *Workers' Way* (*Rabochii Put*) that September, Lenin specifically listed large printing plants among the points of power that revolutionaries must seize. It was necessary, he wrote, "to suppress the bourgeois counter-revolutionary papers (*Speech*, *Russian Word*, etc.), to confiscate their printing plants, to declare private advertisements in the papers a state monopoly, to transfer [both the plants and the ads] to the paper published by the Soviets, the paper that tells the peasants the truth."[16]

On 1 October *Word* expressed doubts about the success of imminent elections for the Constituent Assembly: "In another country, not so immense, with a population more cultured and politically developed, the task of organizing a constituent assembly would not present special difficulties. It is another matter in Russia with its almost universally illiterate people, immense spaces, terrible communications, and polyglot population, especially under conditions of war."

Within two weeks Sytin's editors were accurately focusing on the immediate threat posed by the Bolsheviks. Thus on 14 October *Word* inaugurated a daily column called "Toward the Bolshevik Uprising," there accurately reporting that the Bolsheviks, who dominated the main Soviets, were plotting the transfer of power from the Provisional Government to the All-Russian Congress of Soviets at its second session in Petrograd just days away. On the anniversary of the October Manifesto of 1905, *Word* reminded its readers that the long-sought freedoms won twelve years before had disappeared in the tide of reaction that followed. The victory of February 1917 could just as easily be lost because the Bolsheviks were now openly organizing an armed force to back their planned coup d'état.

Then *Word* detailed the actual takeover, reporting on 24 October that the Military Revolutionary Committee of the Petrograd Soviet, under Leon Trotsky, had seized control of the Petrograd Military District. One day later the second All-Russian Congress of Soviets proclaimed itself the sovereign power, and *Word* condemned the coup by the party of Lenin, who was once again in Petrograd. The day after that, the Moscow Soviet closed Sytin's paper and all others in Moscow opposed to the revolution. Authority for the closures came from Petrograd in the 27 October decree of the Congress's Council of People's Commissars. The purpose of the measure, stated the decree, was to "staunch the flow of filth and slander" from the "bourgeois press." New laws, it promised, would restore full "freedom" to all but those publications that incited resistance, disobedience, or dissent by distorting facts.[17]

At once the Moscow revolutionaries faced a problem: the idled newspaper printers had no income. The local soviet consequently offered to let Sytin and the other owners reopen their papers if they would pay full wages for the closure period. Sytin was among those who agreed, and *Russian Word* reappeared on 8 November.

Meanwhile in Petrograd a one-sided debate on press policy had finally taken place on 4 November during a meeting of the executive committee of the All-Russian Congress of Soviets. There, outnumbered two to one by the Bolsheviks, the Social Revolutionaries vainly insisted that socialism must win support by example and persuasion, not by silencing opposition papers. The Bolsheviks, scorning "antiquated" conventions, countered that to grant any share of the press to the "capitalists" was to abandon socialism, and they easily passed a resolution to that effect.[18] Pending the elections they had long demanded for the Constituent Assembly, however, the Bolsheviks for the moment agreed to tolerate "bourgeois" papers in the two capitals.[19]

When it reopened on 8 November, *Russian Word* continued to criticize the Bolsheviks. Besides printing an attack by Varshavsky, Sytin's attorney, against their press policy, that day's issue called the Bolsheviks "the new autocracy" who would keep power no matter who won the elections to the Constituent Assembly. On 22 November, however, *Word* described the elections as the country's "final hope" against a new despotism. Four days later, when the voting was over and Sytin and his editors rightly assumed that Lenin's party had won a minority of seats, *Word* once again called on the citizenry to fight for democracy and even to arm itself to defend the Constituent Assembly. But this was Sytin's last issue of *Russian Word*, for Lenin, in Petrograd, had ordered the militia of the Moscow Soviet to march that night to surprise all unfriendly papers with closure. He likewise stopped all papers in Petrograd but for Gorky's *New Life* and the Social Revolutionaries' *People's Cause* (*Narodnoe Delo*).

Lenin's Moscow lieutenant, A. Arosev, recalls the initial meeting to lay the seizure plan for both Moscow and Petrograd. "Sitting at a table, Lenin moved his great, heavy head from one palm to the other and ... proposed ... first to close the bourgeois papers, to stop them from publishing, and then to sanction this act by decree. Only then, said Lenin, will our decree not hang in the air."[20] As preparations had advanced Lenin had discussed the operation to its "smallest detail" by phone. "Especially worrying him was whether the newspaper people would begin to protest and consider the action of the military authorities, which was a good thing, as arbitrary, for there was still no decree." Thus Arosev was to "occupy all the printing plants simultaneously," using force if necessary, and leave the military in command. All this was essential to meet Lenin's order "that not a single copy of a paper hostile to us will appear."

Arosev continued with the nocturnal invasion he led "at the printing plant of *Russian Word* (where *Pravda* is now printed). A half hour after the start of the operation, the telephone rang at the printing plant." On the line was Lenin, demanding a report each half hour. "And," concludes Arosev, "only when the occupation of the printing plant was complete and the stores of paper seized, there followed the appropriate decree about the closing of the bourgeois papers in the country where the dictatorship of the proletariat had begun." The closure of enemy papers, then, was the first step in the post-election consolidation of power by the Bolsheviks.

On 28 November the Moscow Soviet officially "sequestered" the printing plant of *Russian Word* as its own, having earlier done the same to Sytin's Moscow Company of Publishing and the Press. Although Sytin was permitted to stay on with his wife in their apartment in the Tverskaia building, the newspaper presses that the old publisher so prized would now rumble two floors below him to print the *Izvestiia* of the local soviet.

Sytin's old editorial staff mainly dispersed, some to head south, where they would briefly publish a paper in the Crimea, behind the lines of the Russian Volunteer Army during the civil war; some to stay nearby and twice to attempt a surrogate version of *Word* in Moscow.[21] Blagov, Rumanov, Varshavsky, and Nemirovich-Danchenko were to emigrate to western Europe. Petrov went to Yugoslavia.

With no thought of emigrating and determined to come to terms with the new regime, Sytin caught the train to Petrograd to see Lenin, the top man in the new government. Over the years he had often travelled north to feel out the officials whose decisions affected him, and now at stake was his critically essential right to work. But, despite getting positive assurances from Lenin, Sytin says nothing about them in the memoirs he prepared for publication under Stalin. The reason seems clear: at least two of the promises that Lenin made would be broken once he was gone.

Grandson Dmitry Ivanovich quotes exactly the private record left by Sytin about his exchange with Lenin: "My paper was the first one subject to nationalization ... I did not object and took no measures in order to avoid any misunderstanding. On the day of the declaration of the transfer of the printing plant [evidently 28 November], I went to Petrograd to Smolny [the institute where Lenin had an office]. I called on Vladimir Ilich."

Not knowing that Lenin had made the closing of *Word* a priority and had personally directed its sudden night-time seizure, Sytin asked first about the confiscation of his newspaper plant. Back came Lenin's answer: "Yes, this is the beginning, and all of your businesses will be nationalized." Calmly accepting this eventuality, Sytin then put forth his main concern: whether he ("I am pointing at myself," he inserted in parentheses) would likewise be "nationalized." And Lenin, Sytin claims, replied: "We will not nationalize him, and, if he is not against us, we will permit him to live freely, as he lived before." Reassured, Sytin had returned at once to Moscow to set to work "with all my machines left to me."

Two others have left their recollections of what Sytin later told them about the meeting. Gessen, the first, quotes Sytin as recalling that Lenin "attentively listened to me, came up to me, put his hand on my shoulder and said, 'I am grateful to you. Ivan Dmitrievich Sytin will help us with his great experience and great knowledge.' " Sytin also related that Lenin had promised him lifetime use of his apartment in the *Word* building and a monthly pension of 250 rubles upon retirement. Motylkov, the second, learned from Sytin that Lenin had approved Sytin's completing all of his own publications already in process and had guaranteed him the right to sell them and the inventory he had stored in his warehouses.[22]

Probably at this meeting Sytin presented Lenin with the autographed copy of *A Half-Century for the Book* that was later found in Lenin's library in the Kremlin. And seemingly soon after this meeting, if not then, Sytin signalled his goodwill by contributing seven million rubles to the Soviet treasury, half of the funds in his personal bank account.[23]

III

Sytin remained in place, then, as the director of Sytin & Co., which continued to operate the old Konovalova plant and the main complex on Piatnitskaia Street. The revolutionaries had too many other tasks during their first months in power to take on a full nationalization of book publishing, but they did impose regulations and otherwise intrude.[24] That December the Moscow Soviet seized Sytin's calendars for 1918 (adoption of the "new style" Gregorian calendar was imminent) and barred the distribution of *lubki*, the simple books for the peasants.

Sytin proceeded to strike deals with the new regime. He sent officials his terms on paper bearing his company letterhead, and they addressed their replies to "Sytin & Co." in Moscow. When, in the first months of 1918, the commissar of education, A.V. Lunacharsky, needed a publisher for the "nationalized" works of fifty-seven Russian writers, he hired Sytin.[25]

But Sytin had nothing more to do with newspapers, as he matter-of-factly explained in his Soviet-published memoirs: "In the first days of the new order, the newspaper and the plant where *Russian Word* was printed, in accordance with the decree on the press, were subject to transfer to state control. I submitted: I felt that I would be useful in the affairs of the new order."[26]

After a short-lived protest strike, many of Sytin's press-room and office workers at the *Word* plant had likewise chosen to stay in place as hirelings of the new regime, but the Menshevik sympathizers among them got on badly with their Bolshevik bosses. Plant productivity, already in decline before the October revolution, deteriorated further.

In January 1918 the Bolsheviks fulfilled *Word*'s prediction by closing the Constituent Assembly on its second day. Two months later they made peace with Germany and declared themselves the Communist

Party of the Russian Soviet Federated Socialist Republic (RSFSR) whose capital was Moscow. Their two national dailies, the Congress of Soviet's *Izvestiia* and the party's *Pravda*, moved with them from Petrograd to resettle in the old *Russian Word* plant, where the first Moscow issue of the Congress's *Izvestiia* was printed on 12 March.[27]

Appalled by the shortfalls he found at Sytin's old plant, the secretary of the directorship for *Izvestiia*, V. Iu. Mordvinkin, filed a report on necessary changes. The "unbearably nervous atmosphere in the plant and the crude treatment of supervisors by the printers has to end," he insisted, but he also cited the incompetence of novice workers.[28] Untrained operators were ruining linotype machines through misuse, while "completely inexperienced compositors" were mixing galleys of type for *Izvestiia* with those of another paper[29] - probably the local *Izvestiia*. Under a directive signed by Lenin on 24 March Mordvinkin joined a three-man commission chaired by V.D. Bonch-Bruevich that was to recommend ways to restore efficiency at the "printing plant of *Russian Word* of Sytin & Co." - the state still not having ratified the plant's confiscation by the Moscow Soviet. The commission was also to establish "mutual relations" with the "owners." Lenin wanted Sytin to take charge again but under Soviet authority.[30]

Lenin had precisely spelled out, says Bonch-Bruevich, that the best means to restore plant efficiency was to "attract specialists for each section, although they might be former owners, if they genuinely, conscientiously, and without any ulterior motives agree to take part. It ought to be noted here that Vladimir Ilich was favourably disposed toward Sytin, valuing his enormous scope, his immense organizing talent." Bonch, however, was among the doctrinaire Marxists who scoffed at the argument, repeatedly put forward by Lenin, that the new state needed the expertise of former capitalists. Bonch thus goes on to deplore the blatant self-interest that the commission found in Sytin. This old overlord responded to their offer, says Bonch, by wondering about the obligations "that third persons would place upon him, and he little inquired into the matter of our Soviet publishing efforts." Although Sytin provided "exhaustive information" about operating the plant, Bonch thought that Lenin's "intended role" for Sytin was wrong because of the publisher's age (sixty-seven), his connections with persons hostile to the new order, and his "compromised [status] in the eyes of the workers."[31]

The commission sent its report to the government on 4 April. There Bonch says that, after hearing out "the general guidelines" for the plant and discussing how best to use "his special knowledge," Sytin had assured the commission of his co-operation only to interject conditions. He said he wanted to recover the two oldest rotary presses in the plant in order to settle an obligation to former colleagues; and, in order to buy paper, hire workers, and pay off some notes due 10 April, he asked for yet more of his "sequestered property."[32] The commission duly reported the terms but did not endorse them.

Sytin's bid to recover, in lieu of salary, some of the property the government had taken from him made sense economically. On the one hand new laws had limited all earnings to modest levels, but on the other hand inflation had made Russian currency nearly worthless. Sytin had large deposits in Russian banks, all nationalized, but no citizen could withdraw more than 250 rubles each week; and the state had further eroded Sytin's fortune by voiding all stocks and dividends. Although he still had deposits in foreign currencies safely abroad, Sytin had decided to salvage what he could of real goods – the one commodity of value. The commission, in turn, saw in Sytin's terms the natural greed of a capitalist.

In this same report, the commission assessed conditions at the plant. Because the Mensheviks were once again "interfering in the printing of *Izvestiia*," it recommended that loyal printers and a new plant director be found. Through tables of figures it showed productivity to have fallen "catastrophically" below pre-revolution levels (see appendix 4). Breakdowns delayed and shortened press runs. Typesetting was two and one-half times slower than the pre-revolutionary minimum, and page make-ups took three times longer. Sytin had handed over a plant that was superbly equipped and stocked (the paper alone was worth 3,213,398 rubles), but present maintenance was deplorable. Scattered, ink-soaked waste paper posed a fire hazard, and critical small parts like matrices for linotypes were missing.

The commission concluded that this "painful state of affairs" existed in all the expropriated plants, not just Sytin's on Tverskaia Street. It therefore called for a centralized publishing agency and a state monopoly on the sale of publications and advertisements. It even proposed building a paper plant in the far north, an idea that must have come from Sytin.

Early in April the Council of People's Commissars met to discuss the recommendations. Although Lunacharsky, who had already found Sytin co-operative, spoke in favour of turning the plant back to him and even letting him revive *Russian Word*, the council decided that its Polygraph Section should control all newspaper plants. It therefore confirmed the confiscation of the *Russian Word* plant and "declined" the services of I.D. Sytin.

Sytin's seeming indifference to new realities had annoyed the council and commission. By demanding payment in material goods for the privilege of serving the people, he had missed the chance to redeem himself. A stern lesson awaited. Before the month had ended, this old capitalist faced the straitened circumstances of a criminal; for, without citing specific charges, zealous revolutionaries had had him locked up in the Moscow jail.

Knowing that Gorky had some influence through his daily, Sytin appealed from jail to his old collaborator: "I rely on your generosity and believe that you do not consider me a criminal."[33] By the time Gorky publicized the arrest in *New Life* on 3 May Sytin was again a free man; but Gorky, who published one of the two unofficial papers still permitted, vigorously condemned the detention. France and England recognized the worth of this eminent enlightener of the people, Gorky wrote, but the "freest country in the world" had sent Sytin to jail after ruining his "enormous, excellent, and technically functioning business." Of course, he continued, "it would have been more intelligent and useful for Soviet authorities to have won over Sytin ... to restore our troubled book publishing industry." Their failure to do so was "out-and-out Russian stupidity."[34]

At odds with Lenin and his circle for some years, Gorky would speak out against the Communists only until mid-July when they closed *New Life*. But because he and Lenin did agree that the new state needed Sytin and all manner of dedicated supporters of Russian culture, the two socialists reconciled on that common ground early in September.[35] Later that same month Gorky served as Lenin's emissary to offer Sytin the government's key directorship in publishing. N.D. Teleshov, who was present in the apartment of Gorky's wife, says that Gorky there relayed a request from Lenin that Sytin head the state's centralized publishing agency, Gosizdat, which would open the next May to nationalize the industry. Sytin, says Teleshov, agreed instead to fill the lesser role of assistant if Gorky would be head, but his counter-offer got nowhere.[36]

Remembering his days in jail, Sytin knew that Lenin's support could not in itself guarantee him a secure place in the new regime. Only days before, on 30 August, there had been another, though subtle, sign of Sytin's being in disfavour in an item in *Izvestiia*. A report there had charged the Russian Union of Trade and Industry with embezzling state property and had named Sytin as one of the union founders.[37]

Reflecting some small credit on Sytin was the fact that his youngest son, Dmitry, was now fighting the civil war in the uniform of the Red Army.[38] (Founded the previous January, the Red Army had commenced to battle "counter-revolutionaries" after the German-Soviet peace treaty of March.)

IV

Sytin also felt disfavour in the increasing strictures at his publishing plant. Now, for example, only the state's Central Technical Publishing Company could print technical books. Worst of all, the government in April 1919 placed a national ban on *lubki* (the 1917 ban was local and temporary). Seizing the initiative again on behalf of the peasants, Sytin at once laid plans to instigate a new series of *lubok*-style books to teach ideas favoured by the new regime, and by mid-year he had convinced the Press Section of the Moscow Soviet to recommend his program to the director of the newly opened Gosizdat. In their endorsement, the Press Section insisted that nothing could rival the long familiar *lubki* as the most "accessible" form of reading "for the broad popular masses." Nor could anyone surpass Sytin in producing them and in marketing them through the pedlar system, just reviving as the civil war wound down. Although the old *lubki* often "promoted ignorance, superstition, and prejudice," concluded the endorsement, Sytin's new series would raise the people's aspirations for knowledge and enlightenment."[39]

Lenin's choice to head Gosizdat, however, was V.V. Vorovsky, a single-minded revolutionary who had more important uses for his short supplies of paper, and he rejected Sytin's proposal.[40] Moreover, Vorovsky's purpose was to phase out this old capitalist, not to defer to him. Sytin had yet some time left in publishing, but strictly on Gosizdat's terms. Vorovsky now had the final say about what paper and printing equipment Sytin got, which manuscripts he could print, what prices he could charge, whom he could hire, and what publishing program he could follow.[41] The Press Section of the Moscow Soviet also gave orders, a typical one requiring Sytin to print the Soviet Constitution on his calendars.

What few books and calendars Sytin published as his own had to be sold through state bookstores, but he mostly printed works commissioned and distributed by Gosizdat.[42] A sticking point, however, was Gosizdat's unwillingness or inability to pay. In August 1919, for example, Sytin urgently requested payment for works long since published and delivered so that he could pay a fuel bill of 4.5 million rubles. Soon after he had to request 1.1 million (of the 2.5 million owed by Gosizdat) to meet his payroll[43] - all these huge sums reflecting the rampant inflation.

As for the performance of this sixty-eight-year-old accustomed to chauffeured independence, Sytin calls himself a "responsible fulfiller" of obligations. Each day he left his apartment and walked more than five kilometres to reach his office by 7 a.m. for a full day's work. There he was "obliged" to meet five times a week with a man from Gosizdat "to get instructions on what to print, on quantity, on quality." Sytin, in turn, finished every order on time and "exactly according to Gosizdat's instructions."[44] No fault of his, he wants the readers of his memoirs to understand, gave Vorovsky cause to dismiss him from the Piatnitskaia plant.

But nationalization had been the plan all along, and it is only remarkable that Sytin stayed on as caretaker as long as he did. A capitalist, however dutiful, ill served a sector that shaped opinion. Thus, in December 1919 Sytin walked out of his publishing plant on Piatnitskaia Street for the last time. He could vividly recall the excitement of moving his enterprise to that site just forty years before, but should he ever again return, he would read a new signplate at the complex - "The First Model Printing Plant" - the name that remains today.[45]

Sytin summed up his departure: "[Vorovsky] said that, unfortunately, he could no longer work with me. So we parted." Still nominally the owner of the Marks plant in Petrograd and the Konovalova plant in Moscow, Sytin got not so much as a thanks for forfeiting the immense centrepiece of his life's work.

Still resourceful, Sytin decided to propose a new project to Gosizdat early in 1920. Shortages of paper, machines, and printers, he stated in his application, made it "virtually impossible" to meet the demand for books within the borders of the Soviet state. Sytin therefore asked to go on an official mission to Finland "with the object of organizing there the printing of text books and other cultural-educational works exclusively permitted and approved by Gosizdat and the Commissariat of Education." Sytin thought he might also see about "sending paper to Moscow."[46]

That trip never came about. Although Vorovsky left Gosizdat about this time, a quote from the new director, O. Iu. Schmidt, shows him equally hostile to Sytin: "It grieves me to say it, but this great worker [Sytin] on whom had been placed definite hopes ... is hurting us more than he is helping us."[47] That December Schmidt nationalized another of Sytin's plants, the old Marks complex in Petrograd that Sytin had promised to the people at his jubilee.

Sytin had expected this takeover, but not the one that followed it when Gosizdat used its authority to seize his inventory of books - private assets that Lenin had said Sytin could keep and sell himself. Sytin again appealed to Lenin for help, and he soon recovered not only his books but also the right to sell them privately through antiquarian bookshops still individually owned and through a small bookstore that his son Ivan would be allowed to open in Moscow. Corroboration comes from the memoir of Doroshevich's daughter, Natalia Vlasovna, who visited Sytin briefly about the start of 1921.[48] Then fifteen years old and en route to Petrograd to find her father, she was told by Sytin that he had been promised his earlier published books from the warehouse to sell. He added that he thought things were picking up for him.

As for Natalia herself, she and Doroshevich had been together in the south until the previous May, when he had returned to Petrograd to find his second wife, the actress O.N. Mitskevich. Natalia tells that his name was still on the door of his Petrograd apartment when Doroshevich reached it; but a stranger dressed in his clothes had answered his knock, and Mitskevich, saying that her life had changed because she thought him dead, had refused even to admit him. Instead she made arrangements for Doroshevich to stay in various rest homes, where his health deteriorated.

Somehow Sytin learned of Doroshevich's difficulties and wrote to tell Natalia about them. As soon as she could, Natalia headed north on a series of freezing trains, and the Sytins gave her a cup of coffee and meat pies in their apartment when she reached Moscow. From that encounter, she recalls the Sytins as "generally hardened, reserved, people ... [who] reacted to events from the viewpoint of what advantage they could draw." They seemed to her very well situated in this year of critical famine (they served scarce coffee from a silver pot), and she wondered at their not offering more assistance to her and her father. Besides telling her about the books he would sell, Sytin mentioned that he was working on orders and helping equip the *Izvestiia* plant.

Natalia Vlasovna proceeded on her way, and in cold, dreary Petrograd, she found her father in a squalid clinic. "My poor, elegant handsome father ... lay on an awful bed, fastened to it by the long sleeves of some kind of astonishing night shirt. Next to him sat a grey, tattered old lady feeding him watery barley soup from a rusty, tin saucer. He raised his yellowish, tormented, vacant eyes to me, and said, 'Finally, you have come. Did you bring anything to eat?' " Already beyond recovery, Doroshevich would die the next year.

During her Moscow visit, Natalia had rightly sensed that Sytin was fully engaged in government work, little realizing what a great turnaround was taking place both for Sytin and for the Bolsheviks. By summer the old capitalist would be on his way to Germany on a high-level economic mission for Lenin.

Open evidence of the sea change had come that March when the Tenth Congress of the Communist Party approved Lenin's New Economic Policy (NEP), which sanctioned private property and profit-making. Here was the first step in the government's drive to break out of its diplomatic and economic isolation (caused, in part, by its nationalization without compensation of material assets in Russia owned by foreigners). As another step, Sytin's long-standing plan to win foreign backing for a huge paper plant on the Kem river, was about to be revived. Already the previous December Sytin had been called in by the Chief Administration for Paper Manufacturing to discuss the country's chronic shortage of paper. Eager for greater involvement and perhaps prodded from above, Sytin had proceeded to submit an outline of his Kem project to Lenin with an impassioned plea: "The book is perishing. Save the book." His covering letter went on: "I want to help Gosizdat, but I ask acceptable conditions for carrying out this work which, in the final analysis will benefit the Soviet government."[49] One of his conditions was a trip to Germany to approach potential backers, especially his old contact, the industrial magnate Hugo Stinnes.

Lenin had immediately forwarded Sytin's communiqué to his commissar of foreign trade, L.B. Krassin, who cleared the way for Sytin to go to Germany "for discussions on the question of organizing within the borders of the RSFSR factories for the manufacture of paper."[50] Sytin was to inform German investors about special concessions from his government, which had no funds to compensate them directly.

This was the time, then, when Lenin had chosen to make Germany the starting place for forging relations with western Europe. Fortunately for Sytin, Hugo Stinnes happened to be the leading advocate in Germany of trade agreements with the Soviet state. Because engaging him in a joint project would encourage other Germans to follow his lead, Sytin emerged as a highly valuable broker for Lenin.

Overtures from Moscow to Berlin had commenced on several fronts in the first half of 1921, and trade minister Krassin himself visited Germany shortly before Sytin arrived there in August. Secret joint military talks were also going forward, in part about the Germans' building weapons and munitions factories in the RSFSR that the Versailles treaty forbade them to build at home. The Treaty of Rapallo between the two countries would result in April 1922 and a joint commercial treaty three years later.[51]

Sytin stayed in Germany from 14 August 1921 to 28 January 1922 and was able to be reunited there with his resident son Peter and daughter Evdokia, who travelled from Poland. As for his negotiations, because he very plausibly claims to have succeeded in persuading Stinnes to invest in the Kem project, Sytin must have returned to Moscow in triumph. His success would, however, be short-lived, for Stinnes would fall ill and die in 1923, and his unsympathetic son would refuse to honour the deal that Sytin had forged.

Immediately after his return, the exuberant Sytin had moved on to a venture of his own under NEP: organizing "The Book Company of 1922," with himself as chairman of the board of directors. He formed a partnership with two other Moscow publishers, V.V. Dumov and M. and S. Sabashnikov, and, by necessity, with Gosizdat. To finance this socialist-capitalist venture, he showed he still had considerable wealth by retrieving from abroad thirty thousand dollars of his own funds. The ban on *lubki*, however, meant he could not publish his specialty.[52]

When *Izvestiia* interviewed him about the company in September 1922, Sytin optimistically described Gosizdat's willingness to put private publishers "on their feet."[53] Under the arrangement, his company would print some books for Gosizdat on a contractual basis and have the right to wholesale its own titles through Gosizdat, the lone large-scale bookseller.

At last, two years after he had described his intentions to the writer E. Lundberg, Sytin had achieved a publishing "syndicate," although one much smaller than he had hoped for. His aim, he had told Lundberg, was to develop a permanent working relationship between private publishers and the socialist state, and his initial task was to overcome resistance from the idled publishers. "They are demanding guarantees. But none of them understands that to begin work, however it is begun, is the best guarantee." The publishers should set aside questions about profit and work together toward the common goal of book publishing. Sytin stated his own credo: "I don't need profits. I need only to work."[54]

One handicap for publishers under NEP that Sytin failed to take into account, however, was the government's refusal to relax its grip on the publishing sector to the same degree that it did on other small businesses and light manufacturing. Rather, just after NEP was announced, the Council of People's Commissars had tightened control on the printing industry by empowering Gosizdat to seize and distribute all paper stocks and by reinforcing its censorship role.[55] Then, on 20 June, V.P. Polonsky (Gusin), a leading publicist for the regime, had spelled out clearly that state leaders could never permit free use of the weapon that had put them in power. As he reminded his readers: "The Communist revolution is victorious not because of bayonets but because of the printing press."[56]

V

In 1923, the sixth year of the revolution, ill health brought on by a stroke cost Lenin his role as pre-eminent leader, and the "Book Company of 1922" failed. I.I. Troianovsky, a writer who had earlier published with Sytin, thought it time to give his old associate something new to think about, and he asked Sytin to help fund an exhibition and sale of artworks in New York to benefit Russian artists. It would "cost a lot," but Sytin could join the accompanying entourage and make his first trip across the Atlantic. A group of Moscow artists, Troianovsky explained, hoped to garner at least $100,000 from rich Americans by offering over nine hundred paintings, sculptures, and graphic prints from the RSFSR. He and Sytin would be the "impresarios" to make the venture possible.

Sytin later recalled that he "agreed with pleasure," but with the prime motive of visiting America to find out about its schools. In the wake of his two failed NEP projects, the paper plant and his book company, Sytin seems to have seized on making himself useful in the field of Soviet education. By going to New York he could discover new methods to enliven Russian schools and enlist Americans to take part in joint educational ventures. Unfortunately, he says, problems dogged the projected art sale from the start. For one thing, his own immediate backing amounted to five thousand dollars, but he had reason to doubt that Troianovsky ever contributed anything. For another, the artists chose to send, in Sytin's judgment, a "motley series" devoid of obviously worthy works.

Difficulties over passports caused another snag, and Sytin did not win his travel clearance until a month after the rest of the delegation had departed without him. Like them, he went next to Riga, Latvia, to obtain a visa from the American consul there because the United States and the RSFSR had no diplomatic ties.[57] Despite the likely challenges for a lone, elderly Soviet travelling abroad, Sytin chose to visit Berlin and Paris en route to New York. As one artist-delegate, Igor Grabar, wrote his wife when Sytin was on his way: "Isn't it true that he is a remarkable old man?"[58] After two weeks of medical exams in the French port of Cherbourg had proved him fit, Sytin set sail for America on the S.S. *Majestic* either a few days before or after Lenin's death on 21 January and just as the new Soviet state was changing its name to the Union of Soviet Socialist Republics.[59] Upon reaching New York late that month, he straight away promised officials on Ellis Island that he would depart within six months and then ferried to Manhattan to find his compatriots bogged down in "Russian quarrels."

According to Sytin, the delegation had by then rented exhibit space but not responded to an offer of aid from the New York chapter of the Russian Red Cross. When, after further delay, Sytin and several delegates had finally called on that group and "encountered some unfriendliness," Troianovsky had the next day hastened to make chapter officials responsible for publicity. That move in turn caused the artist-delegates to insist that news coverage be arranged by Sytin, "who is known in America and whom every paper will help," because he alone could disassociate their fund-raising project from the Soviet government. But, continues Sytin, the Russian Red Cross had already cast the "blot" of a "doubtful reputation" on the art sale and turned all but the "Jewish papers" against it.[60]

The *New York Times* issued its first stories about the impending exhibit on 19 February and 2 March and in both identified the "wealthy Russian publisher" Sytin as being in charge. After the exhibit's opening on 4 March at the Grand Central Palace, the next *Times* report told how Sytin, stationed at the entrance, had greeted the son of Leo Tolstoy, Count Ilia Tolstoy, then living in the United States. The two had last met ten years before when Sytin had published Leo Tolstoy's complete works. Tolstoy, said the *Times*, had relished the old Muscovite flavour of Sytin's speech and marvelled at how little the publisher had changed, but for becoming greyer.[61]

As restless as ever, Sytin had meanwhile made several outings to evaluate local schools and factories; and professors at New York University, he says, had responded to one such visitation by offering to send an exhibit of their methods and texts to the USSR.[62] Favourably impressed overall, Sytin had promptly sent a letter urging his grandson "Dimusha" to educate himself in America. "It is not necessary to live here, but you must study here," he wrote, to discover "things that you will see nowhere else" and to "make contacts for your future." He would prefer Americans to pay more attention to man's "heroic, brilliant spirit," but he closed with this tribute to the vitality of New York: "Your grandpa looks younger."[63]

As for the art exhibit he had helped arrange, Sytin was little surprised that few viewers came and fewer bought anything. The *Times* described the dismal results in a front page story on 6 April headlined: "Debts End Russians' Vision of Gold." A spokesman for the Russian Red Cross in New York, placing blame on the delegation, said that the receipts to the end of March totalled only two thousand dollars.[64]

By mid-April the Russians were reporting profits of thirty thousand dollars, a figure still far short of their goal, and were getting ready to break the collection for separate showings elsewhere in North America. With his obligations ended, Sytin went off on his own to visit Niagara Falls and to mail home several picture postcards. He and Grabar subsequently travelled home together, reaching Riga, en route to Moscow, on 26 June 1924.

Grabar had sent intermittent reports to the USSR throughout his half-year trip, and in one he expressed disappointment that Sytin "turns out under the closest examination to be a man who has gone to seed ... where is the mind and talent he once had? ... he can't be considered a serious businessman any longer."[65] In another, Grabar admitted that the entire delegation had grossly overestimated what the exhibit could earn, inasmuch as "the golden days of the art trade in America had already passed."[66] Sytin, in turn, accepted no blame whatever for the "muddle" of the venture. In the memoirs he wrote for Soviet publication he went so far as to claim that "when I arrived in America ... it was already clear that the exhibition had not succeeded as intended. With a feeling of dissatisfaction over the failure that had befallen us, I left America and returned to Russia."[67] He would have his reader understand that he had had no American experiences whatever.

Home once more in Moscow, Sytin found his credibility, personal strength, and room for manoeuvring greatly diminished. No longer could he call on Lenin for help, and he could expect no favours from Stalin, then fixing an iron hold on the Communist Party. As yet another setback, the Neva River had flooded its banks during his absense to ruin his warehouse full of paper on Basil's island in Petrograd.[68] Then came grief of the profoundest sort of all when Evdokia Ivanovna, his wife of forty-seven years, died that September. In 1924 Sytin issued what would be his last publication: a slim catalogue to list the few books that remained to him to sell from his once enormous inventories.

The next year found Sytin penning a mainly gloomy letter to a close friend, admitting that he sorely needed income to help support his progeny. If only his "old machine" were not redundant in the "new fighting apparatus," he would be less "half-hearted" in his search for work at the "advanced age of 75." But, he confides, "I am tired," and, worse yet, "bored." His two remaining printing plants in two prisons torment him with financial losses, but he expects much more distress to add to the recent deaths of both Evdokia Ivanovna and the wife of his second son. "All this is sad, but it is unavoidable to live through it."

In contrast, Sytin writes glowingly of the one "country of miracles in the world," America, which put no limits on the "rights to live and to work." There, he writes, government "is based on the rule of law," intellectual and physical work hold equal value, and "no one's religious belief can be infringed." Finally, just before signing off, he corrects his age as seventy-four, not seventy-five, and laments: "My head is getting old [and] I am confused."[69]

Only a few months later Sytin again betrayed a loss of acuity by misdating (as "1924") his 28 May application to start another publishing company under NEP. In that same document, moreover, he wrongly cites the year of his trip to America as "1925."[70] Much else in that application tends toward hyperbole. Sytin starts out factually enough to describe himself as a son of the people who had worked all his life in the book trade. All the huge material results of his labour were now nationalized, he wrote, but Lenin had stressed to him that this takeover was merely a result of the general plan. As for the private resources that he still held, Sytin quotes Lenin as assuring him before a witness (N.P. Gorbunov): "If you are not against us, we will allow you to live and work as you lived and worked [before]." Sytin claims then to have replied: "I am certain that my abilities and knowledge can serve the new order." For the seven years since, continues Sytin, he had kept faith with that vow by trying to be useful.

First, from 1917 to 1919, he had "conscientiously worked for Gosizdat. Then, with great difficulty, he had lined up "solid foreign capital" to start an immense paper plant on the river Kem only to see the project fail "because of a single accidental event [Stiness's illness]." Most recently, he had "categorically declined" a number of "advantageous proposals" to stay in America to work in newspaper and book publishing; for he had presumed, he emphasizes, that his homeland needed his knowledge and experience. "Despite my years, I still can and want to work in the booktrade"; and had not one of the journals dedicated to the book trade just described him as the "Russian Ford"? Official approval of his request to start a publishing company, he concludes, "would constitute only elementary justice." But for all his brave words, whether he ever submitted them or not, Sytin had already ended his publishing days.

Meanwhile Sytin completed both the book-length memoir that son Vasily helped to edit and the rambling but engaging "Notes after Visiting America" (see appendix 1) that he wrote entirely on his own. Of the two, the inchoate "Notes" better reflect the personal qualities and mature beliefs of this singular, semi-literate, humane, and devout man. Through them, this septuagenarian veteran of fair stalls describes America as a Nizhnii Novgorod writ large: a free and lively place of diverse people rich with the work and learning opportunities he so prized but short of the spiritual insights he now cherished above all.

VI

With no further work but his own writings, no work place but his apartment, and no possibility for travel, Sytin began a regimen of daily walks in his neighbourhood, cane in hand, with frequent pauses to chat with acquaintances. He also welcomed visitors like A.I. Gessen, once parliamentary and foreign correspondent for *Russian Word*, who says that their last meeting took place when the old publisher was about seventy-five. On that occasion Sytin had shown him a bronze statuette of a high-booted Russian that he identified as Sharapov, the boss who had "reached out his friendly hand" and had "made me a success." Gessen had several times earlier run into Sytin at Gosizdat and recalled him sad-faced and disappointed over once again finding no work.[71]

Another old friend, Al. Altaev, tells of taking the aging, idled Sytin to visit a sect of Old Believers in the mid-twenties. "I stood with Ivan Dmitrievich in a prayer chapel. From under the low arches one could see everywhere the dark faces of the icons, ... black shapes floated silently; women in black with loose schismatics' shawls, with song sheets in their hands. Women serve, women read the gospels, women sing in monotone, in unison. The men wore long kaftans, almost to the ground. Melodious, strange, unhurried, evocative ... Ancient Rus, ancient Rus." Sytin, she noted, "was attentive, his face concentrated, black eyes shining; the usual crafty look had disappeared from them."[72]

Whatever solace came from his religious beliefs, Sytin had lost his ebullience. Sometime in 1926 he reflected on his seventy-fifth year. "To work one's whole life without rest, and now to realize that I cannot work; I have become old," he lamented. "This is the tragedy. But life dictates its own, to live is necessary, and so I am pushed to the next, risky step."[73]

Sytin may by then have read a Soviet book of 1926 which bracketed him with another native entrepreneur then in disfavour – Gorky, who had fled abroad, on Lenin's advice, in 1921. Both men had "lazy" minds, wrote former employee Alexander Kugel, and had relied on "tact" to get along without "special efforts of thought." He seemed to imply that Sytin was the worse for relying, as well, on great sums of money.[74] Even though Sytin by this time lacked even small financial reserves, Kugel's criticism had ominous overtones in a country where official hostility toward the "bourgeoisie" was deep. Perhaps it was these more difficult times that brought Sytin's son Peter, now thirty-three, home from Germany.

During the next year came a harsh and unmistakable signal of official disfavour: a directive to Sytin to move out of the family apartment that Lenin had promised to him to the end of his days. The staff of the trade union paper *Labour* (*Trud*) ostensibly required the space, but the unspoken message was that Sytin deserved no special considerations. As the family at large already well knew, anyone bearing the Sytin name had come under a cloud.

(Grandson Aleksei Vasilievich testifies that in 1939 he qualified for admission to artillery officers' school and remembers the initially kind, encouraging words of the selection committee. Then had come their final question: "There was at one time a publisher named Sytin. Do you have any connection with him?" When he answered affirmatively, "everything changed. I was sent back to the regiment.")[75]

At least the pension that Lenin had promised Sytin was not denied him. Citing his past service to publishing and to popular education, the Council of People's Commissars in October 1927 granted Sytin a monthly stipend of 250 rubles.[76] By then he had completed his forced move to an apartment at what is now 12 Gorky Street, where, recalls Aleksei Vasilievich, "he began noticeably to age, to ache off and on, to seclude himself in his small room; walks along the corridor were rarer."[77] Inert and silent, he now idled through most daylight hours in an armchair wedged between his bed and his familiar old desk.

The month he received his pension was also the tenth anniversary of the October revolution, and, to mark the occasion, Sytin's eldest son Nicholas had helped assemble a book to honour the founders of the Soviet state. But because some of the honourees had since been labelled enemies by Stalin, persons in authority found Nicholas guilty of subversive activity and exiled him, by administrative order, to the Siberian city of Tomsk.[78]

In 1929, on the occasion of her fortieth anniversary jubilee as a writer, Altaev says that Sytin called on her, early in the morning, when it was barely light. He could not come to the observance that evening but had brought as gifts a copy of *A Half-Century for the Book* and a volume from his Great Reforms series. He drank a cup of coffee and then departed, "leaving the sad impression of a fallen colossus." Within minutes, Altaev's domestic worker appeared to describe her encounter with Sytin in the stairwell: "I am coming along and he is standing on a lower landing, holding on to the railing, looking down and asking loudly, 'How do I get out of here? There is no stairway.' I was frightened. Such a man, and like a foolish child ... Well, of course, I showed him the way and watched to see that he made it. Nothing happened. He found his way, and even quickly, not like an old man. But, all the same, he wasn't himself."[79]

Motylkov, the former errand boy at Sytin's St Petersburg bookstore, visited the publisher in his Moscow apartment at about this same time. Seeing him after many years, Motylkov thought back to the active man he had known. It was the "great practical mind, his enormous energy" that had made Sytin "under conditions of capitalism a master entrepreneur of the American type." But, continues Motylkov, Sytin had suffered in the "post-revolutionary order" both as a result of the new rulers' "lack of confidence in a former capitalist" and from his own "inability to adapt."[80]

Meanwhile Stalin had given conciliatory signs to Gorky and brought him home in the summer of 1927 for a triumphal tour. Sytin's old ally had then returned permanently in 1931 to serve as first writer of the state and to reside in a magnificent house in Moscow not too far from the apartment of Sytin. No available records show contacts between the two men, but it is certain that Sytin never gave up hoping that Gorky would come to his aid by endorsing his memoirs so that Gosizdat would finally relent and permit their publication.[81]

But Sytin was thoroughly out of favour, and by 1933 the presses of the government had printed a number of works that mocked the deposed capitalist. Besides the one by Kugel, another three had come from N. Miretsky, once part of the Sytintsy, who consistently used his pen to brand Sytin as a tsarist agent who exploited his workers and his readers simply to get rich.[82] Indictments like these were serious strikes against Sytin.

But the final fatal blows were the frequent illnesses that buffeted the "fallen colossus" in the years after Altaev's celebration. Both the mind and the body of Sytin were failing him. When his death at eighty-three from pneumonia came on 23 November 1934, the year when Stalin's purges began, the passing of a once mighty entrepreneur evoked no official praise, not even from Gorky.[83] Close friends, family members, and a few former employees attended the final rites at Vvedensky cemetery. There were no speeches.

CHAPTER ELEVEN

Epilogue: Ivan Dmitrievich Sytin, Russian Entrepreneur

Ivan Sytin was a most unlikely Russian, as his contemporaries testified. To be sure, they recognized in him a native son, a Russian villager, a commoner. But they also found him altogether uncommon.

Sytin easily fits Joseph Schumpeter's definition of the entrepreneur as a lowly born, risk-taking venturer who puts together "new combinations of productive means." What Sytin effectively combined to build his publishing empire was, first of all, his main product of cheap, brightly illustrated works for the peasants; next, his distribution network of itinerant pedlars; and finally, his advanced printing technology from the West. He was not himself an innovator in the technical aspects of publishing. Publishing for peasants, rather, was his own special bailiwick, and no one before or after him reached and exploited this market so well.

Knowing that fact, Chertkov took his own populist works to Sytin for printing and distribution and thereby linked Sytin with the Tolstoyans, to everyone's benefit. Sytin deserves little credit for seizing an opportunity that arrived, unbidden, in his shop; but through the ideas and suggestions of the intellectuals he came to know, he broadened his own product line to include not only books and pamphlets for all kinds of readers but also periodicals with wide appeal, especially *Russian Word*, whose mass circulation, liberal outlook, and quality journalism made it a decidedly innovative newspaper in Russia.

In turn, by combining more and more printing-related ventures within a single company, Sytin forged a business organization that was new to Russia – a kind of modern holding company. Soviet scholars have consequently seen Sytin as "an example of the progressive tendency toward monopoly in Russian industry,'' a vague charge that avoids labelling Sytin a monopolist, which he definitely was not. War and revolution ruled out two long-planned expansions of his combine: a country-wide network of newspapers supplied by his own machine and type factories, his own telephone/telegraph networks, and by a news-gathering syndicate with international ties that he would organize; and the giant paper plant he envisioned in the north where trees and power were cheap and abundant - again to supply his own presses.

Sytin the combiner of productive means was also Sytin the overcomer of obstacles. Besides hurdling such business challenges as getting what he wanted from his workers, partners, and bankers, Sytin repeatedly passed the test that faces every publisher: acquiring good writers and editors. Some he wooed with high pay; some he attracted with his vast press runs and wide access to markets. On yet another front he proved a skilled negotiator of the snares contrived by officials who were hostile to what he published and worried about how he might influence public opinion. He thereby advanced press freedom in Russia, however temporarily.

Sytin also fits the entrepreneurial profile that has emerged from recent research. Like most of the present-day entrepreneurs in one study, Sytin saw his childhood as deprived, his father as improvident, and his schooling as deficient. And, again like many in that study, he learned his trade and how to run a business as the protégé of a mentor/sponsor. Sharapov served as a surrogate father for Sytin, gave him printing and management experience, arranged his marriage, and provided him with capital to set up his own shop.

Besides having the predictable entrepreneurial traits that several studies have confirmed - openness and flexibility, for example, and the tendency to rely on others with useful skills and higher talent - Sytin had within him the undercurrent of ''delinquency'' recently found common to entrepreneurs. It surfaced in Sytin when he evaded restrictions, broke promises, paid bribes, and made expedient deals - although the degree of his dishonesty and how it compared to that of his peers is hard to gauge. Moreover, when it came to outwitting the autocratic regime, using foul means as readily as fair was then, for many, a matter of honour.

But entrepreneurial traits aside, Sytin's success depended very much on luck. As just one example, the lowly birth that prodded Sytin to rise happened also to enhance his standing at a higher social level. The populism then in vogue had endowed the peasant with special virtues, and intellectuals and the highly born valued the chance to collaborate with someone of just that stamp, especially a proved success in an industry that disseminated ideas. Moreover, his emergence from the lower class to become a high-ranking, self-proclaimed servant of his countrymen exempted Sytin from the guilt that debilitated so many upper-class Russians of his day. As a nouveau riche who invested his resources and energy into expanding his enterprises and who yet lived quite modestly, he felt only passing pangs of guilt for all his millions. Finally, Sytin could blame his peasant upbringing for his conniving tactics and unpredictable behaviour, both of which were very useful to him in business.

In the years before 1917, victories for Sytin far outnumbered defeats, and, whether by cleverness or chance, he never made a catastrophic blunder. In projects of great magnitude such as his proposed paper plant in the north, Sytin seems to have proceeded with care and deliberation. He failed repeatedly to convince others to back him and he would not - or perhaps could not - take the risk alone. As one of the praising articles in his fifty-year business chronicle pointed out, Sytin, when expanding, took care never to jeopardize those business ventures already in place.

Through all these strategies, Sytin established his publishing empire and proclaimed his self-worth, all the while manifesting the strong ego that experts call the primal force within entrepreneurs. The anniversary celebrations he pridefully arranged are sufficient proof in themselves. He saw to it that tributes to himself as "first citizen of the Russian land" and the "real minister of education" were read out before a large and eminent audience, and then he had those tributes published in the biggest newspaper of the land.

To his credit, Sytin built a kingdom worth bragging about. By every major publishing indicator he led the field in Russia, as all six figures in the appendix show. Without question, the accomplishments of Sytin place this Russian peasant squarely in the mainstream of modern western economic development. But even as he proved that pre-revolutionary Russia provided ample manoeuvring room for free enterprisers to build business empires, Sytin the entrepreneur matters most as a modernizer and democratizer of old imperial Russia.

Appendices

APPENDIX ONE

Sytin's "Notes After Visiting America"

During June 1924 Sytin reflected in writing on America and his homeland in pungent but ungrammatical Russian, and my abridged and edited translation follows.[1] (Excluded are his comments on the exhibition and sale of Russian art that he had helped to oversee in New York because they are summarized in chapter ten.) Much more than jottings, these notes are the fullest existing statement of the life philosophy that Sytin distilled over half a century. Never before had the preoccupied man of affairs been in so reflective a mood.

Sytin addressed his thoughts both to fellow Russians and to Americans, and he seems to have hoped that his words would one day appear in print. They do so here for the first time. In the 1920s Sytin could not openly argue for Russia's opening again to the West. At the time when the Bolsheviks were enforcing isolation and their political order as dictates of historical laws, to propose the Russian-American, psychological-spiritual synthesis that he favoured would have made him an enemy of the state. These notes have consequently been in the hands of his family for sixty years.

What Sytin says he found in America were his own rudimentary ideas about freedom and enlightenment but in advanced form. The thrill of discovery was therefore especially sharp for him. He found that the American educational system nurtured initiative and democratic values from nursery school on. He noted the partnership of inventors, capitalists, and workers in the free enterprise system and the readiness of Americans to work hard. Here were the sources of America's social and economic vitality

But he missed in America the spiritual completeness that enriched his beloved homeland. Because Russia and the Russian Orthodox Church dated to ancient times, his own people had acquired a deeper wisdom and closer union with nature. He also sees a new beginning and the emergence of free men for the first time in Russia's long history. He would have tradition and the church play an important role, but he would introduce Russians to the optimistic industriousness of the West.

"NOTES AFTER VISITING AMERICA" BY I.D. SYTIN

We [Russians] have a number of problems because we are humble, old-fashioned, drab bumpkins. Although Yermak long ago occupied Siberia for us, we still do not know what we have and what we own. And we are marking time and whining about land and about the crowded conditions of our life, but this is really [behaving like] a dog in the manger ... Let us stand up, wake up and look at ourselves.

[Russia,] your neighbours went to work a long time ago, your younger sister, dear America, has created miracles. You are the older sister and you have a plentitude of grace, more than other parts of the world, and you have treasures everywhere and in every thing. But you cannot nourish yourselves effectively and well.

Serfdom was for you a terrible time, like a heavy sleep. You have had your freedom for only sixty-four years, and for each freed peasant only 5.4 acres.[2] Through these sixty-four years there has been a struggle for literacy, and you know nothing except the four arithmetical operations ... These problems raise the following comments about what you [Russia] now have and what you must do, not only in the present generation. You have enough seed in you to fill and cultivate the whole area for many centuries. But to do this you need knowledge.

Knowledge. Know about yourself, that you are an ordinary man, but that your strength in unity is immense and mighty. It is not enough to have only theoretical knowledge, but it is necessary to experience life. [For example,] America has a very surprising way of bringing up children. From the age of two the child is left at nursery school every morning at 8 o'clock by his mother for the whole day.[3] Tens of these little ones, whether they are children of millionaires or workers, are together in one big, spacious room, full of children's furniture and rugs, and they do what they want - crawl, play, and mix together. All peacefully, calmly, and in friendly fashion, they amuse themselves and help one another.

[Sytin next explains that his own purpose in going to the United States was to study its educational system.]

... I was in America, and I saw everything, talked pleasantly everywhere. There each person very much wants to work. America is my love, [for in that land] everything is built grandly, skilfully, finely.

It pains me and it is a pity that we do not follow the example of the Americans. They are so terribly rich: they do not know what to do with all their machines, and they have many dollars. [Even so,] America very much resembles us in the organization of workers, [as I found when] I with great pleasure visited a large printing plant and a textile plant. So, too, Americans in their workplaces, in their efficiency, in private conversations very much resemble Russian workers.

At their jobs [Americans] listen attentively to the visitor's queries and quietly and politely explain all the good and bad points of a given machine and the possible ways in which it might be perfected. The mechanic - with the great pleasure and interest of the expert – tells you everything, and it stimulates him very much to do so.

It is another matter in Germany.[4] There the worker is stingy and unwilling with his words, as though he is afraid of competition. He answers briefly or tells you "ask at the office." The French worker pays [a curious visitor] even less attention and he fusses at his work. He is constantly in motion. At your request, he stops for a minute either to wait to see what you want and then answers with one word only. After that, he pays you no further attention, and he continues his fussiness, his watching of his machine. In the big printing plants in London it is still worse. There you can enter only with a representative of the business office, who gives you no explanation. He merely conducts you through the factory and "permits" you not to delay him because his business awaits. His interesting, clean, abundant plant is sad and ponderous; workers here are like automatic machines.

[Sytin next describes his journey by way of Europe to America.]

... On the seventh day [aboard ship], wonderful New York – a city completely its own special world of seven and a half million inhabitants. Here everything is different. One dollar costs two rubles. The fuss and traffic are terribly dizzying. For each three persons there is one automobile; the trains run three stories overhead and three stories below ground. On the many, many busses, you can ride thirty versts [twenty-eight kilometres] for five cents. Nowhere else is found such cheap and elegant food, and it is possible here to speak and to get answers in all languages. This is a world market.

If you come to America, you are like an American citizen right away – a completely free man. Conditions of life are strikingly freely organized; and all your possibilities are achievable in reality ... Making acquaintances is very easy and quick. All nationalities have committees to assist their compatriots and help them to find work. In this respect, the poorest goods are the Russian intelligentsia. They are already in America and they do not like their compatriots [refugees from the Russian Revolution] coming here now; their fellow Russians are for them a harmful element.

As for the undifferentiated Americans, they are not surprised by anything, and you cannot give them anything new. They live with their daily hard work and fill their lives with it. Each devotes himself to productivity in all ways; he is a living machine from 10 until 6 o'clock and his one interest is dollars, dollars, dollars. He gives the rest of his day to his family. Little of his time is lost on theatre, and then mostly in going to the movies, which are plentiful.

Full democracy is everywhere, from the millionaires to the lower classes without exception ... Ninety per cent of the millionaires of New York have private residences but pass their time in public hotels without a single private servant – using only the hotel service and keeping their cars in the public garage. They drive everywhere without chauffeurs. Often one family has two or three cars, and everyone services them himself. Such kindly democratization inside this sensible country has surprisingly changed life and inner culture. The American concentrates on work and business, and he counts it worse than death to be without them.

[Sytin next describes the genesis of the exhibit/sale of Russian art in New York in 1924, his part in it, and why it failed. He also describes his good times.][5]

... Only the recollections [of the trip to America] remain, but here is what stays with me: the children's nurseries ... There little children arrange things for themselves and observe for themselves. With only two nurses for twenty or more children, these little ones become accustomed to crawl about and to play together, all friendly, peacefully. They train themselves to the toilet, ask for drinks, learn the time to eat ... Here are the first lessons at the beginning of life, the first ideas about everything that you need to know, including all the vowels.

I have travelled around Europe and America seeing everything. Europe [for me] paled and grew old; there I found little dynamic movement and improvement. America was quite another matter, aspiring to fly to perfect technology. During my four months in New York, I saw a surprising growth in the number of machines and a perfecting of the methods of production in all the factories.

Everything I was shown in New York was new to me ... [including] a great rotary press. When I spoke with the factory owner and the mechanics about its cost, they were astonished that anyone would consider such a trivial matter:[6] "We constructed a press suited to our work ... and we take all measures ... to improve it [because] it is our business to make sure that the machines of our factory are the most advantageous in speed, simplicity, and efficiency."

This method is characteristic not only of printing-machine manufacturing but of all industries. The goal is to perfect production, so managers and workers have to be very skilfully trained ... I am pleased that I witnessed in America ... this habit of mind, this way of doing things, this handling of work [for it] reminds me of the way we work in Russia.[7] In Germany a lot is automated; the French, with their quick and fussy movements, seem to me to be superficial. It is the Americans who study the operation of each machine in detail, treating it like a favourite woman, lovingly caring for her, looking after her attentively.

All [American] industry works this way, linking all interests together. Each producer must study the market for his own product and know his objectives so that the producer of machines can send the necessary machinery, set it up, and get it ready for production ... Then can you bravely begin manufacturing [because] the machine-maker himself teaches you to use his machinery, and you have credit from him and more from the bank to buy raw materials.[8]

[The next paragraphs further describe the exhibit/sale of Russian art in New York.]

And you, sister America, should be happy that your older sister [Russia] has earlier saved up for you rich resources. You are the young heir, brother, and I will share with you. You are happy with much that is good, new; but my country, my friend, is a greater treasure and remarkable and valuable because of its long, wise, history. That which lives wisely lives eternally. We do not know where the beginning or the end is, [but] it is a great happiness to understand the meaning of life, my dear transoceanic neighbour.

America, how clearly tempting you are, wonderfully splendid, and how I feel your close brotherhood with us. You are a happy, bright, new country. You have gathered together all the strong people, with ready talents and they have set themselves up, and they are working. New world, new people, new thinking.

We are very old. We have lived tragically for long, unfree centuries, living through heavy historical bondage. We Russians have, over the centuries, produced the cruel nobility; but all the same we survived until suddenly there appeared the dawn, the bright sunlight, and bright northern lights with all their brilliance. And the whole people - having been divided into classes of tsars, ministers, boyars, generals, and slaves - emerged without any ranks. All titled majesties vanished and there remained only man himself! And nothing else! Great happiness, what a miracle - Man.

Dear America, for [the first] two months I viewed your treasures without understanding how to approach you, and everything seemed to me to be petty, boring, cheap. It was simply that the markets, posters, bazaars, stores, with their massively spread-out goods for the crowd seemed to me merely diverting. When the moment came for me to write to you and about you, then, My God, I remembered that you are our young daughter. This [immaturity] was why I found you boring and why I felt out of place, dissatisfied with you.[9] Younger sister, our interests are close to yours. Your spirit and our Russian nature are very close. We Russians have a very warm feeling for you; and you for us. But I am not able to say that you go along with or imitate our deep native feeling and spirituality. And what we like in you is the latest developments in culture [that is, democracy, technology, and productivity].

Of greatest importance to man is the spiritual life given by God through the blessings of the great ideas of nature. So precious to man is this spirituality born in the abundant north where [the Russian] was tamed by the most innocent surroundings and natural requirements. With this spirit inside man every deed is blessed. The force of the sacred spirit ... has done everything to awaken in man humility, mercy, forgiveness, and self-sacrifice. Influenced by the idea of a heavenly reward, the whole great mass of the people meekly relives - through piety in childhood and adulthood - the whole higher school of asceticism. They also choose their pastors and their disciples to manifest and take part in the Great Eternal Meaning, both positive and negative.[10] It is a pity when this richest experience, of meekness and goodness, is not used to form a person in his first fifteen years; for this upbringing makes everything accessible to him.

There is also a need to develop in each youth a knowledge of practical work. Utilize him, teach him, do not hinder him, give him scope in his work, be a friend and brother to him; and he will give you a great and happy life. And take strict care to appreciate him so that you will not abuse his rights. Bring out in him human qualities, develop in him a sense of home.

[You who oversee workers,] involve yourself and educate yourself in the experience of your workers. Teach them and you will learn from them. This greatest, happiest university [the workplace] gave me the confidence to take pride in myself and be happy with myself. My 2,500 workers and I educated one another and surrounded ourselves with all kinds of [schooling] ... [for] it is impossible to achieve truth fully without the knowledge of books. And from knowing this has been the source of my happiness from my book business.

Why is it not possible to do the same thing in the textile, mechanical, and all other factories and shops, especially agricultural? Broaden managers' schools and experimental workshops; put in practice new means to give the worker some rights and encourage him to be interested in his work. Then will he strongly, willingly do everything to perfect his work and his machine. Amateur lecturers and master mechanics are required, as is good literature on all subjects. Only then can work reach the perfection of advanced models.

APPENDIX TWO

Total Works Published by Sytin & Co., 1901–10

*Categories**	*Number of titles*	*Number of copies*
Calendars	21	51,038,050
Popular literature (*lubki*)	598	33,959,833
Pictures of religious content	215	30,597,250
Belles lettres	837	15,935,833
Pictures of varied content	322	15,421,130
Basic grammars	58	13,950,640
Spiritual-moral publications	192	13,601,935
Pictures of Tsar, imperial family	58	11,846,865
Children's books	272	4,503,875
Texts and study aids	369	4,168,010
Popular science in different disciplines	562	2,837,755
Publicistic works	140	2,420,320
Natural science books	110	2,320,470
Social-juridical, law, economics, science	89	1,485,950
Pedagogy, didactics	92	1,080,475
Geography, ethnography	42	945,400
Dictionaries, encyclopedias, informational books	84	875,480
Books against drunkenness, other evils	33	705,620
School books	4	650,200
Funeral and prayer books	4	650,000
Criticism	41	621,700
Agriculture	144	513,625
Medicine, hygiene, veterinary	77	400,125
Self-education	94	388,000
Biography	32	367,500
History of literature	24	272,800
Logic, psychology, philosophy, ethics	72	214,720
History	41	128,000
Household economy	32	117,280
Technology	42	102,375
Art	11	24,200
TOTALS	4,838	212,145,216

*Categories are those of Sytin & Co.

Source: I.D. Sytin & Co., *Ocherk izdatel'skoi deiatel'nosti T-va I.D. Sytina* (Moscow 1910), v.

APPENDIX THREE

Publications Owned or Supported by I.D. Sytin (as a Private Investor or through Sytin & Co.)

MAGAZINES

Around the World (*Vokrug Sveta*) [1892–1917] Moscow, weekly, illustrated. Eds.: E.N. Kiselev, E.M. Polivanov, N.V. Tulupov, V.A. Popov.

Dawn (*Zaria*) [1913–16] Moscow, monthly, illustrated. Ed.: N.I. Sytin.

For the Peoples' Teacher (*Dlia Narodnogo Uchitelia*) [1907–16] Moscow, 20 issues a year. Eds.: N.V. Tulupov, P.M. Shestakov.

Friend of Children (*Drug Detei*) [1902–3; 1905–7] Moscow, semi-weekly, illustrated. Eds.: A.V. Melnitskaia, N.V. Tulupov.

Little Bee (*Pchelka*) [1906–7] Moscow, semi-monthly, for children. Ed.: N.V. Tulupov.

Needs of the Country (*Nuzhdy Derevni*) [1907] St Petersburg, weekly, illustrated. Ed.: A.P. Mutvogo.

Small World (*Mirok*) [1911–16] Moscow, monthly, for children. Ed.: V.A. Popov.

Tilled Field (*Niva*) [1916] St Petersburg, weekly, illustrated.

War with Japan (*Voina s Iaponiei*) [1904] Moscow, weekly, illustrated. Eds.: I.I. Mitropol'sky, I.D. Sytin.

JOURNALS

Education (*Prosveshchenie*) [1907] Moscow, semi-monthly. Eds.: V.P. Vakhterov and V.D. Sokolov.

Library of Russian Word (*Biblioteka ''Russkogo Slova''*) [1913–14] Moscow, weekly, serialized fiction. Ed.: I.I. Sytin.

Messenger of Book, Scholarly, and Library Affairs (*Vestnik Knizhnogo Uchebnogo i Bibliotechnogo Dela*) [1907–11] Moscow, 31 issues a year. Ed.: V.A. Popov.

Messenger of the School (*Vestnik Shkoly*) [1914–16] St Petersburg, weekly, for teachers.

Eds.: I.V. Skvortsov, I.S. Ivanov, S.V. Skvortsov.

Northern Lights (*Severnoe Siianie*) [1909] Moscow, monthly, literary. Ed.: I. Bunin.

Voice of the Past (*Golos Minuvshego*) [1913–16] Moscow, monthly. Eds.: S.P. Mel'gunov and V.M. Semevsky.

NEWSPAPERS

Bibliography (*Knigovedenie*) [1906–7] Moscow, daily. Ed.: V.A. Kozhevnikov.

Day (*Den'*) [1912] St Petersburg, daily. Ed.: S.P. Skvortsov.

Duma (*Duma*) [1906] St Petersburg, daily. Eds.: P.B. Struve, F.A. Vinberg.

Early Morning (*Rannoe Utro*) [1916–17] Moscow, daily.

Russian Truth (*Russkaia Pravda*) [1906] Moscow, daily. Ed.: M.M. Gakkebush.

Russian Word (*Russkoe Slovo*) [1897–1917] Moscow, daily.

Sunday (*Voskresenyi Den'*) [1901–16] Moscow, weekly. Ed.: S.Ia. Uvarov, S.K. Uvarova.

Telephone of Russian Word (*Telefon "Russkogo Slova"*) [August 1904] Ed.: F.I. Blagov.

Truth of God (*Pravda Bozhiia*) [1906] Moscow, daily. Ed.: G.S. Petrov.

SUPPLEMENTS (all illustrated)

Journal of Adventures (*Zhurnal Prikliuchenii*) [1916] Moscow, monthly for *Around the World*.

Journal of Fashion (*Modnyi Zhurnal*) [1904–5] Moscow, monthly for *Around the World*. Ed.: E.M. Polivanova.

Messenger of Sport and Tourism (*Vestnik Sporta i Turizma*) [1914] Moscow, monthly for *Around the World*.

On Land and Sea (*Na Sushe i Na More*) [1911–12; 1914] Moscow, monthly for *Around the World*.

Sparks (*Iskry*) [1901–17] Moscow, weekly for *Russian Word*. Eds.: E.N. Kiselev, F.I. Blagov.

World War in Stories and Illustrations (*Mirovaia Voina v Rasskazakh i Illiustratsiiakh*) [1915] Moscow, monthly for *Around the World*.

APPENDIX FOUR

Data on the Production of *Izvestiia* of the Executive Committee of the All-Russian Soviet (in the Plant of *Russian Word*, 1918).

Issue number	*Begin printing*	*Copies printed*	*Copies sold*	*Copies unsold*	*Free distribution*	*Remaining*
46	9:00 a.m.	56,000	25,625	30,375	29,000	1,375
47	9:50 a.m.	41,000	18,711	22,289	20,750	1,539
48	8:30 a.m.	50,000	39,867	21,133	18,200	2,933
49	9:00 a.m.	43,250	26,261	16,989	15,300	1,689
50	10:00 a.m.	33,900	27,923	5,977	4,285	1,692
51	9:00 a.m.	33,100	28,345	4,755	4,250	485
52	9:45 a.m.	31,300	28,751	2,549	1,213	1,336
53	9:00 a.m.	30,050	28,843	3,637	2,215	1,422
54	10:30 a.m.	46,000	28,657	17,343	15,170	2,173
55	7:20 a.m.	32,300	28,060	4,240	2,485	1,755
56	9:00 a.m.	32,200	26,829	5,371	4,033	1,388
57	9:30 a.m.	34,674	29,207	5,467	2,172	3,295
58	7:30 a.m.	39,450	26,312	10,138	6,505	3,633
59	6:30 a.m.	38,500	24,935	3,565	3,045	520

Source: TSGAOR, 130-2-193, sheet 128.

APPENDIX FIVE

Figures

Figure 1 Publishing Income, Sytin & Co.

1883-1915, various years

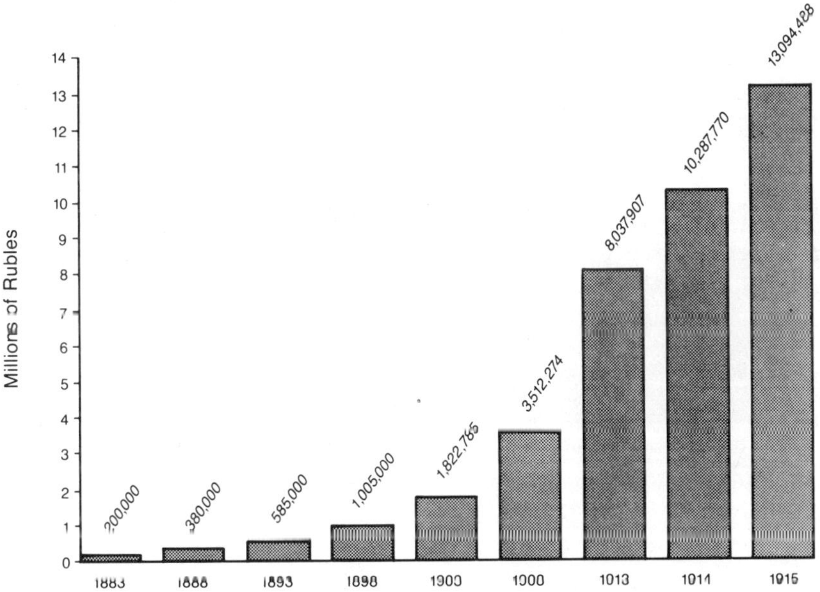

From: *Polveka dlia knigi*, ed. N.V. Tulupov, Moscow, 1916, p. 387

Figure 2 Book Production Value

1904-1914

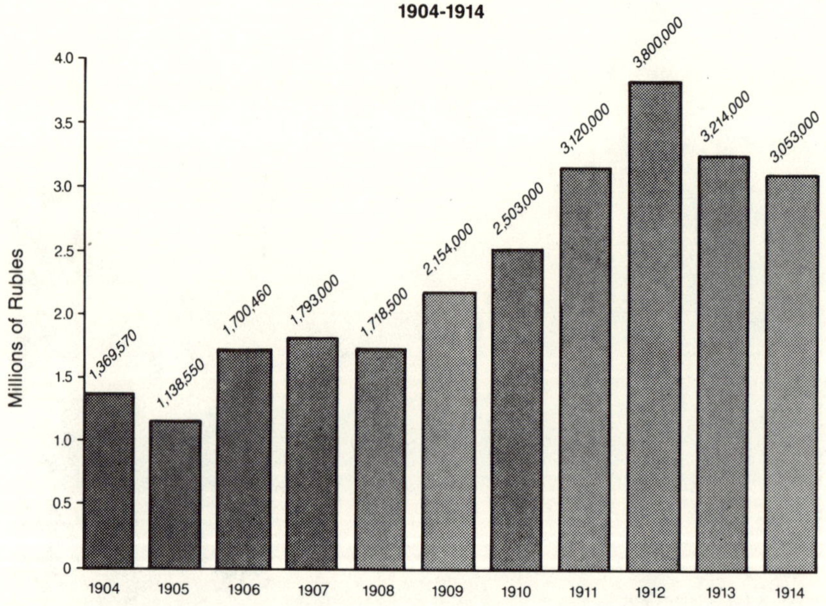

From: N. Sytin and M. Soloviev to the Moscow Revenue Department, (May 1916?), TsGIA Moskvy, 51-10-1166, sheet 65-6

Figure 3 Comparative Profits

Sytin and Four Main Rivals

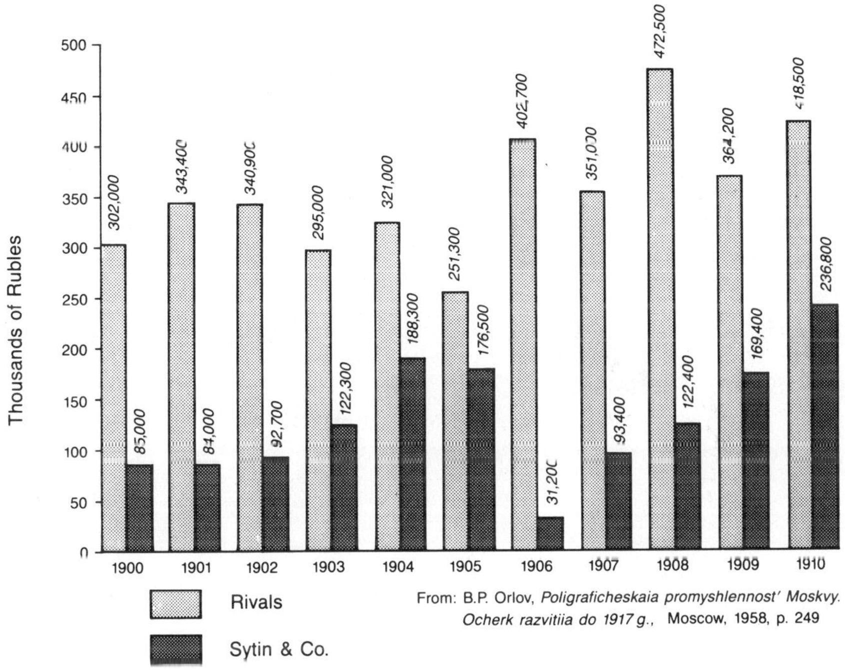

From: B.P. Orlov, *Poligraficheskaia promyshlennost' Moskvy. Ocherk razvitiia do 1917 g.*, Moscow, 1958, p. 249

Figure 4 Major Costs of Russian Word

Each fifth year (1900-1915)

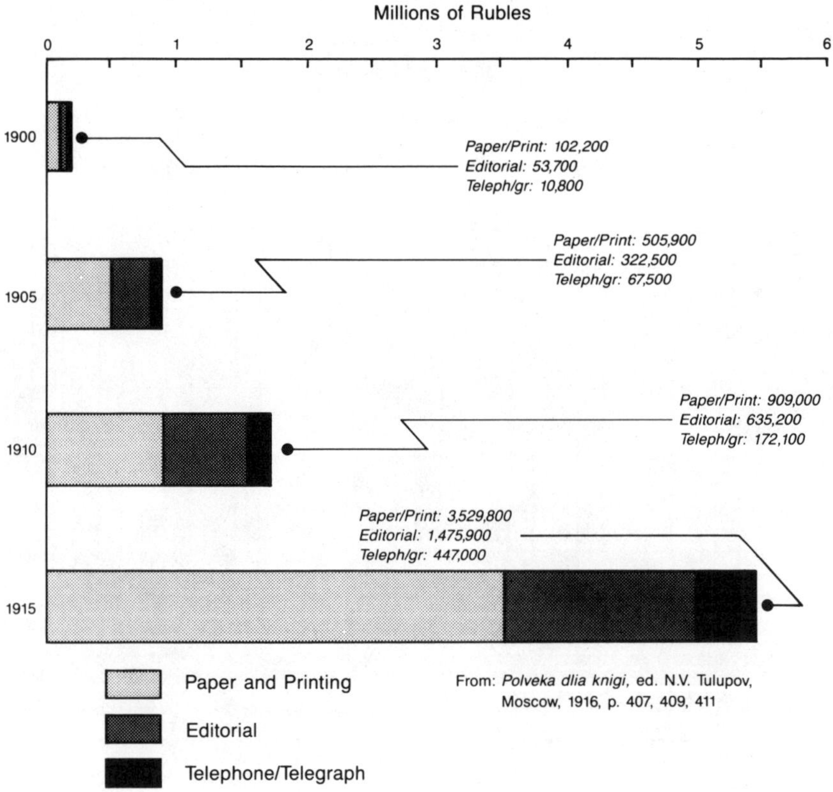

Figure 5 Circulation of Russian Word

1898-1917

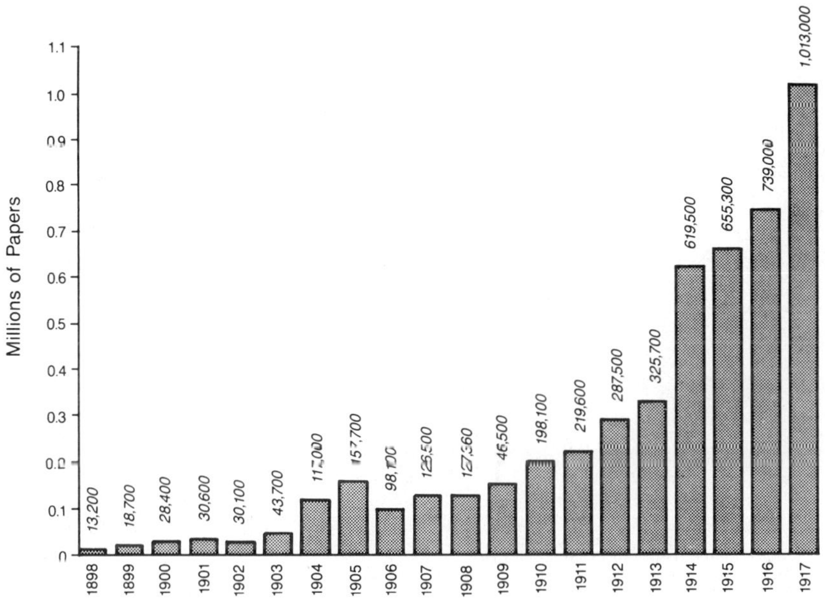

From: Louise McReynolds, "News and Society: *Russkoe Slovo* and the Development of the Mass Circulation Press in Late Imperial Russia" Unpublished Ph.D. Dissertation, University of Chicago, 1984, p. 226

Figure 6 Russian Word Advertising Revenue
1905-1914

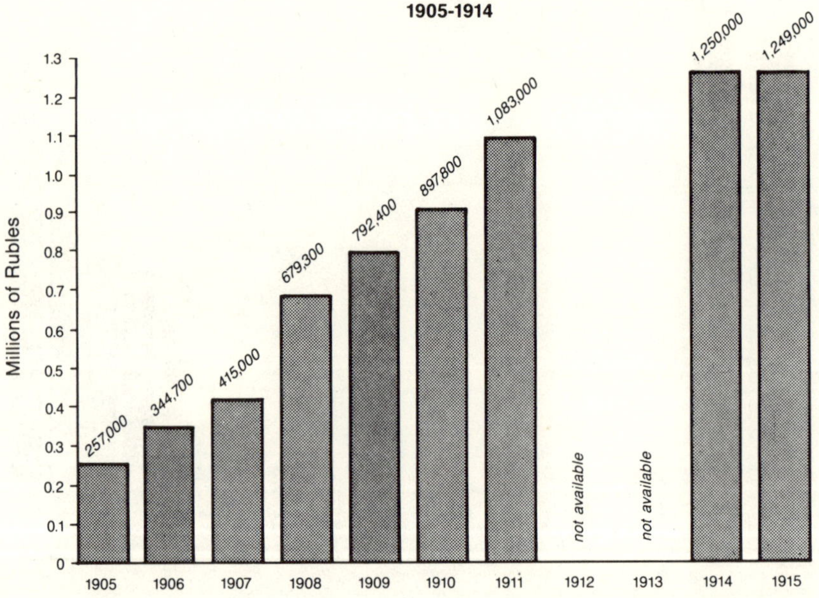

From: *Polveka dlia knigi*, ed. N.V. Tulupov, Moscow, 1916, p. 413

Notes

ABBREVIATIONS

INION — Institute for Scientific Information in the Social Sciences
PSS — Complete Collected Works
PSS i Pisem — Complete Collected Works and Letters
SS — Collected Works
TsGIA — Central State Historical Archive
TsGALI — Central State Archive of Literature and Art
TsGAOR — Central State Archive of the October Revolution
TsGIA Moskvy — Central State Historical Archive of Moscow
RO GBL Manuscript Division, Lenin Library

INTRODUCTION

1 Daniel Goleman, "The Psyche of the Entrepreneur," *New York Times Magazine* (2 February 1986), 31.
2 Cited here is the English translation of Schumpeter's book which appeared in 1934: Joseph A. Schumpeter, *The Theory of Economic Development: An Inquiry into Profits, Capital, Credit, Interest and the Business Cycle* (New York 1934), 90.
3 Ibid., 93.
4 *International Encyclopedia of the Social Sciences*, s.v. "Entrepreneurship."
5 Donald E. Clifford and Richard Cavanaugh, "The Entrepreneurial Corporation," *McKinsey Quarterly* (August 1985), 13.
6 Orvis F. Collins and David G. Moore, *The Enterprising Man* (East Lansing 1974), 70.

7 These are the views of Abraham Zaleznik and Lyle M. Spencer as summarized by Goleman, "The Psyche of the Entrepreneur," 31, 63.
8 The main ones are by E.A. Dinershtein and S.I. Inikova. The others are by A.N. Bokhanov, N.I. Chlenova, and S.V. Belov. All are cited in the notes and bibliography.

CHAPTER ONE

1 I.R. Kugel', "Sytin: Vospominaniia o proshlom russkoi pechati," *Leningrad* 23/24 (1940): 16-19. Parallels in phrasing suggest that Kugel' was countering a tribute to Sytin published in Paris two years before by émigré A.V. Rumanov ("I.D. Styin - izdatel'," *Vremennik druzei russkoi knigi* 4 [1938]: 223-31). Rumanov stressed that Sytin most valued books as tools for enlightenment.
2 I.D. Sytin, *Zhizn' dlia knigi* (Moscow 1960). This memoir includes much of a personal sketch that Sytin, then sixty-five, published in the similarly titled *A Half-Century for the Book (Polveka dlia knigi, 1866–1916)*, ed. N.V. Tulupov (Moscow 1916).
3 P. Krasnov and V. Shevelev, "Na rubezhe dvadtsatogo veka," *Sovetskaia Pechat'* 12 (1961): 46.
4 Konstantin Konichev, *Russkii samorodok* (Leningrad 1966). The second edition was published in Iaroslavl in 1969.
5 S.V. Belov, "Russkie izdatel'stva kontsa XIX - nachala XX v. (Nereshennye problemy)," *Problemy rukopisnoi i pechatnoi knigi* (Moscow 1976), 292-7.
6 Al. Altaev [M.V. Iamshchikova], "Moi starye izdateli: Iz vospominanii," *Kniga: Issledovaniia i materialy* 26, Moscow (1973): 154-82; and A.M. Motyl'kov, "Moia rabota u I.D. Sytina (Iz vospominanii bukinista," ed. A.P. Rusinov, in ibid. 37, Moscow (1978): 156-66.
7 A. Tolstiakov, "Stranitsy bol'shoi zhizni," *Knizhnoe Obozrenie* 5 (31 January 1986): 16.
8 Gnezdnikovo is in the northern part of Kostroma province, close to Soligalich, the town where Sytin was baptized.
9 Sytin or his assistants may have had Glinka's opera *A Life for the Tsar* in mind in naming his jubilee book *A Half-Century for the Book*. Sytin's memoirs, *A Life for the Book*, was similarly named.
10 Sytin, *Zhizn' dlia knigi*, 20.
11 Sytin, "Iz perezhitogo," *Polveka dlia knigi*, 15.
12 Daniel R. Brower, "Urban Revolution in the Late Russian Empire," 327, and Joseph Bradley, "Moscow: From Big Village to Metropolis," 20-3, in Michael F. Hamm, ed., *The City in Late Imperial Russia* (Bloomington 1986).
13 Jo Ann Ruckman, in *The Moscow Business Elite: A Social and Cultural Portrait of Two Generations, 1840–1905* (DeKalb, Ill 1984), 19, generalizes that

"Moscow abounded in new millionaires, many from the peasantry," but the only such peasant she names is Smirnov. Two other books on the businessmen of Moscow cite no peasant millionaires. See Thomas C. Owen, *Capitalism and Politics in Russia: A Social History of the Moscow Merchants, 1855-1905*. (Cambridge 1981), and Alfred J. Rieber, *Merchants and Entrepreneurs in Imperial Russia* (Chapel Hill 1982). Rieber defines entrepreneurs as risk-taking businessmen who wished to play a new social role in Russia. These men, he writes, "sought to break out of the traditional merchant pattern of economic timidity, social inertia, and political indifference by creating regional interest groups" (xxv).

14 James D. White, "Moscow, Petersburg, and the Russian Industrialists," *Soviet Studies* 24, no. 3 (1973): 414-20.

15 Sytin, "Iz perezhitogo," 16-17.

16 Sytin, unpublished chapter of memoir, p. 306, deposited at the Sytin Museum, Moscow.

17 Konichev, *Russkii samorodok*, 37-9.

18 Sytin, "Iz perezhitogo," 18-19.

19 Sytin, *Zhizn' dlia knigi*, 32-3. The fair was notorious for its prostitution. See, for example, Leo Tolstoy's *Kreutzer Sonata*.

20 M.T. Solov'ev, ["I.D. Sytin"], *Polveka dlia knigi*, 135.

CHAPTER TWO

1 Mikeshin to Sytin [1878], S. Belov, ed., *Kniga: Issledovaniia i materialy* 42 (1981): 129-31. Mikeshin (1835-96) provided the graphic sketches used by the sculptors of the bronze and granite statue, "To Catherine II," unveiled in 1873 in St Petersburg.

2 I.D. Sytin, *Zhizn' dlia knigi* (Moscow 1978), 47.

3 Ibid., 37.

4 This lithographic press required three men: one to insert each single sheet of paper, another to lower a platen, and a third to pull away each printed sheet.

5 Sytin, *Zhizn' dlia knigi*, 49. See issues of *Moscow Bulletin* (*Moskovskie Vedomosti*) from April through September 1882 for accounts of the exhibition.

6 Sytin, *Zhizn' dlia knigi*, 50-1. For a description of visual aids printed by Sytin, see I.K., "Nagliadnye posobiia v izdanii T-va Sytina," *Polveka dlia knigi*, ed. N.V. Tulupov (Moscow 1916), 507.

7 Sixteen pages comprise one printer's signature, and books are universally built from that unit of four double pages (from one sheet printed on two sides, cut, stacked, and glued or stitched together). I have a copy of a one-signature book printed by Sytin in 1904 that retells the Japanese folk tale "Meduza." In the original story, the empress dies; in the Sytin version, duly approved by the censor, she lives.

8 Prugavin told the anecdote in *Zaprosy naroda i obiazannosti intelligentsii v oblasti prosveshcheniia i vospitaniia*, 2d. ed. (St Petersburg 1895), 405. See also Sytin, *Zhizn' dlia knigi*, 55.

9 *Polveka dlia knigi*, 35.

10 Sytin paid Chekhov 2,300 rubles for this collection published in December 1884. See Ernest Simmons, *Chekhov: A Biography* (Boston 1962), 329.

11 The charge came after the 1917 Revolution from three former employees, who say that Sytin paid a bribe of twenty thousand rubles about 1885. See *Sytintsy v 1905 godu. Sbornik vospominanii rabochikh I-i Obraztsovoi Tipografii* [*b. Sytina*], ed. E. Rumailo, L. Mal'kov, N. Miretsky (Moscow [192?]), 21.

12 A. Gusev, "Kalendar'," in *Polveka dlia knigi*, 435-42. Several terms in use at the time, including "collections" and "almanacs," referred to calendars. Sytin issued two kinds - table calendars and wall calendars, the latter including the tear-off kind.

13 For an extensive study of the pedlar system in the central provinces around Moscow, see A.S. Prugavin, *Knigonoshi i ofeni (Vstrechi, nabliudeniia i issledovaniia*, 2 vols., pts. i-viii (n.p., n.d.), reprinted from *Severnyi Vestnik*.

14 I.N. Pavlov, *Zhizn' russkogo gravera* (Moscow 1963), 204. The word *lubok* (plural, *lubki*) originally meant a woodcut print. But by Sytin's time the word, in its generic meaning, referred to all cheap, "popular" prints and stories, however printed.

15 Prugavin, *Knigonoshi i ofeni*, 1:96.

16 Ibid. A similar criticism of *lubki* is to be found in V.P. Vakhterev, *Vneshkol'noe obrazovanie* (Moscow 1894), 96.

17 Sytin, *Zhizn' dlia knigi*, 68. Sytin devotes a full chapter (pages 68-71) to his work with the Tolstoyans. For numerous letters and summaries of letters on the Tolstoy-Sytin connection, see L.N. Tolstoy, *Polnoe Sobranie Sochinenii* (hereafter *PSS*), 91 vols. (Moscow 1928–78).

18 A.V. Blium, "Lubochnaia kniga vtoroi poloviny XIX veka," *Kniga: Issledovaniia i materialy* 42 (1981): 97, 99.

19 See the notes and commentary in Tolstoy, *PSS*, 85:122.

20 Chertkov to Tolstoy, 27-28 November 1884, in ibid.

21 Quoted in E.A. Dinershtein, "Vo imia blagogo dela (L.N. Tolstoy, I.D. Sytin i 'Posrednik')," *Kniga: Issledovaniia i materialy* 37 (1978): 78.

22 P. Biriukov, "I.D. Sytin i delo 'Posrednika'," *Polveka dlia knigi*, 115.

23 Chertkov to Tolstoy, 20 December 1885, *PSS*, 85:303. Chertkov also said that up to forty mail orders a day were coming into Sytin's shop "from the most ordinary and half-literate people. They cannot name the title of the book and write something like, 'the book where it is told how the angel lived in the shoemaker's shop.' "

24 Chertkov speaks of that meeting in his letter to Tolstoy of 8 October 1885; *PSS*, 63: 297-8.

25 Robert C. Otto has studied the Mediator archive in Moscow and outlines

the costs for paper, honoraria, and the like that put Chertkov in debt to Sytin & Co. by 4,450 rubles in December 1886. See Robert C. Otto, ''Publishing for the People: The Firm Posrednik, 1885-1905'' (Ph.D. dissertation, University of Wisconsin, Madison 1983), 70-2.

26 Ibid., 74.

27 Sytin, *Zhizn' dlia knigi*, 69.

28 Quoted in Blium, ''Lubochnaia kniga,'' 99.

29 Tolstoy to Chertkov, 6 April 1907, *PSS*, 89:63.

30 Otto, ''Publishing for the People,'' 72-3.

31 Tolstoy himself recommended a number of people to Sytin, among them N.A. Polushin, a populist writer who worked at Sytin & Co. for fifteen years composing educational calendars.

32 I.D. Sytin, ''O monopolii novoi i monopolii staroi,'' *Russkoe Slovo* 20 (25 January 1914). Sytin here further says that the ''participants in Mediator ... chuckling to themselves, left it to Sytin to bow down and be the supplicant ... [to] C.P.Pobedonostsev.''

33 Brian Alderson, ''Tracts, Rewards, and Fairies: The Victorian Contribution to Children's Literature,'' in Asa Briggs, ed., *Essays in the History of Publishing in Celebration of the 250th Anniversary of the House of Longman, 1724-1974* (London 1974), 245-82.

34 N.V. Chekhov, ''Detskaia literatura i izdatel'stvo T-va. I.D. Sytina,'' *Polveka dlia knigi*, 518-19.

35 Sytin, *Zhizn' dlia knigi*, 61.

36 V.K. Lebedev credits the words to Biriukov in ''Iz istorii sotrudnichestva knigoizdatel'stva 'Posrednik' i izdatel'skoi firmy 'I.D. Sytin i ko',''
Russkaia Literatura 2 (1969): 210. Quoting from the same archival *fond* as Lebedev, Otto credits M.P. Vinokurov, a worker in Mediator's St Petersburg warehouse (Otto, ''Publishing for the People,'' 68).

37 Prugavin, *Knigonoshi i ofeni*, 1:289.

38 N.V. Tulupov, *Katalog Otdeleniia ''Narodno-shkol'nykh bibliotek'' pri knizhnoi torgovli Sytina* (Moscow 1897). Saltykov-Shchedrin Public Library in Leningrad holds over sixty book catalogues from the Sytin company covering almost its entire existence. The Historical Library of the RSFSR in Moscow has a smaller collection from 1905.

39 To augment his two bookstores in Moscow, Sytin opened one in Kiev and one in Ekaterinburg in 1893, and another in Odessa in 1900, and yet another in St Petersburg (opening date not known).

40 Quoted in Lebedev, ''Iz istorii sotrudnichestva,'' 210.

41 Tolstoy, *PSS*, 85:189.

42 Chertkov to Tolstoy [September 1887], *PSS*, 86:81.

43 Biriukov, ''I.D. Sytin i delo 'Posrednika','' 115.

44 *Vsesoiuznaia poligraficheskaia vystavka. I-ia Obraztsovaia tipografiia v Moskve* 1 (Moscow 1927). This publication, which has no pagination, summarizes

the mechanical development of the Sytin plant on Piatnitskaia. See also Iu. A. Gorshkov, "Russkii lubok: ot manufaktury k fabrike," *Kniga: Issledovaniia i materialy* 47 (1984): 111. Sytin bought his second rotary press in 1895, two decades after A.S. Suvorin acquired the first one in Russia. These presses work at very high speeds because roll-fed paper continuously meets curved lead castings of raised type. Sytin had previously printed calendars on the flat-bed presses (initially hand-powered and then steam-powered) required for books. In this press, a large roller drum carries one hand-fed sheet of paper at a time to meet the formes, at the rate of several hundred per hour.

45 Vl. Popov, "Vokrug Sveta," *Polveka dlia knigi*, 549-50. Sytin charged four rubles a year. One ruble more entitled subscribers to a monthly, then bi-monthly, literary supplement which serialized the works of Russian authors and foreign favourites such as Jules Verne, Victor Hugo, and Rudyard Kipling.

46 Durnovo to Feoktistov, 12 February 1892, S.V. Belov, ed., "Novye dokumenty ob izdatel'skoi deiatel'nosti I.D. Sytina," *Sovetskie Arkhivy* 5 (1979): 23. Another likely person on the authorities' list was a rich socialite, A.M. Kalmykova, who backed radical causes and would later support the Bolshevik paper of Lenin. She met Sytin about the time Mediator began and sold his works in her St Petersburg bookstore (connected to the local Committee for Literacy), which the police soon shut down. See A.M. Kalmykova, *Polveka dlia knigi*, 125-6.

47 Feoktistov to the Moscow Committee on Press Affairs, 15 March 1892, TsGIA, 777-4-3, sheet 24.

48 Publications for the peasants by all Moscow publishers dropped 43 per cent during the famine of 1891-92. See B.P. Orlov, *Poligraficheskaia promyshlennost' Moskvy: Ocherk razvitiia do 1917 g.* (Moscow 1953), 176.

49 Lebedev, "Iz istorii sotrudnichestva," 211. Petrov, on the recommendation of Chertkov, served as a go-between on matters connected with Mediator.

50 Dinershtein, "Vo imia blagogo," 79. At this same time Sytin responded to Tolstoy's appeal for famine relief for the Volga region by contributing a wagon load of cabbages and potatoes, ten containers of fruit drink, five pounds of dry milk, and a bag of millet. Sytin to I.I. Gorbunov-Posadov, 8 May 1892, Belov, "Novye dokumenty," 133.

51 Lebedev, "Iz istorii sotrudnichestva," 211. After the second refusal, Sytin sold his weekly to Sytin & Co. and had the company apply for the news supplement in September, 1895 – again to no avail. E.A. Dinershtein, *I.D. Sytin* (Moscow 1983), 79-80. Approval finally came in 1898.

52 Quoted in Lebedev, "Iz istorii sotrudnichestva," 211-12.

53 The other houses were S.P. Iakovlev's Print Works (at 475,000 rubles) in 1882; I.N. Kushnerov's Printing and Trading Company (at 350,000

rubles) in 1888; A.A. Levenson's Fast Printing Company (at 210,000 rubles) in 1890; and I. Mamontev's Printing Company (at 300,000 rubles) in 1892.

54 *Polveka dlia knigi*, 370.

55 A.B. Khavkina, "Khar'kovskie kollektivnye trudy v izdanii T-va Sytina," *Polveka dlia knigi*, 500.

56 TsGIA Moskvy, 16-129-224, sheet 1.

57 Quoted in Dinershtein, "Vo imia blagogo," 81.

58 The final break came when Sytin refused in 1904 to publish a costly series of children's stories because they were not directed to the villages. Otto, "Publishing for the People," 87.

59 Durnovo to Delianov, 5 February 1894, TsGIA Moskvy, D3-635-1893, sheets 12-15.

60 Durnovo to Nicholas II, 12 February 1895, TsGIA, 776-1-30, sheet 21. The identity of Ermakov is unclear.

61 Ibid., sheet 22.

62 "Delo Departamenta Politsii," TsGIA Moskvy, D3-635-1893, 15 March 1895, sheets 66, 67, 74, 76.

63 *Polveka dlia knigi*, 388-9. Sytin & Co. also received awards from the Imperial Moscow Economic Society, the Industrial and Artistic Exhibition, and the Imperial Russian Technical Society.

64 The census of 1897 shows an urban population in Russia of 16.8 million, of which 1.3 per cent were "merchants" of the second and first guild and 1.1 per cent were "honorary citizens."

CHAPTER THREE

1 Quoted in George Juergens, *Joseph Pulitzer and the New York World* (Princeton 1966), 16.

2 As quoted in *The History of the Times*, vol. II, *The Tradition Established, 1841–1884* (London 1939), 162-3.

3 Fritz Stern, *Gold and Iron: Bismarck, Bleichroder, and the Building of the German Empire* (New York 1977), 263-6.

4 See the chapter on *Corriere* in Martin Walker, *Power of the Press: the World's Great Newspapers* (London 1982).

5 A. Peshekhonov, "Russkaia periodicheskaia gazeta (statisticheskii ocherk)," *Russkoe Bogatstvo* 3 (March 1901): 17-18.

6 Chekhov to A.S. Suvorin, 18 November 1891, in *The Life and Letters of Anton Tchekhov*, tr. and ed. S.S. Koteliansky and Philip Tomlinson (London 1965), 195.

7 Chekhov to Al. P. Chekhov, 4 April 1893, *Polnoe sobranie sochinenii*, vol. XVI, *Pis'ma 1893–1896* (Moscow 1949), 54.

8 N.I. Gitovich, *Letopis'zhizni i tvorchestva A.P. Chekhova* (Moscow 1955), 351.

9 For letters, see both A.P. Chekhov, *Polnoe Sobranie Sochinenii i Pisem v tridtsati tomakh* (Moscow 1974-8), vol. 6; and A.P. Chekhov, *Sobranie Sochinenii v 12-ti tomakh* (Moscow 1957), vol. 12.

10 Chekhov to Sytin, 4 October [?] 1895 [unsent], Chekhov, *PSS i Pisem*, 6:82.

11 Chekhov to Suvorin, 10 November 1895, Chekhov, *SS*, 12:93.

12 Chekhov to Pavlovsky, 22 May 1899, Chekhov, *PSS i Pisem*, 8:190. Pavlovsky was to meet Sytin in Paris, where the publisher had gone on a business trip. See also Chekhov to Pavlovsky, 5 May 1899, *Oxford Slavonic Papers* 9 (1960): 124-5.

13 Chekhov to Suvorin, 8 December 1893, Chekhov, *SS*, 12:39-40.

14 I.D. Sytin, *Zhizn' dlia knigi* (Moscow 1978), 120. See also "Istoriia gazety 'Russkoe Slovo'," RO GBL 259-1-1, sheet 3.

15 An editor of Tolstoy's works, in a footnote (*PSS*, 85: 175), summarizes a letter from Chekhov to Tolstoy dated 29 April 1885 (and delivered by Sytin) which discusses a newspaper for the people, presumably with the same standards as Mediator. He further specifies that Tolstoy had himself come up with the idea and that Sytin was considering taking part.

16 V.M. Doroshevich, "Russkoe Slovo," *Polveka dlia knigi*, 395.

17 "Istoriia gazety 'Russkoe Slovo'," RO GBL, 259-1-1, sheet 3.

18 B.A. Shchetinin, "V literaturnom muraveinike (Vstrechi i znakomstva)," *Istoricheskii Vestnik* 123, no. 3 (1911): 876.

19 Chief Administration of Press Affairs to Moscow Governor General, 29 July 1892, TsGIA Moskvy, 16-79-197, vol. 1, sheet 8.

20 Secret Section of the Moscow Governor General to the Ministry of the Interior, 16 August 1892, TsGIA Moskvy, 16-79-197, vol. 1, sheets 12-13.

21 Alexandrov to the Governor General, Received 5 October 1892, TsGIA Moskvy, 16-79-197, sheets 14-16.

22 Moscow Governor General to the Minister of the Interior, 6 October 1892, TsGIA Moskvy, 16-79-197, vol. 1, sheet 17.

23 "Pis'ma Pobedonostseva, K.P. Aleksandrovu, A.A.," TsGALI, 2-2-5 (12 January 1894 - 31 March 1896). This file contains eighteen letters.

24 M. Mironis to Alexandrov, 14 April 1895, TsGALI, 2-1-802, sheet 50.

25 F.P. Elenev to Alexandrov, 11 February 1898, TsGALI, 2-1-802, sheet 26.

26 Sytin to Alexandrov, 10 March 1894, TsGALI, 2-1-747, sheet 1.

27 Sytin, *Zhizn' dlia knigi*, 121-2.

28 Alexandrov to the Chief Administration of Press Affairs, 10 May 1894, TsGIA, 776-8-847, sheet 1. Interior's approval is to be found in "Programmy gazety 'Russkoe Slovo' ..." TsGALI, 595-1-2, sheet 1.

29 Dinershtein, *I.D. Sytin*, 83.

30 Sytin, *Zhizn' dlia knigi*, 124-5.

31 Alexandrov to the Chief Administration of Press Affairs, 10 May 1894, TsGIA, 776-8-847, sheet 1.

32 “Programmy gazety ‘Russkoe Slovo’ ...” TsGALI 595-1-2, sheet 1.
33 [N.O. Bocharov], “Semeinaia khronika ‘Russkogo Slova’ i ‘Iskry’,...” RO GBL, 295-1-4, sheet 3. Alexandrov recruited such conservative writers as his printer V.A. Gringmunt; Lev Tikhomirov, a reformed revolutionary; the Archimandrite Nikon; and the official who became the conservative director of censorship in mid-1897, M.P. Soloviev.
34 Sytin, *Zhizn' dlia knigi*, 126.
35 Ibid., 125-6; “Istoriia gazety ‘Russkoe Slovo’,” RO GBL, 259-1-1, sheet 3.
36 Sytin to Alexandrov, 31 March 1895, TsGALI, 2-1-747, sheet 5.
37 Sytin, *Zhizn' dlia knigi*, 126.
38 Dinershtein, *I.D. Sytin*, 84.
39 Ibid., 84-5. In the account of the 1896 grant by a writer who joined *Word* in 1899, Alexandrov published “ten hysterical, quasi-patriotic leading articles, in which the attractions of the petty bureaucratic order were eulogized,” and then “travelled to St. Petersburg and returned with a more or less rich subsidy” (Shchetinin, “V literaturnom muraveinike,” 876).
40 Sytin, *Zhizn' dlia knigi*, 127.
41 “Semeinaia khronika ‘Russkogo Slova’ i ‘Iskry’,” RO GBL, 259-1-4, sheet 8.
42 Attorney A.E. Sirin to Alexandrov, 13 August 1897, TsGALI, 2-1-6, sheet 1. The printing bills then amounted to 2,757.05 rubles for *Word* and *Review* together.
43 “Akt o prodazhe A.A. Aleksandrovym gazety ‘Russkoe Slovo’ Ivanu Dmitrievichu Sytinu (kopiia),” TsGALI, 2-1-540, 28 August 1897, sheet 1; Sytin, *Zhizn' dlia knigi*, 127. Dinershtein, citing archival sources, quotes Sytin as having paid 40,000 rubles for *Word*. Dinershtein explains that the figure includes the 15,000 in the sales agreement plus the required 5,000 ruble deposit to the government, plus “overhead expenses” (i.e., a bribe or bribes) of 20,000 rubles (Dinershtein, *I.D. Sytin*, 89). Inikova states flatly that Sytin paid a bribe in St Petersburg to get permission to buy the paper. See S.A. Inikova, “Gazeta I.D. Sytina ‘Russkoe Slovo’ ” (Moscow 1983), 4, unpublished paper 12927, duplicated at INION, Moscow.
44 Sytin, *Zhizn' dlia knigi*, 121. Sytin suspected at the time that the ober-procurator “very much wanted to make me ‘his’ and attract me to the service of the Synod” (105).
45 Ibid., 130-1.
46 V.A. Giliarovsky, “Russkoe Slovo,” *Izbrannoe*, vol. 2 (Moscow 1960), 215; I.I. Iasinsky, *Roman moei zhizni: Kniga vospominanii* (Moscow-Leningrad 1926), 272. I have inferred the dating of the two writers' comments from the context.
47 Sytin, *Zhizn' dlia knigi*, 131.
48 N.I. Gitovich, *Letopis' zhizni i tvorchestva A.P. Chekhova*, 456.
49 TsGIA, 776-8-847, sheet 31. Blagov became a member of the Moscow city

council and therefore had to belong to the merchant's guild. He practised medicine at least until 1911. The city directory (*Vsia Moskva*, 18 vols., 1896–1936) lists him as a doctor specializing in internal illnesses with daily reception hours from 11:30 a.m. to 1:00 p.m.

50 Sytin to Chekhov, 7 October 1897, S.V. Belov, ed., *Kniga: Issledovaniia i materialy* 42 (1981): 135.

51 Dinershtein identifies this suspected candidate as I.N. Sakharov, secretary of the Moscow Committee for Literacy (*I.D. Sytin*, 88).

52 Grand Duke Sergei Alexandrovich to Soloviev, 15 October 1897, Belov, ed., *Sovetskie Arkhivy* 5 (1979): 23-4.

53 S.E. Zvoliasky to the Chief Administration of Press Affairs, 20 October 1897, ibid., 24.

54 Dinershtein, *I.D. Sytin*, 88.

55 Chekhov to A.S. Suvorin, 14 December 1896, Chekhov, *PSS i Pisem*, 6:251. One grandchild remembers several small snug cottages and says he was born in one of them (conversation with Aleksei Vasilievich Sytin, Sytin Museum, 2 June 1989).

56 TsGIA, 776-8-847, sheet 52.

57 Alexandrov worked for the Ministry of the Interior from 1898 to 1900 and then taught in gymnasiums in Riga, St Petersburg, and Moscow until illness caused him to retire in 1915 on full pension. TsGALI, 2-1-9, 12 December 1915, sheet 1. This same file contains a 1918 document authorizing Alexandrov, as an employee, to eat in the cafeteria of the prime Soviet newspaper, *Izvestiia*.

58 TsGIA, 776-8-847, sheets 62, 66.

59 Shchetinin quotes F.N. Berg's comments on Sytin's complaint about his financial losses: "There [Sytin] sits on his treasure chest, trembles and counts his copecks and ... cries, 'I am carrying more losses.' I answer him, 'You have a real gold mine in *Russian Word*; the name alone is worth something.' 'Buy this gold mine,' he tells me. 'I will sell it for a song'." Shchetinin, "V literaturnom muraveinike," 893.

60 Ibid., 877-8.

61 Sytin to Chekhov, 28 January 1899, Belov, ed., *Kniga: Issledovaniia i materialy* 42 (1981): 136.

62 Chekhov to E.Z. Konovitser, 14 February 1899, Chekhov, *PSS i Pisem*, 8:83; Konovitser's reply is on p. 425.

63 Dinershtein, *I.D. Sytin*, 90.

64 S.I. Umanets, "Iz proshlogo nashei tsenzury," *Nasha Starina* 10 (1915): 956. See also A. Sidorov, "Iz vospominanii o tsenzure," *Golos Minuvshego* 3 (1923): 129.

65 I.I. Iasinsky, "Moi tsenzora: (Iz vospominanii)," *Istoricheskii Vestnik* 123, no. 2 (1911): 551.

66 B.B. Glinsky, "M.P. Soloviev i S.I. Kossovich. Iz tsenzurnogo

proshlogo,'' in Glinsky, *Sredi literaturov i uchenykh* (St Petersburg 1914), 443-4. Glinsky describes comic scenes in Soloviev's office when Soloviev ''fell into a faint and so did his petitioners.''

67 The police kept an eye on Rubakin and recorded in July 1900 that he planned to use an honorarium from Sytin to found a Sunday school for workers (TsGIA Moskvy, 102-DO-396, sheet 16). In 1901 the police sent Rubakin into internal exile for two years and his wife for one (presumably for their active membership in the outlawed Social Revolutionary Party). In 1907 he moved to Switzerland, where he compiled his monumental guide to Russian books, *Among Books* (*Sredi Knig*). Sytin was contemplating publishing Rubakin's collected works when the Revolution began.

68 N.I. to Rubakin, 1 July 1897, RO GBL, 358-235-5, sheet 12; and N. I. to Rubakin, 28 July 1897, ibid., sheet 25. ''N.I.'' was surely Nicholas Ivanovich, Sytin's eldest son (now twenty-one), who was to become one of Sytin's main editors.

69 TsGIA Moskvy, D3-81-1813, sheets 53-4.

70 In 1916 the company as much as admitted its ownership by reporting that it never found out the reason for the store's closure. See ''Tovarishchestvo I.D. Sytina. Istoricheskii Ocherk,'' *Polveka dlia knigi*, 372.

71 Quoted by Inikova in ''Gazeta 'Russkoe Slovo' i tsenzura (1897–1917),'' *Problemy istorii SSSR* 13 (Moscow 1983), 248. *Russian Word* had its highest 1899 press run (21,541) when it covered the Pushkin celebration. ''Istoriia gazety '*Russkoe Slovo*,' '' RO GBL 259-1-1, sheet 7.

72 Inikova, ''Gazeta 'Russkoe Slovo' i tsenzura (1897–1917),'' 248; Dinershtein, *I.D. Sytin*, 80.

73 N.P. Bocharov, ''Kratkaia letopis' gazety 'Russkoe Slovo','' RO GBL, 259-1-2, sheets 2-3. Sytin probably chose the name *Sparks* to denote a publication to ''fire'' the interest of readers. By chance he started it almost exactly as Lenin began publishing, in Europe, his paper *Spark* (*Iskra*), with the purpose of kindling a workers' revolution. The Historical Library of the RSFSR in Moscow holds a full run of *Sparks*, 1900–17.

74 ''Iskry,'' *Polveka dlia knigi*, 559-60.

75 D. Batiushkov, ''O tom, kak I.D. Sytin izdal illiustratsiiu k 'Snu Makara' V.G. Korolenko,'' ibid., 109-12; Inikova, ''Gazeta 'Russkoe Slovo' i tsenzura (1897–1917),'' 249.

76 Sytin, *Zhizn' dlia knigi*, 193-6.

77 Shakhovskoi miscalculated in pressing his case through the most extravagant member of Russia's wealthy when Sytin, as one associate put it, always took pride in living like a Spartan. To make his point, S.V. Iablonovsky, a writer for *Russian Word*, says that, when he first met Sytin in 1901, the already wealthy publisher was limping in boots resoled and made too small by a ''scoundrel'' shoemaker. What's more, Sytin had been suffering in them for three days. He was later chided by Sytin, con-

tinues Iablonovsky, for sitting ahead of him in expensive seats in the theatre and for riding in a phaeton rather than a humble cab. While he also claims that his boss kept the well appointed social rooms of his apartment locked and set aside for special occasions, Iablonovsky warmly praises Sytin for never putting on airs. See S.V. Iablonovsky, "Sytin," *Illiustrirovannaia Rossia* 51 (1934): 4-5.

CHAPTER FOUR

1 N.D. Teleshov, *Zapiski pisatelia* (Moscow 1958), 191 (English edition: N. Teleshov, *A Writer Remembers: Reminiscences*, tr. L.E. Britton [London n.d.])

2 A typed copy of Sytin's remarks on the occasion of the thirty-fifth anniversary is at the Sytin Museum.

3 I.N. Pavlov, *Zhizn' russkogo gravera* (Moscow 1963), 126.

4 *Vestnik knigoprodavtsev*, 36 (1901): 562, 578-9.

5 Leonid Andreev, "Vserossiskoe vran'e," *Sobranie Sochinenii* 1 (1911): 66-76.

6 Gor'ky to Andreev, 26-31 January 1901, *Literaturnoe Nasledstvo* 72 (1965), 82.

7 Gor'ky to K.P. Piatnitsky, 1-2 February 1901, *Arkhiv A.M. Gor'kogo*, 9 vols. (Moscow 1954), 4:19.

8 Andreev to N.K. Mikhailovsky, October 1902, *Literaturnoe Nasledstvo* 72 (1965), 499.

9 Gor'ky to Teleshov, 2 December 1901, *Arkhiv A.M. Gor'kogo* (Moscow 1959), 7:33. Liberals admired *zemstvos* as well-springs for grassroots democracy.

10 Gor'ky to Andreev, 2-4 December 1901, *Literaturnoe Nasledstvo* 72 (1965), 113.

11 I.I. Iasinsky, *Roman moei zhizni: kniga vospominanii* (Moscow 1926), 298.

12 On Doroshevich, see S.V. Bukchin, *Sud'ba fel'etonista: Zhizn' i tvorchestvo Vlasa Doroshevicha* (Minsk 1975); and M. Teplinsky, "Vlas Doroshevich - avtor knigi 'Sakhalin' " in *Sakhalin*, ed. P.E. Belousov (Iuzhno-Sakhalinsk 1962). Louise McReynolds has a chapter on Doroshevich in "News and Society: *Russkoe Slovo* and the Development of the Mass Circulation Press in Late Imperial Russia" (Ph.D. dissertation, University of Chicago, December 1984).

13 Sokolova's obituary in *Istoricheskii Vestnik* 3 (1914): 954-9, gives details of her life. See also A.R. Kugel', *Literaturnye vospominaniia, 1882-1896* (Petrograd 1924), 98.

14 V. Giliarovsky, "Moskovskie gazety v 80-kh g.," *Byloe* 6 (1924): 122.

15 Chekhov to M.P. Chekhov, 19 December 1901, *Sobranie Sochinenii*, 12 vols. (Moscow 1964): 12:424.

16 Kugel', *Literaturnye vospominaniia*, 102.
17 The book was *Kak ia popal na Sakhalin* (Moscow 1903, 1906).
18 Amfiteatrov to Sytin, 31 January 1912, RO GBL, 259-10-23, sheet 7.
19 Quoted in Bukchin, *Sud'ba fel'etonista* 128.
20 A.S. Suvorin, *Dnevnik* (Moscow 1923), 273-4.
21 "Dogovor S. Doroshevichem," Sytin Museum. The agreement is described in Bukchin, *Sud'ba fel'etonista*, 165, and in E.A. Dinershtein, *I.D. Sytin* (Moscow 1983), 96.
22 V.M. Doroshevich, "Russkoe Slovo," *Polveka dlia knigi*, ed. N.V. Tulupov (Moscow 1916), 396.
23 Chekhov to M.P. Chekhov, 17 December 1901, *Sobranie Sochinenii*, 12: 424. There seems no reason for Chekhov knowingly to mislead or to veil his meaning in a private letter to his brother. G.S. Petrov also belatedly learned about the hiring of Doroshevich. He wrote to Sytin in November 1901 that he had just spoken to F.M. Berg, then editor of *Tilled Field*, about joining *Word* as editor only to have Berg reject Sytin as too close with his copecks (Petrov to Sytin, 25 November 1901, RO GBL, 259-19-20, sheets 5-8).
24 I.D. Sytin, *Zhizn' dlia knigi* (Moscow 1978), 141.
25 "Istoriia gazety 'Russkoe Slovo'," RO GBL, 259-1-1, sheet 10.
26 The editorial administration of *Word* is summarized in N.A. Chlenova, "Arkhiv gazety 'Russkoe Slovo'," *Istochnikovedenie otechestvennoi istorii, 1981* (Moscow 1982), 118-30.
27 V. Doroshevich, "Russkoe Slovo," 406. Both Doroshevich and Sytin sought to impart to the staff at *Russian Word* what is now called corporate culture - common values, standards, and forms of behaviour.
28 V. Nazhevsky to the Chief Administration of Press Affairs, 31 August 1902, TsGIA, 776-8-847, sheet 184.
29 V.A. Giliarovsky, *Izbrannoe*, 3 vols. (Moscow 1960), 2.210.
30 Kugel', *Literaturnye vospominaniia*, 99.
31 Giliarovsky, *Izbrannoe*, 317-18.
32 Doroshevich to Turkin, 26 February [1903], TsGALI, 091-1-4, sheets 27, 23.
33 One demand from Blagov's business office that Doroshevich rejected was that advertisers be favourably mentioned, even endorsed, in the news columns.
34 Sytin, *Zhizn' dlia knigi*, 141.
35 Doroshevich, "Russkoe Slovo," 410.
36 K. Chukovsky, "Revoliutsiia i literatura: O Vlase Doroshevíche (epitafiia)," *Svoboda i zhizn'* 5 (1906): 2.
37 Anton Krainy [Z.N. Hippius], "Zhizn' i literatura," *Novaia Zhizn'* 11 (1912): 120.
38 D.S. Mirsky, *A History of Russian Literature*, ed. and abr. Francis J. Whitfield (New York 1955), 406.

39 Staryi Zhurnalist [O.L. Orsher], *Literaturnyi put' dorevoliutsionnogo zhurnalista* (Moscow 1930), 45.

40 Giliarovsky, *Izbrannoe*, 317-18.

41 *Word* gave extensive coverage to the death of Chekhov and his last rites. The paper of 3 July 1904 had a large, line-drawn portrait of Chekhov and a eulogistic feuilleton by Doroshevich covering half of page one and part of page two. Besides praising him, Doroshevich described Chekhov as a victim of the fickle public and of stingy publishers (Sytin published very little by Chekhov).

42 Chekhov to his sister Maria, 19 May 1904, *The Life and Letters of Anton Tchekov*, tr. and ed. S.S. Koteliansky and Philip Tomlinson (London 1965), 297.

43 Chekhov to Maria, 24 May 1903, ibid., 285.

44 *Polveka dlia knigi* (1916): 62.

45 "I.D. Sytin," *Russkoe Slovo* 41 (19 February 1917).

46 The plant on Piatnitskaia is described by the head of the mechanical section, V. Frolov, in "Masterskie Tovarishchestva i ikh razvitiia," *Polveka dlia knigi*, 565-81. Frolov says that while in Berlin in 1913, Sytin stopped to watch a just-perfected photogravure press that printed intaglio and decided to buy one at once for *Sparks*. He placed an order when he got home and had the press running the next year. The press produced deeper-toned and sharper-coloured pictures and required less make-ready time than older presses.

47 V.P. Orlov, *Poligraficheskaia promyshlennost' Moskvy: Ocherk raszvitiia do 1917 goda* (Moscow 1953), 277.

48 "Delo Departamenta Politsii o meshchanine Panteleimone Ivanoviche Nechaeve," TsGAOR, 102-1-573 (1902), sheets 1-146.

49 "Delo Departamenta Politsii ...," TsGAOR, 102-1-573, sheet 5. Three were graphic artists (A.E. Tsygankov, 18; I.A. Ivanov, 21; and V.S. Maksimov) and five were from the lithograph section (Ia. I. Markin, 27; P.M. Birev, 42; P.G. Zinoviev, 27; I.E. Tanakov, 41 - all peasants from beyond Moscow - and V.I. Klang, 27, who was legally of the merchantry).

50 Ibid., sheet 35.

51 Ibid., sheet 43.

52 I.N. Pavlov, *Zhizn' russkogo gravera*, 220.

53 N.A. Troinitsky, ed., *Pervaia vseobshchaia perepis' naseleniia Rossiskoi Imperii 1897 g.*, vol. 2, *Chislennost' rabochikh v Rossii na osnovanii dannykh pervoi vseobshei perepisi naselenii Rossiskoi Imperii*, pt. 1: 178, and pt. 2: 22. As for the total work force in the printing industry, the 1897 census counted 52,175 workers throughout the Empire (including such non-Russian publishing centres as Warsaw, Riga, Vilnius), a number equal to 1.6 per cent of the total industrial work force. V.V. Sher, *Istoriia professional'nogo*

dvizheniia rabochikh pechatnogo dela v Moskve: Materialy (Moscow 1911), 31, gives the figure for 1902.

54 Sher, *Istoriia*, 32.

55 An account of the strike is in ibid., 110-40.

56 Moscow Okhranka report in *Rabochee dvizhenie v Rossii v 1901–1904 gg.*, ed. L.M. Ivanov et al. (Leningrad 1975), 178-81.

57 "Istoriia gazety 'Russkoe Slovo'," RO GBL, 259-1-1, sheets 15-6.

58 Advertisement for new subscribers, *Russkoe Slovo* 1 (1 January 1905).

59 Just before the "Country of the Enemy" series appeared in Sytin's *Russian Word*, Sytin & Co. published a book entitled *The War of Russia and Japan* which put the Japanese in the worst light.

60 *Russkoe Slovo* 17 and 28, (19, 30 January 1905).

61 Ibid., 38 (9 February 1905).

62 Ministry of the Interior announcement, 14 October 1905, TsGIA, 776-8-847, sheets 228, 230, and 256.

63 V.P. Orlov, *Poligraficheskaia promyshlennost' Moskvy*, 279. N.S. Trusova et al., eds., *Nachalo pervoi russkoi revoliutsii, Ianvar'-mart 1905 goda* (Moscow 1955), 282.

64 N.I. Miretsky, *Pervaia obraztsovaia tipografiia, 1876-1933: Materialy iz istorii* (Moscow 1933), 36.

65 Trusova, *Nachalo pervoi russkoi revoliutsii*, 284.

66 Sher, *Istoriia*, 150; A. Borshchevsky, S. Reshetov, and N. Chistov, eds., *Moskovskie pechatniki v 1905 godu* (Moscow 1925), 37.

67 Sher, *Istoriia*, 153.

68 *Russkoe Slovo* 45 (16 February 1905).

69 Vice-Governor to Blagov, letters 6-7 April 1905, TsGALI, 595-1-1, sheets 1-2. Blagov invoked a western tenet on press sources: confidentiality.

70 *Russkoe Slovo* 128 and 129, (14, 15 May 1905).

71 S.I. Sokolov to the Moscow Committee on Press Affairs, 26 May 1905, TsGIA, 776-8-848, sheet 16.

72 Ibid., 9 June 1905, sheet 15.

73 As the law prescribed, the order was published in *Russkoe Slovo* 162 (18 June 1905). The comments about the general direction of the paper were framed in a meeting of the Chief Administration of Press Affairs, 16 June 1905, TsGIA, 776-2-36, sheets 69-74.

74 The press statute of 1865, still in effect, exempted papers in Moscow and St Petersburg from preliminary (pre-publication) censorship, but it required official "warnings" for any that showed a "dangerous orientation" (a vague concept subject to broad interpretation). Three warnings gave cause for temporary suspension or closure, at the government's discretion. See Charles A. Ruud, *Fighting Words: Imperial Censorship and the Russian Press, 1804–1906* (Toronto 1982), esp. chs. 9 and 13.

75 There are no figures showing *Word*'s circulation geographically or by social

class, but its large readership in the several provinces of the central industrial region had to include many in the merchant class and what we now term the middle class. Censors, as has been noted, complained about the paper's influence among the peasants and industrial workers.

76 The conservative *Russkaia Pravda* (1904-6) championed the government under editor M.M. Gakkebush (Gorelov). It sold only on the streets and provides another example of Sytin's eclectic publishing range.

77 A copy of the text of the agreement is in the archive of the Fifth Section of the Moscow Revenue Department, TsGIA, Moskvy, 51-10-1166, 16 November 1915 - 22 September 1917, sheet 87. A.M. Bokhanov concludes that nothing changed in Sytin's holdings as a result of this agreement. See A.M. Bokhanov, *Burzhuaznaia pressa Rossii i krupnyi kapital* [Konets XIX v. - 1914] (Moscow 1984), 63.

78 Bokhanov cites 1910 as the year of settlement (ibid., 62). A calculation based on the profit figures available for *Word* in the annual reports yields the same result. Annual reports for Sytin & Co. for a number of years are in TsGIA, INION, and Lenin Library, all in Moscow.

CHAPTER FIVE

1 V.V. Sher, *Istoriia professional'nogo dvizheniia rabochikh pechatnogo dela v Moskve* (Moscow 1911), 164-5.

2 Report of the Moscow Okhranka to the Moscow Governor General, 12-19 September 1905. L.M. Ivanova et al., eds., *Vserossiiskaia politicheskaia stachka v oktiabre 1905 goda* (Moscow 1955), 55-6.

3 Report of the police of the Piatnitskaia district to the Moscow Chief of Police, 20 September 1905, ibid., 49-50.

4 Iu. Milonov, ed., *Moskovskoe professional'noe dvizhenie v godu pervoi revoliutsii. K dvadtsatiletiiu 1905 goda* ([Moscow 1925]), 166.

5 The police reports for 23, 24, and 25 September are in Ivanova et al., *Vserossiiskaia politicheskaia stachka*, 57-60, 71.

6 Sher, *Istoriia*, 168.

7 The resolutions of the Soviet are in Ivanova et al., *Vserossiiskaia politicheskaia stachka*, 61-2.

8 Ibid., 72. This leaflet, a call to continue the strike, was issued over the name of the Union of Moscow Typographical Workers.

9 Sher, *Istoriia*, 177. Sytin did not negotiate directly with his workers. He said business, not labour, was his concern, and he assigned A.V. Vasil'ev, one of the directors, to conduct talks. See *Zamoskvorech'e v 1905 godu*, comp. N. Morozov-Vorontsov (Moscow 1905), 76.

10 I.D. Sytin Co. to the Chief of Police of the Piatnitskaia District, 30 September 1905, N.I. Miretsky, *Pervaia obraztsovaia tipografiia, 1876-1933. Materialy iz istorii* (Moscow 1933), 55.

11 The settlement is described in Sher, *Istoriia*, 180.

12 "Istoriia gazety 'Russkoe Slovo'," RO GBL 259-1-1, sheet 19.

13 Sher, *Istoriia*, 184.

14 Miretsky, *Pervaia obraztsovaia*, 56-7.

15 Ibid., 60.

16 Konstantin Konichev, *Russkii Samorodok* (Leningrad 1966), 130. This incident has the ring of documented fact because Konichev precisely dates the gift by Sytin as 18 October 1905 and its diversion to MUPW as happening 19 October.

17 *Russkoe Slovo* 292 (6 November 1905).

18 I have elaborated on these events in "The Printing Press as an Agent of Political Change in Early Twentieth Century Russia," *Russian Review* 40, no. 4 (October 1981): 378-95. Witte was chairman of the Council of Ministers, but scholars conventionally call him prime minister.

19 Miretsky, *Pervaia obraztsovaia*, 63.

20 Ibid., 62. For his role in printing *Izvestiia*, Vasily was briefly sentenced to administrative exile that required him to stay at least fifty versts (thirty miles) outside Moscow. He therefore stayed at Sytin's country estate.

21 I.D. Sytin, *Zhizn' dlia knigi* (Moscow 1978), 168.

22 Ibid., 170.

23 Ibid., 172.

24 *Sytintsy v 1905 godu. Sbornik vospominanii rabochikh Pervoi Obraztsovoi tipografii (b. Sytina)*, ed. E. Rumailo, N.I. Miretsky, L. Mal'kov [Moscow 192?], 96-110. There are also excerpts from the transcripts in Miretsky, *Pervaia obraztsovaia*, 65-8. Miretsky appears to have read an account by printers involved in the events (A. Borshevsky, S. Reshetov, and N. Chistov, eds., *Moskovskie pechatniki v 1905 godu* [Moscow 1925], 86) for his article, "Ot Sytina k Pervoi Obraztsovoi tip. (1876-1931)," *Bor'ba Klassov* 5 (1932), which argues that soldiers started the fire.

25 Miretsky, *Pervaia obraztsovaia*, 66-7.

26 *Sytintsy v 1905 godu*, 96. Sergei Dmitrievich Sytin (c.1863-c.1915) is the younger brother whose arrival seemingly forced Ivan to leave school and go to work at twelve. As a profligate youth, he fell under the influence of Tolstoy in the mid-eighties (Sytin began publishing Mediator in 1885) and thereupon joined a rural commune, whose good effects he described to Tolstoy in an 1886 letter. The next year he appeared at Tolstoy's estate, announcing his intention to work nearby and committing himself to Tolstoy's "Agreement against Drunkenness." Tolstoy, in an 1888 letter to his wife, agreed that Sergei had become a "burden," but one he would bear "reasonably and well." Late in the eighties Sergei left for Smolensk province to open a school; but, failing that, he moved to Moscow to live with Sytin and to work as a supervisor at the printing plant. See volumes 50, 64, 84 and 85 of L.N. Tolstoy, *Polnoe Sobranie Sochinenii*, 91 vols. (Moscow 1928-1978).

27 Miretsky, *Pervaia obraztsovaia*, 98.

28 Ibid., 66; *Sytintsy v 1905 godu*, 96-7.

29 Miretsky, *Pervaia obraztsovaia*, 67-8.

30 Miretsky, "Ot Sytina k Pervoi Obraztsovoi tip. (1876–1931)," 84.

31 *Zamoskvorech'e v 1905 gody*, 43.

32 N.N. Malakhov to A.F. Rediger, 20 December 1905, A.L. Sidorov et al., eds., *Vysshii pod''em revoliutsii 1905–1907 gg. Vooruzhenie vosstaniia. Noiabria-dekabria 1905 goda* (Moscow 1955), 725. Both *Moscow Messenger* and *Russian Newssheet* reported the arrest of one of Sytin's sons (unidentified) at the burning plant because he had shot at Cossacks with a machine gun. *Russian Word* termed this allegation "a fantasy of the reptile press."

33 "Informatsionnye soobshcheniia gaz. '*Pravo*'," 18-24 December 1905, Sidorov et al., *Vysshii pod''em revoliutsii*, 702. Teleshov recounts the fire in this way in his memoirs: "The Sytin printing plant was the central point of the Zamoskvoreche's defence and defended by several barricades. Shells from tsarist artillery ignited the printing plant and fire brigades that arrived were forbidden to put the fire out." (Quoted by B. Sibirsky, "Zagrobnoe vozmezdie," *Vozrozhdenie* 127 [1962], 86). In contrast, Bernard Pares, who knew Sytin, wrote: "Sytin was very much cast down at the time because his press had been burnt down by the revolutionaries during the abortive Moscow uprising." See *My Russian Memoirs* (London 1931), 119.

34 This summary of the proceedings is based on a story in *Russian Word* 35 (12 February 1908).

35 Sytin, *Zhizn' dlia knigi*, 172.

36 Ibid., 173-4.

37 The record of prosecutions and fines is in the archive of the Chief Administration of Press Affairs, TsGIA, 776-8-848, 776-8-853, and 776-8-854.

38 Telegram from Osorgin to the Minister of the Interior, 10 November 1905, TsGIA, 776-8-848, sheet 114.

39 Ibid., sheet 119. S.I. Inikova, "Gazeta 'Russkoe Slovo' i tsenzura, 1897–1917," *Problemy istorii SSSR* 13 (1983): 251.

40 Ibid., 252. This source also confirms, by citing two separate court orders for the destruction of an issue of *Word*, one indictment and conviction in 1912 (for a letter to the editor condemning Rasputin) and the same in 1914 (Inikova does not state the grounds but does say that the confiscated copies this time amounted to a handful of the more than 600,000 printed).

41 "Istoriia gazety 'Russkoe Slovo' Ocherk (1894–1914)," RO GBL 259-1-1, sheets 20-1. Later in 1906 Sytin published *Whirlwind* in book form with the title intact. There were no repercussions, for the book ridiculed the "liberals" of 1905 for extreme self-interest.

42 The table below shows the number of times the Committee on Press Affairs asked for indictments against *Word* from 1905 through 1916 and the available figures on administrative fines after their reinstatement in 1907.

Year	*Requests to indict*	*Fine total (in rubles)*	*Year*	*Requests to indict*	*Fine total (in rubles)*
1905	2	–	1911	0	N/A
1906	13	–	1912	6	2,400
1907	1	5,000	1913	1	3,500
1908	1	8,100	1914	4	8,000
1909	2	4,000	1915	2	N/A
1910	2	3,500	1916	1	N/A

Compiled from Inikova, ''Gazeta 'Russkoe Slovo' i tsenzura (1897-1917),'' 254, 256; and TsGIA 776-8-847-853.

43 I.V. Gessen says that he talked with Sytin in 1906 about hiring his presses to print a newspaper for the Constitutional Democratic Party. I.V. Gessen, *V dvukh vekakh. Zhiznennyi otchet* (Berlin 1937), 218. He describes Sytin as a ''half-educated pedlar who very skilfully put himself forward as a simpleton in order to conceal a sharp native wit.''

44 For Petrov's career through 1906, see A.V. Rumanov, *Sviashchennik G. S. Petrov. Biografiia i ist. ssylki v monastyr'* (Moscow 1907). This laudatory account by the head of *Word*'s St Petersburg bureau was published by Sytin in the year that Petrov gave up journalism to serve in the Duma.

45 E.A. Dinershtein, *I.D. Sytin* (Moscow 1983), 102. Proof that high officials were angry with Sytin's paper comes from the minister of finance, who tells that, as the first Duma started, ''*Russian Bulletin*, *Russian Word*, and *Speech* [the Kadets' St Petersburg daily] were quite openly conducting the 'attack on the government' of which Goremykin [then prime minister] had spoken to me and were preaching that now was the time for the representatives of the people to take all authority into their hands.'' See V.N. Kokovtsev, *Out of My Past*, ed. H.H. Fisher, tr. Laura Matveev (Stanford 1935), 124.

46 The combined loss to Sytin & Co. from *God's Truth* and *Duma* was 30,000 rubles. An equal deficit in 1906 came from three established journals: *Little Bee* and *Friend of Children* (both for juveniles) and *Around the World*. In 1907 these three would together lose another 20,000 rubles. See A.N. Bokhanov, *Burzhuaznaia pressa Rossii i krupnyi kapital, konets XIX v. – 1914 g.* (Moscow 1984), 59-60.

47 Petrov to Sytin, 13 August 1908, RO GBL, 259-19-21, sheet 1.

48 The following table shows the relative worth of subscriptions versus single-copy sales of *Russian Word* and *Sparks*, 1907-10:

Year	*Subscription revenue (rubles)*	*Percent of total*	*Single copy revenue (rubles)*	*Percent of total*
1907	505,900	60	343,000	40
1908	515,400	58	357,400	42
1909	560,300	56	440,000	44
1910	691,800	60	472,000	40

Sources: Bokhanov, *Burzhuaznaia pressa*, 63; and the incomplete files of annual reports by Sytin & Co. (*Otchet pravleniia tov. Pech., Izd., i Kn. Tor. I.D. Sytina v Moskve*) in Lenin Library, the Library of Scientific Information in the Social Sciences of the Academy of Sciences, Moscow, and TsGIA Moskvy, 2316-1-1. For overall figures on annual press runs, see Figure 5 (page 209 in this book).

49 "Istoriia Gazety 'Russkoe Slovo'," RO GBL 259-1-1, sheet 23.

50 V. Piast [A. Pestkovsky], *Vstrechi* (Moscow 1929), 214.

51 Tolstoy to Gorbunov-Posadov, 14 November 1906, L. Tolstoy, *PSS*, 76:33. "Shakespeare and the Drama" appeared in 1906 issues of *Russian Word* dated 14, 15, 16, 17, 18, and 23 November.

52 Both the Ministry of Trade and Industry and the Council of Ministers gave their assent on 4 October 1907. *Obshchii zhurnal Soveta Ministrov*, 5 October 1907, TsGIA, 1276-17-37, sheet 78.

53 Sytin to Vas. I. Nemirovich-Danchenko, 26 December 1907, TsGALI, 2571-1-397, sheet 1.

54 Dmitry Ivanovich Sytin, "Iz vospominanii vnuka I.D. Sytina," Sytin Museum, 1.

55 S.I. Inikova, "Gazeta I.D. Sytina 'Russkoe Slovo', 1897–1917" (Moscow 1983), 39 (MS duplicated in INION AN SSSR, no. 12927).

56 A. Ertel' to I.D. Sytin, 24 March 1906, Sytin Museum.

57 The only records of stockholdings are for 1907, 1914, 1915, 1917, and 1919. See note 36 for ch. 8.

58 *Russkoe Slovo* 17 (23 January 1907).

59 P.A. Buryshkin, *Moskva kupecheskaia* (New York 1954), 286.

60 In its reports for 1908-10, the Moscow Press Affairs Committee repeated this evaluation. TsGIA Moskvy, 31-5-734, list 17.

CHAPTER SIX

1 Chekhov to Aleksei Suvorin, 17 January 1897, *Letters of Anton Chekhov*, tr. Michael Henry Heim, ed. Simon Karlinsky (New York 1973), 293.

2 I.D. Sytin, *Zhizn' dlia knigi* (Moscow 1978), 112-16.

3 One of Sytin's primers from the turn of the century (*The World in Stories*

for Children by V.P. Vakhterov and his wife, both educators) would sell spectacularly and go into many editions; its press run in 1910 would be 1,290,000 copies. The engraver who helped prepare the illustrations remembers Vakhterov as a "small dried-up little old man" whose "colossal" earnings amounted to "hundreds of thousands per year." He claims that Tulupov prepared his readers "with the help of paste and scissors" to earn 50,000 rubles per year. I.N. Pavlov, *Zhizn' russkogo gravera* (Moscow 1963), 218.

4 *Katalog izdanii tovarishchestva I.D. Sytina* (Moscow 1905 and 1906).

5 Sytin, *Zhizn' dlia knigi*, 115.

6 N.I. Iordansky, "Uchebnaia literatura v izdanii I.D. Sytina," *Polveka dlia knigi*, ed. N.V. Tulupov (Moscow 1916), 475. Incomplete figures available from the 1880s to World War I show, for example, that Sytin & Co. submitted 412 texts for the first two classes of the higher schools and gained approval for 132, or 32 per cent. Among these, twenty-three of thirty-two "classroom reading" books were approved; seven of twenty-eight arithmetic texts; only three of twenty-one scriptural books. However, of the thirty-nine volumes for school libraries, the ministry approved all but two. See S.I. Inikova, "Tovarishchestvo pechataniia, izdatel'stva i knizhnoi torgovli I.D. Sytina (1883–1917) (Kandidat dissertation, Moscow University 1985), 134.

7 Sytin, *Zhizn' dlia knigi*, 117. The application and accompanying explanatory note are in the archives of the Imperial Ministry of Trade and Industry. TsGIA, 23-12-209, sheets 1-35.

8 Ibid., sheets 3-4.

9 A.V. Rumanov, " 'Mechta' I.D. Sytina," *Polveka dlia knigi*, 33.

10 Inikova, "Tovarishchestvo pechataniia ...," 131.

11 For evidence about the use of the courts against the press, see the article by S.R. Mintslov, "14 mesiatsev 'svobody pechati.' 17 oktiabria 1905 g. – 1 ianvaria 1907 g," *Byloe* 1-4 (March 1907): 123-46. Mintslov lists the confiscations of separate issues of 84 satirical journals, of 113 newspapers and journals in St Petersburg, as well as of 352 books.

12 This trial is summarized in S.I. Inikova, "Tovarishchestvo I.D. Sytina i tsenzura, 1883–1914," *Problemy istorii SSSR* 12 (1982): 164.

13 Ibid., 165.

14 The surviving court documents are in the archive of the Moscow Court of Appeals. See TsGIA Moskvy, 131-73-102, vols. 1 and 2, and TsGIA Moskvy, 131-75-37, vol. 1.

15 TsGIA Moskvy, 131-73-102, vol. 2, sheet 7.

16 S.I. Varshavsky, *Russkoe Slovo* 42 (21 February 1917)

17 The records of this case are in the archive of the Moscow prosecutor of the Court of Appeals, TsGIA Moskvy, 131-73-103, vol. 2; 139-93-103, vol. 4; and the archive of the Criminal Department of the Moscow Court

of Appeals, TsGIA Moskvy, 131-77-69, vols. 1-2.

18 TsGIA Moskvy, 139-93-103, vol. 4, sheets 4-5.

19 The Moscow Court of Appeals ruled against Skvortsov in October 1910 because he, as a company employee, had agreed to contribute stories for nothing to *Friend of Children* and *Little Bee*. TsGIA Moskvy, 131-73-103, vol. 4, sheets 126-7.

20 TsGIA Moskvy, 139-93-103, vol. 4, sheet 30. Sytin's lawyers introduced material from *Knizhnyi Vestnik* on the comparative output of 140 firms in 1908, and below are listed the top five in three categories.

Ruble-value of books published in 1908

Sytin		2,808,055*	
E. Konovalova	582,836		
V. Dumov	519,308	1,877,347	total of other four in top five
K. Rikker	403,203		
Brockhaus, Efron	372,000		

*A much higher figure than the 1,718,500-ruble amount reported for 1908 to the Moscow Revenue Department in 1916 (see figure 2).

Total copies published in 1908

Sytin		12,303,200
E. Konovalova	3,514,870	
Razvlechenie	3,334,000	10,431,148
N. Aleksandr	1,920,508	
Mediator	1,661,770	

Total titles published in 1908

Sytin		718
E. Konovalova	249	
Iurgenson [music printer]	160	
Mediator	154	667
V. Dumov	104	

21 The documents are in the files of the Moscow Court of Appeals, TsGIA Moskvy, 131-92-119, sheets 1-5.

22 *Glasnost'* was a term that in the early years of the twentieth century had loosely taken on connotations of freedom of the press. In its stricter legal definition, traceable to the judicial reform of 1864, *glasnost'* meant "permitted public discussion." Such discussion in the press was exempt from judicial prosecution.

23 "Istoriia gazety 'Russkoe Slovo'. Ocherk (1894-1914)," RO GBL 259-1-1, sheet 28; *Russkoe Slovo* 232 (9 October 1910).

24 Sytin's council tenure apparently lasted five years and followed Blagov's two-year term (1905-7). By law all members had to own substantial property. Sytin's membership in ameliorative organizations included the Society for Protection of Homeless Juveniles Released from Incarceration, the Moscow Orphanage Society, and the State Society for the Care of Children of Public Teachers and Clerks. This information is from the comprehensive professional and business directory, *Vsia Moskva*, 18 vols. (Moscow 1896-1936).

25 A., "Tainy sytinskogo knigoizdatel'stva," *Stolichnaia Molva* 71, 72, and 74 (7, 8, and 17 August 1909). Although a weekly, this publication issued about sixty issues in a year.

26 I.R. Kugel' says he saw a print order in Sytin's office for a certain number of copies of a book by V. Ia. Kanel and shortly thereafter heard Sytin cite a much smaller figure to the author. I.R. Kugel', "Sytin: Vospominaniia o proshlom russkoi pechati," *Leningrad* 23/24 (1940): 17.

27 During this congress, delegates elected Sytin to the Organization Bureau for the next session and endorsed a report by Sytin's attorney, Varshavsky, critical of continuing government controls on publishing. M. Lemke, ed., *Trudy pervogo vserossiskogo s''ezda izdatelei i knigoprodavtsev, 30 iiunia - 5 iiulia, 1909 goda* (St Petersburg 1909), 87-92.

28 For one, see the remarks of G.I. Porshnev on the eve of the 1917 Revolution quoted in note 30 to ch. 9. Even old friend Altaev chose to mention Sytin's opportunistic merchandising in her recollections of him in 1946 (when he was still out of favour). This "completely illiterate capitalist," she wrote, "understood the meaning of 'wise books' " but "conveyed to the markets crude popular pictures, little doll books, little cat books, dog books with doggerel for children." Al. Altaev (M.V. Iamshchikova), *Pamiatnye vstrechi* (Moscow-Leningrad 1946), 296. I.R. Kugel's earlier (1940) article on Sytin, quoted in ch. 1, more starkly described a profiteer and political opportunist.

29 "Knizhnik-farisei," *Moskva* (6 July 1909), 3.

30 Petrov to Blagov, 12, 16 May 1909, TsGALI, 595-1-46, sheets 1-2.

31 Petrov to Sytin (11 May 1909?), ibid., sheet 11.

32 Sytin to Petrov (June 1909?), in S.V. Belov, ed., "Iz perepiski I.D. Sytina," *Kniga: Issledovaniia i materialy* 42 (1981): 139.

33 V.A. Posse, *Moi zhiznennyi put', dorevoliutsionnyi period, 1864-1917 gg.*, ed. B.P. Koz'min (Moscow 1929), 160 1.

34 Bunin to Gor'ky, 26 April 1909, M. Gor'ky, *Materialy i issledovaniia*, ed. S.D. Balukhaty and V.A. Desnitsky, 3 vols. (Leningrad 1934), 2:411.

35 Gor'ky to I.P. Ladyzhnikov, after 23 April 1909, *Pis'ma k pisateliam i I.P. Ladyzhnikovu*, vol. 7 of *Arkhiv A.M. Gor'kogo* (Moscow 1959), 193. At least one of the "other proposals" that Gor'ky had in mind was to start

a radical journal in Russia with Sytin as principal backer. M. Gor'ky, *Sobranie Sochinenii*, 30 vols. (Moscow 1954–55), 29:550.

36 Dinershtein, *I.D. Sytin*, 143. In 1910 Sytin would open a bookstore in Sofia, Bulgaria, with publisher A.S. Suvorin of St Petersburg but fail to lure him into a stock company for jointly operating kiosks in rail stations – seemingly a new approach by Sytin for securing a long-term contract from the rail directors. Sytin to A.S. Suvorin, 3 September 1910, TsGALI, 495-1-4150, sheet 1.

37 Sytin sent Bunin a congratulatory telegram, TsGALI, 44-2-127, sheet 1.

38 Bunin to Gor'ky and M.F. Andreevna, 15 September 1909, *Gor'kovskie chteniia, 1958–1959* (Moscow 1961), 43.

39 Statistics are slippery, but all available sources rank Sytin & Co. first among Russian publishers from 1908 onward. The figures on book production from *Knizhnyi Vestnik* for 1908, already cited above in note 20, place Sytin & Co. first and "E. Konovalova" second in (1) gross worth, (2) total copies, and (3) total titles. More important, they show how greatly Sytin surpassed second-place Konovalova (Sytin's book worth was nearly five times higher; his total copies, three and one half times higher; and his titles, nearly three times higher). In addition, of course, Sytin & Co. had an immense production of calendars and pictures.

40 Sytin to Blagov [June 1910], TsGALI, 595-1-50, sheets 7-8.

41 Sytin to Blagov, 11 June 1910, TsGALI, 595-1-150, sheets 1-4.

42 Sytin to Blagov, [June 1910], ibid., sheets 5-6.

CHAPTER SEVEN

1 Alexandra Tolstoy, *A Life of My Father* (New York 1953), 507.

2 E.A. Dinershtein, "Vo imia blagogo dela (L.N. Tolstoi, I.D. Sytin i 'Posrednik'), *Kniga: Issledovaniia i materialy* 37 (1978): 88.

3 Dinershtein, "Vo imia blagogo," 89. See also the account of the Kursk Station episode in A.B. Gol'denveizer, *Vblizi Tolstogo* (Moscow 1959), 236, 319, 446.

4 Anne Edwards, *Sonya* (New York 1981), 428; Henri Troyat, *Tolstoy* (Garden City, NY, 1967), 683. All the Russian and major foreign papers gave extensive coverage to Tolstoy's death and funeral.

5 Western biographers often wrongly show Sonia totally shut out of decisions on the publication of Tolstoy's works after her husband's death. Although she could not prevent transfer of Tolstoy's literary works to the public domain, she did have a say in deciding what amount Sytin should give her for her lost rights to the pre-1881 works and did receive that amount as entirely her own.

6 The other three were N.K. Murav'ev, the lawyer who drafted the will; N.N. Gusev, a former assistant to Tolstoy; and A.K. Khir'iakov.

7 Company founder A.F. Marks had pioneered in offering periodical premiums and had earlier used the works of Dostoevsky to promote *Field.* See A.G. Dostoevskaia, ''Prodazha prav 'Nive' (Iz vospominanii),'' ed. S.V. Belov, *Kniga: Issledovaniia i materialy* 32 (1976): 147-58.

8 Dinershtein, ''Vo imia blagogo,'' 91.

9 Ibid., 92.

10 Ibid., 93-4.

11 S.A. Tolstaia, *Dnevniki v dvykh tomakh*, ed. N.I. Azarova, O.A. Golinenko, I.A. Pokrovskaia, S.A. Rozanova, B.M. Shumova (Moscow 1978), 2:373. The editors of this source mistake what Sytin ''bought'' with the 100,000 rubles handed to Sonia in April 1912. Sonia uses the term ''books'' in her diary and the Soviet editors have assumed that Sytin purchased the ''remnants in the warehouse of all her editions'' (p. 563) – that is actual books. Cathy Porter repeats this erroneous assumption in her English translation of the *Diaries*: ''Aleksandra Tolstaya suggested to I.D. Sytin that he buy from Sofia Tolstaya all the unsold copies of all her editions still in the warehouse.'' See *The Diaries of Sophia Tolstoy*, tr. Cathy Porter, intro. R.F. Christian (New York 1985), 969. But having paid at the outset for the right to publish any of Tolstoy's books, the publisher was the one who owned all unsold copies. Rather, Sytin gave Sonia 100,000 rubles as compensation for her lost ''rights'' with respect to all future editions of Tolstoy's pre-1881 books. The problem raised by Tolstoy's conceding these rights to Sonia only to revoke them by his will was separate from the controversy between Sonia and Sasha over the rights to the manuscripts and diaries by Tolstoy that had not yet appeared in print.

12 Dinershtein, ''Vo imia blagogo,'' 95. Dinershtein also says that Sytin offered to pay a salary of four thousand rubles to Paul Biriukov (a close associate of Chertkov) to edit the works.

13 I.D. Sytin, *Zhizn' dlia knigi* (Moscow 1978), 174-80.

14 Ibid., 180.

15 Dinershtein, ''Vo imia blagogo,'' 96-7.

16 Russia had a stake in the Balkans conflict (embroiling Turkey, Greece, Montenegro, Serbia, and Bulgaria) that began in October 1912, and V.I. Nemirovich-Danchenko once again went to the war zone to send daily dispatches to *Word*. Elections to the fourth Duma took place in November 1912.

17 N. Valentinov [N.V. Volsky], ''Aleksandr Blok i 'Russkoe Slovo','' *Dva goda s simvolistami*, ed. Gleb Struve (Stanford 1969), 230.

18 Amfiteatrov to Sytin, 9 December 1911, S.V. Belov, ed., ''Iz perepiski I.D. Sytina,'' *Kniga: Issledovaniia i materialy* 42 (1981): 142-3. About this time Sytin had Rumanov approach A.A. Suvorin, the liberal-leaning son of the conservative publisher, with a proposal to become editor of *Russian Word*; but Suvorin said he found the paper too liberal. E.A. Dinershtein, *I.D. Sytin* (Moscow 1983), 108.

19 Dinershtein, *I.D. Sytin*, 109. Alexander Blok mentions in his diary on 30 December 1911 that Doroshevich had left *Word*. Blok, *Sobranie Sochinenii*, eds. V.N. Orlov, A.A. Surkov, K.I. Chukovsky, 8 vols. (Moscow 1963), 7:114-15.

20 Struve's reply is cited in Dinershtein, *I.D. Sytin*, 108.

21 Petrov to Sytin (1912?), RO GBL, 259-18-20, sheet 31. On Struve's journalistic outlook and his ties to the Faction of Peaceful Renewal, see Richard Pipes, *Struve: Liberal on the Right, 1905–1944* (Cambridge, Mass.: 1980), ch. 4.

22 Amfiteatrov to Sytin, 31 January 1912, RO GBL, 259-10-23, sheet 6.

23 Sytin to Rumanov, 17 January 1912, TsGALI 1694-1-730, sheets 16-17.

24 I.R. Kugel', "Sytin: Vospominaniia o proshlom russkoi pechati," *Leningrad* 23/24 (1940): 18.

25 Valentinov, "Aleksandr Blok i 'Russkoe Slovo'," 230.

26 Kugel', "Sytin," 18.

27 Dinershtein, *I.D. Sytin*, 141. For a later reference to Rumanov's role, see Andreev to Rumanov, 12 February 1912, TsGALI, 1694-1-33, sheet 6.

28 Alexander Kaun, *Leonid Andreev: A Critical Study* (New York 1924 [AMS ed., 1970]), 308. In the play, the Romans (the government) carry off the Sabine women (civil liberties) and the Sabines (the Kadets) feebly resort to words, not swords, to get them back.

29 Andreev to Blagov, 12 February 1912, TsGALI, 595-1-44, sheets 1-2.

30 Andreev to Rumanov, 19 February 1912, TsGALI, 1694-1-33, sheet 6.

31 Andreev to Sytin, 6 April 1912, S. Belov, ed., "Iz perepiski I.D. Sytina," *Kniga: Issledovaniia i materialy* 42 (1981): 144; Dinershtein, *I.D. Sytin*, 142.

32 Staff member A.V. Filosofov welcomed Doroshevich's return because "without him *Russian Word* was bland" and because it provided "the best escape from the difficulty [over Kugel']." See Filosofov to Rumanov, 6 March 1912, TsGALI, 1694-1-649, sheets 7-8. Noting the big names at *Word*, he mentions "Gor'ky, Andreev, Merezhkovsky" and should have added Bunin, whose lengthy story, *Ignat*, would be serialized in *Word* in July.

33 Valentinov, "Aleksandr Blok i 'Russkoe Slovo'," 230. In conceding to Valentinov, Doroshevich borrowed two lines from Pushkin's poem, "As down the noisy streets I wander": "... It is the season/For me to fade, for thee to bloom" (Alexander Pushkin, *Collected Narrative and Lyrical Poetry*, tr. Walter Arndt [Ann Arbor 1984], 95).

34 Doroshevich and Sytin signed a 48,000-rubles-a-year, five-year revocable contract, effective 1 March, on 24 February 1912. As in their initial 1901 contract, Doroshevich could write for no other Russian daily or weekly and was to provide *Word* with a signed feuilleton each week; but he had to submit a much higher number of articles and reviews, as well (eighty-eight per year of each). He had final say on their content. The responsible

editor (Blagov) could alone reject "inconvenient" content, but only after justifying that decision. Besides advising the responsible editor on editorial matters, Doroshevich had the right to veto the installation of anyone authorized to reject what he wrote (i.e., any replacement for Blagov). He agreed to reside each year at least three months in Moscow and the same in St Petersburg, being free to submit his work the other six months from wherever he chose. (This 1912 contract is at the Sytin Museum.)

35 The 23rd annual report of the directors of Sytin & Co. can be found in TsGIA Moskvy, 51-10-1166.

36 A. Rumanov, "I.D. Sytin – Izdatel'," *Vremennik druzei russkoi knigi* 4 (1938): 231. Sytin also hoped to buy papers in Kiev and Odessa.

37 Petrov to Sytin (1911?), TsGALI, 595-1-73, sheets 1-2.

38 Sytin says his visit to Stolypin took place shortly before Stolypin went to Kiev in late August 1911. On 1 September Stolypin was assassinated in the Kiev opera house. See unpublished chapter from the original ms of Sytin's memoirs, Sytin Museum, 296-9.

39 Petrov cites the 500,000 ruble figure in a letter late in 1912 as available "three years ago" (Petrov to V.I. Sytin and M.T. Solov'ev, 17 December 1912, TsGALI, 595-1-46, sheet 24). He cites the figure again in 1917 (Petrov to Sytin, 13 April 1917, RO GBL, 259-19-21, sheet 29).

40 Sytin to Rumanov [1911], TsGALI, 1694-1-626a, sheets 34-5. Suvorin's independent-minded son, A.A., was also one of Sytin's candidates to edit *Word* in Moscow. (See above, note 18.) Putilov belonged to the family that owned St Petersburg's largest factory, the Putilov Works. In 1904-5, he was deputy minister of finance under S.I. Witte, who promoted industrialization in Russia based on western precedents.

41 P.A. Sergeenko to Sytin, 8 July 1912, Sytin Museum. "This letter not sent to I.D. Sytin" appears at the top.

42 TsGALI, 595-1-30, sheets 2-3. Because a son's patronymic (second name) is formed by adding a suffix to the father's first name, editor P.D. Zaikin and letter-writer M.P. Zaikin can easily be father and son.

43 TsGALI, 595-1-30, sheet 1.

44 Natalia Vlasovna, Doroshevich's daughter, says in her unpublished memoirs that early in 1911 the Constitutional Democratic Party offered Sytin one million rubles for *Word*, providing that Doroshevich remained as chief writer. She quotes this indignant response from her father. "This little merchant [Sytin] it seems, has got it into his head to sell my newspaper and me along with it! Keep in mind that neither *Russian Word* nor Doroshevich is for sale to any party for any price." Quoted from the archival source by S.V. Bukchin, *Sud'ba fel'etonista: zhizn' i tvorchestvo Vlasa Doroshevicha*, ed. F.I. Kushelov (Minsk 1974), 196. Bukchin concludes that Sytin, attracted by the idea of "getting out of politics," did entertain the offer. Other Soviet specialists accept this view, but no corroborating evi-

dence from the Kadets or others has come to light. Moreover, the Kadets already had an influential daily, *Speech* (*Rech'*). More likely, Natalia Vlasovna was misconstruing Sytin's attempt to hire Struve as editor late in 1911, a move that Doroshevich could have called a "sell-out" to the liberals and one which coincided with his resignation. *Word* was, in any case, worth much more than one million rubles.

45 Valentinov, *Dva goda s simvolistami*, 118-19.

46 Sytin to Rumanov (1912?), TsGALI, 1694-1-626a, sheets 52-4. Sytin also told Rumanov, "Our institution owes Kugel' 20,000 rubles [apparently the compensation for not hiring him at *Word*] and it is necessary to pay him. We promised word of honour to pay him in January as agreed. I don't know of any other conditions."

47 This company's ownership of *Day* is recorded in *Bibliografiia periodicheskikh izdanii Rossii, 1901–1916*, ed. L.N. Beliaev et al., 4 vols. (Leningrad 1958), 1:438. Kugel's account is in I.R. Kugel',"Iz vospominanii," *Literaturnyi Sovremennik* 12 (1940): 121-6.

48 Following Sytin's withdrawal, the Northern Publishing Company of I.R. Kugel', A.S. Zalshupin, E.E. Kedrin, and V.M. Zhukovsky assumed ownership. Lesin seems to have been a silent partner, like Sytin.

49 Another probable cause for the break was an attempt by persons at *Day* to lure Valentinov from *Word*, for an undated letter by Sytin indicates that such an offer came up in 1912 while he yet held an interest in *Day*. In it, Sytin tells Rumanov of having just learned from Valentinov of his defection to *Day* for "around one million rubles" - surely a hyperbolic figure. It was best that this "agitation remain secret," argues Sytin, but they should try to "keep [Valentinov] by offering him something." And Valentinov did stay. A Soviet archivist wrongly dated this letter in 1913. Sytin to Rumanov [1913?] TsGALI, 1694-1-626a, sheets 43-6.

50 Valentinov, "Aleksandr Blok i 'Russkoe Slovo'," 230-1. Gleb Struve provides a sketch of Valentinov's life in English as an introduction to *Dva goda s simvolistami*. Michael Karpovich does the same in the English edition of *Encounters with Lenin* (London 1968).

51 Valentinov to Rumanov, 16 September 1913, TsGALI, 1694-1-106, sheet 10-11.

52 Most newspapers, unlike *Word*, aligned with special interests or received government funds. The Report of the Minister of the Interior on Censorship Affairs, 1912–1917 (TsGIA, 776-1-40-46, sheet 48) shows, for example, that the government in 1914 paid subsidies to forty-one periodicals totalling 592,075 rubles (ostensibly to buy subscriptions).

53 *Uchebniki, uchebnye posobiia i nagliadnye posobiia dlia nizshikh, srednykh i vysshikh uchebnykh zavedenii vsekh vedomstv, i tak zhe dlia samobrazovaniia, 1911-1912* [Moscow 1911]. This is one of seventy separate editions collected in the Saltykov-Shchedrin Public Library in Leningrad.

54 Gosudarstvennaia kantseliariia. Otdelenie obshchego sobraniia Gosudarstvennogo Soveta, "Delo po zaiavleniiu 32 chlenov ...," TsGIA 1148-10-7, 1913, sheets 5-7, 208.

55 " 'Delo po zaiavleniiu 32 chlenov," sheet 263.

56 Ibid., sheets 232-6. A subordinate read the minister's statement.

57 The lengthy speech came on 29 and 31 May 1913. "Rech' na zasedanii IV gos. Dumy," *Stenograficheskii otchet*, sessions 57 and 59 (29 and 31 May 1913), pt. 3, cols. 369-72 and 428-52 (St Petersburg 1913).

58 V.M. Purishkevich, ed., *Shkol'naia podgotovka vtoroi russkoi revoliutsii* (St Petersburg 1913). The quotation is from N.V. Tulupov, ed., *Polveka dlia knigi* (Moscow 1916), 482.

59 Sytin, *Zhizn' dlia knigi*, 183.

60 Gor'ky to E.P. Peshkova, 12 March 1911, A.M. Gor'ky, *Pis'ma E.P. Peshkovoi, 1906–1932, Arkhiv A.M. Gor'kogo* (Moscow 1966), 9:114.

61 Piatnitsky describes the details of the negotiations in his Capri diary, quoted in ibid., 9:332. See also O.D. Golubeva, "Dva izdatelia (I.D. Sytin i M. Gor'ky)," *Gor'ky i ego sovremenniki*, ed. K.D. Muratova (Leningrad 1968), 187.

62 Gor'ky to E.M. Peshkova, 12 March 1911, *Arkhiv A.M. Gor'kogo*, 9.114.

63 Gor'ky to V. Anuchin, 8 November 1912, M. Gor'ky, *Literaturnyi Arkhiv: Materialy i issledovaniia*, 3 vols. (Leningrad 1934), 1:273.

64 Gorky had earlier, in 1910, urged Sytin to credit the "role of the popular mass" in a book on Russian history to mark the 300th year of the Romanov dynasty and had also learned that M.P. Miaklashevsky planned to get Sytin's help to buy *Contemporary World* (*Sovremennyi Mir*) with the goal of making it a "united Marxist journal." See K.D. Muratova, *M. Gor'kii na Kapri* (Leningrad 1971), 25-6, 112. Both facts suggest that Sytin already seemed amenable to leftist projects or was being prodded in that direction.

65 *Letopis' zhizni i tvorchestva A.M. Gor'kogo* (Moscow 1958), 336. Just before Sytin's 1913 visit, Gorky wrote Ladyzhnikov that he saw advantages in *Russian Word* over *Tilled Field* inasmuch as having a "connection with an organ so widely distributed is not bad" (Gor'ky to Ladyzhnikov, 14 May 1913, *Arkhiv M. Gor'kogo*, 7:223). Gorky continued that they could probably "introduce several of our people"; besides Gorky, *Word* would shortly add Vladimir Korolenko, Valery Briusov, and Alexander Kuprin as literary contributors.

66 Valentinov to Rumanov, 31 May 1913, TsGALI, 1694-1-106, sheet 19. The series appeared in four issues of *Word*: "Fuel Oil for the British Fleet" (June 6), "The Excitement over Oil" (June 14), "Manipulating Oil Stock in England" (June 19 and 20). One Soviet historian assumes, without evidence, collusion between *Word* and Russian capitalists to raise the market price of oil stocks. S.I. Inikova, "Gazeta I.D. Sytina 'Russkoe Slovo'," 43.

67 "'Istoriia gazety 'Russkoe Slovo'. Ocherk (1894–1914)," RO GBL, 259-1-1, sheet 2.

68 Sytin's son Ivan edited the *Library of Russian Word* of 1913-14 which serialized the complete works of Tolstoy as a supplement to the paper.

69 Sasha apparently sold the diary excerpts to *Word*. The disputed ownership broke into print when Sasha and Sonia, in separate interviews, each claimed sole rights to the diaries under the new Russian copyright law of 1911. The controversy and its legal implications are discussed in Serge L. Levitsky, *Copyright, Defamation and Privacy in Soviet Civil Law* (Alpehn aan den Rijn, the Netherlands, 1979), 331-4 and 338-44.

70 "Perepiski Prok. mos. Sudeb. Palaty o knige 'Krug chteniia' L.N. Tolstogo," TsGIA Moskvy, 131-83-93, sheets 1-16.

CHAPTER EIGHT

1 N. Valentinov [N. Volsky], "Aleksandr Blok i 'Russkoe Slovo'," *Dva goda s simvolistami*, ed. Gleb Struve (Stanford 1969), 230-1.

2 Petrov to Vladimir Ivanovich [Sytin] and Mikhail Timofeevich [Soloviev], 17 December 1912, TsGALI, 595-1-46, sheets 23-4.

3 Sytin to Rumanov, 2 December 1911, TsGALI, 1694-1-730, sheet 28.

4 A. Blok, *Sobranie Sochinenii v Vos'mi Tomakh*, ed. V.N. Orlov, A.A. Surkov, K.I. Chukovsky (Moscow-Leningrad 1963), 7:115, 130.

5 V. Piast [V.A. Pestovsky], *Vospominaniia o Bloke* (Petrograd 1923), 48. Piast also testifies that any unknown who received a byline in *Word* felt that he received instant celebrity.

6 Blok notes the dismissal of Rozanov in his diary entry for 16 November 1911 (Blok, *SS*, 7:92).

7 Ibid., 115.

8 Blok to L.D. Mendeleeva-Blok, 23 June 1912, *Literaturnoe Nasledstvo* 89 (1978): 282. Vasily, according to his son Mikhail, was the "right-hand" of Sytin at the company. Moreover, he and Sytin lived in close proximity in the *Russian Word* building: Vasily and his family on the fifth floor, Sytin on the third. Mikhail Vasilievich Sytin, "Vospominaniia starshego vnuka," Sytin Museum.

9 Valentinov, "Aleksandr Blok i 'Russkoe Slovo'," 231-2.

10 Valentinov, "Aleksandr Blok i 'Russkoe Slovo'," 232-3. In Blok's "New America," the poet looks out over the terrible vastness of the steppes of "Wretched Rus" and deplores that his "ill-fated home country" seems an old woman, "pious though poor." Then he sees afar the "tall chimneys" of a "many-floored factory building" and discovers there a different dream – of Russia as a young bride who will join with her bridegroom of coal and iron to effect the vision of the last two lines: "Yes, above the bleak steppe-lands, the rising New America shines like a star!" Blok would contribute poetry to *Word* through 1916, but no prose.

11 The editor at *Word*'s foreign desk in this period, K.V. Orlov, testifies that Sytin let Doroshevich impose his will whenever he chose; for, wrote Orlov, "Sytin is a little afraid of Doroshevich and only of him. No single editor of *Russian Word* is possible because each must efface himself with each return of Doroshevich to Moscow. Doroshevich doesn't suffer anyone's opinion and compels everything to be the way he wants it." Quoted in M. Lemke, *250 dnei v tsarskoe stavke* [25 sent. 1915 - 2 iiulia 1916] (Petrograd 1920), 177-8).

12 S.I. Inikova, "Tovarishchestvo I.D. Sytina i tsenzura (1883-1914), *Problemy istorii SSSR* 12, Moscow (1982): 162-3.

13 The correspondence of the prosecutor of the Moscow Court of Appeals is in TsGIA Moskvy, 131-79-81, vols. 1 and 2, sheets 1-10, 1-5.

14 Correspondence of the prosecutor, Moscow Court of Appeals, ibid., 131-81-72, vol. 1, sheets 3-6.

15 Ibid., 131-83-93, sheets 1-16.

16 The family lore in this paragraph and the two before comes from three typescript memoirs in the Sytin Museum: Mikhail Vasilievich Sytin, "Vospominaniia starshego vnuka"; Dmitry Ivanovich Sytin, "Iz vospominanii vnuka I.D. Sytina"; and Aleksei Vasilievich Sytin, "Vospominaniia." Both Dmitry and Mikhail describe their grandmother as strict but very loving and kind.

17 Sytin summed up his mood in 1913 in a brief memoir, "A.M. Gor'ky," which describes his second trip to Capri. It and a second version (denoted " 'A.M. Gor'ky,' second variant") is in the Sytin Museum. The quoted passage about the robbery comes from the first variant.

18 I.D. Sytin, "O monopolii novoi i monopolii staroi," *Russkoe Slovo* 20 (25 January 1914). Sytin was also vigorously marketing books in conventional ways; by 1913 he was publishing twenty book catalogues a year. I.E. Matveeva, "Reklamy v knizhnoi torgovli I.D. Sytina," paper given at the Second Sytin Reading, Sytin Museum, 23 February 1989.

19 Unpublished chapter from the original ms. of Sytin's memoirs, Sytin Museum, 288-91.

20 I.Kh. Ozerov (an economist at Moscow University who often wrote for *Russian Word* on questions in his field), quoted by S.I. Inikova, "Tovarishchestvo pechataniia, izdatel'stva i knizhnoi torgovli I.D. Sytina (1883-1917)" (Kandidat dissertation, Moscow University, 1985), 139.

21 Valentinov to Sytin, 1 March 1914, Sytin Museum.

22 *Novoe Vremia* 13600 (21 January 1914): 5. Indirect evidence strongly suggests that Sytin shared a personal friendship with Kasso, then considered a reactionary for his harsh policies against student unrest in 1911.

23 "Kazennaia monopoliia," *Utro Rossii* 19 (24 January 1914): 5.

24 E.A. Dinershtein, *I.D. Sytin* (Moscow 1983), 184-5.

25 "Kazennaia monopoliia," *Utro Rossii* 20 (25 January 1914): 5.

26 I.D. Sytin, "O monopolii novoi i monopolii staroi;" *Zhizn' dlia knigi*

(Moscow 1978), 117-19; *Polveka dlia knigi*, ed. N.V. Tulupov (Moscow 1916), 485.

27 *Russkii Vestnik* (26 January 1914): 5.

28 Melgunov, who printed his prestigious *Voice* in Sytin's plant beginning in 1913, innovated among scholarly journals by publishing articles and memoirs in social, economic, and revolutionary history. See Iu. M. Kritsky, "Voprosy istorii russkoi obshchestvennoi mysli i revoliutsionnogo dvizheniia v Rossii xviii – nachala xx v. v zhurnale *Golos Minuvshego* v 1913–1923 gg," *Istoriia i istoriki* 5 (1972):79-80.

29 James H. Krukones, "To the People: The Russian Government and the Newspaper *Sel'skii Vestnik*, 1881-1917," (Ph.D. dissertation, University of Wisconsin, Madison, 1983), 301. Sytin's 1912 contract with *Village Messenger* (*Sel'skii Vestnik*) probably resulted from his meeting with Stolypin in mid-1911. The reticence of Sytin about this project stands in contrast to his telling in his memoirs, as a point in his favour, that he had rebuffed Prince Shakhovskoi in 1901 over the same kind of project.

30 Purishkevich overlooked that Sytin at this time was also publishing, in St Petersburg, School and Knowledge's weekly periodical for village teachers: *Messenger of the School* (*Vestnik Shkol*), 1914–16.

31 V.D. Purishkevich, *Pered Grozoiu: pravitel'stvo i Russkaia shkola* (St Petersburg, 1914), 68.

32 I.D. Sytin, *Zhizn' dlia knigi*, 118.

33 The May-through-April fiscal year of the company is here designated by the calendar year in which it begins. Thus the fiscal year from 1 May 1911 to 13 April 1912 is labelled 1911.

34 Dividends for 1910 (10 per cent), 1911 and 1912 (11 per cent), 1913 (8 per cent) and 1914 (8.5 per cent) appear under the entry for "Sytin & Co." in *Aktsionerno-Paevye Predpriatiia Rossi*, ed. V.V. Lavrov (St Petersburg 1917).

35 The Symbolist poetesses who edited *Path*, P.S. Solovieva and N.I. Manaseina, merged with Sytin & Co. as the "Tropinka" section. See N.V. Chekhov, "Detskaia literatura i izdatel'stvo T-va I.D. Sytina," *Polveka dlia knigi*, 530.

36 Minutes for three general meetings (26 September 1907, TsGIA Moskvy, 2316-1-1; 23 May 1914, ibid., 51-10-1166; and 16 October 1915, ibid.) show pre-revolutionary stock ownership. At the 1907 meeting Sytin, his relatives, and certain presumably loyal associates together voted about 500 of the 1,000 outstanding shares. A similar group in 1914 held about 1,000 shares out of 1,800 outstanding and, in 1915, about 2,500 out of 3,400. Sytin personally voted 158 shares in 1907, 761 in 1914, and 2,084 in 1915. In percentage terms, Sytin held 27 per cent of the stock votes at the first meeting, 42.2 per cent at the second, and 61.3 per cent at the third. The Sytin Museum holds a list of ninety-five stockholders at

the post-revolutionary meeting on 27-29 April 1919. Of the then outstanding but worthless 3,400 shares, Sytin held 2,017.

37 "Delo Moskovskoi Kazennoi Palaty," TsGIA Moskvy, 51-10-1166, sheet 85; 51-10-1162, sheet 112.

38 Sytin, *Zhizn' dlia knigi*, 164. The company would double its capitalization between 1914 and 1916 and more than double it again to 22.5 million rubles in March 1917.

39 Sytin to Rumanov [Spring, 1913?], TsGALI, 1694-1-626a, sheets 59-60. Sytin often overstated real or feared setbacks, and this letter sounds much like another in the same Rumanov file. That second letter, undated, centres on the miswording of a contract. Should there be a law suit, writes Sytin, "I'll be dishonoured and deprived of my livelihood ... I'll lose everything. All will go to hell ... and all that is left is to put a bullet in my brain" (sheets 55, 56).

As for the conniving of his paper company partners, Sytin knew how commonly business insiders seized private benefits at others' expense. Major figures in his own firm, for example, routinely used company labour and materials to build dachas and homes for themselves (I.N. Pavlov, *Zhizn' russkogo gravera*, 207).

40 Sytin, *Zhizn' dlia knigi*, 102-10. A work with a similar purpose but directed at a broader readership was *The Patriotic War and Russian Society, 1812–1912*, which appeared in 1912. Among the other valuable and widely read encyclopedic works that Sytin issued just before the First World War were, in 1910–12, *The Popular Encyclopedia of Scholarly, Scientific and Applied Knowledge* in fourteen volumes and, in 1913–14, *The Children's Encyclopedia* in ten volumes.

41 Dinershtein, *I.D. Sytin*, 185-6.

42 Sytin, *Zhizn' dlia knigi*, 102-110.

43 Gor'ky to V. Anuchin, 8 November 1912, M. Gor'ky, *Literaturnyi Arkhiv: Materialy i issledovaniia*, 3 vols. (Leningrad 1934), 1:273.

44 A.M. Motyl'kov, "Moia rabota u I.D. Sytina (Iz vospominanii bukinista), ed. A.P. Rusinov, *Kniga: Issledovaniia i materialy* 37 (1978): 160.

45 Pavlov, *Zhizn' russkogo gravera*, 207, 219.

46 Chekhov to M.A. Chekhov, 10 September 1902, A.P. Chekhov *Polnoe Sobranie Sochinenii i Pisem*, eds. A.M. Egolin and N.S. Tikhonov, 20 vols. (Moscow 1944–51), 19:337.

47 Al. Altaev [M.V. Iamshchikova], "Moi starye izdateli (Iz vospominanii)," ed. N.A. Letova and B.D Letov, *Kniga: Issledovaniia i materialy* 26 (1973): 177-8.

48 Gor'ky to A.M. Tikhonov, 9 June 1913, *Gor'kovskie chteniia, 1953–1957* (Moscow-Leningrad 1959), 45.

49 Gor'ky to Ladyzhnikov, 18 September 1913, *Arkhiv A.M. Gor'kogo*, 7:230.

50 Bertram Wolfe, *The Bridge and the Abyss* (New York 1967), 63.

51 O.D. Golubeva, "Dva izdatelia (I.D. Sytin i M. Gor'ky)," *M. Gor'ky i ego sovremenniki* (Leningrad 1968), 192-3.
52 *My Apprenticeship* appeared in *Russian Word* during November and December of 1915. F.M. Borras, *Maxim Gorky: The Writer* (Oxford 1967), 129-30.
53 Gor'ky to Ladyzhnikov, 15 May 1914, *Arkhiv A.M. Gor'kogo*, 7:233.
54 Gor'ky to Ladyzhnikov, end of May, prior to 10 June 1914, *Letopis' zhizni i tvorchestva A.M. Gor'kogo*, 2:438.
55 Lemke, *250 dnei v tsarskoi stavke*, 544.
56 Sytin, *Zhizn' dlia knigi*, 184.
57 Ibid., 185. T.I. Dubinskaia, "Letopis'," *Russkaia literatura i zhurnalistika nachala xx veka, 1905-1917*, ed. B.A. Bialik (Moscow 1984), 203. That November Sytin would pay 19,190.51 rubles to Sail and in December, 20,000 rubles. He also paid Sail's 7,000-ruble debt to a paper company. O.D. Golubeva, "Knigoizdatel'stvo 'Parus' (1915–1918)," *Kniga: Issledovaniia i materialy* 12: (1966): 113. Records at the Sytin Museum show these additional payments: fifteen thousand rubles from Sytin to Gor'ky, 31 March 1916; ten thousand rubles from Sytin to Ladyzhnikov, 1 April 1916 (specified for *Letopis'*); and one thousand rubles from Sytin to Gorky, 26 September 1916. All these payments total 72,190 rubles, and there may have been more.

CHAPTER NINE

1 Rumanov to the editors of *Russian Word*, 14 September 1914, TsGALI, 595-1-12, sheets 21-3.
2 Ibid., sheet 37.
3 Editors of *Russian Word* to the chairman of the Moscow Military Censorship Committee, 25 October 1914, ibid., sheets 25-6.
4 *Russian Word* to the Moscow Telegraph Agency, 29 November 1914, TsGALI, 595-1-13, sheet 46. To prove delays of an hour or so, the editors enclosed a log for 27 November citing the arrival time at *Word* of sixty-four telegrams (from thirty-seven cities in Russia and abroad) against their arrival time at MTA. On 5 December 1915 they would protest delays of three to seven hours. Ibid., sheet 48.
5 Agreement for the line would be reached on 14 June 1917, ibid., sheet 69.
6 Assistant War Minister to Prince N.B. Shcherbatov, 15 July 1915, TsGALI, 595-1-37, sheet 9.
7 TsGALI, 595-1-37, sheet 18. The account first appeared in the offical *War Veteran* (*Russkii Invalid*).
8 Louise McReynolds, "News and Society: *Russkoe Slovo* and the Development of the Mass Circulation Press in Late Imperial Russia," (Ph.D. dissertation, University of Chicago 1984), 93-9.
9 Maj.-Gen. M. Adabash to S.E. Vissarionov, 5 August 1915, TsGIA, 776-8-854, sheet 9.

10 Vladimir Ivanovich first served in the army in the early 1900s. Following the 1905 revolution, he had taken charge of Sytin & Co.'s wholesale operations and become a director. He re-entered the army again at the outbreak of the First World War, contracted pneumonia while on duty, and died on 2 December 1915.

11 After the Revolution in November 1917 the Soviet government took over the estate for various uses. The manor house later burned and only the foundations now remain.

12 *Russian Word* to the Minister of War, 23 September 1915, TsGALI, 595-1-37, sheet 11.

13 Blagov to the chairman of the Moscow Committee on Press Affairs, TsGALI, 595-1-22, sheet 27.

14 V. Doroshevitch, *The Way of the Cross*, intro. Stephen Graham (New York and London 1916), iii-iv. Graham describes Doroshevich as a "liberal and progressive ... [who] breathes a tender love toward the individual."

15 The poster is reproduced in A.V. Rumanov, "I.D. Sytin - Izdatel'," *Vremennik russkoi knigi* (1934), 4:225. All the posters here described are in TsGALI, 1931-1-9, 17, 38, 39.

16 Just after the trial Chukovsky wrote Rumanov: "Surely Sytin's company has its own solicitor; why didn't he appear in the chamber and explain the essence of the matter? Why wasn't I informed? I would have acted as my own attorney." Chukovsky to Rumanov [1914?], TsGALI, 1694-1-681, sheet 18. Chukovsky revised the book and took it elsewhere for printing.

17 I.D. Sytin, *Zhizn' dlia knigi* (Moscow 1968), 200.

18 Ibid., 192-7.

19 Fr. Georgii Shavel'sky, *Vospominaniia poslednogo protopresvitera russkoi armii i flota*, 2 vols. (New York 1954), 2:210-15. Shavel'sky erroneously places the trip in August or September 1916 but admits that his timing is perhaps wrong.

20 M.M. Lemke, *250 dnei v tsarskoi stavke (25 sent. 1915–2 iiulia 1916*) (Petrograd 1920), 543.

21 Sytin to Rumanov, 2 April 1915, TsGALI, 1694 1 370, sheet 85. Just before seeing the Tsar, Sytin informed Rumanov that he was, by necessity, making his own printer's ink. Sytin to Rumanov, 6 February 1916, TsGALI, 1694-1-730, sheet 96. That spring, to get surer delivery of fuel oil for his generating plant, both Sytin and his company would invest in an oil company. See S.I. Inikova, "Tovarishchestvo I.D. Sytina (1883–1917): ot litografii k monopolisticheskomy ob''edineniiu" (Moscow 1983; unpublished paper duplicated at INION, no. 13928).

22 Lemke, *250 dnei v tsarskoi stavke*, 544.

23 The Okhranka report which summarizes and quotes Sytin's words at the meeting is reprinted in *Burzhuaziia nakanune fevral'skoi revoliutsii*, ed. B.B. Grave (Moscow 1927), 99-100. The same report is in Lemke, *250 dnei v tsarskoi stavke*, 790. Sytin knew several businessmen on the

Information Committee formed in 1914 by members of the Progressist Party and the Constitutional Democrats to establish links with parties on the left. Leopold Haimson describes this committee in "The Problem of Social Stability in Urban Russia, 1905-1917, Part Two," *Slavic Review* 24, no. 1 (March 1965): 4.

24 Unpublished chapter from the original ms of Sytin's memoirs, Sytin Museum, 301-3. Sytin blamed "some weakness in our culture" for such a thin reed as Savva Timofeevich after two "thick oaks" like the serf-born Savva Vasilievich, who founded the family company, and his son, Timofei Savvich, who made it a giant. In the early 1900s, eccentric "Savvyshka" had dressed shabbily, handed radical propaganda to his workers, and generously funded the Bolsheviks and the Moscow Art Theatre. In 1905, afraid of the police and estranged from his family, he had fled to Nice and there killed himself at forty-five.

25 "Obrashchenie I.D. Sytina k Moskovskomu Kupecheskomu obshchestvy," Sytin Museum.

26 N. Sytin and M. Soloviev to the Moscow Revenue Department (May 1916?), TsGIA Moskvy, 51-10-1166, sheet 65-6). This brief cites the ruble value of book production each fiscal year since 1904 (see appendix 5, figure 2). Proof of how copies accumulated in company warehouses comes from a 1916 accounting to author A.S. Prugavin, which showed that 30 per cent (or 1,800 copies) of his *Old Believers* (1904) and 35 per cent (or 3,500) of *The Schism and the Sectarians* (1905) remained unsold. Sytin & Co. to A.S. Prugavin, 22 November 1916, TsGALI, 2167-1-112, sheet 15.

27 Lemke, *250 dnei v tsarskoi stavke*, 827.

28 Commander of the Moscow Military District to V.A. Udintsov, head, Chief Administration for Press Affairs, 2 June 1916, TsGIA, 776-8-854, sheet 176.

29 *New York Times*, 11 June 1916, 2:12.

30 At least one writer, G.I. Porshnev, would respond to the book with well-worn criticism. "Having risen from the depths of the people, self-taught, [Sytin] combined all the deficiencies of the shopkeeper with a great, talented, and ebullient nature," he charged. Sytin sometimes published good books but "he does it more through ... a merchant's habit to operate in bulk and, in part, through literary 'ignorance.' " G.I. Porshnev, "Korol' knigi," G.I. Porshnev, *Revoliutsiia i kul'tura naroda: Sbornik statei po vneshkol'nomu obrazovaniiu* (Irkutsk 1917), 103-12.

31 In 1906 Russian publishers as a whole paid 92.4 per cent of their outlays for new equipment to German firms. V.P. Orlov, *Poligraficheskaia promyshlennost' Moskvy: Ocherk razvitiia do 1917 g.* (Moscow 1953), 170.

32 Sytin bought his first typograph in 1906 and his first linotype in 1908; each displaced six to eight hand compositors. The monotype was the best machine available for casting larger type faces. See Richard E. Huss, *The*

Development of Printers' Mechanical Typesetting Methods, 1822–1925 (Charlottesville 1973), 23.

33 I.N. Pavlov, *Zhizn' russkogo gravera* (Moscow 1963), 206. Pavlov contends that Sytin advanced Frolov because he considered him his "own." Frolov "knew everything there was to know about the work of the printers, their thinking, their mood." Sytin eventually gave Frolov six shares of company stock and made him a director.

34 Orlov, *Poligraficheskaia promyshlennost' Moskvy*, 254. Accusations that Sytin wished to create a monopoly seem to gain substance from these expansionist ventures, but there is no evidence that he actually had this goal in effecting his massive projects. In 1915 a group of Moscow newspaper sellers accused him of forming a syndicate with other publishers to set prices for street sales, but the company made a convincing case against even this charge. TsGIA Moskvy, 212-3-328, sheets 283-7.

35 A.N. Bokhanov, *Russkaia burzhuaznaia pressa i krupnyi kapital, konets XIX v. – 1914 g.* (Moscow 1984), 143.

36 Both firms were known for their high-quality books. Brockhaus and Efron's eighty-three-volume *Encyclopedic Dictionary* (*Entsiklopedicheskii slovar'*) is still an irreplaceable source for pre-revolutionary Russian history.

37 TsGALI, 1694-1-730, sheet 171.

38 *The Times*, 28 October 1916, Russian Supplement, 9.

39 Sytin, *Zhizn' dlia knigi*, 208. Sytin provides no date for the interview.

40 On *Russian Will*, see A.N. Naumova's notes in *Literaturnoe Nasledstvo: Gor'ky i Leonid Andreev: Neizdannye perepiski* 72 (Moscow 1965): 456-8.

41 Gor'ky to Korolenko, 21, 22 October 1916, *A.M. Gor'ky i V.G. Korolenko: Perepiska, stat'i, vyskazyvania*, ed. N.I. Chitovich (Moscow 1975), 80.

42 Gor'ky to E.P. Peshkova, 30 November 1916, *Arkhiv A.M. Gor'kogo*, 9:190.

43 Sytin hired Gor'ky to reorganize *Tilled Field* and assumed the Marks's contract for his complete works which Gork'y had signed on 17 September 1916. *Letopis' zhizni i tvorchestva A.M. Gor'kogo, 1890–1916*, ed. K.D. Muratova, 4 vols. (Moscow 1958), 2:282, 571.

44 Paul Miliukov, *Political Memoirs, 1905–1917*, ed. Arthur P. Mendel, tr. Carl Goldberg (Ann Arbor 1967), 373-81.

45 *Russkoe Slovo* 300, 29 December 1916.

CHAPTER TEN

1 "Protokol zasedanii Iubileinoi Komissii ...," Sytin Museum. The commission consisted of Sytin's long-time friends and collaborators: I.I. Flor, V.P. Frolov, D.A. Varopaev, M.N. Makarevsky, V.V. Popov, M.T. Soloviev, and F.I. Blagov.

2 *Russkoe Slovo* 42, 21 February 1917, contains the speeches of Tulupov,

Varshavsky, Mikhailovsky, Sytin, and others.

3 The Jubilee Commission decided to pay 200,000 rubles for land and 300,000 rubles for the building for Dom Knigi. The building would include apartments for the staff and director. Petrov describes Dom Knigi in *Polveka dlia knigi*, ed. N.V.Tulupov (Moscow 1916), 333-7.

4 Telegrams had also arrived from I.K. Grigorovich, the imperial Russian naval minister; I.L. Mrozovsky, commander of the Moscow military district; V.N. Shebako, the Moscow chief of police; M.D. Mrozovskaia, chairman of the Society for the Assistance to the Poor; N.D. Oboleshev, former commander of the Moscow military district; Maksim Gor'ky; Sen. A.F. Koni, the distinguished liberal jurist; and others.

5 They included representatives from the Society of Mutual Assistance for Writers and Scholars, the Russian Textile Society, the Society for the Dissemination of Commercial Information, and the Moscow Society of Peoples' Universities.

6 *Russkoe Slovo* 42, 21 February 1917. In 1911 Andrew Carnegie had established the Carnegie Corporation of New York on the principle first put forward in his *Gospel of Wealth* (1899), that wealthy men should use their money for the public good.

7 A.M. Motyl'kov says that in 1916 Sytin bought a sanitarium at the Caucasian resort town of Kislovodsk for a half million rubles for the benefit of printers. A.M. Motyl'kov, "Moia rabota u I.D. Sytina (Iz vospominanii bukinista)," *Kniga: Issledovaniia i materialy* 37 (Moscow 1978): 166). Konichev gives the figure of 1,200,000 rubles in *Russkii Samorodok*, 2d ed. (Iaroslavl 1969), 384.

8 N.D. Teleshov, "Drug knigi," *Zapiski pisatelia: Vospominaniia i rasskazy o proshlom* (Moscow 1980), 197. This essay on Sytin also appears as an appendix to I.D. Sytin, *Zhizn' dlia knigi* (Moscow 1978), 268-81. In Teleshov's account, Sytin speaks of three charitable projects, three crucial agents (the pedlars, the Tolstoyans, and Chekhov) and three stages in his life. Notably, Bunin says that Chekhov told him in 1904 that he longed to retreat to a monastery (Ernest Simmons, *Chekhov: A Biography* [Boston 1962], 618), and Tolstoy often made such a vow. Motyl'kov also says he heard from several people prior to the February revolution that Sytin had declared complete his "earthly" business and had vowed to disappear as a "Fedor Kuzmich" – the name, according to legend, that Alexander I assumed as a humble pilgrim when the world thought him dead.

9 Unpublished chapter from the original ms. of Sytin's memoirs, Sytin Museum, 230-40. Sytin speaks of Vtorov, a manufacturer from Siberia, as one of Moscow's richest men, a friend of "generous mind and heart" and "a real European." In contrast, a recent study of the Moscow business elite says that Vtorov "engaged in dramatic speculation and stock raids reminiscent of the American robber barons." Alfred J. Rieber, *Merchants and Entrepreneurs in Imperial Russia* (Chapel Hill, NC 1982), 295.

10 *Russkoe Slovo* 69, 28 March 1917. The head of the Moscow secret police, A.P. Martynov, described Drilikh as an outstanding agent strategically placed at *Word* to gather data on liberal groups like the War Industries Committee. See A.P. Martynov, *Moia sluzhba v otdel'nom korpuse zhandarmov: Vospominaniia*, ed. Richard Wraga (Stanford 1972), 227.

11 Lenin to the Central Committee of the RSDWP, 30 August 1917, in V.I. Lenin, *Polnoe Sobranie Sochinenii*, 42 vols. (Moscow 1962), 34:120. See also Albert Resis, "Lenin on Freedom of the Press," *Russian Review* 36, no. 3 (July 1977): 274-96; and Occasional Papers 121 and 144, Kennan Institute for Advanced Studies (both by Peter Kenez).

12 Lenin, *PSS*, 34:112.

13 This article appeared in *Workers' Way* (*Rabochii Put'*), no. 11, 28 September 1917 (Lenin, *PSS*, 34:208-13).

14 *Russkoe Slovo* 220, 221, and 225, 27 and 28 September and 3 October 1917.

15 Lenin, *PSS*, 34:341.

16 "The Tasks of the Revolution," Lenin, *PSS*, 34:236.

17 "Dekret Soveta Narodnykh Komissarov o pechati," 27 October 1917, in *Izdatel'skoe delo v pervye gody Sovetskoi vlasti (1917–1922): Sbornik dokumentov i materialy*, ed. E.A. Dinershtein et al. (Moscow 1972), 11-12.

18 Fifth Session, Central Executive Committee, 4 November 1917, *The Debate on Soviet Power: Minutes of the All-Russian Central Executive Committee of Soviets, Second Convocation, October, 1917–January, 1918*, tr. and ed. John L.H. Keep (Oxford 1979), 68-89.

19 A Bolshevik participant in the debate would later misstate that Lenin had there insisted on complete press freedom because all opposition papers would naturally disappear as the revolution succeeded. V.D. Bonch-Bruevich, "Konets burzhuaznoi pechati," *Zhurnalist* 11 (1927): 8.

20 A. Arosev, "Kak zakryvali burzhuaznye gazety," *Krasnaia Niva* 4 (1929): 9. Subsequent quotations from Arosev are also from p. 9.

21 Former employees of *Russian Word* would briefly secure presses in or around Moscow to publish *New Word* (closed by the Bolsheviks on 16 April) followed by *Our Word* (closed on 12 May). No evidence connects Sytin to these papers.

22 Dmitry Ivanovich Sytin, "Iz vospominanii vnuka I.D. Sytina," Sytin Museum, 2-3; A. Gessen, "Ivan Dmitrievich Sytin, Vstrechi i vospominaniia," Sytin Museum, 10-11; A.M. Motyl'kov, "Moia rabota u I.D. Sytina (Iz vospominanii bukinista)," ed. A.P. Rusinov, *Kniga: Issledovaniia i materialy* 37 (Moscow 1978): 165.

23 Dmitry Ivanovich, Sytin's grandson, has records of Sytin's bank account following the Bolshevik revolution. I have not seen these documents and do not have the date of the transfer of monies to the new government.

24 For evidence of the extensive private publishing in the first year of Soviet control, see Maurice Friedberg, *Russian Classics in Soviet Jackets* (New York

1962). For titles published by Sytin in the early 1920s, see E.A. Dinershtein, *I.D. Sytin* (Moscow 1983), 222-8.

25 Sheila Fitzpatrick, *The Commissariat of Enlightenment: Social Organization of Education and the Arts Under Lunacharsky, October 1917–1921* (Cambridge 1970), 135.

26 Sytin, *Zhizn' dlia knigi* (Moscow 1978), 210.

27 The citation of "12 March" is the initial date in this text from the "new style" Gregorian calendar henceforth used. The government abandoned the Julian calendar on the "old style" date of 31 January 1918 and decreed the next day to be 14 February, new style. Because the names are thoroughly familiar today, I have not translated *Izvestiia* (*News*) and *Pravda* (*Truth*) in my text.

28 An archival guide to the Manuscript Division of Lenin Library cites a five-page typewritten report by V. Bonch-Bruevich on problems at the *Russian Word* plant entitled "Catastrophe in the publication of the Newspapers in 1918" and refers to a discussion there of "Sabotage by the printers and office workers" and "closing of the plant and the selection of new workers." I have not see this report (although I asked for it in 1984 and 1989), but I deduce that the closure (probably the earlier-mentioned strike) and new hirings (necessarily including many rank beginners) preceded Mordvinkin's arrival. The document is in GBL, *fond* 369, carton 21, document number 29.

29 "Doklad o polozhenii del v tipografii 'Russkoe Slovo'," 4 April 1918, TsGAOR, 130-2-193, sheets 122-23.

30 Ibid., sheet 121.

31 The excerpts from Bonch's memoir are quoted in Dinershtein, *I.D. Sytin*, 216.

32 TsGAOR, 123-2-193, sheets 124-33.

33 Quoted in Dinershtein, *I.D. Sytin*, 172.

34 A.M. Gor'ky, *Novaia Zhizn'* 82 (297), 3 May (20 April), 1918, in *Nesvoevremennye mysli: Stat'i, 1917-1918*, ed. G. Ermolaev (Paris 1971), 202-3.

35 On 4 September Gor'ky became head of the Publishing House of World Literature attached to Lunacharsky's Commissariat of Education. F.M. Borras, *Maxim Gorky, the Writer: An Interpretation* (Oxford 1967), xvii. Gor'ky and Lunacharsky had long been friends.

36 Dmitry Ivanovich Sytin gives an account of the breakfast meeting, quoting written recollections of N.D. Teleshov. Teleshov does not mention the incident in his published memoirs. Konichev describes the meeting in the second edition of *Russkii Samorodok* (Iaroslavl 1969). These are the words that Dmitry Ivanovich quotes from Teleshov: "On one occasion [in 1918, when Gosizdat was being organized] I found Sytin and Gorky at Ekaterina Pavlovna's for breakfast. This was an important event. Gor'ky told Sytin: 'Vladimir Ilich asked me to discuss something with you. One of these days the State Publishing House will open and Vladimir Ilich

absolutely wants you to be director and to become head of it.' Sytin responded that to be head of Gosizdat 'would not do for me' in 'times like ours'." Vystuplenie Dmitriia Ivanovicha Sytina, 19 oktiabria 1966 ..., Sytin Museum, 4-5.

37 "Krupnyi tsentr spekulatsii," *Izvestiia Vserossiiskogo Tsentral'nogo Ispolnitel'nogo Komiteta Sovetov* 186/450 (30 August 1918): 6.

38 In 1924 Dmitry Ivanovich would complete the course at the Marx Institute of the National Economy and work many years as an engineer-economist. He won honours in the Second World War as a navy colonel specializing in submarine engineering. In the two decades before his death in 1973, he formed the collection which has been exhibited at the Sytin Museum.

39 Vypiski iz protokolov zasedanii kolegii Narkomprosa RSFSR, TsGAOR, 395-1-11 (1919), sheet 2, 15.

40 "Project on the division of Functions between the State Publishing House and the Press Sections ...," ibid., sheet 134.

41 TsGAOR, 393-1-3, sheet 229.

42 The archive contains a lengthy list of such books, calendars, brochures, and journals, ibid., sheets 501 and 582.

43 Ibid., sheets 184, 461.

44 Sytin, *Zhizn' dlia knigi*, 211.

45 Sytin says that the plant officially passed to Gosizdat in May 1919. E. Nemirovsky says that nationalization would have come sooner but for the opposition of Lunacharsky, who argued that state direction would ruin a plant so technically complex and cost workers their livelihoods. *Literaturnaia Gazeta* 41 (11 October 1967): 7.

The name of A.A. Zhdanov (a close associate of Stalin who disappeared under peculiar circumstances) prefaced the name of the plant from 1948 until 1988, when the Moscow City Soviet removed it.

46 Sytin to Vorovsky (February-March 1920), TsGAOR, 395-1-86, sheet 298. A certificate permitting the trip was issued by the Commissariat for Foreign Affairs, 24 January 1919. The document is at the Sytin Museum.

47 Dinershtein, *I.D. Sytin*, 236.

48 N.V. Doroshevich, ' "Korol' fel'etona' v poslednie gody zhizni," *Prostor* 1 (1971): 92-103. Natalia dictated this memoir two weeks before her death in April 1955.

49 Quoted in Dinershtein, *I.D. Sytin*, 232. The conditions mentioned by Sytin are not quoted.

50 Konichev prints the "Mandat" ordering Sytin to Germany in *Russkii Samorodok* (1966), 289. The original is in the Sytin Museum, along with the "udostoverenie" (certification) testifying to the dates of Sytin's trip.

51 A discussion of the political background can be found in E.H. Carr, *German-Soviet Relations Between the Two World Wars, 1919–1939* (Baltimore 1951), 48-59.

52 Vorovsky at Gosizdat received a plea in 1923 that he end the ban because "we need our *lubochnaia literatura*, precisely the kind from which Sytin made his money and which satisfies the great demand ... in the deep countryside." If the ban were lifted and "if a new Sytin turns up, he will make a fortune [NEP still being in effect]." M.D. Artamanov to A. Vorovsky, 10 April 1923, "Iz istorii sovetskoi literatury, 1920-1930 godov," *Literaturnoe Nasledstvo* (Moscow: 1983), 583.

53 "I.D. Sytin o Gosizdate," *Izvestiia*, 5 September 1922. Many shared Sytin's hope that the NEP signalled a return to some form of capitalism, and the USSR (expanded from the RSFSR in 1924) did thereby attract badly needed funds for redevelopment, both from citizens like Sytin with foreign accounts and from foreign investors.

54 E. Lundberg, *Zapiski pisatelia* (Berlin 1922), 203.

55 Order of 16 March 1921, *Izdatel'skoe delo v pervye gody Sovetskoi vlasti*, 95.

56 TsGALI, 1328-3-5, sheet 1. V.P. Polonsky was founder and chairman (1921–29) of the House of the Press (a journalists' organization) and editor of *Press and Revolution.*

57 I.D. Sytin, ["Notes After Visiting America"], Sytin Museum. Also see appendix 1.

58 Grabar' to V.I. Grabar', 31 December 1923, in I.E. Grabar', *Pis'ma, 1917–1941*, ed. N.A. Evsina and T.P. Kazhdan (Moscow 1977), 10-11.

59 Sytin says he started on the seven-day voyage on 15 January ("Notes After Visiting America") while Grabar' dates Sytin's arrival in New York on 30 January. Grabar' to V.I. Grabar', 30 January 1924: 95.

60 Sytin, "Notes After Visiting America."

61 *New York Times*, 19 February 1924: 6; 2 March IV: 11; and 9 March IV: 10.

62 Sytin, "Notes After Visiting America."

63 Sytin to Grandson Dmitry Ivanovich (undated, 1924), Sytin Museum. The letterhead was that of the Grand Union Hotel at 32nd Street near Madison Avenue.

64 Robert C. Williams, *Russian Art and American Money, 1900–1940*, (Cambridge, Mass. 1980), 98-9.

65 Grabar' to V.I. Grabar', 10 February 1924: 99.

66 Grabar' to "Friends," 18 March 1924: 118. Another artist-delegate testified that Americans sometimes "reacted in horror or burst out laughing" at the prices on artwork in the exhibit, but he found their tastes to be very primitive. K.A. Somov, *Pis'ma, Dnevniki, Suzhdeniia Sovremennikov* (Moscow 1979), 234-7.

67 Sytin, *Zhizn' dlia knigi*, 213.

68 Two and a half years had lapsed since the nationalization of his Petrograd plant, but Sytin seems to have managed to keep these paper stores as an asset in reserve.

69 Sytin to P.I. Makushin, 12 February 1925, Sytin Museum.

70 I.D. Sytin, "Dokladnaia zapiska," wrongly dated 28 May 1924 (actually 1925).

71 Gessen, "Ivan Dmitrievich Sytin," 9-10.

72 Al. Altaev (M.V. Iamshchikova), *Pamiatnye vstrechi* (Moscow-Leningrad 1946), 293-4.

73 Dinershtein, *I.D. Sytin*, 241.

74 A.R. Kugel' (Homo novus), *List'ia s dereva* (Leningrad 1926), 140.

75 Aleksei Vasilievich Sytin, "Vospominaniia," Sytin Museum, 5.

76 The pension certificate, which took effect 14 May 1928, is reproduced in Konichev, *Russkii Samorodok*, 2nd ed.

77 Aleksei Vasilievich Sytin, "Vospominaniia," 3. The other two grandsons also date Sytin's decline from the time of his move.

78 Konichev, *Russkii Samorodok*, 389-90. Konichev, who is reliable on precise historical detail, also states here that a story about this time in a Belgrade newspaper reported that Sytin himself had been arrested for illegal business dealings with daughter Evdokia Ivanovna, who was living in Poland, although an article in *Izvestiia* dismissed these charges. Mikhail Vasilievich Sytin quotes a journalist (Mikhail Kol'tsov) who ran into Sytin on the street and asked about the recent fuss in foreign papers about his being in Butyrki prison. Sytin reportedly responded: "Those sons of bitches. To invent such nonsense! I beat the liars." "Vospominaniia Starshego Vnuka," 3.

79 Al. Altaev, "Moi starye izdateli: Iz vospominanii," *Kniga: Issledovaniia i materialy* 26 (Moscow 1973): 179.

80 Motyl'kov, "Moia rabota u I.D. Sytina," 166.

81 The first edition of Sytin's memoirs cites the date of their completion as 1922 (Sytin, *Zhizn' dlia knigi*, 5), but the second edition omits that reference. Sytin's hope of an endorsement from Gorky is mentioned by Dinershtein in *I.D. Sytin*, 242.

82 *Sytintsy v 1905 godu: Sbornik vospominanii rabochikh Pervoi Obraztsovoi Tipografii (b. Sytina)*, ed. E. Rumailo, N. Miretsky, and L. Mal'kov (Moscow 192?); N. Miretsky, "Ot Sytina k Pervoi Obraztsovoi Tipografii, 1876-1931," *Bor'ba klassov* 5 (1932): 74-90; and N. Miretsky, *Pervaia Obraztsovaia tipografiia, 1876-1933: Materialy iz istorii* (Moscow 1933).

83 Altaev, "Moi starye izdateli," 179. Gorky was still pre-eminent, but he had already become disenchanted with the regime when Sytin died; and evidence suggests that, at least by 1935, Stalin no longer trusted him. The death of Gorky on 19 June 1936 seems now to have been precipitated by Stalin.

APPENDIX ONE

1 I have given a title to Sytin's handwritten manuscript, now filed at the Sytin Museum, along with a copy of the complete text in English translation.

2 Sytin understates the average allotment. Rather, one-fifth of the peasant households received allotments up to five desiatinas (thirteen and one-half acres) and three-fourths exceeded that amount to a maximum of ten desiatinas. See Lazar Volin, *A Century of Russian Agriculture from Alexander II to Khrushchev* (Cambridge, Mass. 1970), 46.

3 The Russian term "detskii dom" literally means a children's home.

4 Sytin visited factories in Germany, France, and England during earlier trips to western Europe.

5 The best times at the art exhibition came outside business hours during social gatherings held there.

6 Sytin must have hoped to inform Soviet officials about the amazing advances in printing technology that he found in New York. Cost was an important factor.

7 Sytin had in mind here the work of his employees before the Revolution because he knew how sharply productivity had dropped in his former plants since then.

8 Sytin especially liked the generous credit system in America. He had complained that it was too stringent in pre-revolutionary Russia.

9 These words suggest that Sytin came to realize fully the worth of America only after his first two months there.

10 In this especially complicated section, Sytin was developing a metaphor in which he compares the historic Russian people with individual Russian man. Some of these ideas in this section are common to the religious thinking of the Slavophiles, a small group of intellectuals during the reign of Nicholas I. They believed that the church was a living expression of Christian values which the communicant absorbed by free and loving participation (*sobornost*) in the service of the church.

Bibliography

ARCHIVES

Bakhmeteff Archive, Columbia University

P.G. Sobolev, "Zapiski starogo zhurnalista"

Central State Archive of Literature and Art (TsGALI)

2 A.A. Alexandrov
459 A.S. Suvorin
595 *Russian Word*
891 N.V. Turkin
1694 A.V. Rumanov
1931 Posters and Popular Pictures

Central State Historical Archive (TsGIA)

776 Chief Administration for Press Affairs

Central State Historical Archive of the City of Moscow (TsGIA Moskvy)

16 Chancellery of the Moscow Governor General
17 Chancellery of the Moscow Governor
31 Moscow Committee on Press Affairs
51 State Treasury, Moscow Section
131 Moscow Court of Appeals
139 Office of the Procurator, Moscow Court of Appeals
142 Moscow Circuit Court
212 Senior Inspector for Book Publishing and the Book Trade
2316 I.D. Sytin & Co.

Central State Archive of the October Revolution (TSGAOR)

102 (DO) Department of the Police
130, 395 The State Publishing House of the RSFSR

Manuscript Division, Lenin Library (RO GBL)

259 *Russian Word*
358 N.A. Rubakin

Exhibition Centre of the All-Union Voluntary Society of Book Lovers (The Sytin Museum)

PUBLISHED SOURCES

Abramovich, N. Ia. *"Russkoe Slovo" (Ideinyi oblik - Dysha gazety; Vlastiteli ulichnoi pressy; sluzhenie rynku; "Russkoe Slovo" i russkaia zhizn')*. Petrograd 1916.

Altaev, Al. [M.V. Iamshchikova]. "Moi starye izdateli: Iz vospominanii." *Kniga: Issledovaniia i materialy* 26 (1973): 154-82.

- *Pamiatnye vstrechi*. Moscow-Leningrad 1946.

Arosev, A. "Kak zakryvali burzhuaznye gazety," *Krasnaia Niva* 4 (1929): 8-9.

Batiushkov, D. "O tom kak, I.D. Sytin izdal illiustratsiiu k 'Snu Makara' V.G. Korolenko." In *Polveka dlia knigi*, edited by N.V. Tulupov. Moscow 1916: 109-12.

Belov, S.V., ed. "Iz perepiski I.D. Sytina," *Kniga: Issledovaniia i materialy* 42 (1981): 129-48.

- "Novye dokumenty ob izdatel 'skoi deiatel 'nosti I.D. Sytina." *Sovetskie Arkhivy* 5 (1979): 22-6.

- "Pomnit', chtoby idti vpered," *Sovetskaia kul'tura*. 30 January 1976: 6.

- "Russkie izdatel'stva kontsa XIX - nachala XX v. (Nereshennye problemy). In *Problemy rukopisnoi i pechatnoi knigi*. Moscow 1976: 292-7.

- and A.P. Tolstiakov. *Russkie izdateli kontsa XIX - nachala XX veka*. Leningrad 1976.

Biriukov, P. "I.D. Sytin i delo 'Posrednika'." In *Polveka dlia knigi* 113-19.

Biriukov, V. "Smelost' i beskorystie izdatelia (K 125-letiiu so dnia rozhdeniia I.D. Sytina)." *V mire knig* 2 (1976): 81.

Blium, A.V. "Lubochnaia kniga vtoroi poloviny XIX veka." *Kniga: Issledovaniia i materialy* 42 (1981): 94-114.

Brooks, Jeffrey. *When Russia Learned to Read: Literacy and Popular Literature, 1861–1917*. Princeton: Princeton University Press 1985.

Bokhanov, A.N. *Burzhuaznaia pressa Rossii i krupnyi kapital. Konets XIX v. - 1914 g.* Moscow 1984.

Bukchin, S.V. *Sud'ba fel'etonista: Zhizn' i tvorchestvo Vlasa Doroshevicha*, edited by F.I. Kushelov. Minsk 1975.

Chekhov, N. "Detskaia literatura i izdatel'stvo T-va I.D. Sytina." In *Polveka dlia knigi*, 517-42.

"Chestvovanie I.D. Sytina (v sviazi s 35-letiem knigoizdatel'skoi deiatel'nosti." *Vestnik knigoprodavtsev* 37 (1901): 578-9.

Chibisov, V. "Rabochaia zhizn': Detishche Sytina." *Pravda*, 1 April 1922: 5.

Chlenova, N.A. "Arkhiv gazety 'Russkoe Slovo'." In *Istochnikovedenie otechestvennoi istorii, 1981*. Moscow 1982: 118-30.

Costello, David R. "*Novoe vremia* and the Conservative Dilemma, 1911–1914." *Russian Review* 37, no. 1 (1978): 30-50.

Dinershtein, E.A. *I.D. Sytin*. Moscow 1983.

- "O vzaimootnosheniiakh A.A. Bloka c 'Tovarishchestvom I.D. Sytina'." *Kniga: Issledovaniia i materialy* 41 (1980): 89-95.

- "Vo imia blagogo dela (L.N. Tolstoy, I.D. Sytin i 'Posrednik')." *Kniga: Issledovaniia i materialy* 37 (1978): 70-97.

- "Zvanie-prosvetitel'. K 130-letiiu so dnia rozhdeniia I.D. Sytina." *V mire knig* 1 (1981): 75-7.

Doroshevich, N.V. "Zhizn' Vlasa Doroshevicha (1864–1922)." *Prostor*, edited by Vl. Lidin, 4 (1971): 92-103.

Doroshevich, V.M. "Russkoe Slovo." In *Polveka dlia knigi*, 393-422.

"50-letie deiatel'nosti I.D. Sytina," *Russkie Vedomosti* 41, 19 February 1917.

Fedorov, I. "Arkhiv gazety 'Russkoe Slovo'," *Zapiski otdela rukopisei Gosudarstvennoi biblioteki SSSR imeni V.I. Lenina*. Moscow 1939.

Frolov, V. "Masterskie Tovarishchestva i ikh razvitie." In *Polveka dlia knigi*, 565-82.

Gaevsky, V. "O Dorosheviche i ego fel'etonakh." *Novyi mir* 1 (1963): 260.

Giliarovsky, V.A. "Russkoe Slovo," In V.A. Giliarovsky. *Izbrannoe*. 3 vols. Moscow 1960, 2:215-23.

Gol'denveizer, A.B. *Vblizi Tolstogo*, Moscow 1959.

Gol'tseva, Z. "Russkii pisatel' I.D. Sytin." *Panorama* 5 (1972): 142-8.

Golubeva, O.D. "Dva izdatelia (I.D. Sytin i M. Gor'ky)." In *M. Gor'ky i ego sovremenniki*, edited by K.D. Muratova. Leningrad 1968: 184-95.

Iu. A. Gorshkov, "Russkii lubok: ot manufaktury k fabrike." *Kniga: Issledovaniia i materialy* 47 (1984): 103-16.

Grabar', I.E. *Pis'ma 1917–1941*, edited by N.A. Evsina and T.P. Kazhdan. Moscow 1977.

Gredeskul', N. "Sytinskoe izdanie." In *Polveka dlia knigi*, 561-4.

Gusev, A. "Kalendar'," In *Polveka dlia knigi*, 435-42.

Gusev, S. "Chitatel' kalendaria." In *Polveka dlia knigi*, 443-60.

"I.D. Sytin: izdatel' (K iubileiu)," *Utro Rossii* 49, 18 February 1917.

"I.D. Sytin o Gosizdate." *Izvestiia*, 5 September 1922: 5.

Iablonovsky, S.V. [S. Potresov]. "Sytin," *Illiustrirovannaia Rossia* 51 (Paris 1934): 4-5.

Iasinsky, I.I. *Roman moei zhizni: Kniga vospominanii*. Moscow-Leningrad 1926.

Ikskul', Baroness V. "I.D. Sytin." In *Polveka dlia knigi* 120-31.

Inikova, S.A. "Gazeta 'Russkoe Slovo' i tsenzura (1897–1917)." *Problemy istorii SSSR* 13 (1983): 246-59.

– "Tovarishchestvo I.D. Sytina i tsenzura (1883–1914)." *Problemy istorii SSSR* 12 (1982): 157-69.

Iordansky, N. "Uchebnaia literatura v izdanii I.D. Sytina." In *Polveka dlia knigi* 461-92.

"Iubilei I.D. Sytina." *Izvestiia sluzhashchikh v pechatnykh zavedeniiakh* 33 (1916): 398-400.

"Iubilei I.D. Sytina (K 35-letie knigoizdatel'skoi deiatel'nosti)." *Vestnik knigoprodavtsev* 36 (1901): 562-3.

Iunitsky, P. "Na puti k narodnomu bogatstvu. Otdel promyshlennogo obrazovaniia." In *Polveka dlia knigi*, 543-8.

Iuniverg, L. "Predmet osobennykh zabot. K 125-letiiu so dnia rozhdeniia I.D. Sytina." *V mire knig* 5 (1976): 28.

"Ivan Dmitrievich Sytin." *Birzhevye Vedomosti* 16108, 19 February 1917.

"Ivan Dmitrievich Sytin." *Izvestiia sluzhashchikh v pechatnykh zavedeniiakh* 43-44 (1917): 518-20.

Kalmykova, A. "Russkie lubochnye kartiny v ikh prosvetitel'nom znachenii dlia naroda za poslednee 75-letie nashei zhizni." In *Polveka dlia knigi*, 163-202.

"Kazennaia monopoliia uchebnoi literatury." *Utro Rossii* 19 and 20, 24 and 25 January 1914.

Khavkina, L. "Khar'kovskie kollektivnye trudy v izdanii T-va I.D. Sytina." *Polveka dlia knigi*, 493-504.

"Knizhnik-farisei." Moskva, 6 July 1909.

Konichev, Konstantin. *Russkii samorodok*. 1st ed., Leningrad 1966; 2d ed., Iaroslavl 1969.

Konovalev, V.F. "Pis'mo v redaktsiiu [On Sytin's boulevard publishing]." *Utro Rossii* 187, 14 August 1911.

Kostrikova, E.G. "Istochniki vneshnepoliticheskoi informatsii russkikh burzhuaznykh gazet: (na materialakh arkhivnykh fondov 'Rechi' i 'Russkogo Slova')." *Istoricheskie Zapiski* 103 (1979): 275-98.

Krainyi, Anton [Z.N. Gippius]. "Zhizn' i literatura." *Novaia Zhizn'* 11 (1912): 114-26.

Krasnov, P. and V. Shevelev. "Na rubezhe dvadtsatogo veka." *Sovetskaia pechat'* 12 (1961): 43-6.

Kugel', A.R. *List'ia s dereva: Vospominaniia*. Leningrad 1926.

Kugel', I.R. "Novosti Dnia." *Literaturnyi sovremennik* 4 (1939): 154-68.

– "Iz vospominanii." *Literaturnyi sovremennik* 12 (1940): 120-6.

– "Sytin: Vospominaniia o proshlom russkoi pechati." *Leningrad*, 23-24 (1940): 16-19.

Lebedev, V.K. "Iz istorii sotrudnichestva knigoizdatel'stva 'Posrednik' i izdatel'skoi firmy 'I.D. Sytin i Ko'." *Russkaia literatura* 2 (1969): 209-12.

Lemke, M. *250 dnei v tsarskoi stavke (25 sentiabria 1915 – 2 iiulia 1916)*. Petrograd 1920.

Levina, A. "Ia veriu v budushchee russkogo prosveshcheniia" (K 125-letiiu so dnia rozhdeniia I.D. Sytina)." *Komsomol'skaia pravda*, 4 February 1976.

Lundberg, E. *Zapiski pisatelia, 1917–1920*. 3 vols. Leningrad 1930.

Lyndstrom, Thais. "From Chapbooks to Classics: The Story of Intermediary," *American Slavic and East European Review* 16 (1957): 190-212.

Maslianenko, D. "I.D. Sytin," *Istoricheskii Vestnik* 148 (1917): 462-82.

S. Mel'gunov. "S.V. Iablonovsky [Obituary]." *Vosrozhdenie* 31 (1954): 199-200.

Miretsky, N.I. "Ot Sytina k Pervoi obraztsovoi tipografii (1876–1931)." *Bor'ba klassov* 5 (1932): 74-90.

– *Pervaia obraztsovaia tipografiia, 1876–1933. Materialy iz istorii*, Moscow 1933.

Motyl'kov, A.M. "Moia rabota u I.D. Sytina (Iz vospominanii bukinista)." *Kniga: Issledovaniia i materialy* 37 (1978): 156-66.

"Nagliadnye posobie v izdanii T-va I.D. Sytina." In *Polveka dlia knigi*, 505-16.

Nekrasova, E.S. *Narodnye knigi dlia chteniia v ikh bor'be s lubochnymi izdaniiami*. Viatka 1902.

"Newspaper Journalism in Prerevolutionary Russia." *Soviet Studies in History* edited by Louise McReynolds. 25, no. 1 (Summer 1986): 3-106.

Obzor Pervoi Vserossiiskoi vystavki pechatnogo dela. St Petersburg 1895. No. 12: 6-7; no. 27: 2-3; no. 29: 8; and no. 31: 4-5.

Ol'denburg, S. "Stranitsa iz istorii preobrazovaniia lubochnykh knig." *Polveka dlia knigi*, 132-42.

"100 letie izdatel'nosti I.D. Sytina." *V mire knig* 3 (1967): 44-5.

Orlov, B.P. *Poligraficheskaia promyshlennost' Moskvy: Ocherk razvitiia do 1917 g*. Moscow 1953.

Osetrov, E. "Zhizn' dlia knigi. K 125-letiiu so dnia rozhdeniia I.D. Sytina." *Trud*, 5 February 1976.

"Osushchestvlenie mechty. K 120-letiiu so dnia rozhdeniia I.D. Sytina." *Knizhnaia torgovlia* 1 (1971): 52 3.

Pavlov, I.N. *Zhizn' russkogo gravera*. Moscow 1963.

Piast, V. [V.A. Pestovsky]. *Vstrechi*. Moscow 1929.

"Po povodu otveta g. Sytina." *Novoe Vremia*, 24 January 1914.

"Polveka dlia knigi." Niva 7 (1917): 105-7.

Polveka dlia knig: Literaturno-khudozhestvennyi sbornik, posviashchennyi piatidesiatiletiiu izdatel'skoi deiatel'nosti I.D. Sytina, edited by N.V. Tulupov. Moscow 1916.

Popov, V. "Vokrug Sveta." In *Polveka dlia knigii*, 549-59.

Porshnev, G.I. "Korol' knigi." In G.I. Porshnev. *Revoliutsiia i kul'tura naroda: Sbornik statei po vneshkol'nomu obrazovaniia*. Irkutsk 1917: 103-10.

Posse, V.A. *Moi zhiznennyi put', dorevoliutsionnyi period. 1864–1917 gg.*, edited by B.P. Koz'min, Moscow 1929.

"Privilegirovannye izdateli i uchebniki." *Novoe Vremia* 13600, 21 January 1914.

Rumanov, A.V. "I.D. Sytin – izdatel'." *Vremennik druzei russkoi knigi* 4 (1938): 223-31.

– "Mechta I.D. Sytina." *Polveka dlia knigi*, 33-8.

– *Sviashchennik G.S. Petrov: Biografiia i istoriia ssylki v monastyr'*. Moscow 1907.

Samorodov, B. "Zhizn', otdannaia knige (K 125-letiiu so dnia rozhdeniia I.D. Sytina)." *Poligrafiia* 1 (1976): 43-4.

Semenov, M. "I.D. Sytin i narodnyi uchitel'." In *Polveka dlia knigi*, 53-7.

Shavel'sky, G.I. *Vospominaniia posledego protopresbitera Russkoi Armii i Flota*. 2 vols. New York 1954.

Sher, V.V. *Istoriia professional'nogo dvizheniia rabochikh pechatnogo dela v Moskve*. Moscow 1911.

– "Moskovskie pechatniki v revoliutsii 1905 goda." In *Moskovskie pechatniki v 1905 godu*, edited by A. Borshchevsky, S. Reshetov, N. Chistov. Moscow 1925.

B.A. Shchetinin. "V literaturnom muraveinike (vstrechi i znakomstva)." *Istoricheskii Vestnik* 3 (1911): 865-95.

Sibirsky, B. "Zagrobnoe vozmezdie [rev. of I.D. Sytin's *Zhizn' dlia knigi*)." *Vozrozhdenie* 127 (1962): 84-98.

Snezhko, E. "Radetel' narodnogo prosveshcheniia." *Literaturnaia Rossiia*, 27 February 1976: 24.

Syromiatnikov, B. "Vsenarodnaia kniga." In *Polveka dlia knigi*, 203-40.

Sytin, I.D. "Iz perezhitogo. Avtobiograficheskie nabroski iubiliara." *Polveka dlia knigi*, 11-28.

– "Iz perezhitogo." *Russkoe Slovo* 41, 19 February 1917.

– "O monopolii novoi i monopolii staroi." *Russkoe Slovo* 20, 25 January 1914.

– "O torgovle narodnymi knigami v raznoc [Doklad chitan v zasedanii III sektsii, 7 aprelia]." *Trudy Pervogo s"ezda russkikh deiatelei po pechatnomu delu v S.-Peterburge (5-12 aprelia 1895 g.)*. St Petersburg, 1895: 18-19.

– "Pozhar moei fabriki." *Zhurnalist* 12 (1925): 26-7.

– "Tri stupeni zhizni." *Russkoe Slovo* 41, 19 February 1917.

– *Zhizn' dlia knigi*. 1st ed., Moscow 1960; 2d ed., Moscow 1978, supp. 1985.

Sytin, I.D. & Co. *Katalog izdanii Tovarishchestva I.D. Sytina* [and variations on this title]. Moscow 1892–1924.

– *Ocherk izdatel'skoi deiatel'nosti Tovarishchestva I.D. Sytina*. Moscow 1900 and 1910.

– *Otchet Pravleniia tovarishchestva pechataniia, izdatel'stva i knizhnoi torgovli I.D. Sytina v Moskve*. Moscow 1894–1910.

Sytintsy v 1905 godu: Sbornik vospominanii rabochikh Pervoi Obraztsovoi tipografii (b. Sytina), edited by E. Rumailo, N. Miretsky, and L. Mal'kov. [Moscow 1922].

"Tainy sytinskogo knigoizdatel'stva." *Stolichnaia molva* 71, 72, 74; 7, 8, and 17 August 1909.

Teleshov, N.D. "Drug knigi." In N.D. Teleshov. *Zapiski pisatelia: Vospominaniia i rasskazy o proshlom*. Moscow 1980: 159-68.

Tolstiakov, A. "Russkii samorodok: k 125-letiiu s dnia rozhdeniia I.D. Sytina." *Knizhnoe obozrenie*, 30 January 1976: 16.

"Torzhestvennoe zasedanie, posviashchennoe 100-letiiu izdatel'skoi deiatel'nosti I.D. Sytina [19 dekabria 1966]." *Sovetskaia bibliografiia* 1 (101) (1967): 80-1.

"Tovarishchestvo I.D. Sytina." *Izvestiia sluzhashchikh v pechatnykh zavedeniiakh*, 43 and 44, 5 and 20 March 1917.

Tripol'sky, P. "Kazennaia monopoliia uchebnikov." *Utro* [Khar'kov] 2216, 4 February 1914.

Trudy pervogo vserossiskogo s''ezda izdatelei i knigoprodavtsev 30 iiunia - 5 iiulia 1909 v S.-Peterburge, edited by M.K. Lemke. St Petersburg 1909: 87-92, 96, 172, 258, 267-70, 369, 388.

Tulupov, N.V. "Deiatel'nost' I.D. Sytina v otsenke russkogo obshchestva." In *Polveka dlia knigi*, 42-52.

Vakhterov, V. "V zashchitu knigi." In *Polveka dlia knigi*, 247-61.

"N. Valentinov [N. Vol'sky, obituary]." *Novyi Zhurnal* 78 (1965): 275-7.

N. Valentinov [N. Vol'sky]. *Dva goda s simvolistami*, edited by Gleb Struve. Stanford: Stanford University Press 1969.

Varshavsky, S. "Pravovoe polozhenie izdatel'skogo dela v Rossii." In *Polveka dlia knigi*, 262-302.

Vsesoiuznaia poligraficheskaia vystavka: Pervaia Obraztsovaia tipografiia v Moskve. Moscow 1927.

Zorev, L.K. *Pervaia obraztsovaia*. Moscow 1967.

UNPUBLISHED WORKS

Inikova, S.A. "Gazeta I.D. Sytina 'Russkoe Slovo' (1897-1917)." Moscow 1983. (Duplicated at the Institute for Scientific Information in the Social Sciences, Academy of Sciences [INION], Moscow, no. 12927, 2 May 1983.)

- "Tovarishchestvo I.D. Sytina (1883-1917)." Moscow 1983. (Duplicated at INION, AN SSSR, no. 13928, 13 September 1983.)

- "Tovarishchestvo Pechataniia, izdatel'stva i knizhnoi torgovli I.D. Sytina (1883-1917)." Kandidat dissertation, Moscow State University, 1985.

James Krukones. "To the People: The Russian Government and the Newspaper 'Sel'skii Vestnik', 1881-1917." Ph.D. dissertation, University of Wisconsin, Madison, 1983.

Louise McReynolds. "News and Society: *Russkoe Slovo* and the Development of the Mass Circulation Press in Late Imperial Russia." Ph.D. dissertation, University of Chicago, 1984.

Robert C. Otto. "Publishing for the People: The Firm Posrednik, 1885-1905." Ph.D. dissertation, University of Wisconsin, Madison, 1983.

Index